A THOMAS HARDY DICTIONARY

By the same author

ONE RARE FAIR WOMAN
Thomas Hardy's letters to
Florence Henniker, 1893–1922
(*edited with Evelyn Hardy*)

A COMMENTARY ON
THE POEMS OF THOMAS HARDY
THOMAS HARDY: ART AND THOUGHT

Edited for the New Wessex Edition
THOMAS HARDY: TWO ON A TOWER
THE STORIES OF THOMAS HARDY (3 vols)

Edited for the Thomas Hardy Society
THOMAS HARDY AND THE MODERN WORLD
BUDMOUTH ESSAYS ON THOMAS HARDY
THE THOMAS HARDY SOCIETY REVIEW (*annual; editor 1975–84*)

A HARDY COMPANION
A JANE AUSTEN COMPANION
A BRONTË COMPANION
A GEORGE ELIOT COMPANION
A GEORGE ELIOT MISCELLANY
A D. H. LAWRENCE COMPANION
A WORDSWORTH COMPANION
A TENNYSON COMPANION
A T. S. ELIOT COMPANION
A WORDSWORTH CHRONOLOGY
THE COLLECTED SONNETS OF
CHARLES (TENNYSON) TURNER
(*edited with M. Pinion*)

A Thomas Hardy Dictionary

with maps and a chronology

F. B. PINION

MACMILLAN
PRESS

First published 1989

Published by
THE MACMILLAN PRESS LTD
Houndmills, Basingstoke, Hampshire RG21 2XS
and London
Companies and representatives
throughout the world

Typeset by Wessex Typesetters
(Division of The Eastern Press Ltd)
Frome, Somerset

Printed in Hong Kong

British Library Cataloguing in Publication Data
A Thomas Hardy dictionary.
1. Fiction in English. Hardy, Thomas,
1840–1928—Encyclopaedias
I. Pinion, F. B. (Francis Bertram), *1908–*
823′.8
ISBN 0–333–42873–0

Contents

Acknowledgments

This work has originated mainly from my own readings and the numerous investigations to which they have given rise over many years. It contains much that will not be found in my earlier publications on Hardy, including revisions and new points of view. Important information has been derived from *The Life of Thomas Hardy* and R. L. Purdy's bibliographical study (both of which are listed in section D of the reference code which follows).

The New Wessex Edition of Hardy's novels has often proved useful, and a few items have been taken from Lennart Björk's edition of Hardy's notebooks. Joan Rees, *The Poetry of Dante Gabriel Rossetti* (Cambridge, 1981), is the main source of the note on Robert Trewe. For the architectural origin of imaginary travels ascribed to Henry Knight in northern France, I am indebted to an illustrated lecture by Dr Claudius Beatty. The relation between the name Henchard and the Dorchester house of the Trenchards was established by P. J. Casagrande and Charles Lock in *The Thomas Hardy Society Review* of 1978; that of Findon and a scene in *The Hand of Ethelberta*, by Robert Gittings in the 1984 issue of the same annual. The initial route taken by the local travellers of 'A Few Crusted Characters' has been adopted from Denys Kay-Robinson's research.

I am grateful to the following for welcome confirmations or information: Angela Allott of the Sheffield City Libraries; Mrs Gertrude Bugler, and Peter Horton of the Royal College of Music (both on Langdon); Dr Fran Chalfont, West Georgia College; Professor Michael Millgate, University of Toronto; R. N. R. Peers, Curator of the Dorset County Museum; John Pentney and Charles Pettit of the Thomas Hardy Society; Professor J. M. Ritchie and Patrick Short, University of Sheffield; Anthony W. Shipps, University of Indiana; and A. D. Townsend of the Mellstock Band.

In addition, I wish to thank Mrs Valery Rose for her splendid co-operation on behalf of the publishers.

Code of Reference and Abbreviations

A. HARDY'S WORKS

CEF	Candour in English Fiction
CM	*A Changed Man*: (1) A Changed Man (2) The Waiting Supper (3) Alicia's Diary (4) The Grave by the Handpost (5) Enter a Dragoon (6) A Tryst at an Ancient Earthwork (7) What the Shepherd Saw (8) A Committee-Man of 'The Terror' (9) Master John Horseleigh, Knight (10) The Duke's Reappearance (11) A Mere Interlude (12) The Romantic Adventures of a Milkmaid
D	*The Dynasts*
DLa	The Dorsetshire Labourer
DR	*Desperate Remedies*
FMC	*Far from the Madding Crowd*
Gen.Pr.	General Preface to the Novels and Poems
GND	*A Group of Noble Dames*: (1) The First Countess of Wessex (2) Barbara of the House of Grebe (3) The Marchioness of Stonehenge (4) Lady Mottisfont (5) The Lady Icenway (6) Squire Petrick's Lady (7) Anna, Lady Baxby (8) The Lady Penelope (9) The Duchess of Hamptonshire (10) The Honourable Laura
HE	*The Hand of Ethelberta*
HS	*Human Shows, Far Phantasies, Songs, and Trifles*
JO	*Jude the Obscure*
L	*A Laodicean*
LLE	*Late Lyrics and Earlier*
LLI	*Life's Little Ironies*: (1) An Imaginative Woman (2) The Son's Veto (3) For Conscience' Sake (4) A Tragedy of Two Ambitions (5) On the Western Circuit (6) To Please His Wife (7) The Fiddler of the Reels (8) A Few Crusted Characters: (a) Tony Kytes, the Arch-Deceiver (b) The History of the Hardcomes (c) The Superstitious Man's

	Story (d) Andrey Satchel and the Parson and Clerk (e) Old Andrey's Experience as a Musician (f) Absent-Mindedness in a Parish Choir (g) The Winters and the Palmleys (h) Incident in the Life of Mr George Crookhill (i) Netty Sargent's Copyhold
MC	*The Mayor of Casterbridge*
MCR	Memories of Church Restoration
MV	*Moments of Vision and Miscellaneous Verses*
OMC	*Old Mrs Chundle and Other Stories . . .* (London, 1977): (1) Old Mrs Chundle (2) Destiny and a Blue Cloak (3) The Doctor's Legend (4) An Indiscretion in the Life of an Heiress (5) The Thieves Who Couldn't Help Sneezing (6) Our Exploits at West Poley
PBE	*A Pair of Blue Eyes*
PPP	*Poems of the Past and the Present*
PRF	The Profitable Reading of Fiction
QC	*The Famous Tragedy of the Queen of Cornwall* (included in OMC)
RN	*The Return of the Native*
SC	*Satires of Circumstance, Lyrics and Reveries . . . .*
SF	The Science of Fiction
TD	*Tess of the d'Urbervilles*
TL	*Time's Laughingstocks and Other Verses*
TM	*The Trumpet-Major*
TT	*Two on a Tower*
UGT	*Under the Greenwood Tree*
W	*The Woodlanders*
WB	*The Well-Beloved*
WP	*Wessex Poems and Other Verses*
WT	*Wessex Tales*: (1) The Three Strangers (2) A Tradition of Eighteen Hundred and Four (3) The Melancholy Hussar (4) The Withered Arm (5) Fellow-Townsmen (6) Interlopers at the Knap (7) The Distracted Preacher
WW	*Winter Words in Various Moods and Metres*

B. THE BIBLE

(OT: Old Testament. NT: New Testament)

Acts	Acts of the Apostles (NT)	Josh.	Joshua (OT)
		Judg.	Judges (OT)
Chron.	Chronicles I and II (OT)	Kings	Kings I and II (OT)
		Lev.	Leviticus (OT)
Col.	Colossians (NT)	Luke	Luke's Gospel (NT)
Cor.	Corinthians I and II (NT)	Mark	Mark's Gospel (NT)
		Matt.	Matthew's Gospel (NT)
Dan.	Daniel (OT)	Mic.	Micah (OT)
Deut.	Deuteronomy (OT)	Num.	Numbers (OT)
Eccl.	Ecclesiastes (OT)	Pet.	Epistles of Peter (NT)
Eph.	Ephesians (NT)	Phil.	Philippians (NT)
Esther	Esther (OT)	Prov.	Proverbs (OT)
Exod.	Exodus (OT)	Psalm	Psalms (OT)
Ezek.	Ezekiel (OT)	Rev.	Revelation (NT)
Gal.	Galatians (NT)	Rom.	Romans (NT)
Gen.	Genesis (OT)	Ruth	Ruth (OT)
Heb.	Hebrews (NT)	Sam.	Samuel I and II (OT)
Hos.	Hosea (OT)	Sol.	The Song of Solomon (OT)
Isa.	Isaiah (OT)		
James	Epistle of James (NT)	Thess.	Thessalonians I and II (NT)
Jer.	Jeremiah (OT)		
Job	Job (OT)	Tim.	Epistles to Timothy (NT)
Joel	Joel (OT)		
John	John's Gospel (NT)	Tit.	Epistle to Titus (NT)
Jon.	Jonah (OT)	Zeph.	Zephaniah (OT)

C. SHAKESPEARE

References are given in accordance with Peter Alexander's edition of the complete works (Collins, London and Glasgow, 1951), following the line-numeration of Clark and Wright.

AC	*Antony and Cleopatra*	*2.H4*	*The Second Part of King Henry the Fourth*
AYL	*As You Like It*		
Cym.	*Cymbeline*	*H5*	*King Henry the Fifth*
1.H4	*The First Part of King Henry the Fourth*	*Ham.*	*Hamlet, Prince of Denmark*

JC	*Julius Caesar*	*R2*	*King Richard the Second*
KJ	*King John*		
KL	*King Lear*	*RJ*	*Romeo and Juliet*
Mac.	*Macbeth*	R of L	The Rape of Lucrece
M.Ado	*Much Ado About Nothing*	Son.	Sonnets
		TA	*Timon of Athens*
MM	*Measure for Measure*	*TC*	*Troilus and Cressida*
MND	*A Midsummer Night's Dream*	*Tem.*	*The Tempest*
		TGV	*The Two Gentlemen of Verona*
MV	*The Merchant of Venice*		
Oth.	*Othello*	*TN*	*Twelfth Night*
Per.	*Pericles, Prince of Tyre*	V and A	Venus and Adonis
WT	*The Winter's Tale*		

D. MISCELLANEOUS

Books

G.T. — F. T. Palgrave, *The Golden Treasury*.

Hutchins — John Hutchins, *The History and Antiquities of the County of Dorset*, 3rd edition in 4 volumes, London, 1861–73.

Letters — R. L. Purdy and M. Millgate (eds), *The Collected Letters of Thomas Hardy*, Oxford, 1978ff.

Life — (1) F. E. Hardy, *The Life of Thomas Hardy*, London and New York, 1962.
(2) Thomas Hardy, *The Life and Work of Thomas Hardy*, ed. M. Millgate, Basingstoke and London, 1984. A new edition of (1).
References are given to both wherever possible, and the first page-number to (1), the second to (2).

Millgate — M. Millgate, *Thomas Hardy, A Biography*, Oxford, 1982.

Orel — H. Orel, *Thomas Hardy's Personal Writings*, Lawrence, Kansas, 1966, and London, 1967.

Purdy — R. L. Purdy, *Thomas Hardy, A Bibliographical Study*, Oxford, 1954.

S.R. — Emma Hardy, *Some Recollections*, ed. Evelyn Hardy and R. Gittings, London, 1961.

Vulgate — the Latin translation of the Bible, for common use (*editio vulgata*), as authorized by Pope Clement VIII.

Abbreviations

arch.	architecture	It.	Italian
c.	*circa*, about	Lat.	Latin
C. of E.	Church of England	ll.	lines
cf.	compare	m.	miles
d.	died	mus.	music
dial.	dialect	N.G.	The National Gallery
ep.	epigraph	pr.	preface
Fr.	French	ps.	postscript
Germ.	German	pub.	published
Gk.	Greek	vb.	verb

Directions are frequently given in the form:

ENE, east-north-east; SW, south-west.

Introductory Notes

RANGE OF ENTRIES

This work is not a Hardy encyclopedia; its entries are limited to uncertainties and questions which could arise, for many at home and abroad with a good command of English, in the course of reading Hardy. They include notes on references; explanations of words which are either rare or used with rare meanings, from the neologistic and scholarly to the local and rustic; sources of quotations; identifications of fictional places and people wherever they are valid to some degree or other; and information of extrinsic and intrinsic interest on at least five hundred of Hardy's poems, as well as on his most important essays, his drama, and all the novels and short stories. The most extensive comments are on his major works, members of his family, and friends (such as Horace Moule and Mrs Henniker) who are important in his verse and prose. There are also notes of critical significance, bearing on Hardy's symbolism or on literary and philosophical influences (Goethe's, for example) to which he was subject. So coherent and self-contained is *The Dynasts* that there is little need to refer to its historical events and personages; difficulties in the text have not been overlooked, however. Geographical references throughout Hardy's works are omitted unless they have a special interest or are not widely known. Room has not been found for the innumerable titles of dances and song in his verse and prose, since contexts make clear into which category they fall. Terms such as 'ankle-jacks' (*FMC*.viii), 'unhaling' (*TD*.xlvii), and 'kimberlins' (*WB*.I.ii) which Hardy explains in his text are also omitted.

The area covered by this compilation includes

i. all Hardy's novels and short stories, including the prefaces*
ii. all his poems
iii. *The Dynasts* and *The Famous Tragedy of the Queen of Cornwall**
iv. selected essays: (a) The Dorsetshire Labourer (b) The Profitable Reading of Fiction (c) Candour in English Fiction (d) The

* Hardy's previously uncollected stories will be found in *Old Mrs Chundle and Other Stories*, together with *The Famous Tragedy of the Queen of Cornwall*; see *OMC* in the Code of Reference and Abbreviations.

Science of Fiction (e) Memories of Church Restoration (references are made to other prose articles)

v. numerous passages in *The Life of Thomas Hardy* or *The Life and Work of Thomas Hardy* relative to topics and individual works.

Hardy's imagination was enriched by a variety of lasting interests. His love of Church of England worship, and of music and song, both ecclesiastical and secular, was part of a youthful inheritance which was enlarged by that of his first wife, before marriage and after. The study of paintings affected his imaginative concepts more obviously than did his knowledge of architecture, though the latter is more frequently evident in both its literal and its figurative use. Hardy's early interest in astronomy prepared him for the extensive scientific realization of space and time which is inseparable from his philosophy. His imaginative continuum reveals the mysteries of 'the full-starred heavens' in conjunction with a historical perspective which ranges from the geological and archaeological to various more recent periods from the classical to the twentieth century. Jude's tense awareness of the near and unattainable, as he watches the doctoral procession at Christminster, reminds Hardy of inaccessible planets he had seen moving across telescopic object glasses (*JO*.VI.i); the old Weatherbury choir instruments make him think of their being played to celebrate Marlborough's victories (*FMC*.lvii). More persistent was his love of literature; he was 'a born bookworm', and in that respect, and 'that alone', he never changed (*Life* 27/31).

QUOTATION AND LITERARY ALLUSION IN HARDY

So well-read was Hardy and so retentive his memory that he had an apt quotation for most occasions and situations. His earliest works testify to his love of poetry in *The Golden Treasury* (his prized copy being the gift of his friend Horace Moule), his responsiveness to the poetry of Shakespeare, and to the poetic thought of Swinburne, Shelley, and Browning. Poetry was his abiding love, and his works illustrate how extensively he pursued it. Prose quotations occur from the classical period to the contemporary. Quotations from Shakespeare are far more numerous than from any other author, but no influence permeates Hardy's work more than that of the Bible. It echoes his deeper thoughts, and provides him with countless expressions. Biblical characters, events, and images affected his imaginative thinking, so much so at times that, despite his rationalism, he can refer to supernatural events in the Old Testament and the New as if they were historical. Biblical phrases such as 'labour of love' have become commonplace, but Hardy (more aware, we may be sure, of its origin than of its facile conversational use) chooses it for its incomparable appropriateness to his fictional situation. A hint of a quotation from Ecclesiastes may be suspected at the end of 'The sensual hind who ate, drank, and lived carelessly with his wife through the days of his vanity' (*JO*.III.i), but the words are just as likely to pass as Hardy's own reflective observation, without a single overtone.

Some of Hardy's quotations and snatches of song have passed out of currency, and of these, and of contemporary *dicta* which he noted, several remain untraced. It is rewarding nonetheless to observe his literary allusiveness, the hints which he gives for 'right note-catching' to 'finely-touched spirits' who share with him contexts of thought and feeling embodied in imagery and the music of words. For readers tantalized in their efforts to trace the source of such echoes, and for those who have not discerned them, a key to Hardy's quotations, hinted at or acknowledged, may serve to restore some of the full implications of his style. New examples of unacknowledged allusiveness are apt to spring to notice with repeated readings, and more undoubtedly remain to be discovered.

REFERENCES TO HARDY'S TEXT

No consistent attempt at completeness has been made. Where given, references are usually selected to indicate the most important or interesting contexts.

EXCEPTIONAL PLACEMENTS OF ENTRIES

Perhaps it needs to be noticed that in the general alphabetical arrangement

(a) initial definite and indefinite articles are ignored, e.g. 'The Absolute Explains' follows 'Absalom's death', and 'A Hurried Meeting', 'hurdle-sauls';

(b) hyphenated words are regarded as wholes, e.g. 'a-bearing' follows 'Abbotsea', and 'high-piled granary', 'Higher Jirton';
(c) words ending in 's are also regarded as wholes, e.g. 'All's Well' (after 'All-Fours') follows 'Allen-a-Dale', and 'bull's eye', 'The Bullfinches'.

For the sake of compression, two special procedures have been adopted, as a result of which

(1) where a difficulty in a poem does not appear in the general order, a note on it can be expected under the title of the poem;
(2) when a series or close succession of references occurs in Hardy's text, explanations are provided under the first of them, except for those which, having a wider application, appear alphabetically in the general arrangement of the work.

A Hardy Chronology

1777 John Hardy of Puddletown marries Jane Knight.
1799 His son Thomas marries Mary Head (formerly of Fawley, Berkshire).
1801 They occupy the cottage his father has built for them at Higher Bockhampton, on the fringe of the heath. (Thomas Hardy's business as mason and bricklayer – which his son inherits – grows, mainly from work done on the Kingston Maurward estate.)
1837 Thomas Hardy ('the first') dies.
1839 (Dec) His youngest son (Thomas Hardy 'the second') who has remained at the lifehold cottage with his mother, marries Jemima Hand (from Melbury Osmond).
1840 (2 June) Their son Thomas (the author) is born. (24 Nov) Emma Lavinia Gifford is born at Plymouth.
1841 (23 Dec) Birth of Mary, Hardy's sister.
1844 T. H. receives an accordion from his father. Francis Pitney Martin purchases the Kingston Maurward estate (his childess wife Julia Augusta subsequently grows fond of Tommy, and teaches him to write).
1848 He is sent to the new C. of E. school at Lower Bockhampton, which has been provided by Mrs Martin. (About this time his mother gives him Dryden's *Virgil*, Johnson's *Rasselas*, and *Paul and Virginia*.)
1849 Towards the end of the year he travels with his mother by train to London, to stay at Hatfield with his aunt (her sister) and uncle, Martha and John Sharpe, to some extent prototypes of Bathsheba Everdene and Sergeant Troy.
1850 (Late summer) Hardy is transferred to a Nonconformist school in Dorchester, his mother having heard that the headmaster is very able, and a teacher of Latin. He is taken to the harvest-supper celebrations in the barn at Kingston Maurward.
1851 (1 July) Birth of Henry Hardy, Thomas's brother.
1852 Thomas accompanies his father as a violinist at wedding-

parties and local dances (a practice he continues for a number of years).

1853 Mr Last, his headmaster, having acquired a private school, Hardy stays with him, and begins to learn Latin.

1854 A serious outbreak of cholera in Fordington, Henry Moule's parish.

1855 Hardy begins teaching at the Stinsford Sunday School.

1856 (July) Leaves Mr Last's school, and is articled to the Dorchester architect Hicks. About this time (or later) he is given advice on water-colouring by Henry H. Moule, the vicar of Fordington's eldest son. (2 Sept) Birth of his sister Katharine.

1857 (Jan) Death of his grandmother in the home where she had lived since 1801. Hardy's friendship with some of Moule's brothers grows, especially with Horace, who is to help him in the study of Greek. Hardy begins a regular reading of *The Saturday Review*.

1860 (Feb) Purchases a copy of Griesbach's Greek New Testament. (Apr) His sister Mary begins her teacher-training at Salisbury, which Hardy visits for the first time (as an architect's pupil), possibly meeting Horace Moule there.

1862 (Jan) Receives a copy of *The Golden Treasury* from Horace Moule. (17 Apr) Leaves for London, where he is soon employed as a draughtsman in Gothic architecture by Arthur Blomfield at St Martin's Place. He is elected to the Architectural Association.

1863 (Feb) Blomfield moves to 8 Adelphi Terrace, overlooking the Thames. (Apr) Hardy visits his sister Mary, now a teacher at Denchworth, Berkshire, where he sketches the church. (May) Awarded the R.I.B.A. prize for his essay on the application of coloured bricks and terra-cotta to modern architecture. About this time (probably a little later) he moves to 16 Westbourne Park Villas, where he is to become friendly with Eliza Nicholls, a lady's maid in the vicinity.

1864 (Autumn) Travels with Mary from Denchworth to Fawley, Berkshire, where he sketches the old church.

1865 Begins a studious course, which he follows for about two years, of reading and writing poetry. (Whether he read Swinburne's *Atalanta in Calydon* in 1865 or 1866 is not clear.)

1866 (Whitsun weekend) Visits Eliza Nicholls at Findon, Sussex, where he sketches the church. Finally abandons his aim of becoming a country curate. (Summer) Elated by Swinburne's first volume of *Poems and Ballads*.

1867 (20 July) Returns to Higher Bockhampton for the sake of his health. Resumes architectural work for Hicks, and starts his first novel *The Poor Man and the Lady*. Meets relatives in Puddletown, especially at the Antells', where he becomes interested in his young cousin Tryphena Sparks (aged 16) and her pupil-teaching.

1869 (May) To Weymouth, where he is employed by the architect Crickmay. (Autumn) *Under the Greenwood Tree* laid aside, after 'about half' had been written, for *Desperate Remedies*.

1870 (7 Mar) Travels to St Juliot on church-restoration business, and meets Emma Lavinia Gifford, the rector's sister-in-law. (May) Leaves Crickmay for London, where he meets Horace Moule and works part-time for the architect Raphael Brandon. (Aug) Returns to Cornwall, at the rector's invitation, to see Miss Gifford, to whom he is virtually engaged.

1871 (Mar) *Desperate Remedies* published; Hardy resumes work for Crickmay at Weymouth. Here and at Higher Bockhampton he completes *Under the Greenwood Tree*.

1872 (Jan) After two years' teacher-training at Stockwell College, Clapham, Tryphena Sparks is appointed head of a girls' school at Plymouth. (Mar) Hardy leaves Crickmay to help the architect T. Roger Smith in designing schools for the London School Board. Sends for the MS of *UGT*, which, on its arrival in the first week of April, he sends to his publisher Tinsley without looking at it. He had thought of giving up authorship. Good reviews of *UGT* and Tinsley's persuasion change his mind; he begins *A Pair of Blue Eyes* at the end of July. (7 Aug) Embarks from London for Plymouth on his fourth visit to St Juliot. (Late Sep) Gives up architecture to finish his novel at Bockhampton.

1873 (June) To London and Cambridge, where he stays at Queens' College with Horace Moule; then to Bath, which Emma Gifford is visiting with a friend. At home he is busy with *Far from the Madding Crowd*. On 21 September, the day he walks to Woodbury Hill Fair, Moule commits suicide in his college rooms at Cambridge. Hardy attends his funeral at Fordington on the 26th. Helps his father with cider-making for the last time.

1874 After completing *FMC*, Hardy goes to London, where (17 Sep) he and Emma are married at St Peter's, Paddington, by her uncle, Head of King Edward's School, Birmingham, and Canon of Worcester. Their honeymoon takes them to Brighton, Rouen, and Paris. They find accommodation on the outskirts of Surbiton.

1875 (23 Mar) Shortly after their removal to Newton Road, Westbourne Grove, Hardy acts as witness to Leslie Stephen's renunciation of holy orders. (11 May) At Oxford with Austin Dobson, to respond to the Literature toast at the Shotover Dinner. His lifelong friendship with Edmund Gosse begins about this period. (July) He and Emma move (via Bournemouth) to Swanage.

1876 (Jan) *The Hand of Ethelberta* is completed. (Mar) To lodgings at Yeovil. (Mid-May) They set off for two weeks in London followed by a visit to Rotterdam and the Rhine valley. From Brussels, on their return, they visit the field of Waterloo. In London, Hardy discusses the battle with veteran Chelsea Pensioners 'over glasses of grog' at the Turk's Head. (3 July) From Yeovil to Sturminster Newton, where they settle in their first independent home, overlooking the Stour river. They spend Christmas at Higher Bockhampton, Hardy renewing his impressions of the background for *The Return of the Native*.

1877 (Jan) Katharine Hardy, after being a pupil-teacher at Piddlehinton, begins teacher-training at Salisbury. Hardy devotes himself to *RN*, but continues to find time for reading and outings with Emma. At the end of October he travels to Bath, to see his father, who is having treatment there.

1878 (20 Mar) The Hardys leave Sturminster, to be nearer London. (In retrospect he thought they had spent the happiest time in their lives there.) They move to Upper Tooting. (June) He works at the British Museum in preparation for *The Trumpet-Major*. Elected to the Savile Club. From 31 August he is in Dorset for ten days; he calls on William Barnes, and views the pictures at Kingston Lacy. (27 Oct) Visits pensioners at Chelsea Hospital.

1879 (1 Feb) To Higher Bockhampton for visits to Weymouth and other places mainly for background research in connection with *TM*. (Aug) He returns, Emma joining him; after a few days they take lodgings at Weymouth. Hardy's mother stays with them, and accompanies them on outings in this area. (Dec) Attends the inaugural dinner of the Rabelais Club (for virile writers) in a cold London fog.

1880 (Feb–Mar) Meets Matthew Arnold, Browning, and the Tennysons. Later, other people of distinction at club dinners. Several chapters of *A Laodicean* have been written. (27 July) He and Emma set off for a holiday in Normandy. Back in England, he sends off the first instalment of *A Laodicean*, and revises *TM* for volume-publication. (Sep) He spends a few days at Higher Bockhampton, discussing family property and the possibility of land-purchase for building his own house in or near Dorchester. At the end of October, after visiting Cambridge with Emma, Hardy is seriously ill. (He is confined to bed for several months, but completes his novel, with Emma as amanuensis.)

1881 (10 Apr) he goes out for the first time since his return from Cambridge. The three years' lease has expired, but is extended for three months. (25 June) They move to Wimborne, Dorset. During late August and early September they are on tour in Scotland. Henry J. Moule visits them at Wimborne, where they meet Sir George Douglas (destined to become a lifelong friend), who is staying with his brother. *Two on a Tower* planned.

1882 (11 Mar) Hardy and Emma attend a performance of *FMC* at the Prince of Wales Theatre, Liverpool; (29 Apr) after attending rehearsals, he is present for the first night of its production at the Globe Theatre, London. (Sep) On a tour with Emma to Salisbury, Lyme Regis, and Dorchester; they call on Barnes at Came rectory. (Oct) To Paris. (During the year Hardy joins the Dorset Natural History and Antiquarian Field Club.)

1883 (May and early June) Visits to London, 'seeing pictures, plays, and friends' (including Lord Houghton, Mrs Procter, Browning, and Gosse). (June) The Hardys move to a house in Shire-Hall Lane, Dorchester; (July) Gosse is their first visitor. Hardy has obtained land for building his own house.

1884 Romano-British relics are found in digging for its foundations. Hardy reads assiduously at the Dorchester Museum, where Henry J. Moule is now curator. He writes much of *The Mayor of Casterbridge*, and becomes a J.P. After a stay during June and July with Emma in London, he visits the Channel Islands with his brother Henry.

1885 (Mar) Accepting a long-standing invitation, Hardy stays with Lord and Lady Portsmouth in Devon; Emma is unable to accompany him. (17 Apr) *The Mayor of Casterbridge* is completed. (End of June) After some weeks in London, the Hardys move to Max Gate, their new home on the Wareham road. He begins *The Woodlanders*.

1886 In London with Emma much of the spring and summer, Hardy reading at the British Museum with the subject of *The Dynasts* in mind. (His custom is to spend four or five months each year in London or abroad.) He meets Pater, Henry James, Meredith, Gissing (who seeks his advice on novel-writing), Browning, Stevenson, Bret Harte, Oliver Wendell Holmes, and other people of distinction. (End of July) They return to Max Gate, where he resumes *The Woodlanders*. (Oct) They spend a week at the Portsmouths' in Devon.

1887 (Mar) The novel being finished in February, they leave for London, on their way to Italy. In London again from the end of April to the end of July, the season being especially 'brilliant' with Golden Jubilee celebrations in honour of the Queen. (Nov) Hardy outlines plans for *The Dynasts*.

1888 (Spring) In London with Emma. (He has been thinking much about this time of people, and their fictional possibilities, as motivated souls.) At the end of May they travel for a stay of more than two weeks in Paris, after which they meet Pater several times in London. (16 July) Return to Max Gate. By the end of September he is preparing for *Tess of the d'Urbervilles*.

1889 At the end of January, the painter Alfred Parsons visits Max Gate, his mission being to visit Melbury House with Hardy, and prepare illustrations for the serial edition of 'The First Countess of Wessex'. (Apr) Hardy is in London with Emma. (2 July) Meets Mrs Hamo Thornycroft at the Gosses'. To Max Gate at the end of July for work on *TD*.

1890 (Mar) Death of his cousin Tryphena (at Topsham, where she had lived since marrying Mr Gale in December 1877). (Easter) Sir George Douglas at Max Gate. (May–Aug) Hardy and Emma are in London, where he grows tired of 'investigating life at music-halls and police-courts' for novel-padding; Emma's visit is curtailed by her father's illness and death. They take Alfred Parsons to Weymouth in August, at the end of which Hardy goes to Paris with his brother Henry. *Tess of the d'Urbervilles* is finished in the autumn.

1891 Other events besides visits to London and the preparation of *TD* for book-publication include visits to training-colleges in preparation for *Jude the Obscure*; (Apr) Hardy's election to the Athenaeum; (June) his visit to Aldeburgh to see his friend Edward Clodd, banker and rationalist; (Sep) a holiday with Sir George Douglas in Scotland, where he and Emma visit many scenes associated with Scott's writings. (Dec) Working on *The Pursuit of the Well-Beloved* (which he expects to finish by March). (About this time, according to Florence Hardy, Emma began the practice of writing in diaries her worst thoughts of Hardy; to judge by her surviving letters, they could have been absurdly paranoiac and abusive.)

1892 The tenor of Hardy's life is disturbed by reviews of *TD* from January to April. (20 July) Death of his father. (Oct) At Fawley, Berkshire, and at Tennyson's funeral in Westminster Abbey. (Emma's break with Hardy's family during the year makes relations between her and Hardy more difficult for the remainder of their married life.)

1893 (Spring) They meet many people in London. (May) To Dublin at the invitation of the second Lord Houghton, Lord-Lieutenant of Ireland; they meet his sister and hostess Mrs Henniker. After visiting Killarney they return to London; Hardy meets Mrs Henniker and sees three Ibsen plays, then proceeds to Oxford, to make more preparations for *Jude*. The remainder of the year is unsettled, with social visits, time devoted to Mrs Henniker and her literary work, and planning for church-renovation at West Knighton near Max Gate. Little progress made with *JO*.

1894 Hardy at last gets *JO* under way. He and Emma are in London for the spring and early summer; (30 Apr) he visits Meredith at Box Hill. *JO* continued in London and, from the beginning of August, at Max Gate, with many interruptions.

1895 Before *JO* is finished Hardy begins revision work for the uniform edition of the 'Wessex Novels'; in March he accompanies their illustrator Mr Raeburn to 'the neighbourhood of Dorchester and other places in Wessex'. (Nov) *Jude the Obscure* appears in book form; condemnation soon begins.

1896 In London Hardy finds that his friends receive him just the same as ever, unlike 'country friends' (county families) who have 'a pathetic reverence for press opinions'. He has decided not to make any further commitments for prose fiction. After a tour in England during August, he and Emma proceed to Belgium, Emma taking her bicycle; Hardy examines the field of Waterloo. He revises *The Well-Beloved* for book-publication.

1897 After staying in London and Basingstoke, the Hardys leave for a tour in Switzerland; they are in Lausanne on 27 June, the anniversary of Gibbon's concluding *The Decline and Fall of the Roman Empire*. (Aug) They visit Wells, Salisbury, and Stonehenge. (Sep) He cycles with Kipling, who thinks of living near Weymouth. The final plan of *The Dynasts* is prepared. The assembling of old and new poems, and work on illustrations, for *Wessex Poems*, are begun.

1898 (July) Cycling 'more vigorously then ever . . . sometimes with Mrs Hardy, sometimes with his brother'. He makes further sketches for *Wessex Poems* (published in December). (Emma has made two attics comfortable for her own pursuits, which include painting and writing.)

1899 (Apr–July) In London and elsewhere with Emma, meeting society friends; Hardy meets A. E. Housman, and visits Clodd, Swinburne, and Meredith. Much cycling with Emma after their return to Max Gate. (Oct) At Southampton to witness the embarkation of troops for the Boer War.

1900 Their London visit is again followed by cycling with his wife, also with the sculptor Hamo Thornycroft.

1901 (May) The Hardys in London, where they attend concerts, as in previous seasons; at the end of the month the literary Whitefriars Club visits Max Gate, where they are entertained in a tent on the lawn. (Nov) *Poems of the Past and the Present* published.

1902 During the second half of the year Hardy concentrates on *The Dynasts*.

1903 (28 Sep) Part I of *The Dynasts* sent to Macmillan.

1904 (3 Apr) Hardy's mother dies. (Aug) Cycling tours.

1905 (Apr) Receives an honorary degree at Aberdeen. Soon afterwards he and Emma travel to London, returning to Max Gate in July. (Sep) At Aldeburgh with Clodd, attending the celebration which marked the 150th anniversary of the poet George Crabbe's birth. Completes Part II of *The Dynasts*. Near the end of the year, if not earlier, Florence Dugdale calls.

1906 As in each of many previous years, the Hardys stay in London during the spring and early summer. (Aug) He visits cathedrals and Cambridge colleges with Henry; cycles in Dorset and Somerset during the remainder of the summer.

1907 (28 Mar) Finishes the first draft of Part III of *The Dynasts*, before the usual season in London, where he meets Gorky, Wells, Shaw, and Conrad. (22 June) He and Emma are guests at King Edward's garden party at Windsor Castle. (Autumn) Sir Frederick and Lady Treves take a house near Max Gate; Hardy and he have frequent discussions.

1908 (Mar) Hardy finishes his edition of selected poems by William Barnes. (July) From London he goes to Cambridge for the Milton tercentenary celebrations. (Nov) Declines a knighthood.

1909 (Apr) Decides he is unfit to attend Swinburne's funeral. In London (22 May) he attends the memorial service to Meredith in Westminster Abbey. He succeeds him as President of the Society of Authors. (Aug) Hardy and Florence Dugdale are Clodd's guests at Aldeburgh. She accompanies him and Henry on an excursion to York, Edinburgh, and Durham. (Dec) *Time's Laughingstocks* published.

1910 Hardy and Florence Dugdale visit Swinburne's grave at Bonchurch, Isle of Wight. (June) He is awarded the Order of Merit. (16 Nov) Receives the freedom of Dorchester. Florence Dugdale much at Max Gate during the latter part of the year.

1911 Emma Hardy completes *Some Recollections*. (June) Hardy avoids the Coronation by making a visit to the Lake District with Henry, Florence Dugdale, and one of her sisters. (July) Takes his sister Katharine to Devon. (Oct) Writes the 'General Preface' for the Wessex Edition of his novels and poems (first published in 1912). (Nov) Visits Gloucester Cathedral. Emma has *Alleys*, a short collection of her poems, privately published.

1912 (Saturday, 1 June) Henry Newbolt and W. B. Yeats arrive at Max Gate (where they present the gold medal of the Royal Society of Literature to Hardy on his birthday). (July)

Garden party at Max Gate. (Sep) Henry Hardy and his sisters move from their old home to Talbothays, West Stafford, a new house designed by T. H. (27 Nov) Death of Emma Hardy.

1913 (6 Mar) With his brother Henry, Hardy begins his journey to St Juliot. (June) Receives the degree of Litt.D. at Cambridge. (Nov) Installed as an honorary fellow of Magdalene College, Cambridge.

1914 (10 Feb) Marries Miss Dugdale at Enfield. They visit Cambridge in the spring, and meet Hardy's old friend Charles Moule, now President of Corpus College. Travel by car to Exeter and Plymouth, where they search for the graves of Emma's parents. Stay a weekend at Stourhead with Sir Henry and Lady Hoare. (4 Aug) War declared against Germany. (Nov) *Satires of Circumstance* published. They attend a rehearsal of 'Scenes from *The Dynasts*' in London.

1915 (10 June) By car to Exeter and Torquay, where they call on Eden Phillpotts and his wife. (29 Nov) Burial of Hardy's sister Mary.

1916 (June) Visit to Riverside, Sturminster Newton, where Hardy wrote *RN*. (Sep) By train to Launceston and Camelford, to visit some of Emma's cousins at the former place, inspect her memorial in St Juliot Church, and see Tintagel.

1917 (June) Hardy declines J. M. Barrie's proposal to accompany him to the battlefront in France. (July) He and Florence visit Barrie at Adelphi Terrace, where (with Wells, Shaw, and Arnold Bennett) they view the Thames and searchlights sweeping the sky to detect enemy aircraft. She has encouraged him to work on *The Life of Thomas Hardy* (which she was to help him produce). (Oct) A brief visit to Phillpotts at Torquay. (Nov) Publication of *Moments of Vision*.

1918 (11 Nov) End of the 1914–18 war.

1919 (May) Hardy and Florence stay with Barrie; he attends the Royal Academy dinner. (2 June) He takes Florence and his sister to Salisbury by the old road past Woodyates (the old coach-inn) and Harnham Hill (from which Constable painted his view of the cathedral). (Oct) Siegried Sassoon brings a volume in which 43 poets have each inscribed a poem in Hardy's honour. (Dec) Hardy opens the war memorial club-room at Lower Bockhampton.

1920 (2 Feb) He receives the degree of D.Litt. at Oxford, and watches a production of scenes from *The Dynasts* by the Oxford University Dramatic Society. (21 Apr) With Florence, he attends the wedding of Harold Macmillan and Lady Dorothy Cavendish, his last visit to London, staying at Barrie's flat close to the house in Adelphi Terrace 'where he had worked as an architect's assistant nearly sixty years before'. (2 June) On his 80th birthday he receives representatives from the Society of Authors, and many congratulations, including one from George V. (7 June) Made an honorary fellow of the R.I.B.A. (July) Motoring in Dorset with Mrs Henniker. (Aug) Robert Graves and his wife spend a weekend at Max Gate.

1921 (9 June) To Sturminster Newton, where, after a performance of *The Mellstock Quire* by the Hardy Players, he revisits Riverside. (16 June) Walks with Walter de la Mare, his guest, to Stinsford.

1922 (Jan) Writes the Apology for *LLE* when ill in bed. (23 May) *Late Lyrics and Earlier* published. The next day he revisits Riverside, and, two days later, the old home at Higher Bockhampton, which he finds very neglected. (July) Visits from Mrs Henniker, Sassoon, Edmund Blunden, and E. M. Forster. (11 Aug) Returning from Sturminster by Dogbury Gate, he walks (with Newman Flower) to the top of High Stoy for the last time.

1923 (Apr) Finishes the first draft of *The Queen of Cornwall*. (June) He and Florence visit Salisbury (the cathedral and the training-college his sisters had attended) and Fawley (where his grandmother had been born) on their way to Queen's College, Oxford, to which he had been elected Fellow; they visit John Masefield at Boar's Hill. (20 July) The Prince of Wales visits Max Gate. (30 Dec) Bernard Shaw, his wife, and T. E. Lawrence lunch there.

1924 (2 Feb) Attends Sir Frederick Treves's funeral. (1 July) The Balliol Players (Oxford undergraduates) perform a version of *The Oresteia* on the lawn at Max Gate. (22 Oct) Hardy and Florence visit the old barn at Kingston Maurward.

1925 (July) *Human Shows* sent to the publishers.

1926 (29 June) The Balliol Players play *Hippolytus* on the Max Gate lawn. (25 July) Virginia and Leonard Woolf call. (20 Sep) Hardy receives a great ovation at Weymouth, where he attends John Drinkwater's dramatization of *The Mayor of*

Casterbridge. Visits Mrs Bankes at Kingston Lacy. (1 Nov) Visits his old home for the last time, with Mr Hanbury of Kingston Maurward House, the object being to have the Hardy house tidied and secluded.

1927 (6 July) The Balliol Players perform *Iphigenia in Aulis* at Max Gate. (21 July) Hardy lays the foundation-stone of the new Dorchester Grammar School buildings. He has had visits from Siegfried Sassoon and Mr and Mrs Masefield. At Bath in August he feels like 'a ghost revisiting scenes of a long-dead past' (with memories of Emma); at his wish, he and Florence return past the Ham Hill stone quarries. (6 Sep) John Galsworthy and his wife call. (11 Dec) Hardy goes to his study, and finds for the first time that he is unable to work. His strength wanes daily. After Christmas he is unable to go downstairs.

1928 (11 Jan) He dies. (16 Jan) At 2 p.m. three memorial services are held: at Westminster Abbey, where his ashes are buried; at Stinsford Church, his heart being buried in Emma's grave; at St Peter's, Dorchester. (2 Oct) *Winter Words* published.

A

a', all, an.

'a, I, he, it.

a-, in the act or state of, in a (a-pen), on (a-perch), to the (a-coast).

Aaron's serpent-rod (*D*2.v.i), Exod.vii,8–12.

abacus, the uppermost part of the capital (at the top of a pier or column), on which rests the architrave or one side of an arch.

The Abbey Mason (*SC*). John Hicks was the Dorchester architect (d.1869) for whom Hardy worked before and after his period in London with Blomfield. For Hardy's visit to Gloucester, out of which this poem – largely his invention – arose, see *Life* 357/384–5. The contemporary view that the Perpendicular style of architecture began there is no longer supported. Abbot Wygmore (d.1337) was followed by Staunton and Horton. *parpend ashlars*, hewn stones, each passing through a wall from side to side; *sizing*, assuming considerable size; *knife the . . . knot* (cf. 'cut the Gordian knot'), solve the difficult or knotty problem; *Prime* (the first hour of the day), the 6 a.m. service; *embodying*, taking shape; *transom*, horizontal stone bar; *spandrel*, a triangular space between the arch of a window or doorway and the rectangular moulding above it.

Abbot's Cernel, Cerne Abbas, 7 m. north of Dorchester; named after its Benedictine abbey, of which little is left but 'the gatehouse' with its beautiful oriel windows above the entrance (*GND*1). A little to the north is **Giant's Hill**, with an enormous giant of unknown origin cut into the chalk (*TD*.xlviii; *LLI*.8e; *D*1.II.v).

Abbotsea (*TM*.xxvi), Abbotsbury, near the coast, 8 m. NW of Weymouth; cf. **Abbot's Beach** (*D*1.II.v).

a-bearing, proceeding in the direction of.

Aberdeen (*TL*). Written after Hardy had received an honorary degree at Aberdeen University; cf. *Life* 323–4/347–8. *Queen*, Knowledge and Wisdom; cf. the epigraph, Isa.xxiii,6.

Abigail . . . Michal, two wives of David (*DR*.xiv.3), I Sam.xxv, II Sam.iii; **Abigail** (*WT*7.i).

Abishag . . . David (*HE*.xlv), a young virgin and the king in his old age, I Kings i,1–4.

Abraham, flocks . . . ring-straked (*TD*.xix), cf. Gen.xiii,2 and Jacob's method of increasing his flocks, Gen.xxx,25–43. **Abraham . . . Isaac . . . hill together** (*TD*.xlix), Gen.xxii,1–18. **Abrahamic success**, in breeding (*MC*.xxix), Gen.xxii,17. **Abraham's bosom . . . solemn thought** (*DR*.viii.2), cf. Wordsworth's sonnet 'It is a beauteous evening' with reference to childhood serenity or the heaven that 'lies about us in our infancy' (*G.T.*).

Absalom's death (*TT*.xiv), II Sam.xviii,9–15; **Absalont** (*W*.xxix).

The Absolute Explains (*HS*), based on the study of Einstein's theories of Relativity and of Time as a 'fourth dimension', in which past and future are co-existent with the present. The theory is illustrated with reference to Hardy and Emma. *toothless*, non-destructive; *phasmal*, visionary, abstract; *irised*, see **iris-bow**; *bruits*, makes renowned.

the Absolution (*LLI*.8f), the forgiveness of sins pronounced by the priest after the General Confession.

Academician, member of the Royal Academy (for arts and sciences).

accompt, tally, reckoning, count, sum.

'According to the Mighty Working' (*LLE*). The title is taken from the C. of E. burial service. *quick-cued mumming* (acting with no pauses), a rapid cause-effect sequence; *spinner's wheel* (cf. *SC*.The Convergence of the Twain, 31. The wheel image was familiar from FitzGerald's *Rubáiyát* and Browning's 'Rabbi Ben Ezra'.) *onfleeing*, flying or revolving on and on.

accursed swine (DLa), Gadarene swine, Mark v,1,11–13.

accursed thing . . . fire (*JO*.VI.v), Josh.vi,18; vii,1,15.

Achates, trusty friend (*L*.III.iv), cf. Virgil, *Aeneid* i,188.

Acheron, Shade in the Mournful Fields by (*FMC*.xxxiv), *Acherontic shades* (*JO*.VI.iv), spirits of the dead in the underworld by the gloomy Acheron river (classical mythology); cf. Virgil, *Aeneid* vi,295ff.

Achillean moodiness (*W*.xxvii), like that of the Greek warrior Achilles during the Trojan war; cf. *Iliad* i. **Achilles** (*MC*.xii) was educated in the arts by a centaur (half-human, half-horse); Henchard had to learn from the rough-and-tumble of experience.

achromatic (*TT*.iv), telescope with lenses which eliminate colour.

a-croupied, crouched, squatting.

Actaeonic (*W*.xii), from hunting. Actaeon was a celebrated hunter, who, according to classical mythology, was turned into a stag from gazing on Diana when she was bathing.

ad referendum (*D*2.v.i), for reference to others (Lat.).

Adam, the old (*TD*.xlv), sinful nature; cf. I Cor.xv,22. **Adam** (the only man in the world, *RN*.II.i), Gen.i; when he **first saw the sun set** (*DR*.ii.4; *WB*.I.vii); **and Eve** (in the garden of Eden, *FMC*.xvii; *TD*.xx), Gen.ii–iii.

Adams and Leverrier (*TT*.ix). John Adams (1819–92) and Jean Leverrier (1811–77) independently inferred the existence of a planet. Their calculations helped the German astronomer Galle to discover Neptune in 1846.

Addison, Joseph (1672–1719): on the epic (PRF), *The Spectator*, no. 267, 5 Jan 1712, 'nothing should go . . . not related to it'; student at Oxford (*JO*.VI.ix).

Adieu! she cries . . . lily hand (*PBE*.xii ep.), John Gay, 'Black-eyed Susan' (*G.T.*).

Adonis, a beautiful youth with whom Venus fell in love; he was killed while boar-hunting. **Adonis (steed of) . . . told** (counted) **the steps** (*PBE*.xi), V and A,277.

Adullam (*MC*.xxxvi), I Sam.xxii,1–2.

Aeneas, at Carthage . . . brilliant scene (*PBE*.xiv), Virgil, *Aeneid* i,419ff; when the disguised Queen of Love (Venus, his mother) . . . perfume (*RN*.II.vi), *Aeneid* i,402–5; with his father (Anchises, whom Aeneas carried out of burning Troy, *RN*.IV.vii), *Aeneid* ii,624ff; **Aeneas and St Paul** (*L*.IV.iii), pagan and Christian representatives, Aeneas the legendary founder of Rome after the Trojan war, and Paul, who was shipwrecked off Malta and whose epistolary zeal contributed immeasurably to the expansion of the Church in countries bordering on the Mediterranean; **Aeneas** (*D*1.VI.v) as the ancestor of the Roman emperors (so presented in the *Aeneid*).

Aeolian harp, a fashionable instrument in the second half of the eighteenth and during the early part of the nineteenth century; it was placed in a window or tree in the garden, where it could be played upon by the wind (Aeolus, the classical god of the wind). **Aeolian modulations** (*MC*.XI), Shelley, *Prometheus Unbound* IV,188.

The Aërolite (*HS*). *aërolite,* meteorite; *grin . . . opined,* do not indicate grief until understood; *sense,* awareness, sentience. Cf. **the Unfulfilled Intention**.

Aeschylus (what he imagined our nursery children feel; Hellenic happiness is less and less possible), Greek dramatist, 525–456 BC, whose surviving plays include the *Agamemnon* trilogy and

Prometheus Bound. The topic raised by Hardy at this point (*RN*.III.i) had been discussed by Walter Pater in his essay on Winckelmann (see Pater, *The Renaissance*); for 'the defects of natural laws', cf. **the Unfulfilled Intention**. For Hardy, who accepted his tragic viewpoint, he was one of 'the old masters of imaginative creation' (PRF). **Aeschylean phrase** (TD.lix), *Prometheus Bound*,169 (*Life* 243/256). His plays are a precedent for the 'intermittent' drama of *The Dynasts* (*D*.pr.)

Aesculapius (*HS*.In the Evening), the Greek god of medicine.

affined, spiritually related.

afore (dial.), before.

After a Journey (*SC*). *autumn wrought division*, cf. *TL*.The Division; *dawn*, when traditionally ghosts vanish (cf. *Ham*.I.i).

After many days (*PBE*.xxxvii ep.), Eccl.xi,1.

After the Fair (*TL*). For the Casterbridge places, see map B. Chiefly at the centre of Dorchester (the Cross, where the main streets cross, the *carrefour* of *MC*.xxii), mainly Cornhill or Cornmarket Place; St Peter's *chimes*, cf. *MC*.iv; *Clock-corner*, below the Town Hall clock; *Hart*, the White Hart inn.

After the Last Breath (*TL*). Hardy's mother died on Easter Sunday (cf. *Life* 321/344–5). *Wrongers*, the Doomsters of *WP*.Hap who had caused her suffering.

After the Visit (*SC*). When the poem was first published in 1910, before Mrs Hardy's death, there was no dedication to F. E. D. (Florence Dugdale, who became Hardy's second wife); the 'ancient floors' disguise the allusion to Max Gate. *drouthy*, suffering from drought.

afterclap, a setback when everything seems favourably disposed.

Afternoon Service at Mellstock (*MV*). Cf. *Life* 10/16 and, for the scene, *OMC*4.I.i. and *DR*.xii.8 (openings).

against a neighbour's cat (*RN*.IV.vi), cf. *KL*.IV.vii,36–8 and 'dog . . . animal kicked out' (*RN*.V.i).

Agamemnon: 'Chant Aelinon, Aelinon! but may the good prevail' is the refrain in the first chorus of this play by Aeschylus ('Then be your burden sad with sounds of wail But let the happier note prevail' in Lewis Campbell's translation); Hardy holds that 'all really true literature' has, directly or indirectly, such a theme (CEF). From the same chorus (ll. 67–8) comes 'Things are as they are, and will be brought to their destined issue' (*JO*.VI.ii).

Agape (Gk.), love-feast (*TD*.xxxv).

The Aged Newspaper Soliloquizes (*WW*), written for the 135th anniversary number of *The Observer* (a Sunday paper), 14 Mar 1926.

The Ageing House (*MV*). Hardy's note that this is Max Gate suggests that he imagined Emma much younger-looking than she was in 1885–6. The poem's deliberate antithesis gives it a more general significance.

Agnostic (cf. *JO*.v.vi), a word coined by T. H. Huxley about 1870.

'Αγνωστωι Θεωι (*PPP*), Greek: 'To the Unknown God', Acts xvii,23. In this poem Hardy raises a hope voiced by the Chorus of Pities at the end of *The Dynasts*.

A. H., 1855–1912, one of Hardy's uncollected poems. Major-General Arthur Henniker, husband of Mrs Henniker and a friend of Thomas Hardy, died prematurely, after being kicked by his horse and sustaining a broken leg. His wife organized a 'little book for his friends' (pub. 1912), to which Hardy contributed this syntactically imperfect poem.

Ah, my heart . . . poor Love shall live or die (*TT*.title-page), from Crashaw's 'Love's Horoscope'; suggested by Edmund Gosse.

Ahasuerus (*RN*.II.vii), the legendary Wandering Jew, condemned to wander on earth until the second coming of Christ, for having struck him when carrying the cross to Calvary.

Ahimaaz . . . king (*RN*.iv.v), II Sam.xviii,22–7.

Aholah and Aholibah, harlot sisters (*TD*.xiv; *WW*.The Clasped Skeletons), Ezek.xxiii,1–4.

Ailinon! (*HS*.Compassion). See ***Agamemnon.***

aion, aeon, a long period in the history of the universe.

air-castles, daydreams, castles in the air.

Ajaccian (*D*.Fore Scene), of Ajaccio, Corsica, where Napoleon Bonaparte was born in 1769.

The Alarm (*WP*). The tradition relates to Hardy's grandfather. Hardy was uncertain whether the date of the invasion alarm was 1803 or 1804. His first sketch shows the Volunteer on the heath near his home (Higher Bockhampton, where Hardy was born), with the beacon flaring on Rainbarrow; the second sketch shows him at the top of Ridgeway, overlooking Weymouth ('royal George's town', where George III habitually stayed with his family in the summer), with Portland beyond.

alarum, a device for waking by noise (cf. 'alarm clock').

Alas . . . grey shadow . . . (*WB*.III.viii ep.), Tennyson, 'Tithonus',11.

Alastor (*MC*.xxvi), avenging spirit (Gk. Cf. Shelley's 'Alastor').

Albertus Magnus (*RN*.I.vi), a thirteenth-century German monk whose scholarly repute made him legendary.

Albion, a poetical name of ancient origin for Britain.

Albuera (*TM*.v; *D2*.VI.iv), a bloody battle in Spain (1811) between the British and the French.

Alcinous (*RN*.I.vii), King of Phaeacia (later known as Corcyra, then Corfu), off the west coast of northern Greece. He was the father of Nausicaa, who nobly came to the rescue of Odysseus when he was shipwrecked (*Odyssey* vi–viii).

Aldbrickham (*LLI*.2; *JO*), Reading, Berkshire. The George Hotel is actual.

Aldebaran (*FMC*.ii), a star of first magnitude appearing between Orion and the Pleiades; **Aldebaran or Sirius** (*TD*.xxxiv), two of the brightest stars, both in the southern sky.

Alderworth (*RN*; *SC*.The Moth-Signal), on Affpuddle Heath, near the crossroads south of Bryants Puddle (map F).

Alexander the Great (355–323 BC), son of Philip, King of Macedonia; his conquests spread to India (*RN*.III.ii).

Alfredston (*JO*), Wantage, Berkshire; the birthplace of King Alfred, whose statue stands in the market-place; the Bear (hotel) is mentioned.

Alicia's Diary (*CM*3, first pub. Oct 1887) is ultimately an anti-marriage anticipation of *JO*. The Venice and Milan scenes were based on Hardy's recent holiday in Italy (cf. *Life* 192–5/200–3). The Wherryborne setting suggests the Frome valley.

Alike and Unlike (*HS*). Hardy and Emma's impressions of the scenes, as they travelled to Ireland, stopping at Llandudno and driving round Great Orme's Head, were changed, either by some difference between them that day or, more probably, by the 'division' that worsened between them as a result of meeting Mrs Henniker the next (*Life* 254–6/270–2). Emma is imagined speaking.

alive again . . . lost . . . found (*WB*.II.vi), Luke xv,32.

all a-sheenen Wi' long years o' handlen (shining, handling, *FMC*.lvi), William Barnes, 'Woak Hill'.

All hemin . . . autou! (*JO*.II.iii), from the Greek, I Cor.viii,6.

All is vanity (*TD*.xli), Eccl.i,2 ('words of the Preacher, the son of David', i.e. attributed to Solomon).

All Saints', All Souls' (*FMC*.xvi), in 'a certain town . . . many miles north of Weatherbury', and imaginary.

allemand, allemande (a name given to various German dances).

Allen-a-Dale . . . lord (*PBE*.viii ep.), Scott, *Rokeby* III.xxx.

All-Fours, a card game; **on all-fours with**, in accordance with.

All's Well (*WP*.The Impercipient; *PPP*.In Tenebris II), cf. Tennyson, *In Memoriam* cxxvi–vii.

Alma (*CM*5), a river in the Crimea; in September 1854, at the beginning of the Crimean War, British and French forces defeated Russian troops opposed to their crossing it.

Almack's (*CM*.12.iii), assembly rooms in London; cf. *TL*.Reminiscences of a Dancing Man.

Alonzo the Brave . . . laughter . . . blue (*FMC*.lii, section vii), alluding to the appearance of Alonzo's ghost at the wedding-feast of the false Imogene in 'Alonzo the Brave and the Fair Imogene' by M. G. Lewis, 1775–1818.

alters . . . alteration finds (love, *TD*.liii), Son.116 (*G.T.*).

Altruism, a term from the philosophical writings of Auguste Comte (see **Positivist**), indicating concern for the welfare of others, as opposed to self-interest (a principle which dominates George Eliot's fiction). Hardy's use of 'loving-kindness' (from Psalm xxiii, but revitalized by Swinburne's use of it in the first of his 1866 *Poems and Ballads*) – which has the additional meaning of 'loving one's kind' – is almost synonymous (cf. *TD*.xlvii). His altruism or Golden Rule extended to all forms of life: *LLE*.Apology; *MV*.'The wind blew words'; *Life* 224/235, 346–7/373–4,349/376–7.

Amabel (*WP*). The name may be from the heroine of W. H. Ainsworth's *Old St Paul's*, one of Hardy's favourite novels in his youth, possibly with the 'à ma belle' overtone. The poem was almost certainly occasioned by meeting Mrs Martin in London (*Life* 41/43; cf. 18–20/23–5). The hour-glass of his sketch shows the sands of time running out, with the soul (represented by the butterflies) excluded anticipatively until 'the Last Trump' (see **Trumpet**), a surprising conventionality for the heterodox Hardy of 1865.

Amalekites (*D*3.VII.v), a warlike tribe in the Sinai peninsula; cf. Num.xiv,45.

Amazonian, pertaining to women of manly strength (from the Amazons of Asia Minor, a warlike tribe according to classical legend).

Ambition pricked me on (*WT*5.ii), cf. Falstaff, 'honour pricks me on', *1.H4*.v.i,130.

American war (*TT*.i), the War of Independence (1775–83), fought by the colonists, mainly British, against Britain.

Amerigo Vespucci (*RN*.I.iv), a Florentine (1451–1512) after whom America was named, though it had been previously discovered by Columbus.

amoroso (It.), lover, gallant.

amourettes, minor love affairs.

Amy Dudley (*W*.xxxi), the Earl of Leicester's wife, murdered in the expectation that he would marry Queen Elizabeth; cf. Scott's *Kenilworth*.

an if (archaic), if.

Anacreontic (*HE*.vii), elegant and lyrical, in the style of the Greek poet Anacreon (sixth century BC).

Ancient Mariner (*DR*.iii.1), cf. Coleridge's 'The Rime of the Ancient Mariner', 578–85. Hardy (*Life* 252/268) regards the novelist as an Ancient Mariner whose business it is to relate stories outside 'the ordinary experience of every average man and woman'.

An Ancient to Ancients (*LLE*). *tabret*, small tabor (drum), timbrel; *Sir Roger* de Coverley, an old country dance; *The Bohemian Girl* by M. W. Balfe (1843) and *Il Trovatore* by Verdi (1853); *Etty, Mulready, Maclise*, fashionable painters in the early Victorian era; novelists: Edward Bulwer-Lytton, Sir Walter Scott, Alexandre Dumas, George Sand; *Aïdes*, Hades, the mythological underworld of the Greek dead; *Sophocles . . . Homer*, writers and philosophers of ancient Greece; *Clement, Augustin(e), Origen*, scholars and leaders in the early Christian Church.

And calumny . . . known (*OMC*4.I.vii), Shelley, *The Revolt of Islam* IX.xxxi.

And he . . . tree . . . (*OMC*4.II.i), Psalm i.3; cf. **Like some fair tree**.

And here's a hand . . . (*MC*.xxxviii; *fiere*, friend), Burns, 'Auld Lang Syne'.

And I heard sounds . . . wars (*D*.title-page), Tennyson, 'A Dream of Fair Women',19–20.

And she humbled . . . (*JO*.VI ep), Esther (Apocrypha) xiv,2.

And the king rose up . . . nay (*RN*.VI.iv), Solomon to his mother Bathsheba, I Kings ii,19–20.

'And there was a great calm' (*LLE*), written to appear in *The Times* on the second anniversary of the armistice which concluded the 1914–18 war (cf. *Life* 407/437). The title is from Matt.viii,26; the Spirits return from *The Dynasts*. *Huns*, a term of opprobrium for the Germans; *weft-winged engines*, aeroplanes with woven or canvas wings; *peace on earth*, cf. *WW*.Christmas: 1924.

And wilt thou . . . nay (*PBE*.xxxv ep.), Sir Thomas Wyatt, 'The Lover's Appeal' (*G.T.*).

Andean, lofty, like the Andes mountain range in South America.

Andrea Ferara (Ferrara), a famous sixteenth-century Italian maker of swords (*CM*.10).

the Angel Gabriel (*CM*.12.v), guardian of Eden before the Fall of Adam and Eve. **angel . . . John saw . . . sun** (*TD*.xxxiii), Rev.xix,17.

Angelico, Fra (*OMC*4.II.i), Italian painter, 1387–1455.

Anglebury (*DR; HE; RN*), Wareham on the Frome river west of Poole; its Wessex name echoes its importance as a port in Anglo-Saxon times. The Red Lion Hotel is actual.

anigh, near; **anighst**, almost.

animalcula (*D*1.Fore Scene), tiny ephemeral creatures, animalcules (a word used ignorantly for 'animals', *MC*.viii), to which ordinary people are reduced in the philosophical scale; cf. *DR*.xii.3 and *RN*.IV.v, where such creatures wallowing in mud are associated with winged ephemerons, Clym 'being of no more account in life than an insect'; cf. also the end of IV.vi, flies in *TD* (especially xvi), and **gnats**.

Anna, Lady Baxby (*GND*7), a story of the Civil War. Her brother was the Earl of Bedford. See **Baxby**.

An Anniversary (*MV*). The 'stile' recalls Hardy's bitterness in April 1871, when he read a crushing review of his first published novel (*Life* 84/87,507), though this may not relate to the anniversary. Time's changes include the burial of his parents, his first wife, and his sister Mary, at Stinsford.

Anno Domini (Lat.), in the year of our Lord (AD), since the birth of Christ.

The Announcement (*MV*). The deleted MS 'January 1879' and the subject (the chairs to support the coffin) link this with **A January Night**.

Antigone (*LLI*.3.iii), heroine of Sophocles' *Antigone*; by burying her brother she obeys the unwritten law of Heaven, but breaks the law of the state and forfeits her life. **As Antigone said, I am neither a dweller among men nor ghosts** (*JO*.VI.ix), *Antigone*,851.

Antinomianism, the belief that the Christian faith is above moral law.

Antinous (*TT*.v; *TD*.lvii), an eastern youth of whom the Roman emperor Hadrian was so fond that he erected a temple to his memory, and encouraged the belief that he had been changed into a constellation.

Antipodean miscreant (*HE*.xlii), **antipodean absences** (*MC*.xlv): see **Botany Bay**.

Antoinette (*HS*.Music in a Snowy Street), Marie Antoinette of Austria, wife of Louis XVI of France. Both were guillotined in 1793; cf. *TL*.One We Knew and *D*2.v.iv,viii ('the bride's great-aunt').

Antony (*PBE*.xxxv), kissed away . . . provinces, *AC*.III.x,7–8.

Aphrodite, the Greek goddess of love and beauty (the Roman Venus), named after the foam of the sea from which she was born; **Weaver of Wiles** (*WB*.I.ii,II.vi), so described by Sappho; **Aphrodite, Ashtaroth, Freyja** (*WB*.II.xii), Greek, Semitic, and Norse goddesses of love. See **Apollo**.

aplomb (Fr.), confidence, self-possession, poise.

Apocalyptic writer (*JO*.I.iii), St John, author of Revelation.

apogee to perigee, the point in the orbit of a planet when it is furthest from the earth to the orbital point when it is nearest.

Apollo, short of (*TT*.xvi). It would have required divine intervention for Lady Constantine to change her mind; Apollo (who here seems to be regarded as the classical god of the sun) was always presented as young and handsome. **the Apollo** and **the Aphrodite** (PRF), the Apollo Belvedere, in the Vatican Museum, and the Aphrodite of Melos, usually known as the Venus, in the Louvre, Paris.

Apollyon (*JO*.I.iii; cf. *Life* 441–2/476), lying in wait for Christian; see Part I of Bunyan's *The Pilgrim's Progress*.

Apologetica (*JO*.IV.i), a textbook of arguments in defence of Christianity.

Apologia pro vitâ meâ (*WB*.I.vi), defence of my life. Pierston is imagined using this expression before it was used by Cardinal Newman in 1864 as the title of one of his works.

Apostle (Peter) **at the accusation** (*MC*.xxii), Matt.xxvi,69–73 (*bewray*, expose, reveal, accuse). **Apostle's corporeal self** (*WB*.I.ix), St Paul's; cf. I Cor.xv,31 (die daily).

Apostolic Charity (*TD*.xxxvi), St Paul on charity, I Cor.xiii,5.

Apostolic Succession (*L*.I.xii), the transmission of spiritual authority from the apostles of Jesus through succeeding bishops, belief in which was given new impetus in the nineteenth century by the Oxford or Tractarian Movement.

Apostrophe to an Old Psalm Tune (*MV*). Memories of the metrical psalm probably sung to the 'New Sabbath' (*L*.I.i): by Hardy in the Stinsford choir; in London (suggested by 'temple'), modified for *Hymns Ancient and Modern* (1861), of which W. H. Monk had been musical editor; played or sung by Emma Hardy, now dead like **Monk** (W. H. or Edwin) or whoever arranged (*outset*, set out) it. (For this reason it pains Hardy to hear it.) Lastly he hears it at church (cf. 'quired oracles') during war (on 13 Aug 1916, it seems), and recalls it in the form he sang it as a boy. It may last until the Day of **Judgment**.

appetite for joy (*TD*.xxx; cf. *TD*.xvi and *Life* 213/222), Browning, *Paracelsus* i, 92.

apple of discord (*W*.xxxiv; *LLI*.3.iii). Marked 'For the fairest' and thrown into the assembly of the gods by the malevolent goddess Discordia, it created rivalry and dissension between Juno, Minerva, and Venus, thereby ultimately bringing ruin to Troy and much sorrow to the Greeks.

apples, christening of. See **St Swithin**.

Apt to entice a deity (*DR*.xv.1), from 'Rosalynde' (*G.T.*), 'Rosalind's Description' in Thomas Lodge's *Rosalynde*, 1590.

Aquae Sulis (*SC*). The title is the name given by the Romans to the hot springs which made Bath a spa for centuries; literally, the waters of Sul, an ancient British goddess. *interlune*, period between the old moon and the new; *baldachined*, canopied.

A.R.A. (*WB*.I.ix), Associate of the Royal Academy (cf. Royal Academician, I.vi).

Arab existence, nomadic life; **Arabian bedstead**, divan.

Arago, François (*TT*.vii), a French scientist who became director of the Paris Observatory in 1830.

araucarias and deodars, hardly 'shrubs' (*HE*.xxv), the former being 'monkey puzzler' trees, the latter a kind of cedar.

Arcadian, as in Arcadia, a pastoral region of ancient Greece where, according to tradition, people lived in innocence and peace, shepherds playing the kind of pipe or flute associated with their god Pan; (*TM*.ii) harmonizing with the countryside.

Arch, Joseph (DLa), founder of the National Agricultural Labourers' Union. Like Shakespeare, he was born in Warwickshire (1826; d.1919).

Archbishop Tillotson (*LLI*.4.ii), born at Sowerby, Yorkshire; studied at Clare College, Cambridge, becoming a fellow in 1651.

Archimedes . . . Stephenson (*L*.I.xiv), all interested in engineering: **Archimedes**, of Syracuse, mathematician and inventor of the third century BC; **Newcomen**, inventor of a steam-engine (1698), improved by **James Watt** (1736–1819); **Thomas Telford** (1757–1834), builder of bridges and canals; **George Stephenson** (1781–1848), designer of railway engines.

architrave, ornamental moulding round an arch or doorway or window; the lowest division of the **entablature**.

archivault (*TT*.ix), main vault or dome, the whole sky.

Arcturus, the brightest star in the northern hemisphere.

area-door, in the basement, giving access to a sunken area between the pavement and the main building; used by servants and tradesmen.

Argonautic voyaging (*LLI*.4.i), of Jason on the Argo ship, in search of the golden fleece.

argumentum ad verecundiam (Lat.), argument based on modesty or respect for tradition.

Ariadne (*W*.xxxi), deserted by Theseus, after helping him to escape from the Cretan labyrinth.

Ariel sleeps in this posture (*L*.II.vii), *Tem*.v.i,88–90.

Aristodemus the Messenian (*WW*), adapted from the account of the war between the Messenians (in SW Greece) and the Spartans by the Greek historian Pausanias. After being forced to retreat to the mountain stronghold Ithome, the Messenians sent for oracular advice from the sibyl at Delphi. Hardy brings forward the death of the Messenian king Euphaes six years to intensify the dramatic situation. *hendecasyllabics*, lines of eleven syllables in classical metre; *Aépy̆tids*, descendants of Aepytus, who gave his name to a line of Messenian kings; *reavement*, bereavement.

Aristotle, a Greek philosopher of the fourth century BC, famous for his teaching on many subjects: (PRF) Hardy uses the argument in the *Poetics* (ix) that poetry (or art) is truer (more philosophical) than history, because it relates not to what has happened but to what might happen; it can present universal truths. **Aristotelian cathartic qualities** (*JO*.1912 ps. to pr.) a reference to the *Poetics* (vi), where Aristotle argues that tragedy through pity and terror purges these emotions.

ark . . . fly . . . rest (*MC*.xxiii), like the dove, Gen.viii,9; **Ark (of the Covenant) . . . Philistines** (*TM*.xxvii; DLa; *TD*.lii), cf. I Sam.v,11 to vi,14 and **The Subalterns**.

armed man, like an (*TT*.xv), Prov.vi,11.

armigerent (*D*1.VI.v), resorting to arms or war (cf. 'belligerent').

arm-in-crook, arm in arm (arms crooked together).

Arnold, Matthew, 1822–88: (*LLE*.Apology) the application of ideas to life (in poetry), from 'The Study of Poetry', *Essays in Criticism*, 2nd series; Hardy accepts Arnold's view (at the opening of this essay) that people will turn more and more to poetry for an interpretation of life, and that 'most of what now passes with us for religion and philosophy will be replaced by poetry'. (PRF) the arts 'a criticism of life' (from the same essay); (*Life* 146–7/151; cf. Gen.Pr.) on provincialism in literature.

arrant (dial.), errand, mission.

arrière-pensée, a thought which is concealed or kept in reserve.

arris, the edge where two carved surfaces meet.

Arrowthorne Lodge (*HE*). Hardy stated that it was a modern house near 'The Earldoms', a wood north of the New Forest.

Artemis (*W*.xlii), goddess of chastity, contrasted with Aphrodite, goddess of sexual passion; (*TD*.xx) and **Demeter**, goddess of fertility and harvests; **Artemis, Athena, or Hera** (*RN*.I.vii), Greek goddesses corresponding to the Roman Diana (goddess of the moon, hunting, and chastity), Minerva (goddess of wisdom, war, and the liberal arts), and Juno (queen of heaven and wife of Jupiter, represented on a throne, with a diadem on her head and a golden sceptre in her right hand).

Artemisia, one who dotes on her dead husband; named after a queen of Caria, who erected the Mausoleum (one of the seven wonders of the ancient world) in memory of her husband Mausolus (d.353 BC).

Arthur (*PBE*.xiii–xv; *QC*.vi,xxii), a legendary British king who resisted pagan invaders; his birth is associated with Tintagel Castle, and his last battle with Lyonnesse (cf. Malory's *Morte d'Arthur*).

Arthur's Seat (*MC*.viii), a hill of volcanic rock outside Edinburgh; for Hardy's 'jarreny' to Scotland, see Life 150/154–5 and **Farfrae**.

Article Four (*TD*.xviii), the fourth of the thirty-nine articles of the C. of E., asserting the physical resurrection of Christ.

As flies . . . gods . . . sport (*TD*.1892 pr.; cf. 'flies', xvi, xliii and 'sport', lix), *KL*.IV.i,37–8.

As I came . . . Cannobie (*MC*.xiv), Canonbie, north of Carlisle and just within Scotland. Hardy couldn't remember where he saw or heard the song.

As I came in . . . my dearie (*MC*.viii), Burns, 'Bonnie Peg' (adapted).

As long as skies . . . sorrow (*HE*.xvii), Shelley, *Adonais* xxi.

As one, in suffering all, that suffers nothing (*W*.xxx; quoted on

Hardy's father, *Life* 248/262), *Ham*.III.ii.64.

As though a rose . . . (*FMC*.lvii), Keats, 'The Eve of St Agnes' xxvii.

'As 'twere to-night' (*LLE*). In this song Hardy remembers a week in March 1870 when he first met Emma Gifford (*Life* 74–5/77–8); cf. *SC*.A Week.

Ascension, of Christ; cf. Acts i,1–11.

Ascham, Roger (*TD*.xv), quotation from *The Scholemaster* (1570).

a-scram (dial.), shrunken, withered.

ashlar, square hewn stone, usually in thin slabs for facing walls; (vb.) face with slabs of stone.

ashleaf, a variety of potato named after its ashen leaves.

Ashton at the disappearance of Ravenswood (*MC*.xxxvi), in a quicksand: Scott, *The Bride of Lammermoor* xxxv.

Ashtoreth (*FMC*.vii), a Semitic fertility goddess who, to some extent, was a forerunner of the Roman Venus; see **Aphrodite**.

Ash-Wednesday, the first day of Lent, so called from the custom instituted by Pope Gregory the Great of opening this period of abstinence by sprinkling ashes on the heads of the penitent.

asile (Fr.), refuge, retreat, haven.

aspen, tremulous, like the leaves of the aspen (a poplar tree).

Aspern, near Vienna (cf. scene in *D*2.IV.iii); here in 1809 the French marshal Lannes, one of Napoleon's most zealous army commanders, was fatally wounded (*D*3.VII.vi).

Assyrian bas-reliefs, in the style of (*LLI*.5.iii), like the conventionally sculptured hair in the bas-reliefs of ancient Assyria, which Hardy was familiar with in the British Museum and in Biblical illustrations.

Assyrians . . . Destroying Angel (*WT*3.iv), II Kings xix,35.

Astronomer Extraordinary (*TT*.vi), a distinguished astronomer appointed as a supernumerary for special investigations. **Astronomer Royal** (*TT*.i), principal of the Royal Greenwich Observatory.

asymptote, a mathematical line which approaches a given curve, but never quite meets it.

At a Bridal (*WP*). The thought is repeated in *WP*.To a Motherless Child and *JO*.III.viii. The idea of nature as the Great Mother (cf. *DR*.xiii.1, a scene which may have been written in 1867), indifferent to human fate, probably came from Shelley's early poem *Queen Mab* (cf. vi,197ff: 'No love, no hate thou cherishest . . . [the world] Where pain and pleasure, good and evil join,

To do the will of strong necessity'). Darwinism confirmed such a view. The ending (careless of the type) recalls *In Memoriam* lv,lvi, where Tennyson has in mind the disappearance of whole species in the survival of the fittest.

At a Fashionable Dinner (*HS*), a superstition about thirteen being an unlucky number, applied seemingly to Emma Lavinia Hardy.

At a Hasty Wedding (*PPP*), written for the story 'A Changed Man', which first appeared in April 1900. The third line ran 'By lifelong ties that tether zest'; the wedding observer thinks that the hasty marriage will prove unhappy.

At a House in Hampstead (*LLE*). Hardy joined the National Committee for acquiring Wentworth House, Hampstead, where the poet John Keats had lived, in March 1920. His poem appeared in *The John Keats Memorial Volume*, 1921. *Sometime*, formerly; *nightingale . . . Full-throated*, cf. Keats's 'Ode to a Nightingale' (*G.T.*); *Seven famed Hills*, of Rome. Keats died in rooms by the steps above the Piazza di Spagna, and was buried in the Protestant Cemetery, where the white pyramidal tomb of Cestius (cf. *PPP*. At the Tomb of Cestius . . .) points the way to his grave; *ancient tree*, the mulberry in the garden at Hampstead.

At a Rehearsal of One of J. M. B.'s Plays. The rehearsal (of *Mary Rose*) occurred during Hardy's last London visit (cf. *Life* 404/528), and the poem was printed below the frontispiece of Barrie in *The Complete Plays of J. M. Barrie*, 1928.

At a Seaside Town in 1869 (*MV*), Weymouth; cf. *TL*.At Waking. *Morgenblätter*, one of a set of waltzes by the younger Johann Strauss (cf. *Life* 63/65, where Hardy states that the gist of the poem is 'fancy only').

At a Watering Place (*SC*). The scene suggests Weymouth.

At an Inn (*WP*). Hermann Lea states that this was written at the George, Winchester; perhaps Hardy told him it occurred to him there. If so, it was while visiting the city with Mrs Henniker, probably in August 1893, to show her places associated with Tess; cf. *TD*.lix. Hardy wrote of Mrs Henniker in *SC*.Wessex Heights, 'my love for her in its fulness she herself even did not know'. The image and thought of 'severing sea' are from Matthew Arnold's poem 'Isolation' ('Yes: in the sea of life enisl'd').

At Castle Boterel (*SC*). Probably a recollection from Hardy's 1873 visit to Cornwall (*Life* 92/94). His first visit in March 1870 suggests no time for the 'benighted' climb up the old road into Boscastle;

cf. *Life* 74–5/77–8.

At Day-Close in November (*SC*). At Max Gate. *June time*, prime of life (1886? cf. *Life* 173/509).

At Lulworth Cove a Century Back (*LLE*). Hardy's interest in the possibility that John Keats, when the ship taking him to Italy sheltered in Lulworth Cove, walked to see relatives at Broadmayne (3 m. SE of Dorchester) was reinforced from knowing Keatses who lived at Higher Bockhampton; cf. **Kaytes**. *looks up at a star*: there is no confirmation of the tradition referred to in Hardy's note about the time and place of composing this sonnet.

At Madame Tussaud's in Victorian Years (*MV*). Madame Tussaud, a wax-modeller who had practised in Paris, came to England in 1800, and toured with her waxworks; in 1835 she established her museum in Baker Street, London. An added attraction was her orchestra, which Hardy probably first heard during his early years in London.

At Mayfair Lodgings (*MV*). With hindsight Cassie Pole was another 'lost prize' to Hardy; he had known her in youth, when she lived 'in a neighbouring village' (*Life* 267/284,513; cf. Millgate, 149). *for good*, for ever; *less unbending*, had she agreed to marry Hardy.

At Middle-Field Gate in February (*MV*), written when Hardy was working on *TD*. For the names of the bevy he remembered from boyhood, see *Life* 223/233. Middle Field is the second of three on the left from Bockhampton Cross (the crossroads) to Lower Bockhampton.

At Moonrise and Onwards (*LLE*). *Heath-Plantation Hill*, on Puddletown ('Egdon') Heath; *Woman of the waste . . . Lady of all my time*, the moon in space, measuring time month by month.

At Rushy-Pond (*HS*). The reflected moon as a wraith, past and present, of a loved one makes one wonder how much of the poem is fanciful, and whether it is related to *WP*. Neutral Tones, or whether Hardy met Cassie Pole there when she was lady's maid at Kingston Maurward House; cf. **On a Heath**. *substant*, real; *secret year*, period of secret meetings.

At the Altar-Rail (*SC*). The *Fountain* and the *Street of the Quarter-Circle* indicate the park bounded by Albert Road, Dorchester (map B). For the association of woman and sin with the apple, cf. *Paradise Lost* ix (from Gen.iii).

At the Mill (*HS*). Yalbury Brow suggests that the mill is the one which stood in Puddletown, and that the market-town is Dorchester. *borne*, brought forth.

At the Piano (*MV*). A memory of Emma and Hardy at St Juliot rectory (cf. *PBE*.iii), with thoughts of her recurring bouts of mental illness.

At the Railway Station, Upway (*LLE*), at Upwey (in the upper region of the Wey valley) between Dorchester and Weymouth; the convict is probably being escorted to Portland Prison.

At the Royal Academy (*LLE*). For the 1891 note on which this is based, see *Life* 235/246.

At the Word 'Farewell' (*MV*). 'Literally true', Hardy told Mrs Henniker, though later he was not sure whether the event occurred during his first or second visit to St Juliot. The stress on chance in the last stanza recalls that of Browning in 'By the Fire-side'; the feather image, that of the feather-touch in George Eliot's *Middlemarch* xxxi.

At Waking (*TL*). *Dead-white as a corpse*, cf. *W*.iv and *PPP*.A Commonplace Day; *the prize*, cf. *DR*.ii.3, written about the same period.

At Wynyard's Gap (*HS*), SE of Crewkerne (map C). Streams rise on the eastern side and flow NE to join the *Yeo* river; *Crookhorn*, local pronunciation of 'Crewkerne'; *Marshwood*, the vale south of Pilsdon.

Atalanta (*TD*.lvii), a beautiful virgin in classical legend who refused to marry until she was beaten in a race. Those she defeated were slain by her dart; she was defeated by Hippomenes, who threw three golden apples (the gift of Venus) which she stopped to gather as they were thrown at different points along the course.

Athalie (*RN*.I.vii), a tragedy by Racine on a Biblical subject (II Chron. xxii–xxiii), which ends with a march or procession and the crowning of Joash; Hardy probably refers to the 'War March of the Priests' which Mendelssohn wrote for this (1843).

ath'art (dial.), across.

Athelhall (*CM2*; *PPP*.The Dame of Athelhall; *LLE*.The Children and Sir Nameless), Athelhampton Hall (mainly Tudor), east of Puddletown.

Athenians . . . unknown God (*L*.IV.iii), Acts xvii,22–3; **Athenian inquirers on Mars Hill**, Areopagus (*LLE*.Apology), Acts xvii,16ff.

at-home cards, invitations to receptions at stated hours.

Atlantean, like that of Atlas, who (according to classical myth) supported the heavens on his back.

Atlantis (*D*1.IV.vi), some unknown island in the Atlantic (like the fabled Atlantis).

a-topperen (dial.), engaged in knocking the heads of.

Atreus, house of (*JO*.v.iv). Hardy had in mind not so much the tragic horror of Atreus's life as the tragedy of his son Agamemnon and Agamemnon's son Orestes, the subject of Aeschylus's trilogy *The Oresteia*.

Attica, part of ancient Greece around Athens.

atween (dial.), between.

An August Midnight (*PPP*). Illustrative of Hardy's altruism, extending to all creatures (and plants; cf.*PPP*.To Flowers from Italy in Winter), and his imaginative humility: Earth's humblest creatures know secrets hidden from man. *longlegs*, spider; *that . . . I*, that I know not. Cf. William Blake, 'The Fly' (*Songs of Experience*).

aura, tremor, sensation.

Aurelius Antoninus, **Marcus** (*L*.IV.i), Roman emperor and Stoic philosoper, AD 121–80; quotation from *To Himself* (or *Meditations*) viii,5, repeated in *Life* 176/183. It was inscribed by Horace Moule in the copy of *Meditations* he gave Hardy on New Year's Day, 1864 (Millgate,87). See **Pagan moralist** and **Thy aerial part . . . .**

aurora, **aurore**, dawn (from Aurora, classical goddess of dawn).

Aurora Borealis or Northern Lights (cf. *TT*.xx), caused by electrically charged particles from the sun which spiral down open magnetic field lines to form the circle of lights round the magnetic pole. ***aurora militaris*** (*FMC*.xxviii), display by a soldier with effects resembling the Northern Lights.

Austerlitz (*MC*.xx), highest point of success, like Napoleon's when he defeated the Prussians and Austrians at Austerlitz in 1805.

Austral, **austral**, in the southern hemisphere.

Auvergne (DLa), a mountainous region in France. Hardy's evidence came from *The Contemporary Review*, Dec 1882.

Aux grands maux les grands remèdes (*TT*.xxxix), 'Great evils (setbacks) demand great remedies', from the French essayist Montaigne, 1533–92; cf. *Ham*.IV.iii,9–10, 'Diseases desperate grown By desperate appliance are reliev'd . . . '.

Avernus, entrance to the classical hell or underworld.

avore (dial.), before, earlier.

ayless, always.

azew, **go** (of cows) dry up.

B

Babylon, weep by the waters of (*RN*.VI.i; *SC*.God's Funeral; *HS*. The Bird-Catcher's Boy), like the Israelites in exile, Psalm cxxxvii; **fallen** (*TD*.xv), Rev.xiv,8; **witch of** (*TD*.xlvi) and **Whore of** (*JO*.VI.vii), cf. Rev.xvii,1–5. **Babylonish**, sinful. **Babylon the Second** (*PBE*.ii), London, 'a modern Babylon', so described by Benjamin Disraeli in his novel *Tancred*, 1847.

Bacchus, the classical god of wine.

bachelor-apostle (*TD*.xlvii), St Paul.

backbrand, log of wood, laid at the back of a fire (domestic).

back-hair, hair at the back of the head.

backy (dial.), tobacco.

The Bad Example (*WW*). *As you*, As if you; *Meleager*, poet of ancient Greece, remembered by his anthology of epigrams.

Badbury Rings (*TM*.xii), a prominent hill near the Wimborne–Blandford road, with prehistoric concentric ramparts.

ba'dy (dial.), bawdy, improper, wicked.

Bagehot, Walter (1826-77), an economist much of whose *Literary Studies* (1878) Hardy had read *seriatim* in *The National Review* (cf. *Life* 33/37). A quotation from his essay on Milton provides the epigraph for *WW*.A Philosophical Fantasy.

bagman, commercial traveller.

bagnet (dial.), bayonet, stab.

Bags of Meat (*HS*). The MS suggests that this was written at Wimborne. Since a buyer had come from as far as Taunton in Somerset, this must have been a sale of good-quality cattle; the Vale 'down there' is the Frome valley.

baily, bailiff.

baint, bain't, ben't, am, is, or are, not.

Balaam (*RN*.II.iv; *PPP*. The Respectable Burgher), Num.xxii–iv.

balancings of the clouds (*LLE*.Apology), Job xxxvii,16.

Balboa (*FMC*.xlvii), a Spanish explorer (1475–1517) who, from a summit on the isthmus of Panama, was the first European to see the Pacific.

bale, woe, misery, misfortune; **and ban**, suggesting a curse.

Balearic-British times (*WB*.II.iii), British or pre-Roman times, when the inhabitants of Portland, like those of the Balearic Islands in the western Mediterreanean, used slings for defence.

The Ballad of Love's Skeleton (*WW*). During the period of the story George III (his ancestor George I came from Hanover in Germany) and his family spent their summers at Weymouth. The Assembly Rooms for dancing (as described; cf. *Life* 229/239) were at the Royal Hotel (cf. **Stacie's Hotel**). See **Culliford** and map G.

ballet, ballad, song.

ballyrag, scold, abuse violently.

banded, sworn, pledged (possibly from 'Band of Hope', the name given to temperance societies for young people).

bandy, an early name for a hockey-stick, applied to a heavy stick with a bent end which was once used for spreading manure in the fields.

banging, bang-up (slang), fine, 'super', smart, up to the mark.

bankers, stone benches used by masons.

The Banks of Allan Water (*FMC*.xxiii), a song by M. G. Lewis (1775–1818) which supplied the title Hardy had considered for *PBE* ('A Winning Tongue Had He').

banquet-hall deserted (*DR*.vi.3), from Thomas Moore, 'Oft in the stilly night' (*G.T.*).

Barbara of the House of Grebe (*GND*2). This story of cruelty calculated to rouse pity and horror (first pub. on 1 Dec 1890) incurred the inquisitorial misjudgment of T. S. Eliot in *After Strange Gods*, 1934.

Barbary, Saracen countries along the north coast of Africa.

Barleycorn, John, whisky or malt liquor.

barley-mow, barley stack.

barm-bladder, bladder (probably a pig's) in which barm was kept for leavening bread or fermenting liquors.

Barnes, William (1801–86), schoolmaster, philologist, poet, and parson. He was born in the Vale of Blackmoor, which provided the background for his dialect poetry. After being a solicitor's clerk in Dorchester, he opened a school at Mere, on the northern side of the Vale, in 1823. Still a private schoolmaster, he moved to Dorchester in 1835; about twelve years later he bought larger premises, adjacent to the offices occupied by John Hicks in South Street when Hardy became apprentice-architect there in 1856. Barnes was ordained in 1847. After being curate at Whitcombe, he was rector of the neighbouring parish of Winterborne Came from 1862 until his death. He was expert in many languages, and his poems have great lyrical appeal. Hardy wrote an anonymous review of his *Poems of Rural Life in the Dorset Dialect* in 1879, and edited his own selection of Barnes's poems in 1908. For his preface to this volume, his introduction to representative poems in *The English Poets*, his 1879 review, and his obituary recollections and appreciation, see Orel,76–85,94–106. See also *MV*.The Last Signal; *LLE*.The Collector Cleans His Picture, The Old Neighbour and the New; *Life* 28/502,161/167,175–6/181–2,183/190.

barrow, tumulus, grave-mound.

barrow-pig, gelt or castrated pig.

Barthélémon at Vauxhall (*LLE*). Barthélémon composed the tune for Bishop Ken's hymn 'Awake my soul, and with the sun', a great favourite with Hardy (cf. *Life* 10/16), about 1780, when he was first violinist at Vauxhall Gardens, a popular resort not far from Westminster Bridge until 1859. For the occasion which inspired the poem in 1921, see *Life* 414/447. So fascinating was the subject, Hardy made three sketches of it for a story (*OMC*,119–21).

Bartimeus (*HE*.xxvii), Mark x,46–52.

barton, farmyard.

Baruch (*MC*.xv). See 'The Epistle of Jeremy' (verse 9), the sixth chapter of Baruch in the Apocrypha.

Barwith Strand (*PBE*.xx), Trebarwith Strand (*Life* 71/74,295/314).

baseless fabrics of a vision (*L*.1912 pr.), cf. *Tem*.IV.i,151.

basinet, a light type of helmet, closed with a visor.

basket-carriage, carriage with a wickerwork body.

Bath, the Bath (*FMC*.xxxiii; *TT*; *GND*2,3,4; *SC*.Aquae Sulis), a spa (in Somerset) for the gentry. See **Midnight on Beechen**.

bât-horse (*D*3.VII.v), horse for carrying baggage (military).

Battle Abbey Roll (*TD*.i). Kept at Battle Abbey, Sussex, it was thought to be a contemporary list of William the Conqueror's knightly supporters, but was probably compiled later.

Battle of Prague, The (*PBE*.ix; described, *Life* 395/429–30), a popular piece of programme music by Kotzwara, who was born in Prague (1730) and settled in London; cf. *S.R.*14.

Battley, Richard (*DR*.xix.5), a London apothecary (d.1856).

Baxby, the Digby family of Sherborne Castle (*W*.xxiii; cf. *GND*.1). Lady Anna was besieged there (*GND*7); a Lord Baxby and his wife (*LLI*.8e) were guests at the manor house (Ilsington House, Puddletown?).

bays (from laurel for the victor), honour, glory, fame.
Be thou an example . . . purity (*TD*.xxxiv), I Tim.iv,12.
Be you not proud . . . (PRF), Robert Herrick, 'To Dianeme' (*G.T.*).
the Bear (*FMC*.ii). See **Charles's Wain**.
beasts of beating heart (*W*.xxxiii), Shelley, 'The Witch of Atlas' vi.
beater, an old type of watch with a loud tick.
beating up, canvassing for recruits.
Beatrice . . . Dante . . . chariot (*DR*.viii.5), Dante, *Purgatorio* xxx.
Beaumont and Fletcher . . . (*FMC*.xliv): *The Maid's Tragedy*, one of the joint works of the verse dramatists Francis Beaumont, c.1584–1616, and John Fletcher, 1579–1625; *The Mourning Bride*, the one tragedy written by William Congreve, 1697; *Night Thoughts*, a popular poetic work on life and mortality by Edward Young, 1683–1765; *The Vanity of Human Wishes*, a poem by Samuel Johnson, 1749.
beautiful bodies without hearts (*RN*.IV.vi), cf. *TN*.III.iv,351–4.
The Beauty (*LLE*). Hardy's extract was copied into his 1884 notebook from *The Dorset County Chronicle* (16 Oct 1828).
becall, give (a person) a bad name, misjudge.
be-chok'd, a mild oath (may I be choked!); cf. **jown**.
bedad, a form of **begad** (by God), a mild oath.
Bede, the Venerable (*JO*.I.vi), a most scholarly English monk (d.735), whose greatest work is an ecclesiastical history of England.
Bede's Inn (*PBE*.xiii,xxxv), Clement's Inn, one of the old Inns of Court. Knight's chambers were drawn from the office of the architect Raphael Brandon, 17 Clement's Inn, where Hardy worked in the summer of 1870.
The Bedridden Peasant (*PPP*): *some disaster cleft Thy scheme*, cf. **the Unfulfilled Intention**.
bed-tick, the cover or case for a feather-mattress.
bee (*MC*.xxviii), b—— (i.e. bitch). **bee-burning**, when the bees were stupefied with smoke while honey was extracted from the hive.
Beelzebub (*W*.ix), 'the prince of devils', Matt.xii,24, or Satan; his **fork**, which Hardy had been led to believe in (and the bonfire for sinners) in his childhood (*Letters* I,259; cf. *TD*.xiv,1).
Beeny, a high cliff near Boscastle, associated with Hardy's courtship of Emma Gifford; cf. *MV*.The Figure in the Scene, and other poems. With High Cliff (map E) it suggested 'the Cliff without a Name' (*PBE*.xxi-xxii). **Beeny Cliff** (*SC*): *woman riding high*, 10 Mar

1870 (*Life* 75/78); *weird*, mysterious and romantic, partly from the Arthurian legends of Lyonnesse (see also *PBE*.pr.). Two islands off shore are known as the **Beeny Sisters** (*QC*.v).

beest, you are.

beetle, heavy wooden hammer.

Before Life and After (*TL*). See the next two poems in *TL* and *PPP*.The Mother Mourns. Hardy was too subject to moods to be a consistent thinker. How could he profess to be an 'evolutionary meliorist' and wish for human regression into harmony with nature through 'nescience'?

Before Marching and After (*MV*), in memory of Lt F. W. George, son of Hardy's second cousin. He was killed at Gallipoli in August 1915. Hardy and his wife Florence had intended to leave Max Gate (the setting for the poem, though he thinks of his mother) to him (*Life* 370–1/400–1).

Before My Friend Arrived (*HS*). Hardy remembers sitting in September 1873 on the Ten Hatches Weir and sketching the grave being dug by St George's Church, Fordington (its tower eminent beyond the meadows) for his friend Horace Moule, who had committed suicide (*Life* 96/98).

Behold, he standeth . . . land (*LLI*.1), Sol.ii,9–12.

Behold, when thy face . . . pain (*TD*.xxxv), Swinburne, *Atalanta in Calydon*, sixth chorus.

Being reviled . . . day (*TD*.xxvi), I Cor.iv,12–13.

Bel and Nebo (*DR*.xiii.2), Isa.xlvi,1.

beldame, old woman.

Belgae (*CM*6), ancient tribes who crossed to Britain from northern Gaul when the latter was occupied by the Romans.

Bellerophon . . . cankered in soul (*MC*.xvii), *Iliad* vi,200–2. Hardy's concept was probably mediated by Carlyle's essay 'Goethe's Helena' and G. H. Lewes's *Life of Goethe* I.iv.

Bellini, Giovanni (*CM*3.viii), Venetian painter, c.1430–1516.

Belong (*D*1.II.v), i.e. Boulogne, where Napoleon's troops were camped.

beloved son . . . well pleased (*JO*.I.vi), with reference to the Alma Mater or 'bountiful mother', the University; cf. Matt.iii,17 and the starting irony of the two contexts, Jude, victim of heredity and chance, destined like Jesus to be 'crucified'.

Belshazzar (*RN*.I.vi; *WT*.1; *D*2.VI.vii), Dan.v,1–9.

the Belvedere Hotel (*DR*.iv), named after the Belvidere (opened in 1819), Weymouth.

Beneath the shelter . . . (*PBE*.x ep.), Burns, 'The Cotter's Saturday Night'.

benefit (*TT*.xix), malapropism for 'benefice'. **benefit-club staves** (*TM*.xxiii), for use in club-walking processions.

bent-bearded, covered with tufts of long grass; **bents**, tussocks of coarse, usually long, grass.

Bentham, Jeremy (*OMC*6.ii), English writer on jurisprudence and Utilitarian ethics, 1748–1832. **Benthamism** (*HE*.xxxvi), utilitarian ethics based on the principles that men inevitably pursue pleasure and avoid pain, and that all actions are right and good if they promote 'the happiness of the greatest number'. J. S. Mill's modifications of Bentham's theory in *Utilitarianism* are alluded to in 'distorted'.

Benvill Lane (*TD*.xliv,liv; *TL*.The Homecoming), the road from Toller Down towards Evershot (map C).

Bertius's Ptolemy to Rees's Cyclopaedia (*TT*.xxx), a standard edition of Ptolemy's work published at Leyden in 1618, and a standard encyclopedia, 1778–88.

Best Times (*LLE*). The first three recollections of Emma Hardy may all be in Cornwall (the Valency river and St Juliot rectory); the fourth refers to the last time she climbed the stairs at Max Gate, after coming down to entertain Rebekah Owen and her sister (C. J. Weber, *Hardy and the Lady from Madison Square*, Waterville, Maine, 1952, pp. 157–62).

Betelgueux, a star of first magnitude, forming (to the observer) the left shoulder of the Orion constellation.

Bethesda, Pool of (*PBE*.xxx), **quicker cripple at** (*MC*.x), John v,4.

Bethlehem (where Jesus was born), **shepherds** (*TT*.viii), Matt.ii,1–12. (Two stories are confused; cf. Luke ii,4–20.)

Better it is . . . shouldst not vow . . . (*OMC*4.II.v), Eccl.v,5.

better wed . . . mixen . . . moor (*FMC*.xxii), better wed a neighbour than a stranger who lives far off.

between the banks . . . vine (*L*.v.viii), Byron, *Childe Harold* III.lv sequel; cf. Hardy's 1876 tour (*Life* 110/113).

Beware the fury . . . (*RN*.v.i), Dryden, *Absalom and Achitophel* I,1005.

bewildered chimes (*DR*.x.3), Wordsworth, 'The Fountain'.

Beyond the Last Lamp (*SC*). The Hardys lived at Upper Tooting, London SW, most of the time from March 1878 to June 1881. The scene was adapted for *TD*.xxxv. An MS date for the poem is September 1911 (cf. iv).

Bien-aimé (Fr.), well-beloved.
biffins, red winter apples.
big pot, put on the, pretend to be a person of importance.
biggen (dial.), grow big (with child).
Bincombe (*WT*3), a village below the downs north of Weymouth. The two deserters of the York Hussars who were shot in 1801 were buried in the churchyard.
Binegar (*LLI*.4.ii), in the Mendip Hills, not far from Wells.
A Bird-Scene at a Rural Dwelling (*HS*), Hardy's birthplace, first occupied by his grandparents in 1801.
Bissett Hill (*LLI*.8h), on the Salisbury–Blandford road south of Coombe Bissett.
bit of bread, come to a (*FMC*.xxxiii), Prov.vi,26.
bitter weed, mischief-maker.
Black Care (*TD*.xli), from Horace, *Odes* III.i,40.
black witch (*W*.xix), a woman who exerts evil powers (cf. **white witch**).
blackberries, common as (*HE*.xxvii; *MC*.xvi), *1.H4*.II.iv,232.
black-hearts, whortleberries.
Blacklock . . . Sanderson (blind people with an intuitive sense of things outside their experience, *RN*.III.iii): Thomas Blacklock, Scottish minister and poet, 1721–91; Nicholas Sanderson (or Saunderson, 1682–1739) lost his sight in infancy but became a great teacher at Cambridge, where he lectured on Newtonian philosophy and optics, and became a mathematics professor.
Blackmoor (Blackmore) Vale (several references, chiefly *W* and *TD*), pastoral and wooded country north of the chalk hills which include Bubb Down, High Stoy, Nettlecombe-Tout, and Bulbarrow. For reasons given in *TD*.ii, it was once known as White Hart Forest.
Black'on (*TM*.xii, *D*1.II.v,v.iv; TL.At Casterbridge Fair iii), Black Down or Blackdon or Blagdon, a height NNE of Portesham, with a memorial to Admiral Hardy.
blackpot, black pudding (sausages made from pig's blood and suet).
Blackwater (*MC*.xxxii,xli), a deep section of the Frome above Ten Hatches Weir, on the eastern side of Dorchester.
Blackwood (screaming . . . lady, *JO*.ps. to pr.): 'Anti-Marriage League', an attack on *JO* by the novelist Mrs Margaret Oliphant in *Blackwood's Magazine*, Jan 1896 (republished in the Aug 1978 number); cf. *Life* –/287,–/295.

blade, fellow.
bleachy, brackish, saltish.
Blenheim (*TM*.vii), near the upper Danube, where British troops under Marlborough, helped by Prince Eugene of Savoy, defeated French and Bavarian forces in 1704.
blent, blended.
Blessed are the merciful (*HS*.Compassion), Matt.v,7.
Blessed Damozel (*DR*.v.2), cf. the opening line of D. G. Rossetti's poem 'The Blessed Damozel'.
The Blinded Bird (*MV*). So much has this in common with the virtues of Tess (the bird caught in a springe, and the embodiment of Christian charity: I Cor.xiii) that 'Who is divine?' may hark back to the challenging sub-title of the novel, 'A Pure Woman'.
blindman's buff, a children's game in which the blindfolded one has to catch and identify another, who then takes his place.
blinking, 'one-eyed', of little interest; dull (in poor light).
block-book, sketch-book.
bloody warriors, dark-red wallflowers (not a September flower, *MC*.ix).
Blooms-End, Bloom's End (*RN*; *LLI*.7; *D*1.II.v; *WW*.In Weatherbury Stocks). Some of its features were taken from the old Bhompston farmhouse below the Tincleton road. The name applies to Mrs Yeobright's house, on the verge of the heath, and the upper end of the small pastoral valley which runs below Duddle Heath (part of 'Egdon' below Rainbarrow), from a point below Rushy-Pond down to the Tincleton road. (In *RN*, where directions relative to other places are changed, it seems to be nearer Hardy's birthplace; the true topography is found in *LLI*.7). See Map F.
Bloomsbury (*DR*.iii.1 and v.3), a fashionable part of west London.
blooth, bloom, blossom.
blow, bloom.
The Blow (*MV*), possibly the 1914–18 war. The final, more hopeful, view of the Immanent Will in some distant future recalls the ending of *The Dynasts*. *oubliette*, literally a dungeon in which a prisoner could be forgotten.
blow about, proclaim, make known; **blow up**, scold, reprimand; **blow upon**, inform against.
blower, one who pumps the organ-bellows.
blow-hard, blusterer, braggart.
Bludyer (*JO*.1912 ps. to pr.), a merciless and unprincipled book-reviewer in Thackeray's novel *Pendennis* (xxxv).

bluebeardy, like that of Bluebeard, who murdered his wives (in an old popular story).

blue blood or **stock**, high or noble birth.

blue-vinnied, mouldy (from a cheese which turns blue when mouldy).

boam (dial.), trail, travel.

board wages, for servants' maintenance (when the family is away).

boat-cloak, a long black naval cloak.

bob o' the steelyard, heavy attachment that is slid on the arm of a weighing-machine, to show the weight when the arm is in equilibrium.

bobbin, string and attachment fastened to the latch (for opening a door).

Bohemian, unconventional, independent, typical of the artistic world.

boil like a pot (*WB*.III,vi), Job xli,31.

Boldwood (*MC*.xxxi). This 'silent, reserved young man' is the Boldwood of *FMC* at an earlier period (James Everdene, xxxi – cf. xvii – is another reminder of that novel).

Bolland, Baron (*WT*.pr.). 'Baron' is the judge's title. At the Dorchester summer assize, on 29 July 1830, he settled the case concerning a preventive guard's encounter with smugglers at Dagger's Grave (map D); cf. *WT*7.v.

Bollard Head (*WW*.The Brother), Ballard Point, north of Swanage.

bolt, remove bran from flour by means of a sifting contrivance (**bolter**, *TM*.xxii).

Bona Dea (*L*.II.vii), the Good Goddess (worshipped by Roman women as the goddess of chastity and fertility).

Bonaparte (**Buonaparte**), the first Napoleon. The threat of his invasion in 1803 and 1804 made him long remembered as an image of terror in southern England (*RN*.I.ix); it was not removed until the combined French and Spanish navies were incapacitated in the battle of Trafalgar, 1805; cf. *TM*.pr. and *WT*2. The Napoleonic wars from 1805 to 1815 are the subject of *The Dynasts*.

bonhomie (Fr.), good nature.

book . . . strange matter (*RN*.v.iv; cf. *TT*.xxv), *Mac*.I.v,59–60.

boon, jolly, convivial.

boreal, **Boreal**, cold, bleak, Northern.

Börne's phrase (*WB*.I.ix), Ludwig Börne, German political writer (1786–1837), 'Nothing is permanent but change'; cf. *GND*.1 and *Life* 352/380.

borus-snorus, bold or outspoken without fear of consequences.

Bos (*SC*.A Dream or No, A Death-Day Recalled), the sea below Boscastle.

Bosom'd high . . . trees (*PBE*.v ep.), Milton, 'L'Allegro' (*G.T.*).

bosom's lord . . . throne (*TT*.xviii), *RJ*.v.i,3.

Bossiney (*SC*.Self-Unconscious), a cove between Tintagel and Boscastle (map E).

Bossuet, Jacques (*L*.I.iv), French bishop (1627–1704), great in pulpit oratory and a leading controversialist.

Boswell's remarks (Gen.Pr.), in his advertisement to the first edition of his *Life of Samuel Johnson*, 1791.

Botany Bay (*MC*.viii; *HS*.The Fight on Durnover Moor), a settlement in New South Wales, Australia, to which British criminals had been sent from 1788.

bothering, troublesome, annoying.

bottle-holder, second or support, as in pugilism.

Bottom, roaring of . . . dove . . . wits (CEF), *MND*.I.ii,62–74.

bottom, hollow, valley, dell; financial basis, capital, resources; ship (as in *H5*.III prologue).

bottomry security, an investment with a shipowner, his ship being security for repayment with interest.

bouncer, very great or stupendous one, 'whopper'.

Bourbon roses (*RN*.I.vii), free-flowering and often highly scented, with rich colours (usually pink, one variety dark crimson).

bourne, small stream; limit, destination. The **common bourne**, death.

bouts-rimés (Fr.), rhymed endings.

Bowdlerized (*DR*.viii.3), no longer using coarse expressions (from Dr Bowdler, who in 1818 produced an expurgated edition of Shakespeare).

bowed down to dust (*TT*.xxxviii), Psalm xliv,25.

Bower o' Bliss (*JO*.II.vii,VI.vii). The name of this lady of varying moral character comes from Spenser, *The Faerie Queene* II.xii (the ending of which consorts with the porcine imagery of Hardy's novel).

bow–pencil, compasses with pencil for drawing curves.

bowse, drink heavily.

boy's love, lad's love, the aromatic shrub Southernwood.

Brabantio, words of (*GND*.10), *Oth*.I.iii,293.

brace, strain, strenuously prepare.

brachet, small hound.

bradded, fastened with brads or shoe-nails.

Bradshaw, *Bradshaw's Monthly Railway Guide*.

Bramshurst Court (*TD*.lvii–viii), Moyles Court, near Ringwood, Hampshire; a place of ill omen for Tess, for it was from here that Dame Alice Lisle was taken to be executed, like Tess, at Winchester.

brandise, an iron stand used for cooking over a fire.

brave, splendid, capital, fine-looking.

breach, 'breach of promise' to marry; it was possible under English law, until recently, to sue for this and obtain damages.

breasted, confronted.

breast-plough, push this implement (for paring turf) from the chest.

the breath and finer spirit of all knowledge . . . science (*LLE*.Apology), from Wordsworth's preface to *Lyrical Ballads*. Hardy had been reminded of it while reading 'The Study of Poetry'; see **Arnold**.

breath-shotten, breathless, exhausted.

brede, braid, a woven band used either as ornament or belt.

Breeze . . . confess the hour (*PBE*.xxiv ep.), Scott, 'County Guy' (*G.T.*), from *Quentin Durward* iv.

breve-like, sustained (like a musical note).

brick-nogging, timber structure filled in with brickwork.

The Bride of Lammermoor (PRF), Scott's novel, 'an almost perfect specimen of form'.

Bridehead, Susanna Florence Mary (*JO*). Bridehead may suggest marital squeamishness (cf. *Letters* II,99). It was a familiar Dorset name, from the psalm-tune (*Life* 337/363), after Bridehead at Little Bredy. Head was Jude's original surname, from Hardy's paternal grandmother, who lived at Fawley (Marygreen) in her youth. Sue's Shelleyan or epicene traits derive from *Florence* Henniker, perhaps also from Hardy's sister Mary; for Susanna, see **lily**.

The Bride-Night Fire (*WP*). The first of Hardy's poems to be published (1875, bowdlerized, some nine to ten years after it was written), it is rather exceptional in its use of dialect and broad rustic humour. *vail*, veil (probably for dialect pronunciation); *laitered*, loitered; *'ithin*, within; *e'th*, earth.

The Bridge of Lodi (*PPP*). See *Life* 195–6/203–4. Napoleon defeated the Austrians at Lodi in May 1796. *Milan's Marvel*, the cathedral; *Adda*, a tributary of the Po in northern Italy; *palinody*, recantation. For the romantic French tune celebrating the victory, cf. *WP*.The Dance at the Phoenix.

brief transit . . . world (*W*.1895 pr.), from the final page of *MC*.

Bright reason . . . wintry sky (*OMC*4.II.iii ep; *DR*.vi.1; *TD*.xiii), Shelley, 'When the lamp is shattered' (*G.T.*).

brimbles, brambles, blackberry briars.

bring down my hairs . . . grave (*W*.xliii), Gen.xlii,38.

Britton . . . Scott, and other medievalists (*L*.I.i): John Britton, 1771–1857; Augustus **Pugin**, 1812–52; Thomas **Rickman**, 1776–1841; and Sir George Gilbert Scott, 1811–78. Pugin had worked with Barry in designing the House of Commons; Scott's work included St Pancras Station.

broad arrow (*L*.v.xi), marking a convict's uniform.

Broad Sidlinch (*CM*4), Sydling St Nicholas, near Maiden Newton; the old mill (MV.Old Excursions) has been demolished.

broadcloth, black cloth of fine quality (compared with fustian, *L*.VI.iv).

A Broken Appointment (*PPP*), with Mrs Henniker at the British Museum. *time-torn* (originally 'soul-sad'), cf. *SC*.The Ghost of the Past, 21–4.

brood-mare, mare for breeding.

brougham, a one-horsed closed carriage.

Brown House (*JO*), the Red Barn, which stood where Ridgeway crosses the road to Wantage. See map I.

Browne, Dr (*JO*.VI.ix), an Oxford student who graduated as Doctor of Medicine at Leyden and Oxford, and became a distinguished writer of prose (1605–82); usually 'Sir Thomas Browne'.

brown-holland, of unbleached linen (first made in Holland).

bruckle, brittle, erring, unfortunate; **bruckle het (hit)**, mistake, failure.

bruit, proclaim, make widely known.

brumal, wintry; **brume**, fog, mist.

brunt, violent assault.

Brussels (*L*.v.ix; *LLI*.3,4; *D*3.VI.ii,iv,vii). For Hardy's interest in 1876 ('maybe with his mind on *The Dynasts*') and 1896, see *Life* 110/114,284/301.

Bubb Down (*TD*.ii; *PPP*.The Lost Pyx), a wooded chalk hill between Melbury Park and Melbury Bubb, at the western end of the range of hills south of Hardy's Blackmoor Vale. Despite the change to High Stoy in *The Woodlanders*, it remains a key point in the true setting of the novel.

The Buck's Head. See **Roy-Town**.

buckle, hair up in, all crisped and curled.
budget, bag and contents.
Budmouth (Regis), Weymouth, made a fashionable resort by George III's residence there summer after summer at Gloucester Lodge (*TM*.xi). While there from the summer of 1869 to May 1870, working for the architect Crickmay, Hardy wrote some poems and began *DR*. He was at Weymouth in the summer of 1879 when preparing for *TM*. Altogether he knew much about the history of the town and its neighbourhood; he was familiar with its bay and old harbour, with the Old Rooms Inn on the southern side and the Nothe, a projecting point to the east (formerly 'Look-out Hill'), with Sandsfoot Castle and Portland Bay to the south. His references to Budmouth are numerous; see **Weymouth**.
buffer, simpleton; **bufferism**, being an 'old buffer'.
buffeting . . . storm (*W*.iii), Wordsworth, 'The Small Celandine' (*G.T.*).
building upon the sand (*TT*.xxxviii), Matt.vii,24–7.
Built . . . aisle . . . stone (*L*.I.iv), Scott, *Marmion* II.x.
buitenplaatsen (Dutch), country residences.
Bulbarrow (*TM*.xii; *TD*; *SC*.Wessex Heights), a high hill south of Sturminster Newton, in the chalk range which overlooks Blackmoor Vale to the north.
The Bullfinches (*PPP*). *Busy . . . Fiends make havoc in her bands*: Hardy introduces this thought into the action of *TD*.ix, with the sleeping mother, the bullfinches, and Tess's danger from the satanic Alec; cf. ***Tess of the d'Urbervilles***.
bull's eye, a lantern with a thick convex lens for concentrating light on an object.
bull-stake, post to which the bull was tied while baited by dogs.
bundle back (colloquial), leave hastily (cf. 'pack off').
Bunyan . . . dream . . . society (*L*.v.xi), cf. the opening of Part I of Bunyan's *The Pilgrim's Progress*.
The Burghers (*WP*). The house is Colliton House, Dorchester; the doorway in the wall below is described in *MC*.xxi. For *Grey's (Bridge), Dammer's Crest* (the highest point on the western road near Damer's Barn), *Pummery* (*Tout* = Hill), and the *Gibbet* (on Gallow's Hill, where supporters of the rebel Duke of Monmouth were hanged by order of Judge Jeffreys), see map B. *haw*, field or enclosure by the house.
Burleigh, lord of (L.I.xii), an allusion to Tennyson's 'The Lord of

Burleigh' (based on the true story of a lord of Burghley House near Stamford), in which the lord, while landscape-painting, falls in love with a village girl and marries her, before declaring his identity.

burn, brook, stream.

burned, damned (burned in hell).

Burning the Holly (*WW*). Twelfth Night (6 Jan) is the end of Christmas–New Year festive season.

Burns's field-mouse (DLa). See his poem 'To a Mouse, on Turning her up in her Nest with the Plough' (*G.T.*) for this, and 'best-laid schemes' (*DR*.x.1), 'guess and fear' (*DR*.xvi.1), and fieldmouse fear of the coulter of destiny (*MC*.xiv).

burr-stones, millstones of coarse texture for grinding corn.

the burthen of the mystery (*D*.pr), Wordsworth, 'Lines Composed . . . above Tintern Abbey'.

busby, a high fur military cap, with a bag hanging from the top, on the right side.

bushel (*FMC*.xxxiii), a large container for measuring corn, Matt.v,15–16.

busy hum (*FMC*.xxix), Milton, 'L'Allegro' (*G.T.*).

But what is this? . . . (*OMC*4.I.iii ep.), Tennyson, *In Memoriam* lxviii.

Buttermead, Lady Mabella (*WB*.II.i). A passage omitted from Hardy's *Life* shows that this young lady, in muslin and going to a ball, was Lady Marge W——, as seen at Lady Carnarvon's (16 May 1887; *Life* 200/208).

buttery, originally the place where the drinks were kept; here (*TT*.xx), the pantry.

By absence . . . miss her (*HE*.xl), from the poem 'Absence, hear thou my protestation', often attributed to Donne, probably by John Hoskins, 1566–1638; entitled 'Present in Absence' (*G.T.*).

By Henstridge Cross at the Year's End (*LLE*). Written during the 1914–18 war, it first appeared as 'By Mellstock Cross . . . '. Only the latter makes complete sense; all roads taken from the crossroads have led to disappointment: *east*, to London in 1862; *north*, past ancestral farms (*Life* 214–15/223–4); *west*, to Cornwall and marriage; *south*, with troops for ports of embarkation during the war. Henstridge, NW of Sturminster, had more important crossroads in the cardinal directions. The departure point is local in a general, not specific, sense.

By Her Aunt's Grave (*SC*). *the Load of Hay*, some country inn.

By the Barrows (*TL*), Rainbarrows (map A). *Multimammia*, cf. **Cybele** and **Diana**.

By the Runic Stone (*MV*), near the Celtic Cross in the churchyard at St Juliot, above the Valency valley; 'she in brown' is Emma Gifford (*Life* 78/81). The die which is cast may refer to their wedding-engagement ('white-hatted' suggests in the summer).

by-now, a short while ago, just now.

bysm, abysm; **Byss** (Abyss), the great deep, the source of life, the Immanent Will.

C

cabala, secrets (from the Jewish Cabbala, an oral tradition of religious interpretations).

Cabanis (*D*3.IV.iv), French pysician and philosopher, 1757–1808.

caddle, quandary, entanglement.

Cadsand (*D*2.IV.vi), on the coast south of Walcheren island.

Caesar (*RN*.I.vi), Julius, who invaded Britain in 55 and 54 BC; **Caesars** (*DR*.iv.2), the first emperors of ancient Rome and its empire, said to be descended from Aeneas (*D*1.VI.v).

The Caged Thrush Freed and Home Again (*PPP*), clearly related to the previous poem ('An August Midnight') and to the frost symbolism of the poems which follow (see **frost**). *terrene*, earthly; *treen*, trees.

Cagliostro, Count (*TT*.vi), the name assumed by an Italian charlatan (1743–95), whose criminal involvement in the affair of the Diamond Necklace – purchased for Marie Antoinette but never delivered – lodged him for a while in the Bastille.

Caiaphas to Pilate (*JO*.VI.i), Matt.xxvi,57 to xxvii.

Cain (*UGT*.I.vii; *FMC*.x; *MC*.xliii; *W*.xxxix; *TL*.The Flirt's Tragedy), Gen.iv,1–14. His **altar** (*W*.xxxi): Canaanite altars were mainly perpendicular in design, square at the base and top, usually with a horn at each upper corner; **mark** of Cain (*RN*.I.ix), **brand** like Cain's (*WP*.San Sebastian), Gen.iv,15.

cake dough, wish (*FMC*.xxxiii), wish things done were undone.

The Calf, an uncollected poem written by Hardy for Florence Dugdale's *The Book of Baby Beasts*, 1911.

Caliban shape (*TT*.i), ugly, monstrous; cf. *The Tempest*.

call, consider, estimate; **call home**, have the banns of marriage announced in church.

calle (Ital.), street, alley.

Calphurnia's cheek was pale (*MC*.xxxvii), *JC*.I.ii,185.

calvary, suffering (from the Crucifixion on Calvary, a hill outside Jersualem; cf. Luke xxii,33 and *JO*.II.v).

Calvinistic (*TD*.xxvi), following the doctrines of John Calvin (1509–64), the Genevan Protestant reformer. Mr Clare differed from Calvin in believing in the salvation of all who are penitent.

Camelot . . . Priam . . . Calvary (*D*3.VI.ii footnote), the city of the legendary King Arthur, thought to be on a hill near Castle Cary, Somerset; king of Troy during its siege by the Greeks, who after ten years gained possession and destroyed it. See **calvary**.

Camelton, Camelford, Cornwall. Originally the extension of the railway in *PBE* (xxi,xxxix) to Stranton (later named Castle Boterel) was imaginary. It was changed to Camelton in the 1895 edition, after the opening of the Camelford line in 1893.

Can one be pardoned . . . offence? (*PBE*.xxvii), *Ham*.III.iii,56.

Can you keep the bee from ranging . . . love (*JO*.V.iii), Thomas Campbell, 'How delicious is the winning' (*G.T.*).

Candaules' wife, mortification of (*RN*.I.x). When her husband, King of Lydia, allowed Gyges to see her naked, she was so incensed that she ordered Gyges to kill him.

Candlemas (*FMC*.vi; DLa; *MC*.xxii–iii; *TD*.xlvi; *SC*.Lament), 2 February, the feast of the purification of the Virgin Mary, when candles used in Roman Catholic churches are consecrated. In Dorchester a fair was held (*not*, by statute, on the holy day), during which labourers were hired to begin work on **Lady Day**.

Candour in English Fiction (Orel,125–33), Hardy's strongest protest against the shackling of the novelist by Victorian grundyism. The essay, the third and last of a symposium, appeared in *The New Review*, Jan 1890.

cankered heaps . . . gold (*CM*.12.x), *2.H4*.IV.v,72.

Canons and Rubric, laws of Church government, and directions (printed in red) for Church services.

Canopus (*TT*.xl; *PPP*.A Christmas Ghost-Story), one of the brightest stars in the southern sky.

canterbury, music and magazine rack.

canticle (*HE*.i). The speaker probably mistakes 'canticle', a familiar church term, for 'cant' (stock phrase).

cantilever, support for a balcony or projecting upper story, extending from side to side.

Canto coram latrone (*PBE*.iii), I sing in the robber's face (adapted from Juvenal's *Satires* x,22).

the Cape, the Cape of Good Hope, South Africa.

Capella (*FMC*.ii; *TT*.vii), a bright winter star which appears halfway between the Pole Star (the North Star) and the belt of Orion.

Capharnaum (*MC*.xlv; *JO*.VI.vii), Capernaum, where the people sat in darkness before seeing a great light, Matt.iv,13–16.

capital, head or top of a column or pillar.

Capitol, and **triumphal chariot** (*MC*.xxvii), the national temple of ancient Rome to which consuls processed in triumph on taking office.

Capitoline (**gladiator**, PRF), the statue of the dying Gaul in the Capitoline Museum, Rome (not a Dacian, as was thought: cf. Byron, *Childe Harold* IV.cxl).

cappel-faced, with white cheeks and muzzle.

captain with the bleeding hole . . . bewitched ship (*JO*.I.iii), from a story by the German writer Wilhelm Hauff, 1802–27.

caqueterie (Fr.), cackling, chatter.

car, carriage (horse-drawn).

card, by the, in exactly the manner or style (cf. *Ham*.v.i,133, where it means 'precisely').

Cardinal Bembo's Epitaph on Raphael (*PPP*), a translation of the cardinal's Latin epitaph on the tomb of the great Italian painter in Rome; see **Raffaelle**.

Care, thou canker (*PBE*.xxix ep.), gnawing anxiety. Untraced.

cark, harass; heavy anxiety.

Carlton House (*TM*.vi; cf. *D*2.vi–vii), home of the notorious Prince Regent, later George IV.

Carlyle, Thomas (1795–1881), as he *said of Cromwell* (*OMC*6.i), in *Heroes, Hero-Worship, and the Heroic in History* vi.

Caro, Avice (*WB*). The surname was adopted because it sounded like a Portland name and means 'dear' in Italian (possibly indicating Roman lineage, II.iii); 'Avice' is an old English name, and Hardy used it because of its historical connection with his father's small Talbothays farm (*Life* 6/10).

Caroline, pertaining to the reign of Charles I, 1625–49.

Caroline, Lady (*GND*3), probably of Wilton House, west of Salisbury and near the Avon river. Originally, the Marchioness of Athelney.

Carpe diem (*RN*.III.v), enjoy life while you can, Horace, *Odes* I.xi.

Carrara, in northern Italy, famous for its white-marble quarries.

carrefour (*MC*.xxii), place where four roads meet (Fr.)

carrel (dial.), carol.

The Carrier (*HS*). *Exon Towers* are those of Exeter Cathedral; *Sidwell Church*, by Sidwell Street in Exeter.

Carriford (*DR*), largely an imaginary village, though mainly within the Stinsford area; its railway station is on the London line not far below the Max Gate site.

carte-de-visite (Fr.) photographic portrait mounted on a small card.

Carthaginian . . . Tarentine . . . Baian (with reference to Budmouth, *RN*.I.x). Carthage was built quickly on Queen Dido's orders; Tarentum, a Greek city on the coast of southern Italy, was noted for indolence and luxury; Baiae, near Naples, was famous as the health-resort of Roman senators.

Cassiopeia's Chair (*FMC*.ii), a constellation on the opposite side of the Pole Star to the Great Bear, and about half way, it appears, to the Square of Pegasus.

cast, interpret, divine, forecast.

cast off (*UGT*.I.vii), observer the progressive or 'casting off' pattern of the dance, couples moving down the set successively and dancing figures with other couples, then working their way back in the same style until the top couple has regained its starting-point.

cast up by rages of the se (*WB*.I.i), from *The Itinerary of John Leland* (pub.1710–12; Leland died in 1552).

Casterbridge, Dorchester, its Wessex name alluding to its past as an important Roman military centre (*castra*) by the river. The Walks, on the levelled remains of the Roman walls, were planted with avenues of trees at the beginning of the eighteenth century. On the NE side its boundary is the Frome, which, after passing the hangman's cottage, flows below the prison and on past Fordington ('Durnover'). The present County Goal, which preserves the 'classic archway of ashlar', dated 1793 (*WT*4.ix), above which executions took place, was completed in 1885. The road east from the High Street passed over Swan Bridge into the country, crossing 'Durnover Moor' and Grey's Bridge, with Ten Hatches Weir on the northern side. At the centre of the town, where Cornhill meets High Street just below St Peter's Church, was the market-place. Lucetta's house (from Glyde Path Road) was imagined here (hence the name High-Place Hall), overlooking the obelisk pump; until 1847 the entrance to North Square or Bull Stake was a narrow arched thoroughfare under a balconied building. The upper part of this was the Town Hall, which extended east over the Corn Exchange (where its successor with the clock-tower was built from 1847 to 1876), with the King's Arms hotel a little lower down High East Street. The curved pavement (now set back) on the St Peter's side of the entrance to North Square was called the Bow. As one turns south via Cornhill, the Antelope hotel is on the right just beyond the pump; further on, in South Street, the Old Greyhound inn had stood to the left. Some way beyond, on the same side, is the house of the town-clerk which served as the original of Henchard's when he was Mayor. Further still, on the right hand, next to where William Barnes kept his school, was the office of the architect John Hicks, with whom Hardy served his apprenticeship. The County Museum, referred to in *MC*, stood in Trinity St, behind the Antelope, from 1851 to 1883, when the present (above St Peter's) was completed. Sessions and assizes were held in the County Hall (in High West Street), the area above which (the west end) was known as Top o' Town. The chapel-of-ease (*CM*.1.iii) was situated beyond the Bristol road, opposite the NW corner of the town, near the cavalry barracks. Maumbury, the Roman amphitheatre (Orel,225–31), is not far from the SW corner of the town; the SE corner of the old town is known as Gallows Hill, from the hangings that took place there as a result of Judge Jeffreys' 'bloody assize' after the failure of Monmouth's rebellion in 1685. See map B.

The Casterbridge Captains (*WP*). Identified as J. B. Lock, T. G. Besant (who returned), and J. Logan. Many British soldiers were massacred in the Khyber Pass on the Indian frontier when being withdrawn from Afghanistan in 1842; Lock (and presumably Logan) fell while trying to come to their aid.

Castilian, characteristic of Spanish nobility in Castile.

Castle Boterel (*PBE*; *SC*.At Castle Boterel), Boscastle, 2 m. from St Juliot, Cornwall (map E).

the 'Castle of Indolence' (*RN*.II.i). In the second canto of this allegorical poem by James Thomson (1748) all those who have been lured to this castle are roused from torpor by the bard

Philomelus who accompanies the liberating knight of Art and Industry.

Castle Royal (*D*2.VI.v), Windsor Castle; cf. **Royal-tower'd Thame**.

Castor and Pollux (*FMC*.ii; *TT*), the two brightest stars of a constellation named Gemini (the Twins) after them.

Casuistry (*HE*.xxxvi), that part of Ethics which resolves cases of conscience, including *disciplina arcani*, the discipline of keeping an important secret.

casus conscientiae (Lat.), a case or issue for exercising moral probity.

cat will after kind (*L*.VI.iv), *AYL*.III.ii,93. **I would not have done it . . . neighbour's cat . . . fiery day as this** (*RN*.IV.vi): see **against**.

The Catching Ballet of the Wedding Clothes (*WW*). Set in the period of William IV (1830–7), when belief in witchcraft was still common in rural England; see **white witch**.

catenary, such as would be assumed by a chain hanging freely between two points laterally apart.

A Cathedral Façade at Midnight (*HS*). Hardy's note of 10 Aug 1897 (*Life* 296/314) on the west front of Salisbury Cathedral at midnight provided the background for the imagined regret that scientific thought had rejected Christian belief based on the comforting pre-Copernican assumption that the Earth was the centre of the universe, and that the sun, moon, and stars were made for man's benefit (MS date, 1897).

Cato the Censor (234–149 BC) was such a rigid reformer that the term for his office became permanently attached to his name (*DR*.iii.2).

Catullus says, 'Mulier . . . vento – ' . . . wind and water (*PBE*.xxvii): see his 70th poem. **Catullus: XXXI** (*PPP*), a free translation of the poem in which the Roman poet celebrates his return from Bithynia in Asia Minor to his home on the Sirmione or Sirmio peninsula, Lake Garda.

Caudine Forks (*OMC*6.vi), a narrow defile in mountains near Capua, where a Roman army was trapped by the Samnites in 321 BC.

caul, membrane sometimes found on the head of a child at birth, and thought at one time to be a good omen, especially against drowning.

causey (dial.), causeway, raised pavement.

Caxtons, books printed by William Caxton, the first English printer

(c. 1422–91).

Cedit amor rebus (*FMC*.xxvi), Ovid, *Remedia Amoris*, 144.

Cedric (DLa; cf. 'Gurth's collar of brass', *MC*.xxix), Scott, *Ivanhoe*.

celebrate (*HE*.xii), a malapropism for 'celibate'.

celestial machinery (*D*.pr.), the working (first found in classical epics) of gods, goddesses, or other heavenly beings on mortals below.

cellaret, a cabinet for drinks.

Central Sea, the Mediterranean.

centurions (*TD*.xxx). Tess probably means officers, having learned, with reference to the Bible, that a centurion commanded a hundred soldiers in the Roman army.

ceorls, the lowest order of freemen in Anglo-Saxon times.

Cercle (Fr.), social club.

Cerealia (*TD*.ii), celebrations in honour of Ceres, Roman goddess of harvests. Any primeval connection with May rites may be less significant than the anticipation of Tess's 'harvest', marked in two harvest scenes (xiv,xlvii).

Cernel Giant. See **Abbot's Cernel**.

cerule, azure, heavenlike.

cess, impose a tax or levy.

cetrer, the rest ('et cetera')

'Ch, I (an Anglo-Saxon survival; cf. *Life* 221/232). **'Ch woll**, I will; **er woll**, he will (both *W*.xvii).

Chain Salpae (*FMC*.ix), marine animal which belongs to a chain-formation, and reproduces such.

chainey, china (local pronunciation).

chairmen, men pushing Bath-chairs (for the old or disabled).

Chaldeans, an ancient people who lived between the Tigris and Euphrates; their capital was Babylon. Many were famous astrologers.

Chaldon (*WT7*), East Chaldon (Chaldon Herring), NW of Lulworth Cove.

Chalk-Newton (*TD*), Maiden Newton, 8 m. NW of Dorchester. For its instrumental choir, see *Life* 10/14; *UGT*.I.iv; *CM4*. The White Horse inn was removed in 1900 (cf. *WT6*.iv and *Life* 214/223).

Chambers (*L*.I.i), Sir William, 1726–96, author of *A Treatise of Civil Architecture* and designer of Somerset House.

chamfered, with angle-edges cut off.

chammer (dial.), chamber, bedroom, room.

chance. Hardy allowed a little for the exercise of free-will (*LLE*.Apology) but insisted on 'the compulsion of circumstances, the tragic force that overrides the human will' (a quotation from a passage on Victor Hugo which he transcribed in 1886). 'The best tragedy . . . is that of the WORTHY encompassed by the INEVITABLE' (*Life* 251/265); elsewhere (*WT*5.viii) Hardy wrote on the cruelty proceeding from 'the whimsical god . . . known as blind Circumstance'. Chance includes hereditary endowments affecting character (*HS*.Discouragement), and character is fate (*MC*.xvii). The substitution of 'Time and Chance' for 'Providence' at the opening of *MC* is a mark of Hardy's sincerity. Tess's 'inherent will to enjoy', after her rally, is defeated by 'the circumstantial will against enjoyment' (*TD*.xliii). For significant comments in Hardy's poems, cf. *WP*.Hap, Ditty; *PPP*.The Bedridden Peasant; *LLE*.Mismet, An Opportunity; and *WW*.'We are getting to the end', where the 'demonic force' of an international situation expresses what may be seen at work in *D*2.I.iii.

chance and change (*WP*.The Temporary the All: *PPP*.pr; *HS*.To C. F. H.), Shelley, *Prometheus Unbound* II.iv,119.

Chancery, a division of the High Court of Justice.

The Change (*MV*). The date confirms Hardy's regretful memory of Emma (*the deodar*, in the garden of the St Juliot rectory); the ending suggests he met her at Paddington Station, when she was visiting her brother in London (*S.R.*,59–60). *a week*, cf. *SC*.A Week and *Life* 74–5/77–8 (Mon. to Sat., 7–12 Mar 1870); *mocking note*, cf. *WW*.The Prophetess.

A Changed Man (*CM*.1). Completed in January 1900, it may be regarded primarily as a tribute to the work done during the Fordington cholera outbreaks, in 1854 especially, by the Revd Henry Moule (cf. *Life* 390–1/423).

A Changed Man (1913). Some of these stories (1881 to 1900) were written late in fulfilment of agreements made before Hardy relinquished prose fiction, soon after the publication of *JO*, for verse; he had several stories in mind at the time. He felt obliged to include some he wished to 'snuff out', because pirated editions were being imported from the States.

Channel Firing (*SC*), before the outbreak of the First World War, August 1914. *blow the trumpet*, on the Day of Judgment, when the dead are raised (I Cor.xv,52); *Parson Thirdly*, of 'Weatherbury' (cf. *FMC*.xlii), so named for his emphasis on 'Thirdly' in his sermons (cf. Elfride, on writing her father's, *PBE*.iv); *Stourton Tower*, on a hill near Stourhead, marking the site where King Alfred raised his standard against the Danes.

Channelcliffe, the Countess of (*WB*.II.i), based most probably, as the name suggests, on Lady Portsmouth. As early as the summer of 1884 Hardy was friendly with her and her family; he stayed with them early in 1885 (*Life* 170/176–7,210/219,211–12/220).

Chanticleer's comb is a-cut (cock's comb = coxcomb), the conceit is taken out of a person.

chap o' wax, a clever, promising fellow.

chapel-of-ease, a church built for the convenience of people who live too far from their parish church.

The Chapel-Organist (*LLE*). The date 185– suggests that Hardy's flamboyant story developed from an actual scandal; whether it was connected with the Dorchester chapel, on the Fordington side of the east end of High Street, which Hardy knew well when he was apprenticed to the architect Hicks (cf. *Life* 29–30/34) is conjectural. *Old-Hundredth*, cf. **On the Tune Called the Old-Hundred-and-Fourth**; this and the following were names of hymn-tunes. *Tallis . . . Ken*, cf. *Life* 10/16 and *LLE*.Barthélémon at Vauxhall. *'The grave . . . bed'*, from Bishop Ken's evening hymn 'Glory to Thee, my God, this night'; cf. *JO*.II.i. *vinaigrette*, smelling-bottle; *red as scarlet*, like the whore of Babylon (Rev.xvii,4–5).

chaps (dial.), cheeks.

charactery, expression, features (cf. **characters**, writing, letters).

Chard (*LLE*.Growth in May), a town in Somerset, west of Crewkerne.

Charity seeketh not her own (*TT*.xli; *JO*.VI.iv), I Cor.xiii,5; and **tinkling simples** (*W*.xxxiv), cf. I Cor.xiii,1.

Charles's Rest (*L*.v.ii), a literal translation of 'Carlsruhe'.

Charles's Wain . . . chimney (DLa), the constellation Ursa Major (The Great Bear or the Plough or the Dipper) in the Pole Star region of the northern sky (*1.H4*.II.i,2–3); cf. waggon and horses TT.xx).

Charmley (*UGT*.IV.v–vii), Charminster, north of Dorchester.

Charmond, Felice (*W*). The name suggest a wordly woman, 'a bit of a charmer', as Winterborne says; it recalls Charmian in *Antony and Cleopatra*, and may hint at the flesh as well as the world (Fr.).

charnel-minded, carnal-minded (malapropism).

Charon, the ferryman who took the souls of the dead across the river Styx into the underworld of classical myth.

The Chase (*GND*2; *TD*), originally part of the extensive forested area known as Cranborne Chase; in *TD* it is limited to woodland near Pentridge.

Chaseborough (*TD*), Cranborne, a small town south of the road from Blandford Forum to Salisbury; the Flower-de-Luce is the Fleur-de-Lis inn.

chassez-déchassez (*MC*.ix) a sideways glide as in dancing (a 'Terpsichorean figure'), followed by ordinary steps.

châtelaine, mistress of a country-house (1855).

Chaucer . . . fine loving (*GND*3), Prologue to *The Canterbury Tales* (Wife of Bath); **time of Chaucer** (*CM*12.iii), second half of the fourteenth century.

chaussée (Fr.), causeway, high road, carriage-way.

chaw, bite, mouthful; chew. **chaw high**, have superior tastes.

Cheap Jack (*D*1.IV.vi), one who offers deceptively cheap bargains.

che-hane, an old Wessex expression, meaning possibly 'I'm snug'; cf. *MV*.The Pity of It for the Anglo-Saxon origin of 'che'; 'hane' (dial. and archaic) suggests enclosure.

chemisette, bodice.

Chene Manor (*GND*2), Canford Manor near Wimborne; some of the old buildings still stand, including 'John of Gaunt's kitchen'.

Chesil Beach (*PBE*.xxix) or **Chesil Bank** ('Pebble-bank' in *WB*), a ridge of shingle which helps to link Portland with the mainland and sweeps NW for 11 m. to Abbotsbury, enclosing a narrow strip of water known as the Fleet. 'Chesil' means 'Pebble'; the pebbles decrease in size from Portland to the Abbotsbury beach. Hardy refers to the gale of November 1824 which blew a brig over Chesil Bank into the Fleet (*W*.xxvi).

Chesterton, G. K. In *The Victorian Age in Literature* he described Hardy as 'a sort of village atheist brooding and blaspheming over the village idiot'. On his death-bed Hardy dictated a few lines on the unscientific outmodedness of this 'literary contortionist'; cf. *Life* –/381.

cheval-glass, a full-length mirror swung on a frame.

chevalier d'industrie (Fr.), one who lives by his wits.

chevroned (arch.), with zigzag ornamentation.

chevy, pursue.

chick, child.

Chickerel (*HE*), the surname of Ethelberta's family, after the village of Chickerell near Weymouth.

chiel, child; a kindly term used to a child or young person. **chiel taking notes** (*PBE*.xiv; *JO*.VI.iii), cf. the fifth line of Burns's poem 'On the Late Captain Grose's Peregrinations'.

Childe Harold's Pilgrimage (*OMC*4.I.iii), the poem which made Lord Byron famous (Cantos I and II, 1812; III, 1816; IV, 1818).

Childhood Among the Ferns (*WW*), adapted from experience (*Life* 15–16/20) here and in *JO*.I.ii. Cf. the Horatian *WW*.A Private Man on Public Men (both inspired by the same thought, and both published in *The Daily Telegraph* during the same week of March 1928) and *WW*.He Never Expected Much.

The Children and Sir Nameless (*LLE*), based on a tradition or fancy relating to a battered effigy in the Athelhampton Chapel of Puddletown Church. Hardy admitted that he had dated the effigy a century further back 'to get rid of the doubt about the ruff'. Cf. the Weatherbury reference in *RN*.I.iii.

Children of Israel, crossing the Red Sea (*WB*.I.v), Exod.xxiv,19–22.

Chillington Wood (*CM*.12.iii-v), retained from the first Wessex setting of the story, and suggested by 'Pallington', the name of the heath east of Tincleton and not far from Clyffe House.

chimbley, chimley-piece (dial.), chimney or chimney-stack.

chimerical, based on a wild fancy.

The Chimes (*MV*), of St Peter's Church, Dorchester; they played the Sicilian Mariner's Hymn in Hardy's boyhood (cf. *MC*.iv). Their change seems to parallel the course of his love; the far-away person, in two senses at two different periods, is Emma Gifford/Emma Hardy.

The Chimes Play 'Life's a Bumper' (*LLE*). The chimes sound as if there is something to celebrate as Hardy leaves home for London (1862–7), again for his wedding (1874), and, ironically, as his wife is buried.

chimley (dial.), open fireplace. **chimley-tun**, chimney-stack.

chimmer, cf. **chammer**.

chimney-crook, an iron hook and chain, or a notched iron, to which cooking-pots could be suspended over the fire.

chimp, produce offspring (**chimp**, young shoot).

chinchilla, small South American rodent with *greyish* fur.

chine, projecting rim of a cask or barrel; backbone of animal with the adjacent meat; a coastal ravine or cleft cut by water.

chiney, china; cf. **chainey**.

chip hat, straw hat.

Chippendale and Sheraton (*MC*.x), two famous English furniture-designers of the eighteenth century.

Chippenham (*PBE*.xxxix), in Wiltshire.

chips-in-porridge, like, of no consequence, making no difference.

chit (dial. for shoot), young person, child (used disparagingly).

chitlings, chitterlings, small intestines of a pig (fried for food).

chiton (*LLI*.1), the ancient Greek tunic.

The Choirmaster's Burial (*MV*). The choirmaster is Hardy's grandfather, who died in January 1837; the story was told by Hardy's father (tenor violin). There was no 'quiring' over his grave, as the remainder of the players were among the mourners (cf. *Life* 10–13/16–17). According to one of the Hardy music-books, 'Mount Ephraim' was played to a verse of a psalm which began 'The Lord God Jehovah reigns'. The supernatural vision suggests that the story is told by Michael Mail; cf. *HS*.The Paphian Ball.

Chok' it all!, a mild oath (probably from 'May I be choked!').

chopstick, churl, peasant.

chord, straight line joining the extremities of an arc (geometry).

chore, chorus or choir, chancel of a church.

The Chosen (*LLE*). Cf. the 'conjoint emotion' of Fitzpiers (*W*.xxix), who 'noticed himself to be possessed by five distinct infatuations at the same time'. The 'Christ-cross stone' recalls Cross-in-Hand and Alec d'Urberville, another womanizer (see *PPP*.The Lost Pyx). Yet this libertine presentation is not realistic; the Greek epigraph reads, 'Which things are an allegory' (Gal.iv,24). It may contain what Hardy thought a general truth, that a new love atones for shortcomings in the old.

Christ, by the well (*JO*.II.vii), John iv,5–14.

The Christening (*TL*). Cf. the view put forward in *JO*.v.i and v.iii, where Thomas Campbell is quoted on fettered love in marriage.

Christiad . . . Pauliad (*TD*.xxv). Mr Clare was swayed more by St Paul's Epistles than by the Gospels.

The Christian Year (*JO*.II.iii), a book of devotional poems by John Keble (1827), who later helped to promote the Tractarian movement.

Christian's companion . . . Hill Difficulty (*CM*6). Bunyan, Part I of *The Pilgrim's Progress*.

A Christmas Ghost-Story (*PPP*). For the full force of the poem, cf. *WW*.Christmas: 1924. For the association of peace with Jesus, who was crucified, see Luke ii,1–14. See Orel,201–3, for Hardy's reply to a critic.

Christmas in the Elgin Room (*WW*). Hardy imagines what the Elgin Marbles in the British Museum thought when they first heard Christian bells. They had been purchased by Lord Elgin and brought to England in 1816, from the ruins of the Parthenon, a temple sacred to Athena. The poem was begun in 1905, and completed in 1926 (cf. *Life* 444–5/479). *Pheidias*, the sculptor responsible for the statue of Athena and the decoration of the Parthenon; *Borean*, northern (from Boreas, the classical name for the north wind); *Athenai's Hill*, the Acropolis; *Helios*, the Greek sun-god; *Ilissus*, a river near ancient Athens; *Poseidon*, the Greek god of the sea; *Persephone*, goddess-queen of the underworld.

Christmas mummers: cf. *RN*.II.iv-v. The reference in *D*.pr (last par.) relates to the kind of expression Hardy thought possible for a certain kind of drama in the future, a style somewhat like that of the mummers he heard in his youth. In suggesting that he had such a style in mind for *The Dynasts* (with philosophical implications for the role of the participants in the historical drama) critics have misled; see Hardy's rebuttal of critics who objected to 'the stage-form' of *D* (Orel,144).

Christmas: 1924 (*WW*). *Peace on earth*, Luke ii,14.

Christmastide (*WW*). *Casuals' gate*, at the Union, Dorchester. See **workhouse**.

Christminster (*DR*.i.1; *JO*; *LLE*.Evelyn G. of Christminster), Oxford. The name originated when Hardy was planning *JO* with its crucifixion theme. The change from the 'Marquis of Trantridge' to the 'Marquis of Christminster' in *GND*6 took place in 1891; the reference in *DR* did not appear until 1896. **Beersheba**, 'Jericho', mainly the parish of St Barnabas, where the church (**St Silas** in the novel) was completed in 1869, after being designed by Blomfield, the London architect for whom Hardy had worked; **Biblioll College**, Balliol; **Cardinal College**, Christ Church (with its 'ogee dome' and great bell – the Tom Tower – and the Cathedral), founded by Cardinal Wolsey and originally known as Cardinal College; **Cardinal Street**, St Aldate's Street; **Chief Street**, High Street; **the church with the Italian porch**, St Mary's; the singularly built (II.vi) **circular theatre**, the old theatre of Wren (VI.i), the Sheldonian; **the college by the bridge**, Magdalen; **the cross in the pavement**, marking the spot in Broad Street where Latimer and Ridley were burned to death for their faith

(1555); **Crozier College in Old-time Street**, Oriel College in Oriel Lane, Hardy subsequently believed; **Crozier Hotel**, the Mitre; **Fourways**, Carfax; **the great library**, the Bodleian; **Oldgate College**, New College; **Rubric College**, Brasenose, Hardy thought in retrospect. **Sarcophagus College** (indicating intellectual death) is unidentifiable, and intended to have general significance, though *named* probably after Corpus Christi College. **All Angels** (*TT*.xxv) may be All Souls. See **Oxford**.

Christminster, one of its **luminaries** (*JO*.v.v), Matthew Arnold; for 'Greek joyousness' and 'sickness and sorrow', see his essay 'Pagan and Medieval Religious Sentiment', *Essays in Criticism* (1865).

church, formalize (marriage) in church. **to be churched**, see **churching**. **church-hatch**, churchyard gate. **church-hay**, churchyard.

church not 150 miles from London (MCR)., Stinsford; for the fashionable actor, see **Lady Susan**.

A Church Romance (*TL*), as it began between Hardy's father and mother (cf. *Life* 13–14/18–19, where 1836, the correct date, is given). His mother came to Stinsford, where she was in service, in November that year. *New Sabbath, Mount Ephraim*, old hymn tunes (cf. *Life* 10/16).

The Church-Builder (*PPP*). The cancelled title was 'Nil Dominus Frustra' (cf. Psalm cxxvii,1, '*Except the Lord* build the house, they labour *in vain* that build it'). *fillet*, a narrow flat band between mouldings; *dossal*, ornamental cloth behind the altar; *And powerful wrong . . . style* (cf. *PPP*.In Tenebris ɪɪ,13–14); *truss*, supporting beam.

Churchill, Charles (*D*1.ᴠɪ.vi), a satirical poet whose *Rosciad* (1761) brought him fame with its satire on London actors.

churching, religious service for women after childbirth.

Cicely, Lady (*OMC*3), Caroline, daughter of the Duke of Dorset. She married Joseph Damer; see **The Doctor's Legend**.

Cicero, Roman orator and statesman, 106–43 BC; **riches of frugality** (*L*.ɪ.v), cf. the sixth of his *Paradoxa Stoicorum*: **the library** the 'soul of the house' (*PBE*.xiii; *TT*.vii), *Ad Atticum* iv.8.

ci-devant (Fr.), former, heretofore.

cima-recta. See **cyma-recta**.

Cinderella *L*.ɪ.iv), the despised sister of a fairy-tale, whose wishes to attend a ball are granted to her by her fairy godmother; here she meets a prince, who is charmed by her, and marries her after she has proved that her foot fits the shoe she left behind.

ciphering, arithmetic, working with figures.

Circe or Calypso . . . sailings (*TT*.v), an allusion to Ulysses' adventures after the Trojan war in Homer's *Odyssey*. He stayed a year with Circe, who changed his companions into swine, and seven with Calypso.

circular notes, letters of credit from a banker enabling one to draw from banks elsewhere.

circulus . . . diabolus (Lat. *WT*.1), a circle in the centre of which is the Devil.

Circumdederunt . . . (*HS*.An Inquiry ep.), The sorrows of death compassed me (Vulgate, Psalm xvii,5; English version, Psalm xviii,4).

Circus-Rider to Ringmaster (*HS*). The MS adds '(Casterbridge Fair: 188–)'. See *Life* 166/172 for Hardy's circus-craze in Dorchester from 1883 to 1885. *tan-laid*, covered as a protective measure with bark refuse, after the bark had been used in tan-pits for the preparation of leather.

Cistercian (*TD*.xxxv; see **Wellbridge**), of the Cistercian order of monks which began in France at the end of the eleventh century.

cit, citizen. **citizen of the world** (*L*.II.ii), from the title of a series of essays by Oliver Goldsmith, 1728–74.

the Civil War, between supporters of Charles I and the parliamentarians, or Cavalier forces and Roundheads (led by Cromwell), 1642–6.

clam, clog, make sticky, become (feverishly) moist.

clamped book (*MC*.ii), the Bible.

clane (dial.), clean; completely.

clap, put, place, set down. **clap-net**, a net used by fowlers and entomologists which can be brought down and drawn tightly round one's prey.

Clare, Angel (*TD*). Though drawn to some extent from Charles, younger brother of Horace Moule, and an academic who became President of Corpus Christi College, Cambridge, he is intellectually much more akin to Hardy (cf. xviii). Angel has Shelleyan qualities, but his name (recalled from a memorial beneath which the boy Hardy sat in Stinsford Church) was chosen not so much from Arnold's description of Shelley as 'a beautiful and ineffectual angel' as from I Cor.xiii,1: 'Though I speak with the tongues of men and of angels, and have not charity . . . '.

Clare, James (*TD*), father of Angel; drawn partly, as Hardy told Mrs Henniker, from the Revd Henry Moule (1801–80), for many years vicar of Fordington.

Clarendon (*GND7*), Edward Hyde (1609–74), first Earl of Clarendon, statesman and historian.

Clarke's Homer (*JO*.I.v), Samuel Clarke's translation of the *Iliad* i–xii, 1829.

The Clasped Skeletons (*WW*). In September 1922 Florence Hardy informed Paul Lemperly that a barrow near Max Gate had been opened the previous week, and eight skeletons discovered. Perhaps it was this discovery (on Ridgeway Hill near Bincombe) which excited Hardy's imagination. The thought of a clasped paid of skeletons recalled famous lovers: Paris and Helen of Troy, David and Bathsheba (II Sam.xi), Jael and Sisera (Judg.iv), Aholah (Ezek.xxiii), the Greek statesman Pericles and his wife Aspasia, Alexander the Great and Thais, Antony and Cleopatra, Procula pleading with her husband Pontius Pilate for the life of Jesus (Matt.xxvii,19), and the twelfth-century French theologian Abelard, privately married to the beautiful young Héloïse (for which he was mutilated).

cleavers (*MC*.xxxix), chopping instruments, used (like the tongs) for noisy accompaniment.

clef (*D3*.VII.vi), key (music).

Cleopatra, failure of courage (*L*.IV.ii; *WT3*.iv), *AC*.III.x–xi.

clewing up (*HE*.xxxiii), raising sails by their lower corners up to the yard before furling them.

climacteric, climax.

climm (dial.), climb.

Climmerston (*LLI*.8b). As the magazine serial version gives 'Climmerston Ridge' for Waterston Ridge (*LLI*.8d), Climmerston is probably Higher Waterston in the Piddle valley NE of Dorchester.

clink off, make off, run off (away).

clipse, embrace, clasp.

clitch, crook of arm or leg.

Clive . . . Gay . . . Keats (*RN*.III.i) and the 'waggery of fate': Robert Clive (1725–74) became a soldier and did much to win India for the British empire; John Gay (1685–1732), best remembered for *The Beggar's Opera*, became a successful poet and dramatist; John Keats (1795–1821) proved to be one of the great poets who died young.

clock-line, cord suspending the weight which actuates the clock.

Cloton (*OMC*2). The mill suggests Netherbury (south of Beaminster), where Hardy worked for Crickmay on structural alterations to Slope House in *1871–2*.

clots, clods, turves.

cloud . . . man's hand (*DR*.xii.4; *LLI*.4.iii), I Kings xviii,44. **clouds drop fatness** (*MC*.xxviii), Psalm lxv,12, Common Prayer version.

clout (dial.) piece of cloth; **clouts**, rags.

cloven foot, sign of the Devil.

cloven tongues (*W*.xl), as of fire, Acts ii,3. Cf. *Life* 165/172 (and *W*.xliii for the 'chut-chut-chut').

clown, rustic, yokel.

cloze (rustic pronunciation), clothes.

club, club-walking (*UGT*.II.viii,v.i; *FMC*.xxxiii; *RN*.I.v; *TD*.ii). A club was a parish 'friendly society' or benefit association; it joined the procession during Whitsuntide festivities.

clue line (*MC*.xxii), that which guides or threads the way through a maze or obscurity (from 'clew', a ball of yarn or thread; cf. the classical story of Ariadne and Theseus).

Clyffe-Hill-Clump (*TL*.Yell'ham-Wood's Story; *HS*.The Paphian Ball), a wooded hill above Clyffe House, near Tincleton.

Coal Sack (*TT*.iv), a region in the Milky Way (apparently near the constellation of the Southern Cross) where the light of the stars is hidden by cosmic dust).

coats, skirt, petticoat.

cob, sturdy middle-sized horse.

Cochin (hen), originally from Cochin-China (now southern Vietnam).

cock, haycock; shoot woodcocks. **cock-o'-wax**, opponent with little courage (cf. 'fighting-cock'). **cock-pit**, enclosure for cock-fighting. **cocking-party** (*LLI*.1896 pr.) either to watch a cock-fight or shoot woodcocks.

coddle (dial.), self-indulgent person.

Code (*JO*.II.v). It contained many regulations on pupil-teachers; see **Revised Code**.

cohue (Fr.), crowd, the conventional many.

coigns of vantage (*WB*.II.ix), convenient places of concealment for observation; cf.*Mac*.I.vi,7 (corner, recess).

coil, trouble, disturbance, turmoil; **coil of things** (*RN*.II.vi), from Swinburne's 'The Triumph of Time' in *Poems and Ballads*, 1866, where it implies the conflict of mind and body, morality and happiness (from *Ham.*III.i,67). **coiled**, involved (in trouble).

cole, coll (dial.), embrace.

Coleridge, Samuel Taylor, poet and philosopher, 1772–1834: 'precipitance of soul', *DR.*ix.1; his morbid poem 'The Three Graves' (a poem of the supernatural begun by Wordsworth), *PBE.*xix; his proof that a versification of any length neither can be nor ought to be all poetry (cf. *Life* 203/212), *LLE.*Apology; 'that willing suspension of disbelief . . . poetic faith' (*Biographia Literaria* xiv), *D.*pr. **or an Emerson** (*OMC*6.vi), Ralph Waldo Emerson, American poet and philosophical essayist, 1803–82.

The Collector Cleans His Picture (*LLE*). The speaker is the poet William Barnes (d.1886) of Came rectory; he had been a picture-collector before entering the Church. The climax of Hardy's story is probably an ironic invention. There is some disguise in 'soon-reached city' and 'adjacent steeple' (Barnes's church at Winterborne Came was a considerable distance from his rectory). Compounds such as 'artfeat' and 'grimefilms' are in Barnes's style. *Fili hominis . . . plaga*, Son of man, behold, I take away from thee the desire of thine eyes with a stroke, Vulgate, Ezek.xxiv,16. *subserved*, served (my) purpose; *Astarte*, in ancient Babylon, *Cottyto*, goddess of debauchery in ancient Greek cities; *dew-fleece*, fleecelike covering of dew; *luthern*, dormer-window.

Colman's (*TM.*xxx). The MS indicates that the play was *The Heir at Law*, one of the many plays written by George Colman the Younger, 1762–1836. Jack **Bannister** was a famous actor of the period, trained by David Garrick.

Columbus (1451–1506), discoverer of America; floating seaweed renewed his hope when he was about to abandon his Atlantic voyage (*FMC.*xiv).

comb-washings, the last drainings of the honeycomb.

Come forward . . . equality in society (*OMC*4.I.vii ep.), from Thackeray's concluding observations in *The Book of Snobs*.

Come Not; Yet Come! (*HS*), written possibly with Mrs Henniker in mind when she was abroad in August 1895. *tear*, cf. 'time-torn' in *PPP.*A Broken Appointment.

Come out from among them . . . Lord (*TD.*xlv), II Cor.vi,17.

Come, woo me . . . consent (*HE.*xi), *AYL.*IV.i,61–2.

The Comet at Yell'ham (*PPP*), Encke's Comet, visible in October 1858. *sweet form*, probably Hardy's sister Mary, to whom he was much attached.

The Coming of the End (*MV*) is devoted to Emma Hardy, as

'Afterwards', the other finale poem, is to Hardy; her life is conceived as an *orbit*. 'Better close no prevision could lend' probably implies that her death was sudden. Hardy thinks of her far from the (madding) crowd (he first wrote 'in the west') in Cornwall, at Sturminster Newton, and at Max Gate, then of her refusal to join him on his weekly visit to his mother.

coming-on, responsive, forward.

Coming up Oxford Street: Evening (*HS*). Written when Hardy was in London, working for the architect Robert Smith (*Life* 87/89).

commandments, see the **ten commandments**. The **eleventh** (*RN*.VI.iii) is the new commandment of Jesus, that ye love one another (John xiii,34).

Commination, a C. of E. service denouncing sinners.

A Committee Man of 'The Terror' (*CM*8). The story originated from a few lines in *The Journal of Mary Frampton*, 1885, the actual being transferred (in Hardy's opening scene) from the Strand, London, to Budmouth. The Committee of Public Safety was set up in revolutionary Paris in 1792; the worship of the *goddess* Reason began there late in 1793. The story was not completed until 1896 (cf. *Letters* II,101,126,129).

A Commonplace Day (*PPP*). The thought is the obverse of the ending of *MV*.He Wonders about Himself, and of Browning's 'Christina', 17–32. *corpse-like*, cf. the opening of *W*.iv; *wakens my regret*, an echo of Tennyson's *In Memoriam* cxv.

Compassion (*HS*). Written at the request of the R.S.P.C.A.; cf. *Life* 346/373,349/376–7 on the 'Golden Rule', the extension of altruism to 'the whole animal kingdom'. *from Columbia Cape to Ind*, generally, from the Arctic (NE tip of Canada) to tropical India.

compass-mentas (i.e. *compos mentis*, of a sound mind), sensible.

Complaint of Piers the Plowman (DLa). *Piers Plowman*, a fourteenth-century poem by William Langland, is a Christian plea for the suffering poor.

Compuesto no hay muger fea (*L*.I.xiii), a well-dressed woman is not ugly (*Compuesta*, to be exact), a Spanish proverb.

Comte (CEF; *LLE*.Apology), see **Positivist**. Among Hardy's extensive notes from Beesly's translation of Auguste Comte's *Social Dynamics*, soon after its appearance in 1876, is one on social progress 'like "a looped orbit", sometimes apparently backwards, but really always forwards', with this illustration: . *pour mieux sauter* (Fr.), to make a better or bigger leap forward.

***Comus*, disappeared . . . crew of** (*MC*.xxxix), like the rabble in Milton's poetic play.

con, read, study, learn, gaze upon, examine.

con amore (It.), enthusiastically.

conceits, fancies.

Concerning Agnes (*WW*). Lady Grove's death in December 1926 recalled dancing with her at Rushmore near Shaftesbury. The Larmer Avenue is named after the Larmer Tree by which, according to tradition, King John's huntsmen assembled. See *Life* 269/286,281/298. *Kalupso*, Calypso, a daughter of Oceanus; *Amphitrite . . . Mid-Sea*, wife of Neptune . . . Mediterranean; *Nine*, Greek Muses.

the conclusion of the whole matter (*HE*.xxvii end), Eccl.xii,13.

concordia discors (*HS*.Genitrix Laesa; cf. *D3*.After Scene, 'the chordless chime of Things'), Horace, *Epistles* I.xii.

Concurritur – Horae Momento (*FMC*.liii title), Things come to an issue; soon (comes swift death or joyful victory), Horace, *Satires* I.i,7–8.

Condol's crown (*QC*.xi), Condolden Barrow (1000 ft high), overlooking the Tintagel coast.

coney, rabbit.

Coney, Christopher (*MC*), cf. 'coney-catcher', a cheat or swindler ('why should death rob life o' fourpence?')

confervae, green algae.

A Confession to a Friend in Trouble (*WP*). See **Moule, Horace**. *outer precincts*, cf. *DR*.xvi.4 (penultimate par.) and *MC*.xlii (ending), 'There is an outer chamber of the brain . . .'.

Congreve's Millament . . . bleed for me (*W*.xxix), the heroine of William Congreve's comedy *The Way of the World*, 1700; cf. the song in III.xii.

Conjecture (*MV*). *Emma, Florence, Mary*, Hardy's first wife, his second, and his sister Mary; *highway*, of life.

conjurors or 'wise' people were inheritors of folk-medicine, to whom other powers, including witchcraft, were sometimes attributed. Hardy presents three: Trendle of Egdon (*WT*4.iv–vi); Fall or 'Wide-oh', the weather-prophet of *MC*.xxvi; and Mynterne of Owlscombe (*TD*.xxi). Owlscome is Batcombe, a village below Batcombe Hill and Cross-in-Hand (map C). According to tradition, his horse leapt over the church, knocking off one of its pinnacles, and he was buried (in accordance with his instructions, after quarrelling with the vicar) partly outside the church and partly in, his tomb protruding from the northern wall.

the Conquest, the Norman conquest of England, beginning in 1066.

consumed (*HE*.xlii), malapropism for 'consummated'.

contrabasso, the largest and deepest-toned instrument of the violin class, the double-bass.

convenances (Fr.), proprieties, convention (*TD*.xx; cf. *Life* 213/222).

The Convergence of the Twain (*SC*), on the sinking of *The Titanic*, a luxurious liner which collided with an iceberg on 15 Apr 1912, on her maiden voyage from Southampton to New York. The poem was written for the souvenir programme of the Dramatic and Operatic Matinée at Covent Garden on 14 May. *Pride of life*, for its wordly connotation, see the first epistle of John ii,16 (NT).

A Conversation at Dawn (*SC*). The story may have been one Hardy had in mind when he decided (after the publication of *JO*) not to write any more prose fiction except what he had agreed to supply. The 'isle' and 'yonder shore' suggest the Isle of Wight. *frustrance*, frustration, disappointment.

coomb, valley, especially within the flank of a hill.

Coomb-Firtrees (*TL*.Yell'ham-Wood's Story), on a hill near Coomb eweleaze, between Puddletown and Puddletown Heath.

Copernicus (*TT*.iv; *WW*.Drinking Song), a Polish astronomer (1473–1543) who overthrew the Ptolemaic theory that the earth is the centre of the universe, and proved that the earth and other planets revolve round the sun.

copyholders (DLa), holders of property belonging to manor estates.

Copying Architecture in an Old Minster (*MV*). Hardy had lived in Wimborne from 1881 to 1883; 'ail-stricken mankind' and a 'trouble-torn' world suggest that the poem was written during the 1914–18 war. The tomb-references are actual; the Saxon king is Ethelred, elder brother of Alfred the Great. *quatre-foiled*, ornamented with quatrefoils (each having cusps which give the impression of four radiating leaves or petals); *parle*, conversation; *passager*, bird of passage.

corbelled, with projections for supporting ornamental structures.

Corfiote, from the Greek island of Corfu.

Corin (DLa), a shepherd, never at court and described by Touchstone as 'a natural philosopher'; **he that wants money . . . friends**, *AYL*.III.ii,11–45.

Corinthian (arch.) elegantly decorated; elegantly dissolute.

Corn Trade . . . repeal of the Corn Laws (*MC*.pr.). The Corn Laws of 1815, restricting imports of corn to protect the farmers, created widespread hostility in working-class populations (cf. *Life* 21/26,501); after a bad harvest many could hardly afford a loaf of bread. The repeal of the Corn Laws in 1846 steadied prices, but a generation passed before foreign competition (mainly from North America) 'revolutionized the trade in corn' (*MC*.xxvi).

The Coronation (*SC*). Hardy avoided the coronation of George V in June 1911 by going to the Lake District; he refused to oblige Clement Shorter with an ode for the grand occasion, preferring to write this amusing fantasy. Knowledge of English history reinforces the appropriateness of the comments, which reflect character and fate in the monarchs concerned. *Hal*, the 'many-wived' and 'self-widowered', is Henry VIII; *he who loved confession*, Edward the Confessor. *Rimmon*, a false god (II Kings v), refers to Henry's defiance of the Pope.

A coronet covers . . . sins (*HE*.xlvi), cf. I Pet.iv,8, on charity.

Correggio (*DR*.xii.3; *PBE*.i; *L*.I.iii; *MC*.xvi; *TD*.xxv), Italian painter (c.1489–1534), named after the town where he was born in northern Italy.

Corsican ogre (*TM*.xxxiii; *WT*2), Napoleon Bonaparte, born in Corsica.

Corvsgate Castle (*DR*.ii.4; and its history, *HE*.xxxi; *OMC*.1), Corfe Castle, between Wareham and Swanage. For Hardy's visit when working on *HE*, cf. Millgate,178.

Coryphaeus (*PBE*.x; *HE*.xxv), leading speaker of the Greek chorus. Hardy had probably noted the use of the term in *Pelham* xl, a novel by Edward Bulwer (later Lord Lytton).

costard, a large kind of apple.

cot, cottage.

couch, bring to rest, lay low; improve vision (by removing a cataract). **couch-grass**, a coarse thickly-spreading weed; **couch-heap**, couch-grass heaped for burning; hence **couch-fire**.

The Country Wedding (*LLE*). The names (verse iv) indicate Puddletown, and Jim with his serpent is one of its instrumental choir. Members of the Stinsford or 'Mellstock' (cf. *UGT*) choir have walked across Puddletown Heath to join him. Hardy may have heard the ill-omened story at home when he was a boy; his grandfather had spent his early years at Puddletown, and his mother had relatives there.

coup, move, stroke. ***coup d'audace*** (Fr.), daring stroke. ***coup de grâce*** (Fr.), death-blow. ***coup-de-Jarnac***, treacherous blow (from the manner in which Baron de Jarnac killed his opponent in a duel, 1547). ***coup d'oeil***, view taken in at a glance.

courage . . . screwed (*TT*.xvii), *Mac*.I.vii,60–1.

course of love (*UGT*.III.iii,IV.v; *TM*.xxxvii; *L*.v.xi), *MND*.I.i,134.

court-patched (*TD*.xxv), spotted (from splashings) as if with beauty-patches, once facial adornments for ladies of fashion.

court-roll, deed of tenure kept by the lord of the manor; copy of, see **copyholders**.

the Cove (*WT*2), see **Lulwind**.

coved, with concave arches.

Coventry, like the good burghers of (*W*.xxxi). According to tradition, the citizens of this Midland town remained indoors, with eyes averted, as she had wished, when Lady Godiva (d.1080), to relieve them of the heavy taxes imposed by her husband, rode naked through the market-place.

covers, draw neighbouring (*TT*.xvi, a fox-hunting term), look locally for a husband.

Cowper's *Aprocryphal Gospels* (*JO*.IV.i), published in 1874.

coz, dear (from 'cousin').

cozen, deceive.

crab-catchings, mistakes by rowers when blades miss the water.

crabs, crab-apples (green, unripe and sour).

cramped, cramp-afflicted.

Cranstoun's Goblin Page (*MC*.ix), in Scott's *The Lay of the Last Minstrel* VI.vii–ix.

craters (dial.), creatures.

cream and mantle (*L*.v.iv), *MV*.I.i,89.

creation groaning and travailing (*RN*.III.ii; *JO*.VI.ii,viii; *PPP*.The Lacking Sense; *HS*.Freed the Fret of Thinking), Rom.viii,22.

the Creed (*LLI*.8f), 'the Apostles' Creed', in which the minister and congregation declare their belief in the Trinity (the Father, the Son, the Holy Ghost or Spirit).

creep in . . . vows . . . kings (*TT*.xiv), Son.115.

creeping up (dial.), growing up, life.

Cresscombe (*JO*), Letcombe Bassett, a village with a water-cress stream, between Fawley and Wantage (map I).

Creston (*DR*.iii.2; *CM*.1), Preston, north of Weymouth Bay.

Cretan labyrinth (*RN*.II.iii), the maze designed by Daedalus for the Cretan king Minos, whose daughter Ariadne laid a clue of thread for Theseus to escape from it. **Cretan, lie like a** (proverbial), cf. Tit.i.12.

cribbed and confined (*TT*.vi), *Mac*.III.iv,24.

criddled (dial.), curdled.

Crimmercrock Lane (*TD*.liii; *TL*.The Dark-Eyed Gentleman, The Homecoming), originally 'Cromlech Crock Lane', part of the road from Maiden Newton leading up towards Toller Down on the way to Crewkerne.

crimp, seize, arrest, impress (for naval service).

Cripplegate Church (*HE*.xxvii), St Giles's, Cripplegate, London. See **Milton's monument**.

Crivelli, Carlo (*DR*.ix.4; *L*.v.i; *TD*.liii, the 'Pietà' in the N.G.), Italian painter, 1435–93; cf. *Life* 177/183.

crochet, crocket; see **crocketed**.

crock, a bulging iron pot.

crocketed, with crockets, carved ornaments, usually of buds or leaves.

Cromwell (*OMC* 6.i; *TD*.xviii), Oliver Cromwell (1599–1658), leader of the Ironsides (the Parliamentarian army) against Charles I in the Civil War, and subsequent Protector of England.

Crookhill, Mr (*LLI*.8h). For his story Hardy improved on an account he read in *The Dorset County Chronicle* (2 Apr 1829) of an army deserter who was arrested in the clothes of a gentleman at whose home, and in whose bedroom, he slept the previous night.

crooking, getting out of line, become crooked.

crooks dangling from a cotterel or cross-bar (*TD*.xviii): cf. **chimney-crook**.

crooping, crouching, squatting down.

crope, crept.

cross, sit astride (a horse).

cross-dadder. The dadder is one who chases a player; if he does not catch up quickly, he must, one after another until he is successful, pursue another who crosses his path.

Cross-in-Hand (*TD*.xlv), a stone pillar on the road along the ridge from Holywell to High Stoy. See map C and *PPP*.The Lost Pyx.

croud, an ancient type of fiddle.

the Crown, the State, represented by the monarch.

crowner (dial.), coroner.

'cruit, 'cruity, recruit.

crumby (slang), plump, luscious.

crush, crowded party.

Crusoe. See **Robinson Crusoe**.

crusted, having developed a protective covering or crust of prejudices or fixed habits and notions.

cry . . . in my trouble (*TD*.xlviii), Psalm cvii,28.

Cry of the Homeless (*MV*). Written at the request of Henry James in 1915 for *The Book of the Homeless* (ed. Edith Wharton) on behalf of war victims.

Cubit (*TD*.iii), Cupid is meant (see below).

Cuckoo Lane (*UGT*.IV.i; *MC*.xl), the road running north from Bockhampton Cross to the Dorchester–Puddletown road (map A).

cuckoo-cry, heard but not regarded (*PBE*.xxxii; *HE*.xxv). Cf. *1.H4*.III.ii,75–6, in a speech which is drawn from in 'not regarded' and 'Enfeoffed . . . too much' (*HE*.ii,xxiv). **cuckoo-father**, cuckolder, lover guilty of cuckoldry (from the cuckoo, which lays its eggs in other birds' nests).

Cui bono? (*DR*.xiv.3),For whose benefit? (Cicero, *Pro Milone* xii,32).

Cui lecta . . . ordo (PRF), Whoever takes pains to chose his subject aright will lack neither fluency nor orderly arrangement (Horace, *De Arte Poetica*).

cuirassier (Fr.), horse-soldier with armour-plate (originally of leather) for the body.

Culliford Tree (*WW*.The Ballad of Love's Skeleton), from 'Cuilvertestrie', AD 1195, the name of the large county area or 'hundred'; now applied to a tree-crowned tumulus on the chalk down east of Came Wood ('Culliford Wood' probably; cf. *Life* 173/508–9 and map G).

culpet (dial.), culprit.

Cunigonde (*GND*.1). The German writer Schiller tells the same story as Leigh Hunt in 'The Glove and the Lions' and Browning in 'The Glove', of the lady (Kunigunde in Schiller's 'Der Handschuh') who tests her lover by throwing her glove, for him to rescue, into a pit of lions.

cunning-man, wizard ('knowing' man).

cup-and-ball (*D3*.I.iv), bilbocatch, an eighteenth-century game, the object of which was to toss the ball and catch it as many times as possible in the cup to which it was attached.

cup-eyed, hollow-eyed.

Cupid, the god of love in classical mythology, usually represented with a bow and quiver full of arrows. **Cupid's Entire XXX** (*L*.II.ii) implies 'passionately in love'. Applied to beer, 'Entire' indicates a blend of all the best flavours; 'XXX', as opposed to 'XX' (medium), indicates a strong brew.

cups, in his, drinking freely.

Curate of Meudon (*HE*.xl), Rabelais (c.1494–1553), author of *Gargantua* and *Pantagruel*.

The Curate's Kindness (*TL*). For Pummery (Poundbury Camp), Ten Hatches (cf. *MC*.xli), and the Union see map B.

Curius (*DR*.ix.6), a Roman who conquered the Samnites and Sabines, and told ambassadors of the former when they visited him in his cottage that he wished to command the affluent while he lived in poverty.

curse . . . lifelong . . . hearse (*WW*.'We are getting to the end'), cf. the eclipsing curse of birth in Shelley's *Adonais* liv.

'The curtains now are drawn' (*LLE*). A memory of Emma at St Juliot rectory; now buried at Stinsford.

Cushi . . . David (*DR*.x.5), II Sam.xviii,19–32.

cusp, the projecting point formed by the meeting foils or curves in tracery or in the ornamentation of arches; **cusping-marks**, indicating the position of the cusps (on the architect's plan).

cust (dial.), cursed.

cut off, run off, off you go.

cwoffer (dial.), coffer, chest.

Cybele the Many-breasted (*TD*.xlii), Cybele, the 'Great Mother' (goddess) in ancient Greek mythology, often represented with many breasts as a symbol of the earth's fertility.

Cyclops (*FMC*.xix). The name ('round eye') was applied by the Greeks to the single-eyed cannibal giants of their mythology.

cyma-recta (cima-recta) curve, or **ogee** (*RN*.I.vii; *MC*.xxii), a moulding (arch.) which is concave in its upper part and convex below: wavy, flexuous.

***Cymbeline*, two mourners in** (*W*.xlv), IV.ii ('sweeten . . . grave', 221).

cyme, cornice moulding (on the highest point of the entablature).

cypher, calculate, prolong notes unduly; secret code.

Cyprian (*TD*.xlv), of Cyprus, where Aphrodite (Venus) rose from the sea. The image is that of Tess to Alec; the legend with which it combines may be that of Iphigenia, saved from the sacrificial altar by Artemis (Diana), a hind being substituted; if so, Hardy renews the hint of Tess's death that began with the white hart of Blackmoor Vale (*TD*.ii).

Cyprus . . . Galilee (*JO*.II.iii), associated with Venus and Jesus, sex and Christianity.
cyst, cavity, grave, body from which life has departed.

D

dab, expert, adept.
daddlen, and hawken, and spetting, dawdling, clearing [his] throat, and spitting (instead of making a proposal).
Daedalian (SF), showing ingenious artistry (after the legendary Daedalus of ancient Athens).
Dahl, Michael (*PBE*.v), Swedish portrait-painter, 1656–1743.
dally with false surmise (*PBE*.xxix), Milton, 'Lycidas', 153.
dame school, a private school, usually in the schoolmistress's home, to which young children were sent for a small fee.
Damer, Mrs (*D*1.I.v scene), Anne Seymour, the sculptress, 1744–1828; see **The Doctor's Legend**. **Damer's Wood** (*TM*.ii), probably Came Wood, named after the Damer family of Came House; see map G and **Middleton Abbey**.
Damocles' sword (DLa), suspended by a hair over his head (see a classical dictionary), a sign of imminent peril.
Danby, Francis (*FMC*.xx), Irish painter, 1793–1861.
The Dance at the Phoenix (*WP*, a story based on fact, Hardy told Edmund Gosse. Most of the places will be found on map B. *The Wain by Bullstake Square*, Charles's Wain (the constellation) as seen from North Square. *Parret*, *Yeo*, and *Tone* are Somerset rivers in apple-growing country (*blooth*, bloom).
dand, dandy.
dang (dial.), damn.
Daniel . . . nonconformity (*FMC*.xiii), cf. Dan.vi,7–17; **Daniel and the den** of lions (*PPP*.The Respectable Burgher), Dan.vi,10–20.
Danish fleet (*HE*.xxxiii). It was destroyed in a storm off Swanage in 876 or 877, during the reign of Alfred the Great, while bringing reinforcements to the Danes in Exeter.

Dantesque gloom (*LLI.*7), characteristic of scenes in Dante's *Inferno*.

dapes inemptae (*TD*.xxv), free banquets (Virgil, *Georgics* iv,133).

Daphnean (*W*.xl), like that of Daphne, who fled from the amorous Apollo, and was changed by the gods into a laurel in answer to her entreaties.

daps, likeness, image.

dark lantern (FMC.xxiv), one that can be carried invisibly at night though lit, a 'door' or shutter being opened for its use, as Hardy explains.

Dark Valley. See **Valley of the Shadow**.

darkle, grow dark. **darkling** (archaic), in the dark.

The Darkling Thrush (*PPP*), first printed as 'By the Century's Deathbed' on 29 Dec 1900. The thought (recalling the wisdom and humility of *PPP*.An August Midnight, and reflecting 'the determination to enjoy' in all nature, *Life* 213/222), was prompted by 'The Twenty-first Sunday after Trinity' in John Keble's *The Christian Year*. The description of song and setting is so like a passage on the midwinter song of the missel-thrush, with the same striking use of 'fling', in W. H. Hudson's *Nature in Downland* (xiii), 1900, that one must conclude, for lack of further MS evidence (we know that its date was changed from 1899 to 1900) that the poem was finished, if not written, in 1900. *scored* has musical overtones. *wind . . . death-lament*; cf. 'Thou dirge of the dying year' in Shelley's 'Ode to the West Wind'.

darkness visible (*TT*.xli), Milton, *Paradise Lost* i,63.

Darton, Farmer Charles (*WT*6), perhaps the son of the farmer Darton mentioned near the end of *MC*.xvii.

the Darwinian theory (*LLE*.Apology). Hardy had in mind, as the sequel shows, the theory of evolution (which appeared heretical in tracing man's development from apes), but it is not likely that he overlooked the struggle for existence (one species preying on another throughout nature) and the survival of the fittest (from Charles Darwin's *The Origin of Species*, 1859, and *The Descent of Man*, 1871; Hardy maintained that 'he had been among the earliest acclaimers' of the former, *Life* 153/158).

David . . . giant-slayer . . . banjo-player (*PPP*.The Respectable Burgher), I Sam.xvii,38–51 and xvi,23; **would see the battle** (*D*1.v.ii), I Sam.xvii,28; **and Bathsheba** (*WW*.The Clasped Skeletons), II.Sam.xi.

Davies (*WT*4), the hangman at Casterbridge gaol. Hardy said that 'Davies' was his real name, and that he had been a friend of his family at Higher Bockhampton.

Davy's locker, go to (*TM*.xxxix), drown at sea (proverbially Davy Jones's locker).

a daw in eagle's plumes (*HE*.xxxiii), an upstart or pretender (like the jackdaw in Aesop's fable that tried to be an eagle).

The Dawn After the Dance (*TL*), one of the 'dramatic monologues' (*TL*.pr.); see *Life* 64/66.

Day, Keeper (*UGT*), see also *FMC*.viii.

days of his vanity (*JO*.III.i), cf. Eccl.ix,9.

Days to Recollect (*HS*), a day in Emma's life at Swanage in the autumn of 1875, and the day of her death. The first shows the origin of a description (thistledown . . . comet) in *HE*.xxxi. *Saint Alban's Head*: see **St Aldhelm's**.

daysman (*TL*.He Abjures Love), arbitrator (cf. Job ix,33).

daze (dial.), damn.

D.D. (*JO*.I.vi), Doctor of Divinity.

DD (*FMC*.xxxvi), an octave below middle D.

de Leyre (*PBE*.iii), Alexandre Deleyre, French writer, 1726–97.

De Quincey . . . combat with Opium (*DR*.xii.5), Thomas de Quincey (1785–1859), *Confessions of an Opium-eater*.

de rigueur (Fr.), expected, required by etiquette.

Dea (*WB*.II.i), Goddess (Lat.).

dead . . . alive again (*WT*5.v), cf. Luke xv,24.

The Dead and the Living One (*MV*). Though described by Hardy as 'a war ballad of some weirdness' (*Life* 372/402–3), it is typical of his Spirit Ironic.

dead leaves . . . wind (*TD*.xxxvi), in one who as a lover was 'less Byronic than Shelleyan', xxxi; cf. Shelley, 'Ode to the West Wind' (*G.T.*).

The Dead Man Walking (*TL*). The MS shows 1896 as the date of composition. *The goal of men . . . iced*: for Hardy's reluctance to make life 'a science of climbing', see *Life* 53/54,87/89,104/107. *my friend*, Horace Moule (d.1873); *my kinsfolk*, grandparents, and his father (d.1892); *In hate of me*, when relations between Hardy and his wife were exacerbated by *JO*.

dead man's eye (*FMC*.v). It implies a curse. For this and its association with a star-dogged horned moon, the death of two hundred, and 'glittered', see Coleridge, 'The Ancient Mariner', 209–62.

Dead March (*UGT*.I.viii; *CM*5.v), from Handel's *Saul*. Its playing by the Scots Greys in Dorchester at the funeral of a 'comrade' in the early 1850s created 'a profound sensation'.

The Dead Quire (*TL*). The Mead of Memories is Stinsford churchyard above the Frome valley; *Moaning Hill*, in a field above the church, gets its name from the wind in a clump of elms (now removed). From Lower Bockhampton, where the 'dormered inn' stood, *Bank-walk* leads into Church Lane (*Church-way*), the route followed by the choir in *UGT*.I.v. The poem turns on the old belief that Christmas day should be kept sacred (cf. *UGT*.I.vii). *Old Dewy*, William Dewy (see below); for the remaining players, see *UGT*. *While shepherds watch'd*, a Christmas hymn based on the Nativity (Luke ii,7–20).

Dead Sea, like a drying (*MV*.The Clock-Winder), a diminishing interval of life offering no solace (like the undrinkable salt Dead Sea, SE of Jerusalem).

Dead 'Wessex' the Dog to the Household (*WW*). The Hardy's dog died on 27 Dec 1926 (*Life* 434–5/469–70); cf. **A Popular Personage at Home**. *path . . . hill*, from Max Gate to Conygar Hill (map G).

Deadman's Bay (*WB*; *D*1.II.v,v.vii), west of Portland; named after the many shipwrecks in its waters during storms.

dead-reckoner, one who calculates a ship's position from the distance run and courses steered, with various corrections (as for currents), but without astronomical observations.

The Dear (*TL*). Hardy informed Henry Newbolt that the poem was based on a real incident; whether the hill called Fairmile (a 'fair' mile long) was on the old Dorchester–Sherborne road or between Honiton and Exeter is uncertain.

Dear my love . . . coffin for me! (*TT*.xi). From verses by the German lyrical poet Heinrich Heine, 1797–1856.

Dearly Beloved Brethren . . . After Me (*FMC*.viii), the opening and closing words of the minister's exhortation before the General Confession.

Death in the Revelation, and his horse (*W*.xxxv), Rev.vi,8.

Death . . . lend . . . Life . . . borrow (*W*.xxvii), Shelley, *Adonais* xxi.

The Death of Regret (*SC*). Written first for one of Hardy's cats, which was buried by a sycamore at Max Gate after being found strangled in a wire rabbit-snare not far away on Conquer Barrow.

debouch (of soldiers), spread out after passing through a narrow passage (e.g. a street or defile).

dee, d—— (damn, damned).

deedy, earnest, serious.

deep, skilled in hidden arts such as witchcraft.

Defoe, Daniel (1660–1731), an English author best remembered for *Robinson Crusoe*. Hardy was attracted by his 'affected simplicity', and tried a similar style in *The Poor Man and the Lady* (*Life* 61/63); he draws attention to Defoe's literary merits in *HE*.xiii,xvi, and *Life* 391/424.

degrading thirst . . . stimulation (*LLE*.Apology), Wordsworth, 1802 preface to *Lyrical Ballads*.

Deïopeia (*L*.I.iv), the fairest of all Juno's nymphs.

Del Sarto (Andrea del Sarto) . . . **Carlo Dolci** (*JO*.III.ii), Italian painters of the sixteenth and seventeenth centuries, except **Spagnoletto** ('The Little Spaniard'), Jusepe de Ribera, a Spanish painter of the seventeenth century.

Delborough (*W*.xlii), named after East and West Chelborough, to the west of Melbury Park; 'One-Chimney Hut' stood near it.

Delia's . . . Georgian times (*TT*.xix). Delia and Amanda were common names of heroines in eighteenth-century fiction; the Georgian period (George I to George III) extends from 1714 to 1820. A powder-closet was a small-room in which powder was applied to the hair.

Delphian ambiguity, like that of the oracles uttered in the temple of Apollo at Delphi in ancient Greece.

Delphin editions (*JO*.I.v), Latin classics prepared for the use of the Dauphin (*ad usum Delphini*), son of Louis XIV, and frequently reprinted.

Delta, applied to territory crossed by diverging mouths of a river, as in Holland. In *MV*.An Appeal to America . . . Hardy thinks of neighbouring Belgium.

the Deluge (*HE*.xliii), Gen.vi–viii.

Demeter, the Greek goddess of fruit and harvest (the Roman Ceres).

Demetrius of Ephesus in west Asia Minor (*WB*.II.ix), Acts xix,21ff.

demise, determination of a, cessation of the conveyance or transfer of an estate.

Demoniac (Daemonic) Sabbath (*MC*.xxxix), a midnight of orgy for demons or witches presided over by the Devil, and assumed in medieval times to take place annually.

descant (archaic), hold forth, comment (on).

(as) Desdemona said (*W*.xxxix), men are not gods, *Oth*.III.iv,149. **Like Desdemona, she pitied him** (*WT*3.ii), *Oth*.I.iii,128–69.

désinvolture (Fr.), ease of manner.

Desperate Remedies (1871) was almost completed at Weymouth and Higher Bockhampton from the autumn of 1869 to March 1870; it was finished and revised in the autumn of 1870, after Hardy's virtual engagement to Emma Gifford (cf. end xiii.5). Though suspense is maintained to the end in a highly complicated plot, where everything is meticulously linked, there are times when probability is strained, and a mystery-thriller, influenced by Wilkie Collins and Miss Braddon, degenerates into rather crude sensationalism, a factor which explains Hardy's pre-publication anxiety (*Life* 83/85), and his ranking *DR* below *The Poor Man and the Lady* (*Life* 64/66). He drew considerably from this rejected novel (including passages which were reproduced in *OMC*4), as well as from at least one of his poems. The element of chance or 'dicing Time' (*WP*.Hap) is stressed (ix.3,xiii.1), and Hardy's rustic humour is already to the fore. Dryden's translation of Virgil is evident, but the most notable source of quotations, particularly in the Weymouth scenes, is Palgrave's *The Golden Treasury*. Anticipations of *WB* will be found in i.2 (the opening) and x.4. Hardy drew from the elaborate scenic symbolism of xii.6 for *RN*.III.v; and repeated significant features of the story in the tragic development of Tess: the heroine's altruistic self-sacrifice in marriage, the hero's 'too late, beloved' arrival to prevent this, her one life ruined (xiii.3–4,xviii.2), and the related image (the essence of a chapter in George Eliot's *Romola*) of the drifting boat (xii.6); cf. *TD*.xxv,lv. For possibly the joint origin of the title, see ***Aux grands maux . . .*** .

despising the shame (*TT*.xxxviii; *LLI*.4.v), Heb.xii,2.

Destiny and a Blue Cloak (*OMC*2). Hardy's first short story ('an impromptu', written on request shortly before his marriage) was published in *The New York Times*, 1874. Its use of actual, non-Wessex place-names (except 'Cloton') suggests that he did not regard it very seriously. Its revelation of a young woman's revenge on a rival who had attracted her admirer is effectively held back until the end. The ruse by which she ensures that this rival does not escape a loveless marriage like her own was adapted for the lighter ending of *HE*.

determined, terminated. **determinism** (*TD*.xxv), the belief that everything is determined by circumstances (and not by free-will).

Deuteronomy, woman in (*TT*.ii). For the words which Hardy's reading in 1866 of Swinburne's 'A Ballad of Burdens' helped him to remember, see Deut.xxviii,67. Cf. *DR*.xi.3.

Devil . . . Temptation (*RN*.I.iii), cf. Matt.iv,1–11.

The Devil's Door (*CM7*), the Devil's Den, a dolmen or 'Druidical trilithon' in the upper part of Clatford Bottom, 2 m. west of Marlborough.

Devil's head in a cowl, like the: said of a hypocrite (Dorset).

The Devil's Kitchen (*TD*.xliv). See **Dogbury Gate**.

the Devil's pitchfork (*TD*.1892 pr.). Cf. *TD*.xiv and *Letters* I,259, where Hardy states that, as a child brought up according to strict Church principles, he had devoutly believed in the Devil's pitchfork (and hell-fire). An allusive visual reminder will be found in Alec and the burning on the allotment (*TD*.l).

Devil's Table-Cloth (*TT*.xli), a white cloud on Table Mountain.

devils, like the . . . tremble (*TD*.xlvi), James ii,19.

devise, the terms or conditions of a will or legacy.

dévote (Fr.), devoutly religious woman.

dewbeat. This dialect word implies heavy footing (in dewy grass).

dew-bit, 'snap' or 'bite' before breakfast.

dewfall-hawk, nightjar, nighthawk.

Dewy, Reuben (*UGT*; *WP*.Friends Beyond; *TL*.The Dead Quire; *LLE*.The Country Wedding; *HS*.Winter Night in Woodland). Though the Dewys' house is drawn from the Hardys' house at Higher Bockhampton, its Christmas festivities had other sources (cf. **The House of Hospitalities**), possibly including parties Hardy attended when he accompanied his father on the violin. He said there were no family portraits in *UGT*. Some of Reuben's characteristics came from the local tranter or carrier (one of the Keatses; cf. *Life* 92/94,202/211) and from James Dart, a violinist in the Stinsford choir (*Life* 97/98).

Dewy, William (*UGT*; *TD*.xvii; poems as for Reuben above, except The Country Wedding), a legendary figure at times, linked with Hardy's grandfather (both 'cellists) and based to some extent on him and stories heard of other choir instrumentalists in the locality (cf. *Life* 10/14).

diachylon plaister, medical plaster based on lead oxide.

Diana, the Roman goddess of chastity. **Diana Multimammia**, many-breasted Diana, goddess of the Ephesians (*MC*.xlv; cf. *TD*.xlii); see Acts xix,23–35.

diapered, with ornamental pattern-work cut into the surface.

dibs, an old game of 'toss and catch' played with pebbles or sheep's knuckle-bones.

Dick Whittington (*JO*.II.i). He walked to London when he was a boy, became famous as its Lord Mayor, and left his wealth to charity (d.1423).

Dictionnaire Philosophique* to Huxley's *Essays (*TD*.xlvi), rational or scientific works which undermined the supernatural in Christian theology, from Voltaire's work, 1764, to the essays of T. H. Huxley, 1825–95.

Diderot (*JO*.ps. to pr.), a versatile French author who wrote on marriage and the natural law in the *Encyclopédie*, 1755.

Dido, woes of (*JO*.I.v), the Queen of Carthage when deserted by Aeneas, *Aeneid* iv; **his Dido dear** (*D*1.IV.vi), Lady Hamilton, Nelson's mistress.

Didymus (*L*.II.i), doubter, John xx,24–9.

diffraction-rings . . . circles (*TT*.xxxiv). When the telescope lenses are perfectly set, the diffraction rings caused by light waves are symmetrical about the centre of the image.

dimant, diment (dial.), diamond.

Diocesan Synod (*TT*.xxv) **and Visitations** (*TD*.xxv), assembly of the clergy of a diocese or area over which a bishop presides, and his visits to parishes in his diocese.

Diogenes Laertius (*PBE*.xxxii), an epicurean philosopher (d.222 AD) who wrote *Lives of the Greek Philosophers* in ten books.

Dionysus (*L*.II.iii), statue of Bacchus (the Greek Dionysus), usually presented as youthful and effeminate.

diorama, scenic representation viewed through an aperture the sides of which are continued towards the picture; different effects were obtained by changes of light and of its angle of projection.

dip, dip-candle (made by dipping a wick into tallow); **dipper**, maker of dip-candles.

disastrous chances . . . accidents . . . field (PRF), *Oth*.I.iii,134–5.

Discouragement (*HS*). *naturing Nature,* an expression (Lat. *natura naturans*) applied by Spinoza to the divine being, God in nature. Here Nature, which produces the natures of species and individuals, is a helpless and suffering instrument of 'her unfaithful lord', the First Cause or Prime Mover; cf. **the Unfulfilled Intention**.

The Discovery (*SC*). A recollection of Hardy's first journey to St Juliot, where he fell in love with Emma Gifford; cf. *Life* 65/67 (for the fires, *PBE*.ii). *on her my heart*, on her whom my heart.

dish (slang), circumvent, cheat.

Dissolution (*JO*.IV.i) of the monasteries by order of Henry VIII

(1535–6).

distaff . . . spindle . . . shears (*RN*.I.vii), alluding to the three classical fates who presided over life: Clotho, with her distaff, presiding over birth; Lachesis spinning the thread; and Atropos cutting it with her shears.

A distant dearness in the hill (*PBE*.xx ep.), Tennyson, *In Memoriam* lxiv.

The Distracted Preacher (*WT7*), a romance, first pub. in April 1879, which arose from smuggling stories heard at Hardy's home in his boyhood (cf. *WT*.pr. and *Life* 164/170), from accounts of smuggling techniques heard at Swanage (*Life* 107–8/110–11) and in the Weymouth area (map D), and newspaper reports of trial proceedings.

Ditty (*WP*). Written with Emma Lavinia Gifford in mind, and the rectory at St Juliot in Cornwall where Hardy first met her in 1870; cf. *SC*.'When I set out for Lyonnesse'. 'Spread a strange and withering change' is an inverted statement (a strange . . . change spread); the change is subjective, like the radiance of *WP*.Her Initials. 'Here is she!' seems an answer to Richard Crashaw's 'Wishes to his supposed mistresse': 'Whoe'er she be, That not impossible she That shall command my heart and me; Where'er she lie . . . '; cf. *DR*.x.4 and *WB*.ep.

diurnal round (*MV*.While Drawing in a Churchyard), from Wordsworth, 'A slumber did my spirit seal' (*G.T.)*.

divination by Bible and key (*FMC*.pr.), cf. *FMC*.xiii.

Divine Comedy (*L*.III.iii), an allusion to the title of Dante's main work, which implies a blissful ending.

the divinity who shaped the ends (*W*.xv), *Ham*.v.ii,10.

The Division (*TL*), written perhaps in July 1893, when Hardy was in London, seeing Mrs Henniker (*Letters* II,26–7), with his wife at Max Gate, little more than a hundred miles off 'as the crow flies'. For the 'division', see **Alike and Unlike** and *SC*.After a Journey.

Do as ye would be done by (*WP*.The Burghers), an old saying based on Luke vi,31.

Doctor Syntax (*FMC*.xliv), three tours in comic and satirical verse (1812–21) by William Combe, illustrated by Thomas Rowlandson.

The Doctor's Legend (*OMC3*) was first intended, as its framework shows, for *GND*. Not wishing to offend a neighbouring family, Hardy was content to have it published in New York (Mar 1891). Joseph Damer of Came House, who became first Earl of

Dorchester, had bought Milton Abbey, built a mansion beside it, and removed the village to extend his grounds; his son married the sculptress Anne Seymour Conway in 1767, and committed suicide in 1776. Hardy discovered much of the background to his story from local tradition, Hutchins, and the letters of Horace Walpole, whose first cousin, Henry Seymour Conway, was Anne's father. With reference to her husband's death Walpole repeated his epigram 'this world is a comedy to those that think, a tragedy to those that feel', the deeper truth of which made a lasting impact on Hardy; cf. *TD*.xx,xxi, and the Spirits of the Years and the Pities in *The Dynasts*.

Doctors' Commons, a London registry which dealt with the probate of wills, the issue of marriage licences, etc.

doff, put or take off (originally of clothing).

Dogbury Gate (*HS*.Life and Death at Sunrise), a stretch of the Dorchester–Sherborne road between Dogbury Hill on the eastern side (*TM*.xii; *W*.xxviii; *TD*.ii,xliv) and High Stoy.On 10 Sep 1867 Hardy, probably on a visit to his sister Mary, who was teaching near at Minterne Magna, sketched Dogbury Hill from 'The Devil's Kitchen', the dell along which Dogbury Gate runs.

dogcart, open vehicle with two back-to-back seats.

dog-days, the hottest period in England, from early July to mid-August, associated with the rising of the greater (Sirius) and of the lesser (Procyon) Dog-star.

doggery, roguery.

dogs, a pair of andirons to support burning wood in a fireplace (**dog-knob**, the ornamental top at the front of each).

dole, deal or portion out.

doleful-bells, snake's head flowers, a kind of fritillary.

dolorifuge (possibly coined by Hardy), dispeller of sorrow.

Domesday, the Domesday Book, a survey of the lands and properties of England, instituted by William the Conqueror in 1086.

Domicilium (*Life* 4/8–9 footnote), the first of Hardy's surviving poems. It was written between 1857 and 1860, giving a description of his birthplace with his paternal grandmother's recollections of it and the heath more than half a century earlier, when it stood alone and heath-croppers were welcome friends; cf. the note on the tranter, 25 Sep 1887 (*Life* 202/211).

don, put on (clothing), assume.

Don Quixote (*JO*.IV.i), one misled by illusions, like the eponymous hero of the novel by the Spanish writer Cervantes, 1547–1616.

Donaghadee (*HS*), written when Hardy received a letter from a stranger at this place (with the appealing name) in County Down, Northern Ireland. He is reminded of Irish songs.

done . . . not be undone (*DR*.v.3), *Mac*.v.i,66–7. Cf. *RN*.I.iv; *TD*.xxxviii.

done . . . ought . . . left undone (*L*.I.iii) from the General Confession (C. of E.).

done that which was right . . . (*JO*.v.vi), cf. Judg.xvii,6.

Donn, Arabella (*JO*). Hardy's note of 1 Mar 1888 (*Life* 206/215) gives Rachel H—— and her 'clever artificial dimple-making' as 'probably in some respects' her original.

Donna Clara (*DR*.viii.1), Sheridan, *The Duenna* (1775) III.iii.

Donnegan's *Lexicon* (*LLI*.4.i), see **Liddell and Scott**.

Doom and She (*PPP*). The 'lord' responsible for Fate is the insentient First Cause or Immanent Will. For Nature as world-weaver, cf. *PPP*.The Lacking Sense,3.

Doomsday (*WB*.I.vi), at the end of the world, when the dead are raised and judged by God.

Dorcas, or Martha, or Rhoda (*LLI*.4.iii), a devoted supporter of the Church (cf. Luke x,38–42, Acts ix,39 and xii,12–13). **Dorcas meeting** (*TT*.vi), of ladies for making and distributing clothes; cf. Acts ix,36.

Dornell, Betty (*GND*.1), Elizabeth Horner, 1723–92, mother of **Lady Susan**.

Dornell, Squire Thomas (*GND*.1), Thomas Horner of Mells Park, Somerset, husband of **Susannah** (*GND*.1), Susannah Strangways of Melbury House. After her husband's death she rebuilt the church at Melbury Osmond ('King's Hintock') in 1745; among her many charities to his memory, a free school there for twenty poor children was completed in 1754.

dorp, hamlet or village, thorp.

The Dorsetshire Labourer (Orel,168–91), pub. in *Longman's Magazine*, July 1883; some of its descriptive detail appears in *MC* and *TD*.

Doubtless . . . pleasure and ennui and **When we have made our love . . . score** (*L*.II.iv), Byron, *Don Juan* XIV.xvii–xviii.

douce, sweet, amiable, pleasant.

Douw, Gerard (*FMC*.ix), Gerrit Dou, Dutch painter, 1613–75.

doxology, a form of praise to God. Longways (*MC*.xviii) probably means 'theology' (cf. *D2*.III.ii); the universality of his argument in 'Why *should* death rob life o' fourpence?' suggests an artistic quintessentializing of a sharp exchange near the end of the opening chapter of Dickens' *Our Mutual Friend*.

drabbet, twilled undyed linen.

drag, make a long-drawn-out journey; a braking-device; a chain (**drag-chain**) for coupling and pulling railway vehicles.

draught, drawing.

draw . . . soul out of . . . body (*LLI*.7), *M.Ado* II.iii,54–5.

draw up (a clock), wind up (a process drawing up the activating weights).

draw-latching, drawlacheting (dial.), idle, good-for-nothing.

The Dream is – Which? (*LLE*). The date confirms that the poet's memories have been of Emma from 1870 (by the Valency river) to her death and burial at Stinsford.

dream of, not to tell (*HE*.xviii), Coleridge, 'Christabel' i,253.

Dream of the City Shopwoman (*LLE*). For the obverse (also written in 1866) see *TL*.From Her in the Country. *this eternal wheel . . . grime*, cf. 'This hum of the wheel – the roar of London! . . .' (*Life* 171/178) and *WW*.To a Tree in London.

A Dream Question (*TL*). *as Moses wrote*, Num.xi,1; *fourth dimension*, see **The Absolute Explains.**

The Dream-Follower (*PPP*). Probably occasioned by looking from Max Gate across the Frome meadows to Kingston Maurward, Stinsford, and thinking of Julia Martin whom Hardy loved when a child, and the shock of seeing her aged in London. See **She, to Him**.

dree (archaic), suffering; three (dial.)

Drenghard, Sir George (*GND*8), Sir George Trenchard, who lived at Wolfeton House (a mile north of Dorchester, near Charminster) in the reign of James I. The **Drenkhards** (or Drenghards) were among the Wessex families for whom Angel Clare had little respect because they had declined (*TD*.xix); they are mentioned in *GND*4, one of them in *GND*2. See **A Man**.

Dresden days (*D*3.VII.ix), a brief period reflecting the glory of Napoleon's last important victory (the battle of Dresden, Aug 1813).

drink my cup to the dregs (*JO*.VI.ix), part of the novel's Crucifixion theme; cf. Luke xxii,42.

Drinking Song (*WW*). History proves the pretentiousness of theories to explain the universe, and Hardy concludes that modern scientific theory on the subject should not be taken very seriously. 'The Scheme of Things is . . . incomprehensible' (*Life*

410/440). *Thales*, a Greek philosopher of the sixth century BC; *Hume*, a Scottish philosopher and historian (1711–76) who did not believe in miracles; *God's clockwork*, an allusion to the eighteenth-century view that everything in the universe is mathematically explicable, and that it runs like clockwork; Dr *Cheyne* (1841–1915), a Biblical scholar who rejected belief in the virgin birth of Christ; Albert *Einstein* (1879–1955), a mathematical theorist whose work on the relativity of the universe made Hardy conclude that the universe 'seems to be getting too comic for words'. See **Copernicus**.

A Drizzling Easter Morning (*LLE*). Easter Day celebrates the resurrection of Jesus, who, according to Christian teaching, died to save (ransom) mankind from their sins (cf. Matt.xx,28). Hardy asks if men will wish to be resurrected from the dead ('pass again their sheltering door'), thinking that when they die they prefer 'endless rest' from toil (cf. *WP*.Friends Beyond).

Dromios (*TM*.xxxix), twin slaves in Shakespeare's *The Comedy of Errors*; when they appear separately, their identities are usually mistaken.

drong, a lane or passage between hedges or walls.

drool, slaver, talk childishly or idiotically.

dropping of the lives. See **life-holders**.

drops (wine) . . . **for the stomach's sake** (*HE*.xxxiii), I Tim.v,23.

droudge, drudge, toil.

drough (dial.), through.

drouth, drought.

Droz, Jacquet (*FMC*.xl), a Swiss clockmaker who invented various mechanical devices, 1721–90.

Druidical, pertaining to the Druids, priests or soothsayers in ancient Britain who regarded mistletoe on oak trees with religious veneration.

Drummer Hodge (*PPP*), 'a native of a village near Casterbridge', Hardy disclosed; see **Hodge**. *kopje*, hillock; *veldt*, open pasture lands; *Karoo*, extensive barren plateaus; *Bush*, uncleared or untilled land.

dry . . . remainder biscuit . . . voyage (DLa), *AYL*.II.vii,39–40.

Dryads, classical nymphs presiding over woods.

Dryden . . . a rent-charge on Providence (*HE*.xxiv), John Dryden, poet and dramatist, 1631–1700; a rent-charge is bestowed from property which the beneficiary does not own.

Dualism, the belief that mind and substance, or God and nature, are separate realities, as opposed to **Monism**; cf. *Life* 369–70/399–400, and *WW*.Our Old Friend Dualism.

The Duchess of Hamptonshire (*GND*9), Hardy's second short story, and the first of his to be published in England (Apr 1878). His Wessex map suggests Tottenham House near Marlborough for Batton Castle (named possibly from the historic neighbouring borough of Bedwyn; Hardy named it first Croome Castle, then Stroome Castle).

duck-hawk, marsh-harrier or moor-buzzard.

duck-shot, bullets for shooting wild duck.

ducking-stool, chair at the end of a plank to which offenders were tied before being ducked in water for punishment.

Duddle Hole (*TM*.ix,xxvi), perhaps Duddle Farm or near, east of Lower Bockhampton.

The Duel (*MV*). In the Countess of Cardigan's *My Recollections*, 1909 (p. 124), Hardy read how Anne Brudenell in the guise of a page held the Duke of Buckingham's horse during the duel in which her husband, the Earl of Shrewsbury, was killed by him in 1668.

A Duettist to her Pianoforte (*LLE*), in memory of Emma Hardy and her dark-haired sister Helen Catherine Holder of St Juliot rectory (cf. *Life* 74–5/77–8, where 'The Elfin Call' is mentioned). Emma is seen, with her old piano, at Max Gate.

Dugdale, Florence E. See **Hardy, Florence Emily**.

The Duke's Reappearance (*CM*.10; pub. Dec 1896). See **Monmouth** and **King's Hintock**.

Dulcianner (*HE*.xl). The dulciana, an organ stop for producing a soft string-like tone, is meant.

Dumas, Alexandre (*W*.ix), French novelist, 1802–70. Both he and François **Méry** (1797–1866) wrote books on their European travels.

dumble, **dumbledore**, bumble-bee; cockchafer.

Dumpy level, spirit-level with a short telescope for land-surveying.

Duncliffe Hill (*JO*.IV.iv), 2 m. west of Shaftesbury.

Dundagel (*PBE*.xxi; *SC*.'I found her out there'), Tintagel Castle; 'grim Dundagel throned along the sea' is from *The Quest of the Sangraal* by the Cornish parson-poet R. S. Hawker, 1803–75. The headland is famed through the legendary association of its castle with King Arthur's birth and the love story of Tristram and Iseult. See **Tintagel**.

dunder-headed, slow, unintelligent.

dun-fly, gad-fly (a pest to horses and cattle).

Durbeyfield, Teresa (Tess), named possible after Hardy's cousin Teresa, who lived at Higher Bockhampton. She and another cousin said that what happened to Tess happened to one of their relatives. This may have been Hardy's paternal grandmother, when she was in Berkshire before her marriage; his Reading and Fawley references (*Life* 282/299,420/453) point to this; see Millgate,18. 'Durbeyfield' indicates descent, social and lineal, from the Turbervilles who came over from Normandy with William the Conqueror. Their early splendour is represented by the tombs and the heraldic arms of the stained glass window in the Turberville Chapel of Bere Regis Church. One family lived at the manor house at Wool, and both this and the chapel figure in *TD* scenes. In person Tess owes much to Gertrude Bugler's mother Augusta Way, when she was a milkmaid at Kingston Maurward farm, and also to the wife of the sculptor Hamo Thornycroft (cf. *Life* 220/230 and **Elizabethan simile**).

Durdle-Door (*HS*.The Bird-Catcher's Boy), a rock which projects into the sea, forming a natural arch west of Lulworth Cove.

dure, duration.

Dürer (*RN*.I.iii), German painter and engraver, 1471–1528.

During Wind and Rain (*MV*), based on scenes evoked by memories of Emma Hardy's youth at Plymouth in *S.R.*, which Hardy did not discover until after her death.

durn, doorpost or wooden framework of a doorway.

Durnover (many references including *MC; CM*5; *D*3.v.vi; and *HS*.Before My Friend Arrived), Fordington, on the SE side of Dorchester. Hardy's close knowledge of it grew from his friendship with sons of the vicar Henry Moule, Horace in particular. The Revd Henry Moule had made himself unpopular by his reforming zeal, but his bravery in fighting cholera outbreaks, especially in 1854, turned him into a hero; Hardy recalled it in his story 'A Changed Man'. His name for Fordington derives from the Roman name for their Dorchester camp, 'Durnovaria', from the earlier British name (cf. **Var**) which meant 'the settlement by the dark river'. **Durnover Moor** is flat marshy meadowland through which the divided Frome river runs, mainly in two streams, immediately east of Dorchester and NE of Fordington, the old Mill Street of the latter being the original of Mixen Lane. The manor of Fordington belongs to the Duchy of Cornwall, and its land to the south of Dorchester and further west is extensive, including Fordington Field, north of the prehistoric camp of Mai-dun or Maiden Castle, the 'Durnover Great Field and Fort' of *WP*.The Alarm. See map B.

Durotriges (*CM6*), a British tribe (probably among the **Belgae** immigrants) in the Dorset region before the Roman occupation.

dust and ashes (*MC*.xix; *TD*.xii,xlii), Job xxx,19.

dust-hole, a hole or bin for refuse.

Duty of Man. See **The Whole Duty of Man**.

Dux Bellorum (*QC*.vi), leader in the wars (Lat.).

dying fall (*L*.I.ii), *TN*.I.i,4.

The Dynasts, composed at various times from the end of 1897 to March 1907, after Hardy had considered the subject and ways of presenting it for many years, and published in three parts: Jan 1904, Feb 1906, Feb 1908. In 1875 he had in mind a series of ballads, 'forming altogether an Iliad of Europe from 1789 to 1815'. Making Napoleon his central human figure, however, and England the leading protagonist, he wisely dropped the Revolutionary period, and began the action in 1805. His 'overworld' view takes the reader from scene to scene in cinematic style, and supports the role of the observing Spirits, suggested principally by Shelley's *Prometheus Unbound*. The most important, those of the Years and the Pities, represent the philosophical and emotional views of Hardy; the Spirits Ironic and Sinister, registering other human reactions to a destructive world, continue the role of Goethe's Mephistopheles. The unreasoning force which sways nations and leaders is part of the Immanent Will at work within the universe; its influence is visualized by Hardy and acknowledged repeatedly by Napoleon, especially when fate turns against him. However dramatically important the characters – and some, women especially, are enhanced by pity – they are seen as puppets and mannikins of little significance in the process of time. This perspective is confirmed by aerial views; detached fragments of a vast Austrian army move like molluscs on a leaf, and a procession of carriages bearing royalty and nobility from Vienna is 'no more than a file of ants'. A few scenes seem unduly long, but excellent proportions are generally kept, and many constitute most vivid and artistic distillations of history. There is too much reiteration of fixed philosophy in the verse, which is artifically concentrated but often admirable in texture. Wessex folk, and common service-men provide comic relief, and descriptive scenes contain some of Hardy's finest prose – economical, clear-cut, with bright poetic flashes. The more hopeful ending (from the chorus of the Pities) was Hardy's idea, but Man's unreason as Europe drifted towards the 1914–1918 war made him regret that he had risked it. Though read by few, *The Dynasts* is a colossal achievement, the culmination of Hardy's greatest single ambition during his literary prime. See *Life* 319–21/343–4,517–18;334–5/360–1;368/398;454/491–2.

***The Dynasts*, Prologue** and **Epilogue**. Both were written at Harley Granville-Barker's request for his production of an abridged version of *The Dynasts*, a patriotic promotion during the early part of the First World War; it ran from 25 Nov 1914 to 30 Jan 1915 at the Kingsway Theatre, London, but was not a success. The Prologue and Epilogue were used again in 1916 when *Wessex Scenes from 'The Dynasts'* was produced at Weymouth and Dorchester.

dys – what do you call it – (*JO*.VI.iii), dysentery.

E

Each to the loved one's side (*PBE*.xxxix ep.), from the song 'The sun upon the lake is low' (*G.T.*) at the opening of Scott's poetic drama *The Doom of Devorgoil*.

Early Flourballs and Thompson's Wonderfuls, varieties of potato.

early-Christian face (*TT*.iv), typical of early Christian paintings, Italian especially.

ease after torment . . . (*FMC*.xxi), from Edmund Burke's *A Philosophical Enquiry into the Origin of our Ideas of the Sublime and Beautiful*, 1757, I.iv.

east, more or travel east.

East Egdon (*RN*), Affpuddle, a village 3 m. east of Puddletown.

East Quarriers (*WB*), Easton, Portland (map H).

An East-End Curate (*HS*). Mr Dowle (Do-well? Cf. 'Dow-well') in the East End, the poorer side of London, recalls *JO*.III.i, on the 'true religion', with 'a touch of goodness and greatness in it', of a humble curate, 'wearing his life out' in a city slum; Hardy seems less sanguine than Jude. *Novello's Anthems*, published by Vincent Novello, 1781–1861.

East-India Stock (*GND*4), shares in the East India Company, a prosperous English trading group.

easting, turning toward the east (the chancel end) of the church, to recite the Creed.

the eastward position (*JO*.VI.ii), alluding to the controversy on whether a priest celebrating the Holy Communion should face east, with his back to the congregation; the Archbishop of Canterbury declared it was compatible with the Book of Common Prayer rubric. The context and the name 'Rubric College' indicate Hardy's impatience with a Church apt to lose sight of its Christian mission in debates on outward signs and formalities.

Ecclesiastes (*FMC*.iv), an Old Testment book the keynote of which is the vanity of all earthly things; see **Old Eccl'iastes**.

échelon, in, with army divisions parallel to each other, and none aligned (cf. *D*3.VII.viii).

Echo (*RN*.II.vi), daughter of Earth and Air. After displeasing Juno by her loquacity, she fell in love with Narcissus; on being rejected by him, she pined away and became no more than a voice.

éclat (Fr.), publicity.

ecliptic, the path of the sun, seen from the earth, in the Zodiac.

écorché (Fr., literally 'skinned'), an anatomical subject or model showing the muscular system.

the Eddas (*D*.pr.), old Norse poetry and traditions.

Eden, the curse of (DLa), weeds, Gen.iii,17–19; **Eden of unconsciousness** (*TT*.i), state of innocence, sexual unawareness.

'ee, 'e (dial.), you.

een (archaic), eyes.

Ees (dial.), Yes.

effet, eft, newt, small lizard.

Egdon (many references, especially *RN*; *MC*.xlv; *WT*4; *LLI*.7). The name was suggested by 'Eggardon', that of an ancient hill-fortress in west Dorset, but it is applied to the heath which stretches eastward from Hardy's birthplace as far as the area north of Wareham and Poole Harbour. For *RN*, where most of the scenes are imagined on Puddletown Heath, with 'Alderworth' several miles further east, Hardy imagines the Frome river and 'Shadwater Weir' near the Tincleton road and 'The Quiet Woman' inn. Egdon is a symbol of life as it has been, and has to be, endured in a world of natural defect and chance. Its most powerful scenes are either dark or gloomy or fiercely torrid and cruel; the former dominates. It varies according to temperament: Thomasin is at home there; for Eustacia it is Hades. Clym Yeobright's face expresses 'the view of life as a thing to be put up with'; abandoning the vanities of Paris, he is one of those ascetics who could feel they had 'a natural right to wander on Egdon'. For Hardy too it is 'absolutely in keeping with the moods of the more thinking among mankind' (cf. *TL.*Yell'ham-Wood's Story). It represents a Darwinian view of Nature which is opposed to civilization; hence the symbolical significance of the plantation which suffers from the stresses of the storm, while the open natural heath feels it is lightly caressed. 'Egdon was made for such times as these' (III.vi). This symbolism is restricted to *RN*. In the preface to this novel and in *WT*4, Hardy expresses his belief that Egdon Heath witnessed the suffering of the Wessex King Ina, afterwards presented as King Lear. During the present century the face of Egdon has successively changed as a result of afforestation and clearance.

Egypt . . . Land of Promise (*TD.*li,lii). After bondage in Egypt the Israelites escaped to Canaan, the Promised Land (Exodus–Joshua).

Egyptian capitals, lettering of a special type (as printed, *DR.*xxi.1).

Egyptian plague of darkness (*FMC.*xxiv, **ninth plague of Egypt**; *HE.*iii; *RN.*v.vii), Exod.x,21ff.

Einstein (*LLE.*Apology). See **Drinking Song**.

El Greco (*HS.*In a Former Resort after Many Years), Spanish painter of Cretan origin and Italian training, 1541–1614.

eleventh commandment (*RN.*VI.iii). See **commandments**.

Elijah and Elisha (*DR.*xii.5): Hardy kept to the August church-readings prescribed for the year 1865; cf. I Kings xvii–xix, II Kings ii. And **fire from Heaven** (*W.*xliv), II Kings i,9–12; **the still small voice** (*PBE.*xix), see **Quid Hic Agis?**

Elizabeth (*FMC.*xx), Queen of England, 1558–1603; dauntless when England was threatened by the Spanish armada.

Elizabethan simile of roses filled with snow (*TD.*xxiv; cf. **Durbeyfield**), Thomas Campion, 'Cherry-Ripe' (*G.T.*).

Elliston (*TM.*xvi), Robert William (1774–1831), a well-known actor in Bath and London, with some experience as a manager of provincial theatres.

Elm-Cranlynch (*GND.*1), Charles Phelipson's home, named after

Great Elm and Cranmore, Somerset (not more than 2 m. from **Falls-Park**).

Elsenford (*CM*2), substituted for 'Homeston Farm', which suggests Bhompston Farm; cf. **Bloom's End**.

eltrot, wild parsley, cow parsley.

Elymas-the-Sorcerer pattern (*FMC*.viii), feeling blindly in the dark, Acts xiii,6–11, perhaps after a cartoon of part of a tapestry by Raphael in the Victoria and Albert Museum.

Elzevirs (*HE*.xxxix), beautiful editions of the classics printed by the Elzevir family in Holland during the seventeenth century.

Embarcation (*PPP*). At Southampton, Vespasian had landed with his Roman legions (c.43 AD); Cerdic, founder of Wessex, in 495 AD. Henry V embarked here with troops for France, defeating the French at Agincourt in 1415.

embowment, embrace.

embroidery of imagination upon the stuff of nature (*JO*.I.vii), an **iris-bow** thought, typical of Hardy and of Carlyle, from whom it may originate.

Emmaus, two disciples . . . haloed figure (*MC*.xxvi), Christ's appearance after his resurrection, as recorded by the **evangelist** Luke: xxiv,13–35.

emmet, ant.

Emminster (*TD*), Beaminster (in *OMC*2), 6 m. north of Bridport.

empery, rule, empire, imperialism.

Empress, the way is ready . . . Eve (*TD*.1; **old Other One**, Satan), Milton, *Paradise Lost* ix,626–31.

en (dial.), him, it.

En avant! (*D*3.VI.v), Forward! (a French order: German, **Vorwärts!**). ***en famille***, as a member of the family. ***en garçon***, as a bachelor. ***en l'air***, in the air, in a state of uncertainty. ***en masse***, in general. ***en papillon***, using the butterfly stroke in swimming. ***en plein . . . à cheval***, betting on one number . . . taking two chances. ***en rapport with***, in sympathy or having an affinity with.

Enckworth Court (*HE*.xxxviii; *OMC*.1), Encombe House in a beautiful valley NW of St Aldhelm's Head (map D). Hardy transferred some features of Kingston Maurward, Stinsford, to it, including the George III 'Brick, brick' story.

End of the Year 1912 (*LLE*). Hardy thinks of Emma before and after her death in November. *Life's mad spinning*, cf. *LLE*.According to the Mighty Working; *six bells*, of Fordington Church, ringing in the New Year.

Endelstow (*PBE*), St Juliot, Cornwall, and probably named after Endellion, a village 12 m. SW; the topography is disguised. **Endelstow House** is drawn from Lanhydrock House near Bodmin, 'at a spot several miles south of its supposed site' (pr.).

Endor, witch of (*RN*.I.vi; *MV*.Apostrophe to an Old Psalm Tune; *LLE*.Apology), I Sam.xxviii,3–20.

Endorfield, Elizabeth (*UGT*.IV.iii–iv), named after the witch of Endor.

endure the ills . . . others (*TD*.xxxvi), *Ham*.III.i,81–2.

***endured* the cross, *despising* the shame** (*LLI*.4.v, with the Greek), Heb.xii,2.

the Enemy (*JO*.III.x), the Devil. **enemy . . . sow . . . tares** (*D*1.II.v), Matt.xiii,25. **enemy to our house** (*MC*.xvii), cf. II Sam.iii,1.

Enfeoffed . . . popularity . . . (*HE*.xxiv; the continuation of this passage is echoed in 'not regarded', *HE*.ii), *1.H4*.III.ii,69–73.

Enfield's *Speaker* (*GND*4), a selection 'from the best English writers', with an essay on elocution, 1777.

Enfin les renards . . . pelletier (Fr.), Foxes eventually reach the furrier's, *L*.VI.iv.

engine, contrive, engineer; contrivance, mechanism.

engined, carried through (of a plan).

entablature, that part of a building, above the column, including architrave, frieze, and (at the top) cornice; ornamental top (of pier-glass).

entail, legal securing of property to a predetermined line of successors.

Enter a Dragoon (*CM*5), begun November 1899, completed January 1900 (cf. *Letters* II,238,246. The scene is at Higher Bockhampton, the house and garden being opposite the common well in the lane.

enterprise . . . pith (*CM*.11.iii), cf. *Ham*.III.i,86.

Entertained a breast . . . rest (*OMC*4.I.iv), George Chapman's translation of Homer's *Odyssey* xvii,313–14.

entresol, between the ground floor and the first floor.

epeisodia (Gk.), episodes.

ephemerons (*RN*.IV.v), ephemera or insects which live only a day in their winged state. See **animalcula**.

Ephesians (*FMC*.xxi), a short book in the New Testament.

Ephraim, grapes of . . . Abi-ezer (*TD*.xlix), Judg.viii,2 **Ephraim . . . idols . . . alone** (*FMC*.lvii), Hos.iv,17.

epiderm, the outer or superficial layer (of the skin).

Episcopalian, of the episcopal or Anglican Church.

Epitaph on a Pessimist (*HS*). 'Smith' and 'Stoke' were chosen because they are common among English family and place names.

equatorial, a mechanism which causes a telescope to revolve with the apparent motion of the heavenly bodies, so that any particular observation can be continued or renewed without readjustment.

equinoctial lines . . . topics (*TT*.xxxviii), lines showing the celestial equator; old Mrs Martin is unable to remember 'the Tropic of Capricorn'.

er (dial.), he. **er woll**: see **'Ch.**

Eros (or **Cupid**), the Greek god of love.

erotolepsy (*JO*.II.iv), seizure by sexual passion.

Esdraelon, plain of (*D3*.VII.viii; *TL*.Panthera; *LLE*.Jezreel), where a huge army assembled against Israel; cf. Judith (in the Apocrypha) vii.

espièglerie (Fr.), roguishness.

Establishment, Established Church, the Church of England.

Esther . . . Vashti (*FMC*.xliii; *W*.xxxi; *PPP*.The Respectable Burgher), cf. the book of Esther (OT). Esther became queen after Ahasuerus, King of Persia, had divorced his consort Vashti. *JO*.VI ep. quotes Esther xiv,2 from its continuation in the Apocrypha.

et praeterea nihil (Lat.), and nothing else.

Eternal City (*WB*.III.i), Rome (a description found in Ovid and other Latin authors). **the pilgrim's Eternal City** (*L*.1896 pr.), the highest ideal goal, as in Bunyan's *The Pilgrim's Progress*, from the City of Destruction to the Celestial City.

ethereal . . . spirit . . . limbs (*JO*.III.ix), Shelley, 'Epipsychidion', 75–82.

The ethereal substance . . . (*WB*.I.v), Milton, *Paradise Lost* vi, 330–1.

Ethiopic (*TD*.xxiv). 'Ethiopia', the Greek name for the country south of the Sudan, means 'burning'.

Etna, a volcano in Sicily.

étourderie (Fr.), silly, reckless behaviour.

Etruscan youth Tages (*L*.II.iii), the first to teach the people of Etruria (ancient Tuscany) the science of augury and divination; said to have been found in the form of a clod by a Tuscan ploughman, and to have assumed a human form to teach this nation.

Euclid, a Greek mathematician of about 300 BC whose rational proof of geometrical principles has provided a standard course for centuries.

Eudoxus (*TT*.vii), a Greek astronomer of the fourth century BC.

Euryalus, feats of (*PBE*.ix), in making a night attack with Nisus on the camp of the Rutuli (Virgil, *Aeneid* ix,314–449).

Evangelicals (*TD*.xxv), a party in the Church of England who laid greater stress on conversion and repentance than on the sacraments.

Evangelists (*CM*2.vii), Matthew, Mark, Luke, and John.

Eve and the Fall (*TT*.xxxv), cf. Gen.ii–iii; **the Eve** (*TT*.xiv), woman's weakness; **put off the old Eve** (*W*.xxxix), cf. 'the old Adam' for degenerate man, and Eph.iv,22–4.

Evelyn G. of Christminster (*LLE*), on the death (6 Sep 1920) of Evelyn Gifford, daughter of the archdeacon who married Emma (her cousin) and Hardy. See *Life* 101/103,397–8/432,407/437, and **Christminster**.

even, evening; (vb.) equal.

Evening Hymn, 'Glory to Thee, my God, this night' by Bishop Ken (1637–1711); cf. *Life* 10/16.

An Evening in Galilee (*WW*), a verse essay in **higher criticism** (as from Nazareth in Galilee). *Carmel*, Mt Carmel; *Tiberias' strand*, the shore by Tiberias on the Sea of Galilee; *the Temple*, in Jerusalem (Matt.xxi,23–7 or Luke ii,41–51); *Who is my mother?* (Matt.xii,46–50); *one other*, Panthera (cf. *TL*.Panthera); *woman of no good character*, cf. **Magdalen**; *outmarking*, indicating; *towards Jezreel*, ominously (cf. **Jezreel**).

Evening Shadows (*WW*). *Pagan mound*, Conquer Barrow, a prehistoric tumulus near Max Gate; *Gospel news*, Christianity, revealed in the four New Testament gospels. For the final thought, cf. *D*1.I.vi,2–9.

the evening star, Hesperus (the planet Venus).

Everdene, Bathsheba (*FMC*), modelled to some extent on Hardy's aunt Martha (his mother's sister), with whom he stayed at Hatfield, Hertfordshire, before she and her husband (see **Troy**) settled in Canada (*Life* 17/21–2; Millgate,44).

Everdene, James, Bathsheba's uncle; mentioned in *MC*.xvii,xxxi.

Evershead (*WT*6.ii; *GND*.1; *TD*.xliv–v; *CM*.10), Evershot, a village about 12 m. NW of Dorchester (map C).

Everything by starts, and nothing long (*L*.I.vi), Dryden, *Absalom and Achitophel* I,548 (Zimri).

Everything Comes (*MV*). Hardy thinks of Emma at Max Gate, first when it was exposed and cold, then sheltered by trees, finally of her dying.

the evil (*MC*.xxvi), scrofula, once thought curable by the king's touch. For the 'toad-bag' treatment, see *Life* 112/115.

ewe-lamb (*FMC*.xxvi; *RN*.I.ix; *TM*.xxxvi; *GND*.1). Cf. II Sam.xii, 1–10.

eweleaze, meadow or down grazed by sheep.

ex-cathedrâ, authoritative.

ex post facto (Lat.), retrospective.

'Excelsior' (*JO*.II.vi), a poem by H. W. Longfellow.

exclaim against . . . succession (*TD*.xxvi), *Ham*.II.ii,346–7.

Exeunt Omnes (*SC*). The MS title 'Epilogue' was deleted. The poem, which is symbolical ('All depart'), was written on Hardy's 73rd birthday.

exits and entrances (*WB*.I.vii), *AYL*.II.vii,141.

Exonbury, Exeter, south Devon: *PBE*.viii; *TM*.xxi,xxiv; *W*.xl; *LLI*.3; *CM*.12 (previously Casterbridge); *WP*.My Cecily; *MV*.In a Museum (Exeter). See **The Carrier**.

An Experience (*LLE*). 'My friend' (cf. **Before My Friend Arrived**) may indicate stimulating discussions with Horace Moule in the Dorchester region. It could be no more than a dramatic device (cf. *LLE*.Fetching Her). *astound*, astonishment; *cobwebbed, crazed*, as if Hardy did not fully realize what was said, his perceptions being fragmentary.

An Expostulation (*HS*). The setting (dancing in masks, with patches for ladies' facial adornment) suggests the eighteenth century. *featness*, dexterity (in dancing; cf. **foot . . . it featly**); *rare*, splendid; *lines*, see **lines . . . fallen**.

extenuate nothing (*MC*.xlv), cf. *Oth*.v.ii,345–7, 'nothing extenuate . . . one that lov'd not wisely, but too well'.

external and internal contact (*TT*.xl). The first refers to the moment when Venus appears to touch the sun's circumference, either when ingress is about to begin or egress about to end; the second applies to such contacts either when ingress is just completed or when egress is about to begin.

exuviae, cast-off skins.

the eye sees . . . means of seeing (PRF), slightly adapted from a quotation in Thomas Carlyle, *The French Revolution*, at the opening of 'Realised Ideals' (I.ii).

eyelids of eve (*D*3.VI.viii), cf. eyelids of the morning, Job xli,18.

eyes . . . pine at (*DR*.iii.2), Keats, 'Ode to a Nightingale' (*G.T.*).
eyne (archaic), eyes.
Ezekiel's vision (conclusion of *GND*.1), Ezek.xxxvii,1–14.

F

Fabian success (*PBE*.xii). Fabius Quintus Maximus, called Cunctator or *delayer* after his campaign against Hannibal, preferred skirmishes and harassment of the enemy to pitched battles.
fable of the well-bonded fagot (*HE*.xxxv), by Aesop, emphasizing the weakness of individuals (sticks), and the strength that comes from unity.
The Face at the Casement (*SC*), probably a fiction prompted by remembrance of a jealous pang in Cornwall; cf. *MV*.The Young Churchwarden. *Saint Cleather*, see map E; *Love is long-suffering*, cf. I Cor.xiii,4; *jealousy . . . cruel . . . grave*, see **Jealousy**.
face . . . book (*TT*.xxv), cf. *Mac*.I.v,59–60.
The Fading Rose (*HS*). Cf. **The Spell of the Rose**.
faeces, excrement.
fain, glad, eager, yearning; gladly, dearly.
Fair, beautiful woman.
fair vestal . . . west (*PBE*.i ep.), *MND*.II.i,158.
fairing, fairling, gift (originally a gift bought at a fair).
Fairland (*OMC*4.II.iv), Higher Bockhampton; cf. 'Monk's Hut' and the 'hermit-group of dwellings' in *CM*5 and *Life* 99/102.
Faithful Wilson (*WW*), suggested by the generalization of an epigram by Strato, an ancient Greek who lived at Sardis in Asia Minor.
Falernian (*L*.v.ii), a wine praised by Roman poets including Horace.
fall, autumn; a woman's veil; yeaning, birth. **the Fall**, of Adam or man, when sin entered the world: Gen.iii.
The Fallow Deer at the Lonely House (*LLE*), at Hardy's birthplace, especially when it 'stood quite alone' by the heath; cf.

'Domicilium' (*Life* 4/8–9). *fender*, a low metal guard round the open hearth.

Falls-Park (*GND*.1), Mells Park, a manor house near Frome, Somerset; it belonged to the Horner family.

Falmouth (*TM*.xxxv; *MC*.iv,xli; *CM*.11.vi), in Cornwall.

Falstaff's favourite beverage (*TM*.xvi), sack, a Spanish wine; cf. *1.H4*.I.ii,2.

familiar, attendant (to a magician or witch).

Family Portraits (*WW*). Whether the remote ancestral drama hinted at in this imaginary scene is connected with Hardy's progenitors is doubtful, though a picture of an eighteenth-century member of the Childs family (one of his maternal ancestors) which came to Hardy in 1917 and which bore a likeness to him (Florence Hardy thought, *Letters* v,216) may have started this. The speaker's hereditary interest is forward-looking, and could not apply to Hardy. (The poem first appeared at the end of 1924, and was much revised later.) *white-shrouded*, ominous (cf. **Standing by the Mantelpiece**); *puppet-like*, as if heredity is compulsive.

family, servant, ox . . . neighbour's wife (*TD*.1892 pr.), alluding to the Commandments, the tenth especially (Exod.xx,2–17).

Famine and Sword (*PBE*.xxix; *RN*.v.ii), Isa.li,17–20.

The Famous Tragedy of the Queen of Cornwall, begun in 1916 after Hardy's visit to Tintagel with his second wife Florence, and completed in 1923 for local performance; the following year it was set to music by Rutland Boughton. Slight expansions for the second edition of 1924 (to which references are made in this work) include the division of scene xiii into three (xiii–xv), principally to make clear how the presence of Tristram at Tintagel is betrayed to Mark. Hardy first visited the Castle ruins with Emma Gifford in 1870; he recalls her ('an Iseult of my own') in the 'lily-rose' of Iseult of Ireland, and more especially in the 'corn-brown hair' and white robe of Iseult of Brittany, whose final words

> Dearer in that our days there were so sweet,
> Before I knew what pended me elsewhere!

express Hardy's regret that his wife's Cornish romance had proved tragically unhappy for both of them. Observing the Greek unities, with no scenery (cf. Orel,139), and with one continuous action in its twenty-four scenes, the play was 'arranged as a play for mummers', this seeming to imply (to judge by the ending of *D*.pr.) a rather 'monotonic' presentation, to suggest a dream re-enactment of old unhappy far-off things conjured up by the magician Merlin. The style tends to be plain and archaic, in conformity with an unsophisticated age which was often crude and barbaric; it is workmanlike rather than inspired, with most appeal in some of the lyrics and Iseult's pleading with Tristram (xvi), which draws considerably from *PBE*.xxxiv–v. Most effective of all perhaps is the staging-technique. Hardy's dedication is to those intimately connected with his Tintagel: Emma Lavinia Hardy, the Revd Caddell Holder, his wife Helen Catherine (Emma's sister), and Florence Emily Hardy. See *Life* 78/81,234/245,422–4/456–7.

fancy-free, not in love. **fancy-free meditation** (*DR*.ii.2), cf. *MND*.II.i,164. **fancy-man**, lover, sweetheart.

fantastic tale . . . family paper (*JO*.ps. to pr.). See ***The Well-Beloved***.

fantocine, puppet.

Far from the Madding Crowd, concluded in July 1874, after rather more than a year of industry, appeared anonymously as a serial and sometimes the better for the advice of its editor Leslie Stephen, in *The Cornhill Magazine* throughout 1874, its authorship being disclosed in the February review of *The Spectator*, after a reviewer had conjectured that the opening chapters were the work of George Eliot. Her *Adam Bede* undoubtedly suggested ideas for Hardy's plot; and imagery relating to her hero, both in this novel and 'Mr Gilfil's Love-Story', may explain why he chose 'Oak' for the name of his hero. The ironic title of his novel (from Thomas Gray's 'Elegy') was probably suggested by the penultimate paragraph of her Introduction to *Felix Holt*. Hardy combines the 'noiseless tenor' or timelessness of rustic life (notably in topics discussed at Warren's malthouse and in the presentation of the 'great barn' at shearing-time) with the sensationally tragic; he lingers expansively in humorous scenes to which his melodramatic crises form startling contrasts. As in *UGT* he was more at home with his background than with that of *PBE*, his 'pastoral' owing much to his deliberate association with the labouring community of Puddletown as well as to his local heritage at Higher Bockhampton, where the novel was written. (Here, during a night of thunder and lightning, he wrote the description of the storm that puts Bathsheba's corn-stacks in jeopardy.) Of three of the principal characters she is the least extraordinary. A Diana in instinct and temperament, she is impulsively indiscreet, and a prey to flattery; 'guileless', she falls to the flattering effrontery of the shallow, self-indulgent Troy. Boldwood's jealousy in love unmans him; his emotions overpower his reason. Oak preserves his judgment despite his expressions of jealousy. Bathsheba accepts him in the end, realizing that she depends on his experience and loyalty; she is tamed, as she knew she needed to be at the outset, but only at the cost of bitter suffering. The novel portrays three kinds of love, and suggests very strongly (lvi) that the author who wrote the last chapters 'at a gallop' (*Life* 100–1/103) knew the superiority, as a basis for a stable marriage (his own not far off), of affection between 'tried friends' with common interests over romantic idealizings. Scenic metaphor, striking in both *DR* and *PBE* (cf. xxxii in the latter), advances impressively in *FMC*, making powerful contributions to its imaginative appeal; cf. the end of 'A Pastoral Tragedy' (v), 'Outside the Barracks', 'Effect of the Letter – Sunrise', 'The Hollow amid the Ferns', Bathsheba's enlightenment during the storm (xxxvii), the woodland swamp (xliv), and 'The Gurgoyle's Doings'. The novel is varied in tempo and strategy; it is worth noting that the hero is first presented with detached amusement, and that the All Saints and All Souls satire of circumstance (xvi) was an afterthought.

far in the Unapparent (*D*.pr.), Shelley, *Adonais* xlv.

fare, farrow, litter.

Fare thee weel awhile (*PBE*.vi ep.), Burns, 'My love is like a red red rose'.

Farewell . . . too dear . . . estimate (*HE*.xxiv), Son.87.

Farfrae, Donald (*MC*). His name indicates a wistful Scot, *far from* home. Some of his traits were drawn from the 'good-looking and ingenuous young cabman' who drove the Hardys about Edinburgh in August 1881. His use of the Scottish language was checked by Hardy's Scottish friend Sir George Douglas. The 'ruddy and of a fair countenance' description (vi) declares his role as David to Henchard's Saul (cf. I Sam.xvii,42).

Farinelli (*RN*.I.v), a famous Italian singer (Carlo Broschi, 1705–82) who impressed the Spanish royal family and was made a grandee.

Faringdon Ruin (*TM*.xxxviii). Part of a windowed gable-end is all that remains of the church and the village which once stood here, in meadowland west of Came House (map G).

Farmer Lynch's short way (*RN*.IV.iv), probably Charles Lynch, a Virginia planter who, during the American Revolution, headed an irregular court to punish loyalists; the word 'lynching' implies excesses committed in the name of such self-constituted courts, without legal authority. **short way**, an echo of Defoe; cf. **The Shortest Way . . . .**

Farnese Hercules (*TM*.v), a statue of this hero of classical mythology, at one time in the Farnese Palace, Rome.

Farnfield, Neigh's estate (*HE*.xxv). Hardy states that it was 30–40 m. SW of London. Further off, at Findon in West Sussex (where he visited Eliza Nicholls and sketched the church in 1866), Hardy must have witnessed, as others did, evidence used for his macabre fog-enshrouded scene in which emaciated horses are kept to be killed, and hounds howl to get at joints of horses suspended from tree-trunks.

farrel, cover or binding of a book.

fasciae (arch.), long flat surfaces.

the Father (God), **in the name of** (*WT*.1), the opening of a common prefix to C. of E. sermons, followed by 'and of the Son, and of the Holy Ghost'.

Father Time or **Little Father Time** (*JO*), a strange conception of a child (MS, the 'Ancient') who inherits all his parental tribulations, and the cares, it seems, of previous generations: at times 'his face took a back view over some great Atlantic of Time, and appeared not to care about what it saw'. Hardy's obsession with heredity (he had been reading Weismann's *Essays on Heredity*) was intensified when he read Sarah Grand's *The Heavenly Twins* (1893) not long before he began the writing of *JO*. Father Time undoubtedly owes something to the child of the syphilitic father in Sarah Grand's novel – old-looking, unsmiling, and dumbly asking why he had ever been born. His appearance on the train (*JO*.v.iii) seems to be based on evidence, but whether Hardy saw this for himself, or read or heard about it, is unknown; *MV*.Midnight on the Great Western seems to be a symbolical refashioning of the subject.

Fathers (*JO*.I.v,vi), early authorities on Christian doctrine.

Faust (*MC*.xvii), as described in Carlyle's essay 'Goethe's Helena'.

Faustina . . . Phryne (*TD*.liii): Faustina, wife of the Roman emperor Antoninus, and notorious for debauchery; **Cornelia**, Pompey's wife, renowned for her virtues; **Lucretia** (raped by Tarquinius), a model of chastity; Phryne, a beautiful Athenian courtesan.

Faustus, Devil . . . penny book (*W*.ii). The story of Faustus, who sold his soul to the Devil to procure all his wishes, was the subject of cheap chapbooks hawked by pedlars. In this popular story the Devil appears to the accompaniment of music during a thunderstorm.

Fawkes, Guy (*HE*.xxxviii), one of the conspirators in the plot to blow up the Houses of Parliament (5 Nov 1605); he was caught red-handed and hanged. To celebrate this Catholic failure, Guy Fawkes Day is traditionally celebrated with firework displays throughout England.

Fawley, Jude (*JO*). His surname is the name of the Berkshire village ('Marygreen' in *JO*) where Hardy's paternal grandmother was unhappy in her girlhood. Many attempts have been made to explain the significance of 'Jude', and such details in the epistle of Jude as 'spots in your feasts of charity', 'clouds . . . without water' (cf. *JO*.v.vi), 'having men's persons in admiration because of advantage', 'hating even the garment spotted by the flesh' (verses 12,16,23) are all pertinent. The most satisfying explanation is that Jude as the patron saint of lost causes is most relevant to Jude's forlorn hopes in Christminster (Oxford, 'home of lost causes' to Matthew Arnold). Jude's self-education in the classics and his periodical fits of drunkenness owe much to Hardy's uncle John Antell, the Puddletown shoemaker; his drunkenness, also to the scholar Horace Moule, who lived for a time in the Close, Salisbury (Melchester).

fawlocks, muskets with flintlocks for firing, firelocks.

fay, faith, luck, fortune, fairy; prosper, succeed.

Fear and be slain . . . death! (*PBE*.xviii), *R2*.III.ii,183–4.

a fearful joy (*FMC*.xxiii; *RN*.II.vi) Gray, 'Ode on a Distant Prospect of Eton College' (*G.T.).*

fearful wildfowl (*L*.IV.iv), *MND*.III.i,29.

feather, in highest, in very high spirits, most cheerful.

feet . . . little mice (*PBE*.vii), Suckling, 'A Ballad upon a Wedding'.

fell, cruel, severe; skin.

fell into hand, or **fell in**, 'lapsed to the lord of the manor' (Hardy's note in his edition of selected poems by William Barnes). See **life-holders**.

felloe-rim, iron hoop enclosing the wooden circumference of a wheel.

Fellow-Townsmen (*WT*5). This novelette, illustrating the workings of 'the whimsical god . . . blind Circumstance' in unhappy marital life, appeared first in April 1880. The original opening, which emphasized the contrast between the Barnet and Downe homes, presented features of Bridport in recognisable detail.

fellow-watcher of the skies (*TT*.xiv), Keats, 'On First Looking into Chapman's Homer' (*G.T.*).

fellow-yearsmen, friends or companions of the same age.

felo de se (legal Lat.), suicide.

felon, whitlow, inflamed sore near the nail.

felze, a covering structure for a gondola.

Female forms . . . beam with mind (*WB*.II.i; cf. *MC*.xlv), Shelley, *The Revolt of Islam* I.liv. The original subtitle of the poem (1818) was 'The Revolution of the Golden City: A Vision of the Nineteenth Century'.

femme de trente ans (*W*.xxxii), woman of thirty (regarded as the ideal age by some French authors), alluding to the title of a novel by Balzac; hence '*édition définitive*', final edition.

fence, defence, plans for defence; keep or ward off.

Fencibles, men called up for full-time service (to supplement the regular army) in the defence of Britain during the Napoleonic war.

fend hands against, guard against.

fendless, against which there is no defence, inescapable.

Fénelon, François (*TT*.xxv), a French writer on religion and education (1651–1715) who became Archbishop of Cambrai in 1695.

Fensworth (*JO*.I.viii,xi), Letcombe Regis, Berkshire (map I).

fess, proud, eager, active, strong.

fetch, recover; (an) indrawn breath.

Fetching Her (*LLE*), based on Hardy's marriage to Emma Gifford from the Cornish coast. *expugn*, vanquish, overcome.

fête carillonnée (Fr.), grand holiday, marked by bell-ringing.

fetichistic, implying the belief that an inanimate object is animated by a spirit.

feu-de-joie (Fr.), a victory firing salute (*D*3.IV.v).

fever and fret (*HE*.xxxiv; *L*.I.ii; *TT*.vi; *W*.xxxiii; *JO*.1895 pr.), Keats, 'Ode to a Nightingale' (*G.T.*).

A Few Crusted Characters (*LLI*.8) was serialized in a monthly magazine from March to June 1891. As in *GND*, the stories are given a fictitious framework; see **Lackland**. They are suited to their audience, two being very entertaining. Two were transferred to the **Longpuddle** region (there may have been others): Hardy's letter of 20 May 1924 states that the miller-moth incident (c) was said to have taken place at Buttock's Spring, Melbury Osmond, and the MS shows that 'The Winters and the Palmleys' (g) belonged to the same region; the noise of the waggon bearing the coffin was heard in the Holway Lane direction (map C), and Harriet and her husband, unable to continue living at King's Hintock, moved to Lewgate. The carrier did not proceed directly to Longpuddle; he seems to have called first at Charminster, before travelling north on the old Bristol coach-road, then turning off for Piddlehinton (map A).

fictile, ceramic, capable of being moulded or worked by hand.

The Fiddler of the Reels (*LLI.7*). Written for an American 'Exhibition Number' (May 1893) to mark the Chicago World Fair, it associates a tale of seductive dance-music with the earliest passenger-trains Hardy remembered and the Great Exhibition of 1851. Unlike that of *RN*, its topography with reference to Bloom's End, the Quiet Woman, and Mistover, is accurate.

fidgets, trifles which create a fuss, fiddling things; restless creature.

fief, service; property held in fee by tenants, i.e. on condition of certain services to the lord of the manor (the owner).

fieldmouse fear . . . coulter. See **Burns's field-mouse**.

fifteen days, the time for the marriage banns to be read in church on three consecutive Sundays, or for residence in a parish by one of the parties if the marriage there is by licence (cf. *PBE*.xi; *TT*.xvii).

The Figure in the Scene (*MV*). Hardy's sketch of 22 Aug 1870 shows Emma Gifford in the rain, with Beeny Cliff in the background. The poem is related to the next, 'Why did I sketch'. *quizzings*, questions; *gauze*, the rain like a transparent fabric across the scene; *Genius*, spirit of the place (the Roman 'genius loci').

fillet, quirk, arris (*HE*.v): (arch.) a narrow flat band between two mouldings; a hollow between part of a moulding and the fillet; see **arris**.

fined, made fine, pure, quintessential.

fineless, endless.

finger of fate touched (*W*.xxv), cf. Tennyson, *In Memoriam* lxxxv, 20.

First Consul (*TM*.xiii), Napoleon Bonaparte; he had been given this position as head of the French empire at the end of 1799. In

1802 he was made Consul for life.

The First Countess of Wessex (*GND*.1) was published first in *Harper's New Monthly Magazine*, Dec 1889, with illustrations of its actual setting. The reference to Little-Hintock, 'several miles eastward', shows that Hardy, anxious not to give further offence to descendants of the countess (see **Reynard**) at Melbury House, was already anticipating the transfer of his setting for *The Woodlanders*; see ***The Woodlanders***.

First dead . . . yode (went: *FMC*.lv), Scott, *Marmion* III.xxxi.

fishers of men (*DR*.iv.2,xii.3), Mark i,17.

fish-seines, fishing-nets.

fist, attempt, effort.

fitful fever (*W*.xlv), life's . . . , *Mac*.III.ii,23.

the Five Orders (*L*.I.i), styles of classical architecture, affecting chiefly columns and entablature: Greek (Doric, Ionic, Corinthian); Roman (Tuscan, Composite).

The Five Students (*MV*). The highroad is life; the seasons reflect stages on its journey. Hardy (*Life* 405/434) identified one as Horace Moule (who committed suicide in 1873), presumably the 'dark He'. The poem may have been suggested when he read (*S.R.*36), 'My sister and I . . . , she dark and I fair' (Mrs Holder of St Juliot rectory died in 1900). Who the 'fair He' is remains conjectural; he could have been included to complete the pattern of the poem. Perhaps he was Henry J. Moule (d.1904; cf. Orel,66–73). In this case, Hardy remembers brothers and sisters he had known very closely. Emma Hardy died in 1912.

five-handed reel (*LLI*.7), a dance for five persons, with heys in the figure of 8.

flags, leaves of the wild iris; pavement (flagstones).

Flamborough . . . St Bees (*PBE*.xxi), English headlands on the coasts of Yorkshire, Kent, Sussex, Dorset, Cornwall, Cumbria.

Flaminius (*OMC*6.iv), the Roman consul whose army was disastrously penned in by Hannibal near Lake Thrasymene in Italy.

flanconade, thrust in the side (fencing).

flash, showy and transitory.

flat, simpleton.

Flaxman, John (*FMC*.xxxviii), English sculptor and draftsman, 1775–1826; the reference is to his illustration of the *Odyssey* (xxiv), with the suitors of Penelope slain by Ulysses (Odysseus).

flèche (Fr.), spire.

fleed (dial.), flew, flown.

the Fleet (*TM*.xxxiv). Its outlet is now crossed by a bridge connecting **Chesil Beach** and Portland with the mainland (map H).

Flemish ladder, perhaps a local term in Hardy's youth. His contexts (*HE*.xli; *TM*.xviii; *MC*.ix) suggest a strongly supported set of wooden steps.

Flemish Last-Suppers (*W*.x), pictures of the Last Supper (Matt.xxvi,17–35) by Flemish painters of the fifteenth and sixteenth centuries.

flesh is weak (*PBE*.xix; *MC*.xiii), Matt.xxvi,41.

flick-flack, thoughtless talk.

Flintcomb-Ash (*TD*; *WW*.We Field-Women). Although it was first called 'Alton Ash Farm', Hardy's map of Tess's wanderings places it further east, almost south of Nettlecombe Tout. The topography of the novel suggests it was roughly NE of Alton Pancras, within a chalky plateau south of Church Hill, with the 'summits' of Nettlecombe Tout to the east and Bulbarrow beyond rather to the NE.

flipped, said flippantly.

flitch, side of a pig (meat).

flounce, flopping sound, splash; flop or throw down, splash heavily.

flummery, nonsense, humbug.

flushest, brilliant, highly colourful.

fluted, ornamented with longitudinal grooves.

fly, a light, covered, one-horse carriage.

Flychett (*HE*.ii,xliv), Lytchett Minster, 4 m. from Wareham on the road to Poole and Bournemouth (map D).

flying (*FMC*.xlv), splintering, cracking.

Flying Isle of San Borandan (*DR*.xviii.3). The legendary Irish saint Brendan or Brandan sailed in search of the Islands of Paradise.

fly-wheel, acting as a regulator (on a machine); cf. *HE*.xv.

foil, arc or hollow between two cusps; leaf.

the folding star (*W*.xxvii), Vesper or Hesperus, the evening star that 'bids the shepherd fold' (put his sheep in the fold).

folly to be wise (*DR*.xvii.3), Gray, 'Ode on a Distant Prospect of Eton College' (*G.T.*).

fondly (archaic), foolishly.

Fontainebleau, St Cloud, the Bois (*RN*.III.iv), places visited by Parisians on holiday outings: the Palace of Fontainebleau, south of Paris; the Bois de Boulogne on the western side, with St Cloud immediately beyond, on the left bank of the Seine.

Fonthill (*JO*.III.ii), Fonthill Abbey, 14 m. west of Salisbury, the remains of a mansion rebuilt in gothic style for William Beckford at the end of the eighteenth century.

foods of love (*LLI*.7), music, cf. *TN*.I.i,1.

Fool'd . . . by thee! (*PBE*.xxxi), Milton, *Paradise Lost* x,880.

foot it . . . featly (*CM*2.iii), *Tem*.I.ii,379.

foot-pace, the step or raised floor on which the altar stands.

footy (dial.), mean, base.

For Conscience' Sake (*LLI*.3). Published in March 1891, it is, like 'The Son's Veto', an anti-clerical story belonging to the period of preparation for *JO*. For the turning-point, cf. facial changes noted by Hardy: *Life* 177/183 (wrought by cold weather) and *MC*.xix (brought by sleep).

for his kin . . . defiled (*L*.v.i), cf. Lev.xxi,2–3.

'For Life I had never cared greatly' (*MV*). The star is vague. Whether Hardy is thinking of Swinburne's line (*JO*.II ep; *Life* 345/372) and adherence to what seems true, or to the gospel of loving-kindness (*SC*.A Plaint to Man) is conjectural. The concluding optimism is less typical of Hardy than the title.

For there was . . . like her! (*JO*.III ep.), translation from Sappho.

For Thou, to make . . . great and **My days . . . fade** (*PBE*.xxvii), from Psalm cii (Tate and Brady version).

For what man . . . Jewish law-giver (*JO*.V.iv), Moses, Deut.xx,7.

For who knoweth . . . sun? (*JO*.VI.i), Eccl.vi,12.

For wisdom is a defence . . . (*JO*.II.ii), Eccl.vii,12.

foreshades, is foreshadowed.

the Forest, the New Forest (**Great Forest**).

forgetting . . . marble (*DR*.iii.2), cf. Milton, 'Il Penseroso' (*G.T.*).

Forms more real . . . (*LLI*.1), Shelley, *Prometheus Unbound* I.i,748–9 (*G.T.* 'The Poet's Dream').

forrard (dial.) forward.

Fort meeting Feeble (*FMC*.xxxiv), the sword-blade near the hilt against the part of it near the point.

fortune . . . threatening eye (*L*.I.xv), *KJ*.III.iv,119–20.

Fountall (*LLI*.4; *CM*.1.iii), Wells, Somerset. It takes its name from the springs which well up from the Mendip Hills. As it has been an ecclesiastical centre for centuries, Hardy's name has also an ironical significance.

Four bells, eight bells (*PBE*.xxix), heard at 2 a.m. and 4 a.m. A bell is struck to indicate how many half-hours of watch-duty (which usually lasts four hours) have been completed on the vessel.

Four in the Morning (*HS*). *cerule*, azure (cf. opening of *TT*.xviii);

Great Nebula, the brightest of the nebulae, which appears in the constellation Andromeda; *this vale*, the Frome valley at lower Bockhampton.

four pieces previously published (*WP*.pr.), 'The Fire at Tranter Sweatley's' in *The Gentleman's Magazine*, Nov 1875; 'The Sergeant's Song' in the 1881 edition of *The Trumpet-Major*; 'The Stranger's Song', *Longman's Magazine*, Mar 1883, and *WT*.1, 1888; 'Lines', *The Pall Mall Gazette*, July 1890.

four-centred . . . arch (*MC*.vi), embodying arcs described architecturally from four centres.

fourteens (*UGT*.I.ii), small candles, fourteen to the pound (weight).

fout (dial.), fought.

frail barque of fidelity . . . (*W*.xv). Cf. 'Who to a woman trusts his peace of mind, Trusts to a frail bark, with a tempestuous wind' (George Granville, Lord Lansdowne, 1667–1735).

Frankenstein (*L*.III.ii), hero of Mary Shelley's novel *Frankenstein*, 1818; he creates a monster which ultimately destroys him.

Franklin (*RN*.I.x), Sir John (1786–1847), the Arctic explorer who was lost after discovering the Northwest passage.

freak with (*SC*.The Elopement), play a trick with, possibly with the added sense of streaking with colour. **freakful**, capricious.

Frederick . . . Archduchess, Napoleon . . . Queen of Prussia (*RN*.I.x): Frederick the Great of Prussia when he attacked Austria (1740), ruled by the Archduchess Maria Theresa; after defeating the Prussians at Jena (1806), Napoleon refused to consider Queen Louisa's pleas (cf. *D*2.I.iii–vi).

Frederick William's Patagonians (*TM*.xxiii), tall soldiers recruited for the Guards of Frederick-William I of Prussia (1688–1740), father of Frederick the Great. The South American Patagonians were said to be the tallest known people.

free will (*LLE*.Apology; *Life* 335/361,449/487). Hardy allows a 'modicum' within a world of necessity (*Life* 337/363–4), when 'the mighty necessitating forces' are 'in equilibrium'. For an application of the theory, possibly from Spencer's 'Equilibration' in *First Principles* (1862), see *FMC*.xviii with reference to Boldwood.

Freemason, member of a secret brotherhood, which began with travelling skilled masons and was extended to friends; it is widespread and wealthy.

freestone, any fine sandstone or limestone that can easily be sawn.

French critic (PRF). See **Taine**. **French window**, a tall window constructed in two halves that open full-length on vertical hinges.

Friar Laurence . . . violent ends (*TD*.xxiii), *RJ*.II.vi,9.

Friar Tuck, one of Robin Hood's merry men.

friend and eulogist of Shakespeare, etc. (*JO*.II.i). Hardy supplied the key to Mrs Henniker (Letters II,95): *eulogist*, Ben Jonson; *recently . . . silence*, Robert Browning (d.1889), who had been awarded an honorary degree by Oxford University; *musical one*, Swinburne; *enthusiast, poet, and formularist*, John Henry Newman, John Keble, and Edward Pusey (Tractarians); *statesman . . . sceptic*, Bolingbroke (1678–1751); *historian . . . Christianity*, see **Lausanne**; *apologized for the Church in Latin* (i.e. defended the Church; Hardy couldn't remember who this was); *saintly . . . Evening Hymn*, Bishop Ken; *itinerant preacher*, Charles Wesley; 'home of lost causes . . . Beautiful city . . .', Matthew Arnold, Preface to *Essays in Criticism*, 1869; *Corn Law convert*, Robert Peel (speech in the House of Commons, 15 May 1846); *sly author*, Gibbon, *The Decline and Fall* xv; *last of the optimists*, Robert Browning, 'By the Fire-side'; author of the *Apologia [pro Vita Sua]*, J. H. Newman; *no polemic*, Keble, from *The Christian Year* (1827), 'Twenty-fourth Sunday after Trinity'; *Spectator*, Addison, *The Spectator*, no. 26 (1711); *gentle-voiced prelate*, Ken in his 'Evening Hymn'.

frise (*D*2.IV.v), defence against cavalry charges, as in '*cheval* (or *chevaux*) *de frise*' (Fr.).

From Victor Hugo (*PPP*), a translation of 'A une femme' from *Les Feuilles d'Automne*, 1831. For Hardy's tribute to Hugo, see *Life* 311/334.

From whose foundation . . . (*JO*.IV.i), from Drayton's *Polyolbion*, 1622.

Froom (many references), the Frome river. It rises at Evershot, flows through Maiden Newton, past Dorchester, Fordington, and Lower Bockhampton, then on to Wareham and Poole Harbour. Before reaching Dorchester it divides into two main streams, one flowing below the flank of Pummery or Poundbury camp; on the north-eastern side of Dorchester, this stream is so dark that Hardy calls it (*MC*.xix) 'the Schwarzwasser of Casterbridge' (naming it after a 'black' German river), not to be confused with the Blackwater pool of the other division (*MC*.xxxii). These Frome streams flow respectively under the Swan Bridge and Grey's Bridge, uniting on the eastern side of Fordington. Hardy sometimes gives the Frome its ancient name of **Var** (which is preserved in 'Wareham'); cf. **Durnover**.

Froom-Everard House (*CM*2), Stafford House, formerly Froom-Everard, on the southern side of the Frome below Lower Bockhampton.

frost or **winter**, symbols of adversity (from Shelley: cf. *The Revolt of Islam* IX.xx–xxvi, 'Ode to the West Wind', 'The Sensitive Plant', 'When the lamp is shattered'). For examples, see *HS*.Discouragement (probably 1865–7); *WP*.Neutral Tones, Heiress and Architect (both 1867); *DR*.xiii.1 and 4; *W*.iv (opening), xviii (end), xxx–xxxi, and the name 'Winterborne'; *TD*.xliii; *PPP*.The Caged Thrush Freed and Home Again ('the Frost's decree'), The Darkling Thrush, In Tenebris I; *MV*.Before Knowledge; *HS*.The Frozen Greenhouse; the title 'Winter Words' and *WW*.Standing by the Mantelpiece.

The Frozen Greenhouse (*HS*). Hardy revisited St Juliot after his wife Emma's death, and the second frost is metaphorical; see above.

fruitful as the vine (*D*2.v.ii), Psalm cxxviii,3. Cf. **His wife**.

frustrate ghost (*W*.xlvi), Browning, 'The Statue and the Bust', 246.

fuddle, tipple, booze.

fuel to maintain its fires (*DR*.v.3), Thomas Carew (?1595–1640), 'He that loves a rosy cheek' (*G.T.*).

fugle, direct, control. **fugleman**, an expert or model whom soldiers at drill must copy.

fulfil their joy (*D*3.After Scene), cf. Phil.ii.2.

Full of sound . . . nothing (*FMC*.iv), *Mac*.v.v,27–8.

full-buff, suddenly, face to face.

full-butt, violently, with full force.

Fuller's *Holy State* (*JO*.VI.vi), Thomas Fuller, *The Holy and the Profane States*, 1642–8.

furmity, or frumenty, a dish made of wheat boiled in sweetened milk, with cinnamon and other ingredients.

the Furnace (*WP*.The Burghers), Dan.iii,13–30; and **the Fourth Figure** (*MV*.The Interloper), 'the son of God', Dan.iii,25.

futtock-shrouds, ropes in the topmost rigging.

G

gaberlunzie (Scottish), wandering beggar.
gaffer, old man, master.
gaingiving, misgiving, deep anxiety; cf. **such a kind of . . . .**
Gainsborough, Thomas (*D*1.vi.vi), English landscape and portrait-painter; from 1760 to 1774 he worked at Bath.
galanty-show (*D*2.v.viii), a pantomime of shadows.
Galen, a Greek physician of the second century AD, and a voluminous writer on medicine and philosophy. **Galen, Hippocrates, and Herophilus** (*W*.xxiii), medical doctors of ancient Greece.
Galilee, northern Palestine. See **The Wood Fire**.
Gall, Franz Joseph (*TM*.xxxviii), a German phrenologist (1758–1828) who advanced the theory that a person's qualities and talents conformed to the development of 'organs' or compartments within the brain.
gallicrow, scarecrow.
gallied, alarmed, scared.
gallipot, glazed earthenware pot.
gallopade, lively dance rhythm.
Gallows Hill (*MC*.viii). See **Casterbridge**.
galls . . . kibe (*TD*.1892 pr.), hurts . . . chilblained heel, *Ham.* v.i,137.
Gambart's . . . Faye's (*TT*.x), comets associated with the French astronomer Gambart (but usually known as Biela's, 1826), the Holy Roman Emperor **Charles V** (1556), Edmund Halley (Swithin was delirious; **Halley's** Comet had appeared in 1835, and was not expected again for over seventy-five years), the French astronomer Faye, 1843. The comet of 1811 referred to a little later in the text is that discovered by the French astronomer Flaugergues.
gammer (dial.), grandmother, old woman.
gam'ster, gambler, fortune-seeker, trickster (cf. 'play up').
Ganymedes, a beautiful youth who was carried off by Jupiter to be the cupbearer to the gods.
Gard Castle (*QC*.i). See **Joyous Gard**.

the garden. Ultimately behind this symbolical image there is the thought of the garden of Eden before sin entered the world; Hardy's image is more directly related to Shakespeare, Samuel Richardson, Shelley (cf. 'this world of life Is as a garden ravaged', 'Epipsychidion',186–7), and Swinburne. *DR*.xii.6, cf. Swinburne's 'Ilicet' (*Poems and Ballads*, 1866), and Shelley, 'The Sensitive Plant' (mandrakes); *TD*.xix (Tess's blighted world), cf. 'Ilicet' and *Ham*.I.ii,135–7,

> 'tis an unweeded garden,
> That grows to seed; things rank and gross in nature
> Possess it merely.

The old garden (*TD*.ix; cf. liv) enclosed by a wall over which Alec leaps is intended to recall Satan's manner of entering the garden of Eden (*Paradise Lost* iv,172ff); his Satanic role is continued in the allotment scene (l). Hardy's garden, with its parasitic or Darwinian ivy and its pet birds, owes more to Richardson's *Clarissa*, where the Satanic Lovelace is the 'wall-climber'.

The Garden Seat (*LLE*), at Max Gate, with thoughts of the dead, Emma Hardy in particular.

garde-robes, wardrobes.

garland . . . heifers . . . (*JO*.v.iv), Keats, 'Ode on a Grecian Urn'.

the Garter, like . . . the hostess of (*L*.II.i), cf. *2.H4*.II.i, with a reference to l.112; Hardy has confused the Boar's Head, Eastcheap, with the Garter Inn of Shakespeare's *The Merry Wives of Windsor*.

garth, churchyard, enclosure (as for home and garden).

gather grapes . . . thistles (PRF), Matt.vii,16.

gawkhammer (dial.), gaping fool; empty-headed, stupid.

Gaymead (*LLI*.2; *JO*.v.vi). Hardy's Wessex map shows clearly that this is Theale, WSW of Reading.

Gaza . . . desert (DR.i.1), a town in south Palestine, near desert country (cf. Acts viii,26).

the general, most people, the public (cf. 'caviare to the general').

The General Preface to the Novels and Poems (Orel,44–50), first published in the Wessex Edition of *Tess of the d'Urbervilles*, 1912.

Générale (Fr.*D*3.VI.ii), call to arms.

Genesis, phrase in (*TD*.xiv), Gen.xxxv,18 ('Benoni' means 'son of my sorrow'); whether Hardy has this marginal note in mind or refers to Gen.iii,16 is uncertain.

Genitrix Laesa (*HS*). The Latin title means 'The Wounded Mother'; for the subject, cf. *PPP*.The Mother Mourns. *Sarum*: The metre is that of Adam of St Victor in *Sequence from the Sarum Missal* (cf. *Life* 306/329; 'Sarum' is the name for old Salisbury).

genius loci (Lat.), the presiding spirit of the place.

Genoa and the Mediterranean (*PPP*). cf. *JO*.III.ix. *Central Sea*, the Mediterranean, *epic-famed* by Homer (the *Odyssey*) and Virgil (*Aeneid*); *Torino*, Turin (It.); *up-browed*, with raised eyebrows; *Superba*, the proud.

Genoese filigree (*PBE*.xi). Hardy means Genoese lace.

Gentiles, people of non-Jewish nations.

gentleman . . . turned Christian . . .: 'He does but give us of his best' (*TD*.1892 pr.), Andrew Lang in *The New Review*, Feb 1892.

Geographical Knowledge (*TL*), a memory of Mrs Coward, postmistress at Lower Bockhampton. *Gib*, Gibraltar.

George Herbert, a 'flat delight' (*W*.xliii), from the poem 'Vanitie' in *The Temple*, 1633.

George Meredith (*TL*). The poem alludes to Hardy's first meeting with the poet and novelist (1828–1909), when he was reader for Chapman and Hall, and advised Hardy on his first (unpublished) novel *The Poor Man and the Lady*; secondly, to their meeting in 1894 at Meredith's home near Box Hill in Surrey. After seeing the announcement of Meredith's death on a London poster, Hardy went to the Athenaeum, where he wrote the poem, which was published in *The Times* on the day of the funeral in Westminster Abbey. See *Life* 60–2/62–4,263/280,345–6/372, and Orel,151–4.

George III, King of Britain, 1760–1820 (*UGT*.III.i; *TM*; *D*1.IV.i, *D*2.VI.v). Hardy observes his 'What, what' mannerism; cf. **Budmouth** and **Enckworth Court**.

Gérôme (*Life* 76/79,206/215), French painter, 1824–1904.

Gethsemane, agony in (*RN*.V.vii), Matt.xxvi,36–46.

ghosts . . . fleeing (*FMC*.xliv), Shelley, 'Ode to the West Wind' (*G.T.*).

Giant Despair (DLa). See Bunyan, *The Pilgrim's Progress*, Part I.

Giant's Hill, Giant o' Cernel. See **Abbot's Cernel**.

Gibbon, Edward (*W*.1895 pr.), 1737–94, author of *The Decline and Fall of the Roman Empire*; Hardy quotes from the 15th chapter. See **Lausanne**.

gibbous, protuberant, rounded.

Gibeon, sun . . . stand still upon (*L*.v.iv), Josh.x,12–14.

Gibraltar of Wessex (*WB*.I.i), Portland, called Vindilia by the Romans, and the Home of the Slingers by Hardy (from its ancient form of defence).

gi'd, gi'ed (dial.), gave, given; **gie, gi'e**, give.

gig, a light, two-wheeled, open carriage.

Gil Blas (*LLE*.Apology), the eponymous hero of a long novel by the French writer Le Sage, 1688–1747. He makes copies of an archbishop's sermons, and is told by their author to inform him whenever they appear to fail. He does so when the archbishop is suffering from a stroke, and is promptly dismissed.

Gilpin's rig (spree, adventures occurring as a result of an outing on horseback; from the poem 'John Gilpin' by William Cowper, 1782), *FMC*.xxxiii; **detained by important customers**, *MC*.xxx.

giltycup (dial.), buttercup (golden).

Ginevra of Modena (in northern Italy: *L*.I.ix). During a game on the day of her wedding, she hid in a chest which had a springlock; it snapped shut, and she was not discovered for many years (fifty, according to 'The Mistletoe Bough', a ballad on the subject by T. H. Bayly, 1797–1839).

Ginnung-Gap (*W*.iii), the void of Norse mythology, before the earth was created.

Giorgione (*L*.VI.v), Italian painter, 1475–1510.

Giotto (*TD*.lix; *Life* 190/197), Italian painter, c.1267–1337. The reference is to a fresco fragment Hardy saw in the N.G. This is now entitled 'Two Haloed Mourners', and attributed to Spinello Aretino.

gipsying, a picnic, open-air festivities; on picnics, at 'gipsy-parties'.

gird at, smite, attack.

Give us grace that (we may cast away the works of darkness), a recollection (*FMC*.xliv) from the collect for the first Sunday in Advent.

glane (dial.), sneer, leer.

Glenfinlas (*PBE*.xxvii; *TT*.xx), a Scottish glen; for the supernatural story see Scott's poem 'Glenfinlas'.

glode (archaic), glided.

the glory and the dream . . . passed away . . . yore (*PBE*.xx,xxxii – cf. the iridescence at the beginning of the chapter; *RN*.I.xi; *JO*.II.i), Wordsworth, 'Intimations of Immortality' (*G.T.*).

glower (dial.), glare.

glued . . . thawings (*W*.xvii), Keats, 'In a drear-nighted December'

(*G.T.*).

glum (dial.), gloom.

glutch (dial.), swallow, gulp. **glutchpipe**, throat.

gnats, wailing (*DR*.xii.6; *RN*.III.v; *L*.I.i; *TD*.xiv), cf. Keats, 'To Autumn' (*G.T.*).

go down to the sea in ships . . . wonders in the deep (*TM*.xxxiv; *HS*.A Night of Questionings), Psalm cvii,23–4.

god, make a god of.

God disposes (*HE*.xxvii), man proposes, God . . . , from Prov.xvi,9.

God has set a mark upon me (*RN*.VI.iii): cf. **Cain**.

Goddess Reason (*D*1.VI.vii). In 1793 French revolutionaries instituted her worship in Notre Dame Cathedral.

God-Forgotten (*PPP*). That this poem turns on a fanciful thought on the Unknowable is confirmed in *D*1.Fore Scene,20–9. *tainted*, cf. the 'blighted' world of *TD*.iv.

God's acre or **allotment**, churchyard.

God's Funeral (*SC*). Cf. *Life* 354/381. *foreborne*, carried in front; *jealous*, cf. Exod.xx,5; *Darkling*, an allusion to the 'darkling plain' of Matthew Arnold's poem 'Dover Beach', which presents the ebbing of Christian faith; *hied*, hurried off; *wanderers*, alluding to Arnold's 'wandering between two worlds', with the old faith dead, and another 'powerless to be born' ('Stanzas from the Grande Chartreuse',85–6); *positive gleam*, cf. **Positivism** and the end of *SC*.A Plaint to Man; *Each mourner shook his head*, cf. *Life* 146/150–1 on Positivism.

God's *not* in his heaven . . . world (*TD*.xxxvii), the negative of the heroine's song in Browning's play *Pippa Passes* I,227.

God's 'ounds, by God's wounds (those of Jesus crucified); see **'Od's blood**.

Goethe (*L*.v.i). He studied law in Strasbourg, 1770–1. His influence on Hardy owed much to Carlyle's writings; cf. **Bellerophon**. The 'optical poem' (*L*.II.vii, with Dare as Mephistopheles) is a Victorian parallel to the Witch's kitchen scene in Part I of Goethe's *Faust*, where the loveliest form of woman is revealed in a mirror to the hero. Dare (associated with lightning and thunder in *L*.II.i, as Manston is in *DR*.viii.4; cf. **Faustus . . . penny book**) is Mephistophelian in a conspiratorial role associated with smoke and fire. It is continued with Louis Glanville (*TT*), though the smoke and fire are reduced to the habitual cigar; there are reminders of it with Fitzpiers and Felice Charmond (*W*). Baron von Xanten (*CM*.12) is Mephistophelian in a more gentlemanly and romantic style; see **The Romantic Adventures** . . . . The cigar, smoke, and Satanic associations are more obvious in Alec d'Urberville. Comments by the Sinister and Ironic Spirits in *The Dynasts* are in the Mephistophelian vein of Goethe's *Faust*. In Carlyle's *Sartor Resartus* (I.viii) Hardy very early met Goethe's conception of the universe as the garment of God, woven on 'the roaring Loom of Time'; cf. **web**. See also ***The Well-Beloved*** and the conclusion of *Faust*, Part II.

goings-out . . . comings-in (*TD*.xxvi), Psalm cxxi,8.

gold-beater's skin, used for separating leaves of gold foil during beating, and as a plaster for wounds.

Golgotha: see **Kranion**.

Goliath the Philistine, his death (*D*3.VII.v), I Sam.xvii,38–54.

gone down into silence (*PBE*.xl; *TD*.1895 pr.), Psalm cxv,17.

Gonzalo and a 'dry death' (*FMC*.xlvii), end of *Tem*.I.i.

good deed in a naughty world (*DR*.iv.1), *MV*.v.i,91.

good sheep and wicked goats (*PBE*.xxvi), cf. Matt.xxv,31ff.

good that I would do . . . evil . . . I do (*D*2.VI.v), Rom.vii,19.

good-hussif, container for needles, thread, scissors, etc.

goodman, husband, master of the house.

good-now, to be sure (from 'good enow', i.e. 'sure enough'); (in the form of a query) I guess.

got handy (dial.) reached (got to) opportunely.

Gothic (*TM*.ii), probably medieval, the word being usually used with reference to the architecture that developed after the Norman Conquest; **ceorls** were the lowest class of Anglo-Saxon freemen; **villeins** were serfs or peasants owing service to the lord of the manor.

Gott (Germ.) God.

gourd . . . prophet (*FMC*.xxxviii; *TD*.lv), Jon.iv,4–9; hence **gourd-like** (*WB*.III.viii), ephemeral.

governor of a steam-engine, a revolving mechanism with heavy metal spheres at the end of arms, to regulate the working of the machine.

Gozzoli, Bonozzi (*OMC*4.II.i), Benozzo G., Italian painter (c.1420–97), noted for his fresco work.

Gracian (quoted, *RN*.III.i), a Spanish Jesuit (1601–58) whose writings are imbued with practical ethics. Many of his maxims were copied into Hardy's notebook by his wife Emma, and some of them contribute to the boringness of Sir William de Stancy (*L*).

grammer, grandmother, old woman; cf. **gammer**.
grandfer (dial.), grandfather.
grandsire triples, a special ringing of church bells, interchanging in three sets of two.
The Grave by the Handpost (*CM*4). It is strange that this doubly suicidal action, though honourable, should have been published in Christmas numbers in England and America (1897).
grave end of the gamut, lower end of the musical scale.
The Graveyard of Dead Creeds (*HS*). The last line shows no optimism, though new religions will continue to emerge. *Catholicons*, panaceas; *caustic*, destructive, life-reducing, ascetic.
gravitation (*TT*.xxxiv), used in the astronomical sense, i.e. 'moving or tending towards a centre of attraction'.
Great Bear (*PBE*.xi). See **Charles's Wain**.
great circle. The shortest distance between two places is an arc of a great circle (a circle which passes between them and of which the plane passes through the earth's centre); usually followed by long-distance navigators.
Great Dame (*WP*.At a Bridal). See **Great Mother**.
Great Forest, the New Forest in Hampshire.
Great Hintock (*W*), Melbury Osmond. See **the Hintocks** and **King's Hintock**.
Great Mother (*DR*.xiii.1; *FMC*.xxxvi), Nature, from 'Magna Mater' (Lat.), the title given to Cybele, a goddess personifying Nature's fecundity.
the Great Plain (*TD*.lviii; *LLI*.5; *SC*.Wessex Heights), Salisbury Plain.
Great Things (*MV*). Cf. **Ridgeway**. *Soul . . . thee*, cf. Luke xii,20.
great trumpet (*MC*.i), announcing the Day of Judgment or the end of the world; cf. I Thess.iv,16.
Greater (or **Great**) **Bear**, cf. **Charles's Wain**. Two stars at the end of this constellation point to the Pole Star.
a greater than himself, no answer to the critical question (*TD*.lviii), Jesus (John xix,9).
Grebe, Barbara (*GND*2), originating from Barbara Webb, who married the fifth Earl of Shaftesbury.
Grecian nose, straight and in line with the forehead (side view).
Greek astronomer's wish (*TT*.xiv). This seems to refer to the Socrates who is presented as an astronomer high in the sky, to observe the sun, in Aristophanes' satirical play *The Clouds*.
Greek poet, 'A perplexing and ticklish possession is a daughter'

(*W.*xii), Menander, writer of comedies, c.343–291 BC.

Greek . . . Spectacle . . . hocus-pocus . . . (*D*3.After Scene), an allusion to a passage near the end of the second chorus in Aeschylus's *Agamemnon*.

green as emerald (*W.*xxvii), Coleridge, 'The Ancient Mariner' I.

green in judgment (*WB.*I.ix), *AC.*I.v,74.

green malt in flour (*TD.*iv). Hardy explained this as having a daughter in childbed before marriage, green malt being immature, and a floor of malt being the outspread malt for steeping.

Green Park (*DR.*vii.3), between Piccadilly and Buckingham Palace.

green wound, one that is fresh and tender.

Greenhill (several references, *Life* 96/98 and *FMC* especially), Woodbury Hill on the eastern side of Bere Regis; it had been a Roman camp, with a chantry or chapel on its west side (Hutchins; cf. *PPP.*The Well-Beloved). 'Greenhill' may have served to preserve the memory of Hardy's journey with his sister Mary past Greenhill Down on their way to Fawley in 1864.

Greenwich Observatory (*TT.*ix,xxxii,xxxiv). See *Life* 151/155–6 for the way Hardy contrived a visit there when he was working on his novel.

Gregorian (*W.*xiii), plain chant or plainsong, traditionally the invention of Pope Gregory I.

Greuze (*DR.*iv.2; *PBE.*ix), French painter, 1725–1805. The first reference is to a portrait (in the N.G.) thought at the time to be by Greuze.

Grey's Bridge (*UGT*; *FMC*; *MC*; *LLI.*8 Introduction; and poems), a stone bridge commissioned by Lora Grey of Kingston Maurward House, over a division of the Frome river, on the main road east of Dorchester.

Grey's Wood (*UGT.*IV.i), on the northern side of the Dorchester–Puddletown road from Hardy's birthplace.

griddle, grill or broil on a gridiron.

Griesbach's text (*JO.*I.v), the revised text of the Greek New Testament, prepared by the German scholar Johann Griesbach and published in 1774–7; used by Hardy (*Life* 29–31/34–5). For the Greek quoted from it in *JO.*II.iii, see I Cor.viii,6.

griff, claw, grip.

griffin, a kind of apple.

Grimm's Law (*JO.*I.iv), formulated by the German philologist Jacob Grimm in 1822, on the inevitable pattern of consonant-mutation from Indo-Germanic to modern German forms.

grinning-match (*TM*.xxvi), through horse-collars (*D*1.II.iv and IV.i), once an amusing competition at rural celebrations.

grintern, a compartment in a granary.

grisly story (*W*.xli), Edgar Allan Poe, 'The Fall of the House of Usher'.

gristing, flour from corn which is gleaned.

grizzel, grizzle, turn grey; grey.

grog-blossom, pimple or redness created by heavy drinking.

gross, open, palpable (MCR), like Falstaff's lies, *1.H4*.II.iv,218–19.

ground-dressing, spreading manure.

ground-lines, outlines.

A Group of Noble Dames (1891). Most of the stories were based to some degree on gossip retailed by 'old family servants of the great families'; 1, 2, 6, 7, 8 owe much to Hutchins' history of Dorset. The framework developed from that provided for 2–7 when they appeared in the Christmas number of *The Graphic*, 1890. Narrators, suitably selected for their stories, were imagined as members of the Dorset Natural History and Antiquarian Field Club (which Hardy joined when he was living at Wimborne) at meetings in the new County Museum (opened Jan 1884), Dorchester. Much concealment is suspected in the setting of some of the stories.

Grub Street, London (CEF), notorious in the seventeenth and eighteenth centuries as the centre for hack-writers; Hardy implies novelists who depend on writing for their maintenance.

guess and fear (*DR*.xvi.1). See **Burns's field-mouse**.

Guido (*PBE*.xxvii; *JO*.III.ii), Guido Reni, Italian painter, 1575–1642.

Guildenstern . . . happy (*FMC*.xxii), *Ham*.II.ii,227.

guilty thing, like a (*WT*4.iii), *Ham*.I.i,148.

guilty thing surprised (*HE*.xxiv), Wordsworth, 'Intimations of Immortality',148 (*G.T.*).

guindée (Fr.), starched and prim.

guisers, actors, mummers.

gunnel, gunwale, the upper edge of a ship's side.

Gunpowder Plot (*RN*.I.iii). See **Fawkes**.

Gurth (*MC*.xxix), a Saxon slave in Scott's *Ivanhoe*.

gutta serena (*FMC*.liii), blindness, without a visible change of the eye; cf. 'drop serene', Milton, *Paradise Lost* iii,25.

gwine (dial.) going.

H

Η ΚΑΙΝΗ ΔΙΑΘΗΚΗ (*JO*.I.vii), Greek: 'The New Testament'.

habilimental hulls and husks (the metaphor sustained in 'kernels'), clothes, outer coverings (*TT*.xxi).

habited, dressed.

hackle, straw roof of a beehive.

Had I wist (known) **before I kist** (*PBE*.xxxii ep.), from the lament in the ballad 'Jamie Douglas' (*G.T.* 'The Forsaken Bride').

Had You Wept (*SC*). The 'deep division' has suggested Emma Hardy as the subject of this poem; the 'large and luminous' eyes seem to point to Florence Hardy before or after her marriage. Neither explanation, especially the second, is adequate. More probably the reading of 'had I but wept' in Mrs Henniker's translation from a Spanish poem reminded Hardy of what he had written about Tess, and the poem reflects Angel's thought; see the paragraph in *TD*.xxxvii beginning 'That was all she said . . .'. Her large eyes are emphasized in ii; their unusual brightness at the time of her break with Angel is commented on in xxxvii.

Hadrian (*MC*.xi,xx), a Roman emperor who visited his troops in England early in the second century; he was responsible for the wall built against the Picts and the Scots. **Posthumus** and the **Constantines** were also Roman emperors, the former being the rebellious Postumus who was recognised as emperor throughout Gaul, Spain, and Britain, the latter including Constantine the Great.

hae (dial.), have.

Haggardon (*TM*.xxvi; cf. My Cicely), Eggardon Hill, a prehistoric fortress about 5 m. ENE of Bridport.

haggler, dealer or middleman, hawker.

hag-rid, hag-rode, afflicted with nightmares, ridden by a witch.

hairbreadth escapes (*WT7*.vii), *Oth*.I.iii,136.

hairs . . . sorrow . . . grave (*W*.xliii), Gen.xliv,29.

Hallam says of Juliet (*DR*.vi.3), Henry Hallam, *Introduction to the Literature of Europe*, 1837–9, on the heroine in *RJ*.

halter-path, bridle-path.

Hambledon Hill (*TD*.ii,1), a chalk hill near Iwerne Courtney or

Shroton, east of Sturminster Newton; here Hardy nearly lost his way in the fog, among the earthworks, after attending Shroton Fair (*Life* 116/119–20).

Hambro' grape (*PBE*.xxi), a black, hothouse grape (Hamburg).

Ham-hill (*W*.viii,xxv), Hamdon Hill, near Yeovil, the source of stone for many fine old buildings in Somerset and Dorset.

Hamilton, Lady (*OMC*4.II.i; *D*1.II.i, v.iv, v.v), c.1765–1815, the subject of many paintings by Romney, and mistress of Nelson at Naples.

Hamlet play scene (*TM*.xvii), cf. *Ham*.III.ii; **Hamlet to the Ghost** (*OMC*6.ii), *Ham*.I.v,142ff; **Hamlet-like fantasticism . . . of augury** (*HE*.xxxiv), *Ham*.v.ii,203–12.

hammer-cloth, cover for the driver's seat or box in a family coach.

Hammers of Heretics (*TD*.1892 pr.). In the singular, the phrase has been applied to a number of people, notably to the president of the council which condemned John Huss to be burned in 1415, and to Torquemada, the first inquisitor-general of Spain in 1483, who is remembered for his infamous cruelties.

Hammersmith (*DR*.iii.1,xxi.3), west of London, near the Thames.

hammochrysos (*HE*.xl), a sparkling, yellowish stone mentioned by classical writers.

Hamptonshire, the old name for Hampshire (*GND*9; *JO*.VI.xi). It occurs in the MS of *GND*6 for 'Southwesterland'.

hand, handbreadth, used for measuring the height of horses; **a Hand** (*CM*.1.iii), 'the hand of the Lord' (Biblical), God.

The Hand of Ethelberta (first pub. serially in *The Cornhill Magazine*, July 1875 to May 1876) depends on a cleverly – at times implausibly – contrived plot, which draws from Hardy's observations (contemporary and earlier) in London, his honeymoon visit to Rouen, and impressions in and around Swanage, where much of the novel was written. Reacting against the imputation that *FMC* was influenced by George Eliot, Hardy gave up work on another rural novel (ultimately *W*), and turned to society or 'manners' in an attempt to show that he 'did not mean to imitate anybody' (cf. *Life* 102–4/105–7). His London scenes being based on observation, they lack the imaginative assurance which characterizes most of *FMC*, though they have a special *Upstairs, Downstairs* interest in presenting 'the drawing-room' from the angle of 'the servants' hall'. His heroine's careerism enables Hardy to resurrect the class-resentment of *The Poor Man and the Lady*, from which he probably lifted some choice satirical passages (cf. xxiv,xxviii); unlike Thackeray (as Macmillan had written), he did not mean fun but *mischief*. There are entertaining scenes, particularly when Lord Mountclere is intent on marrying Ethelberta, and her relatives are indignant that their family should be connected with such an old *roué*. Ethelberta is calculating but not cold; she is as much concerned for her family as for herself, in accordance with the principles of J. S. Mill's Utilitarianism. The worship of Mammon is indicted, in a world where Neigh's success depends on knackery. Hardy's mother's pre-marital plan to set up a 'club-house' in London (*Life* 8/12), and his own social embarrassment, including a difficult situation with a butler (Millgate,149–50), contribute to the plot. The title is ambivalent, Ethelberta's managing 'hand' (proleptically symbolized in the adroitness of the wild duck in the opening chapter) being evident in the Sequel (to the last word). Hardy's sympathies are with Julian; he has no inclination for life as 'a scientific game' (cf. *Life* 53/54,87/89,104/107).

hands across (*UGT*.I.vii). Although it has been claimed that this indicates the dance 'Hands Across', the way the expression is presented and the immediate sequel (the opening of I.viii) suggest no more than a call to get ready for the next (see **six-hands-round**), joining right hands being the first movement of partners at the start of a dance.

Handsome-does . . . Handsome-is (*PBE*.xxviii), cf. the proverb 'Handsome is as handsome does.'

handwriting on the wall (*W*.xxv), as at Belshazzar's feast; cf. Dan.v,5.

hang-fair, public execution.

Hannah Dominy (*OMC*6.i; *MC*.xxviii), an illiterate interpretation of 'Anno Domini', i.e. 'in the year of our Lord' (from the birth of Christ).

Hannibal (*D*3.VII.ix), a Carthaginian general who swore eternal enmity to Rome, and proved his genius by victorious campaigns in which he led his troops over the Pyrenees and Alps (218 BC).

hap, chance; **hapless**, unlucky; **haply**, perhaps, perchance.

hapeth (dial.), halfpennyworth.

Hapsburgian (*W*.iv). The royal Austrian family of the Hapsburgs developed and maintained links by marriage with a number of European countries over a long period.

The Harbour Bridge (*HS*). *painters*, ropes to prevent boats from drifting; *cut black-paper portraits*, silhouettes (common at seaside resorts like Weymouth before the days of the cheap camera: cf. *UGT*.I.i).

Hardy, Captain Thomas Masterman (*TM*; *D*.pr, *D*1.IV.i,V.ii,iv,vii) one of the descendants of the Hardys of Jersey who settled in Dorset centuries earlier. He lived at Portesham, was captain of Nelson's flag-ship at Trafalgar, and became Vice-Admiral Sir Thomas Hardy. The monument erected to his memory on Blackdown Hill in 1844 is alluded to in *TM*.xii.

Hardy, Emma Lavinia (née Gifford, 1840–1912). After girlhood in Plymouth, she moved with her family to Kirland, near Bodmin, in Cornwall. When her sister married the Revd Caddell Holder in 1867 she joined her at St Juliot, where she met Hardy in 1870 (see *S.R.*). Her vitality and happy spirit brought new life to Hardy, and her faith in his future as a novelist sustained him. He recalled 'her golden curls and rosy colour as she rode about, for she was very attractive at that time' (*Letters* IV,299); she was called 'the peony' when she was young, she told Bertha Newcombe in 1900 (cf. *SC*.After a Journey). She was a talented painter, with literary aspirations beyond her gifts. She gave Hardy considerable help as his amanuensis. Unfortunately, like her father, she suffered from fits of social superiority; periodically she was afflicted with mental instability, as Hardy noticed before their marriage in 1874. In conjunction with her own form of religious orthodoxy, these weaknesses created strains and discords as Hardy's intellectual self-confidence asserted itself in his later fiction. After the publication of *TD*, their division became wide and unbridgeable, though they accommodated themselves to a style of living together. She was a campaigner for good causes, and prominent in the movement for women's suffrage; in Dorchester she was remembered for her wild cycling downhill in knickerbockers. During her last years literary illusions and domestic loneliness (with Hardy retired to his study) made her convert the Max Gate attics into a comfortable flat; they met for their main meals. She wrote poems and continued her diaries; the latter became so bitter and hostile that they preyed on his mind after her death and were destroyed. (She had destroyed all his love-letters.) His expiation took the form of pilgrimages to Cornwall and Plymouth (in which interest had become particularized by *S.R.*) and innumerable poems of remembrance, among which will be found some of Hardy's greatest poetry. Many bear directly on their relationship, and had a confessional cathartic value for him; others are more allusive or clothed in fictional disguise. *Identifications are given for individual poems, wherever they are certain or most probable.*

Hardy, Florence Emily (née Dugdale, 1879–1937). Daughter of an Enfield headmaster, she taught for a time and then became a writer, particularly of books for children. She first met Hardy in 1905, it seems, helped him occasionally with research at the British Museum when he was at home, and typed for Emma Hardy at Max Gate when the latter was bent on authorship. After Emma's death she took charge of Max Gate, and saved Hardy from intrusive visitors; they were married at Enfield in February 1914. Subject to her feelings, she could easily be depressed (especially as Hardy's poems on Emma continued) and highly jealous at times. Her part in helping to compile *The Life of Thomas Hardy* is usually underestimated. (His private wish was that the whole work would be put into correct literary form by an experienced writer and scholar.) After his death she turned to social work, especially in the poorer parts of Fordington. See *TL.*On the Departure Platform; *SC.*After the Visit, To Meet, or Otherwise, A Poet; *MV.*Conjecture; *LLE.*'I sometimes think', A Jog-trot Pair.

Hardy, Jemima (Hardy's mother, 1813–1904). She spent her early years in or near Melbury Osmond (cf. the **Hintocks**). Like her mother (*Life* 6–7/11–12), she was a great reader, and Hardy owed much to her 'store of local memories', reaching back to the time when ballads were commonly heard. Her 'good taste in literature was expressed by the books she selected for her children' (*Life* 321/344–5); her ambition for Thomas is indicated by her gift of Dryden's *Virgil*, Johnson's *Rasselas*, and *Paul and Virginia* when he was little over eight. She met his father when she was in service at Stinsford House, after acting as a cook to another of the Strangways families, both at Maiden Newton and in London, where she had hoped to take some of her brothers and sisters to live with her (an idea germinal to the plot of *HE*). Her initial disappointment when Hardy gave up architecture for writing has its parallel in *RN*. She and her mother's family had suffered hard times in her youth, and her views undoubtedly affected her son's. 'Mother's view (and also mine)', he wrote at the end of October 1870, 'that a figure stands in our van with arm uplifted, to knock us back from any pleasant prospect we indulge in as probable.' See *PPP.*In Tenebris III; *TL.*A Church Romance,

The Roman Road, Night in the Old Home, After the Last Breath, She Hears the Storm; *MV*.Looking Across.

Hardy, Mary (née Head, 1772–1857), Hardy's paternal grandmother. Her girlhood was spent at Fawley in Berkshire (cf. **Durbeyfield**). She married Thomas Hardy of Puddletown in 1799, and they occupied their new house at Higher Bockhampton in 1801. Her recollection of events during the French Revolution (cf. *Life* 215/224) and the Napoleonic era made an indelible impression on her grandson. See **Domicilium**; *WP*.The Alarm; *TL*.One We Knew.

Hardy, Mary (Hardy's sister, 1841–1915). She and her younger sister Katharine (1856–1940) attended the teacher-training college at Salisbury, and eventually taught together at the Dorchester Girls National School in Icen Way, where Mary was headmistress (both retiring early to help their mother at Higher Bockhampton). She was a talented painter, and a church organist in more than one parish during her teaching career. She and Hardy were very close friends from childhood. See *Life* 371/401–2. There may well be a reflection of her in Thomasin Yeobright (*RN*). See also *WP*.Middle-Age Enthusiasms; *MV*.Conjecture, Logs on the Hearth, Molly Gone, Looking Across (iv), In the Garden; *LLE*.Sacred to the Memory, The Sun's Last Look on the Country Girl; *HS*.Paradox.

Hardy, Thomas, 'Thomas the First', Hardy's grandfather, 1778–1837. He was a builder, and the 'cellist of the Stinsford choir. During the period when Napoleon threatened to invade England he was a Volunteer (cf. *TM*.xxiii). His copy of Gifford's *History of the Wars Occasioned by the French Revolution* (in illustrated magazine numbers) initiated the interest which led to *The Trumpet-Major* and *The Dynasts*. Cf. *Life* 8–9/12–13,10–12/16,16–17/21,248/262–3,250/264, **Dewy, William**, **Yeobright, Mr**, and *WP*.The Alarm.

Hardy, Thomas, 'Thomas the Second', Hardy's father, 1811–92. He continued his father's building business, and married Jemima in 1839. For many years he was a violinist in the Stinsford string choir and at local parties and festivities. His small farm at West Stafford was called Talbothays. His character is reflected to some degree in Giles Winterborne (*W*). See *Life* 13–15/17–19,21/25–6,23–4/28,248/262,318/342,444/479; *PPP*.The Self-Unseeing; *TL*.A Church Romance, Night in the Old Home; *MV*.To My Father's Violin, Looking Across (i); *LLE*.On One who Lived and Died where he was Born.

HARDY, THOMAS, the author, 1840–1928. His knowledge of architecture, astronomy, music (sacred and secular), painting, literature (poetry especially), the Bible, and Church worship is copiously illustrated throughout his work. His references to paintings have sometimes been dismissed as pedantic intrusions; more rightly they will be found integral to his conceptions, their study being indivisible from one of his fictional aims, to create scenes that the reader can visualize. His scenery is rarely a mere backcloth; it reflects the moods and dilemmas of his principal characters. His poetic intuition made him ready not only to adopt fine phrases from other authors but also to adapt features and situations from great literature to some of his most successful Wessex fiction. In this he aimed at artistic or organic form (cf. PRF and *Life* 95/98,170–1/177), though his MSS and admissions show that he was not a slave to blue-print methods (cf. CEF and *Letters* II,93). The best of his poetry, influenced in the earlier stages of its post-novel development by the more lyrical verse of Wordsworth and Browning, owes much to his policy of creating a style which is conversational in idiom and syntax. At its worst it is near the borderline of the prosaic or, more often, cluttered with artificialities, and quaintly – if not perversely – idiosyncratic in diction. His prose is often laboured, occasionally heavy and clumsy, either from attempting undue compression or from using faulty constructions (particularly with unrelated participial phrases). As novelist and poet, nonetheless, he is supremely successful – more in both capacities than any other English writer. Most of his fiction is unusually thoughtful; it concentrates, but rewards more than it exacts. We read too often that Hardy was content to succeed as a serial writer in Victorian magazines; his statement on the subject (*Letters* I,28) should leave no doubt that his aims were always high. How high can best be seen in PRF and in the General Preface, where he finds no irreconcilability between provincialism and literary greatness. Such was his philosophical and creative vision, and so intimate became his knowledge of the Wessex he inherited – features of which (including superstitions) he continued to memorialize in his later years – that he was richly endowed with what T. S. Eliot regarded as the essentials of an author who is a landmark in national literature: 'strong local flavour' combined with universality.

hare (eyes), wide, staring.
hark back, return.
harlican. Hardy (*Letters* III,124) gives the meaning as applied to a small boy: wild-looking urchin, object, scarecrow.
harmless as a dove . . . serpents (*HE*.vi), Matt.x,16.
harnet (dial.), hornet.
Harpy, faeces of a (*DR*.xvi.4), *Aeneid* iii,216–18. ('foedissima . . . ora'): Virgil describes the harpies as birds with girls' faces, 'a most revolting discharge from their bellies, claws for hands, and faces always pallid' (with hunger).
Harrison, Frederic (*LLE*.Apology), a Positivist evolutionary philosopher and eminent professor of law, 1831–1923. Hardy's 'quotation' sums up the disagreement with his philosophy which Harrison expressed in a review of Hardy's *Collected Poems*, 1919, in *The Fortnightly Review*, 2 Feb 1920.
Hartmann (*LLE*.Apology), Karl Robert von (1842–1906), a German philosopher noted for his theory of the Unconscious as the Creator. On this subject Hardy's principal views were formed before he read much on von Hartmann in English journals.
harum-scarum, reckless, wild, flighty.
harvest-home (*FMC*.xxxvi and pr.), celebrations on the farm when harvesting was completed (cf. the opening of 'The Harvest Supper' in George Eliot's *Adam Bede*).
The Harvest-Supper (*HS*). Hardy's return to the barn at Kingston Maurward in 1924 (*Life* 426–7/460) reminded him of his boyhood experience when he saw the redcoats (soldiers from Dorchester barracks) participating in the dances after the harvest-supper, and heard the traditional ballads sung (cf. *Life* 19–20/24–5 for this and particulars of the ballads he remembered and refers to in this poem). *the Scotch-Greys*, the old name for the Scots Greys, a cavalry unit (cf. *D3*.VII.ii and footnote).
The Hatband, an uncollected dramatic verse narrative, commemorating an old Wessex custom. At a funeral, and the following Sunday service, the chief mourner wore a black hatband, which hung behind to the waist, and was tied to the hat, if the deceased were a young unmarried woman, with a bow of white ribbon.
hatch, small gate. **hatches**, sections of a weir which can be raised or lowered to control the flow of water.
Hath misery . . . loved? (*OMC4*.I.vi ep.), Byron, *The Corsair* III.viii.
Haunting Fingers (*LLE*), imagined possibly at the Horniman

Museum, London. *Amphion,* a musical genius of classical mythology, to the sound of whose lyre the walls of Thebes sprang up; *dampered,* subjected to a device for preventing string-vibration; *reverbed,* reverberated; *Cecilian,* from St Cecilia, patroness of church music.

Havannah, cigar manufactured in Havana, Cuba.

Havenpool (*LLI.*6; *CM*8,9; *LLE.*The Chapel-Organist; *WW.*The Mongrel), Poole, Dorset, a port long engaged in 'the Newfoundland trade'.

Havill, Mr (*L*), named after the Avill river which flows past Dunster ('Stancy') Castle.

hawk, clear the throat.

Hawksgate (*OMC*4.I.iii), 'a remote hamlet', but not far from Stinsford, since Edgar Mayne walked across Tollamore Park to school.

Hawks'-Hold Counts (*D1*.VI.v), the Hapsburgs or Habsburgs (descended from Roman nobility). The first of the dynasty took his title ('Count of Hapsburg') from the eleventh-century castle on the Aar called 'Habichtsburg' (*Habichts,* hawk's; *burg,* castle, fortress, or hold). Francis II of Austria, who relinquished the title of Holy Roman Emperor in 1806, is linked with Charlemagne, the first to accept it in 800.

hawse-holes, cylindrical holes in the bow of a vessel for the cables to pass through.

Hayling Island (Gen.Pr.), immediately east of Portsmouth.

Haylock (*UGT.*IV.iv), a Casterbridge butcher whose name and shop probably recall Robert Hayward's of High East Street, Dorchester, 1851.

He comes . . . bondage held (*CM*4), from the hymn 'Hark! the glad sound!'

He Follows Himself (*LLE*). The yew (a traditional symbol of death and immortality) indicates a churchyard, almost certainly that at Stinsford, where Hardy's first wife was buried (confirmed by the MS deletions: 'Love's', 'Love', and 'her' originally, for 'friend's', 'friend', and 'his').

He heard her musical pants (*PBE.*xviii ep; cf *FMC.*xxxvii), untraced.

He, like a captain . . . relies (*OMC*4.II.i ep; *DR.*xii.5), Dryden's translation of Virgil's *Aeneid* v,439–42.

He Prefers Her Earthly (*MV*). Hardy's views of life-after-death have changed from the subjective (cf. Her Immortality). *firmament-riding,* riding in the heavens; cf. *LLE.*A Woman Driving.

He Resolves to Say No More (*WW*). *O my soul . . .*, a line translated from the Greek epigrammatist Agathias; *Pale Horse*, of death and slaughter (Rev.vi,8). *Let Time . . .*, an allusion to the theory then becoming current ('Magians' indicates Hardy's scepticism) that time could flow backward; whatever they think, he can anticipate the future. *By truth made free*, John viii,32 (cf.*LLE*.Apology). Hardy could see developments leading to the Second World War.

He Revisits His First School (*MV*), at Lower Bockhampton, where he worked at the rule-of-three in Francis Walkingame's primer (*Life* 16/21). Published as *The Tutor's Assistant* in 1851, it remained the most popular arithmetic book in England and America for a long period.

He set in order many proverbs (*PBE*.xiii ep), Eccl.xii,9.

He that is accursed . . . (*FMC*.xlvi), based possibly on Gal.i,8–9.

He that observeth the wind . . . sow (*MC*.xxiv), cf. Eccl.xi,4. For **the Preacher** (Solomon), see Eccl.i,1–2.

He turn'd . . . terror . . . eyes . . . star . . . fix'd (*TT*.xxxvi), from the first part of Swinburne's *Tristram of Lyonesse*, which appeared in 1882 (when Hardy was writing *TT*).

He was the only son . . . widow (*LLI*.8g), Luke vii,12.

The Head Above the Fog (*MV*). Whether remembered or imagined, this tryst is in the Frome valley; for the circumstances, cf. *TL*.Former Beauties,7 and *SC*.Wessex Heights,22. The image of the head made trunkless by thick low-lying white fog had been used in *CM*.12.vii.

Heads of Houses (*JO*.VI.i), masters of colleges.

heard his days . . . (*LLI*.4.ii), cf. Tennyson, 'Locksley Hall',110.

heart . . . knoweth . . . bitterness (*TD*.xxxvi), cf. Prov.xiv,10.

heathcroppers, stray animals, usually ponies, on the heath.

Heaven, far nearer (*DR*.vi.1), cf. the ending of Thomas Hood's 'I remember, I remember' (*G.T.* 'Past and Present').

heaven lies about . . . then (*JO*.I.iv), in infancy; from Wordsworth, 'Intimations of Immortality',66 (*G.T.*).

Heaven's high tower (*FMC*.lvii; *D3*.VII.v), see **The Lord look'd . . . tower**.

Hebe, a woman of youthful bloom like Hebe, the cupbearer of the classical gods.

Heber, Bishop (*TT*.xli). Poet and hymn-writer, he accepted the see of Calcutta in 1823, and died in 1826.

Hebrews (the epistle to the), quoted (*LLI*.4.v), xii,2; (*TD*.xviii), xii,27.

hedged by his own divinity (*W*.xxv), cf. *Ham*.IV.v,120.

heft (dial.), weight.

Heine (*L*.v.x). Hardy recalls (perhaps from a guidebook) the description of Amiens Cathedral by the German Heinrich Heine, 1797–1856; for his own description, cf. *Life* 138/142. The Titans were giants who made war against the gods of Greek mythology. **Dear my love . . . coffin for me!** (*TT*.xi), translation from Heine's *Lieb' Liebchen*; **Above the youth's . . . eyes . . . fool's-cap rise!** (*JO*.II.vi), translated from Heine's 'Götterdämmerung'. **Heine observed nearly a hundred years ago that the soul . . . will not be darkened by statutes, nor lullabied by the music of bells** (*LLE*.Apology).

Heiress and Architect (*WP*). In London, from 1863 to 1867, Hardy worked for the architect Arthur Blomfield at 8 Adelphi Terrace, chiefly on church-design and restoration. He may have presented him a copy of the poem when he left. It is marked by originality and disciplined structure. The arch-designer is fate; the reductive theme, based on 'the Frost's decree' or the 'Life offers – to deny!' philosophy, is grim. *engrailed*, ornamented.

hele (dial.), pour out.

Helen (*OMC*2), beautiful young woman, like Helen of Troy.

Helicon, a mountain in Greece, with fountains and springs, once sacred to the muses of poetry, music, painting, and the liberal arts.

heliographic science, photography.

hell-and-skimmer, like, 'like blazes', at a furious pace.

helm (vb. from 'helm', a ship's steering-wheel), steer.

Héloïses . . . Cleopatras (*RN*.I.vii). Héloïse was a beautiful girl who fell in love with the great theological scholar Peter Abelard (1079–1142) when he lectured in the cathedral school of Notre Dame. They fled to Brittany, where she bore him a son. After their separation, she became a nun. Cleopatra (as in Shakespeare's *Antony and Cleopatra*) represents the more sensual, luxurious type of love.

Hence will I . . . tell (*OMC*4.II.vi ep.), end of *RJ*.II.ii.

Henchard, Michael (*MC*). As Henchard was first conceived as a stonemason, Hardy may have had in mind the intractable personality of *PPP*.A Man, whose knell none sighed to hear and who was soon forgotten. His connection with the Trenchard house in Dorchester, and the fact that it was occupied by a Henning of the same family when he became the Mayor of

Dorchester in 1840 seem to supply the portmanteau origin of 'Henchard'. Henchard's most powerful imaginative qualities undoubtedly have literary sources (Saul in particular; see ***The Mayor of Casterbridge***), but his strength of character and his irascibility owed something to the reputation of the town clerk Mr Giles, who lived in the South Street house which is the original of the Mayor of Casterbridge's. Late in life Hardy told Elliot Felkin that he had thought of naming his hero Giles.

hender (dial.), hinder.

Hendford Hill (*LLI*.4.iv), in Yeovil, on the main road south. (Hardy almost bought a house on Hendford Hill before deciding to build Max Gate.)

Henley Regatta (*WW*). The annual regatta at Henley-on-Thames, near Reading, is still an important event.

Henniker, Mrs Florence, daughter of Lord Houghton, and hostess to her brother at the Vice-regal Lodge in Phoenix Park, Dublin, when he was Lord-Lieutenant of Ireland and the Hardys were guests in May 1893. Hardy, at odds with Emma, found Mrs Henniker (whose ambition as a novelist made her cultivate his acquaintance) a 'charming, *intuitive* woman'. They met frequently in London that summer (when Hardy was still planning *JO*: cf. *Life* 254–7/270–3). Later that year they collaborated in a short story (see **The Spectre of the Real**). Mrs Henniker lived for a time at Southsea (cf. **An Imaginative Woman**), and she and Hardy met occasionally in Salisbury and Winchester. He followed her husband's fortunes in the Boer War with great interest and concern. Her campaigning against cruelty to animals strengthened Hardy's promotion of altruism to all living creatures. He had fallen in love with her at first, and recovered; their friendship lasted until her death in 1923. She returned what remained (about 150) of his letters to her, rightly assuming that their preservation had biographical value. See ***Jude the Obscure*** for her influence on that novel, and *WP*.At an Inn; *PPP*.A Broken Appointment; *SC*.A Thunderstorm in Town, Wessex Heights ('one rare fair woman'), In Death Divided; *MV*.'He wonders about himself' (cf. 'He views himself as an automaton', *Life* 260/276); *HS*.Come Not; Yet Come!, The Month's Calendar, Last Love-Word.

Henry the Eighth's Castle (*WB*), Sandsfoot, south of Weymouth; built by Henry VIII in 1539, when an invasion prompted by the Pope was feared.

hent (dial.), hint.

Heptarchy, the seven kingdoms of Anglo-Saxon England, including Wessex.

Hepzibah Pyncheon's chicken (*HE*.xl), in Nathaniel Hawthorne's *The House of the Seven Gables* (vi).

Her Death and After (*WP*). The Field of Tombs is Dorchester Cemetery, adjacent to the Roman amphitheatre (Maumbury Rings), 'the Cirque of the Gladiators' (cf. *MC*.xi).

Her Definition (*TL*). Whether Hardy's 'sweetest image' in 1866 was the Idea or Ideal of *W* and *WB* or an actual person is unknown. *outfigure*, delineate; *fitless*, unfitting.

Her Father (*TL*). This was written at Weymouth in 1869 (MS).

Her father did fume (*PBE*.ix ep.), Scott, 'Lochinvar' (*Marmion* v.xii).

Her Haunting-Ground (*HS*). Though her graveyard at Stinsford was not 'slighted', this must have been written with Emma and St Juliot in mind.

Her Immortality (*WP*). This kind of 'subjective immortality' gained ground, as a substitute for the belief in life-after-death, when Darwin undermined Christian theology. Hardy's inventive narration was probably written with his cousin Tryphena in mind; cf. *PPP*.His Immortality, The To-Be-Forgotten. His sketch shows the track he took with her from Stinsford across the fields to Higher Bockhampton; at the time she was young, living at Puddletown, three miles further, across the heath.

Her Initials (*WP*). The second initial in Hardy's accompanying sketch is Z; the first, probably F, rather than Y. For the thought – a common one with Hardy – cf. *TL*.At Waking, also written in 1869.

Her Late Husband (*PPP*). The insistence of Hardy's maternal grandmother that her husband (d.1822) should be buried by his mistress in Melbury Osmond churchyard is the source for this poem (Millgate,13). See **King's Hintock**.

Her Reproach (*PPP*), for studious days in London; cf. *Life* 48–9/50–2. Hardy may have imagined this reproach from Eliza Nicholls (see Millgate). The subject was suggested by Milton's 'Lycidas', 64–72. *water*, nourish.

Her welcome . . . (*PBE*.xvii ep.), Scott, 'The Maid of Neidpath' (*G.T.*).

Hercules, pillars of (*FMC*.xlvii), Gibraltar and Ceuta, two promontories flanking the entrance to the Mediterranean.

According to classical mythology they were joined until severed by Hercules.

Here . . . And nothing wanting . . . (*L*.v.xii), cf. the end of 'Phoebus, arise!' by William Drummond, 1585–1649 (the second poem in *G.T.*).

Here we suffer . . . part no more (*TD*.li), from 'Heaven Anticipated', a popular hymn by T. Bilby (1832).

Heredity (*MV*). Cf. the note for 19 Feb 1889 (*Life* 217/226), the germ of *The Well-Beloved*.

Hermia and Helena (*L*.III.vi), cf. *MND*.III.ii,198–214.

Hermon, dew of (*JO*.II.iii), Psalm cxxxiii,3.

Herne the Hunter (*JO*.I.iii), a legendary wild huntsman in Windsor Forest (cf. Shakespeare, *The Merry Wives of Windsor*, IV.iv,27–37). The youthful Hardy read about him (and Cardinal College, Oxford) in Harrison Ainsworth's novel *Windsor Castle*; see *Life* 25/30.

Herod, died like (*OMC*3.iii), of worms, Acts xii,23.

Herrick, Robert (PRF), lyric poet, 1591–1674; aptly quoted lines from his poem 'To Dianeme' (*G.T.*).

Herschel, the younger (*TT*.xl). Sir John Herschel (1792–1871), who pioneered celestial photography, travelled to the Cape to extend his father's sky-sweeps.

Hesiod . . . Thucydides (*JO*.I.vi), a Greek poet (c. eighth century BC) and a Greek historian (fifth century BC).

het (dial.), swallow, 'knock back' (literally, hit, knock); hot, heat. **het or wet**, sunshine or rain. **het across**, take a short cut across.

hev (dial.), has (have).

hey, a country dance with weaving or serpentine movements.

hidebound, little but skin and bone.

hie (archaic), hasten, pass quickly.

higgler, cf. **haggler**.

high thinking, plain living (*RN*.III.ii; *TD*.xxv; *LLE*.Apology), Wordsworth, 'Written in London, September 1802' (*G.T.*).

highday, high-day, a day for special celebration.

The Higher Criticism (*PPP*.The Respectable Burgher), a historical and scientific assessment of Biblical legends and traditions; it spread from Germany towards the middle of the nineteenth century, and subjected the supernatural to a withering light.

Higher Crowstairs, originally 'Higher Polenkill' (*WT*.1), a sheep-farmer's lonely house on a down less than 3 m. from Casterbridge. Hardy told Rebekah Owen that the hangman would come from the north or NE; the third stranger from 'Shottsford' had probably followed cross-country roads and lanes north of Puddletown (see map A). The house therefore might well have been to the NE rather than to the north of Dorchester.

Higher Jirton (*LLI*.8d), probably Higher Forston, 4 m. north of Dorchester.

high-piled granary (PRF), cf. Keats, 'When I have fears . . . ' (*G.T.*).

Highridge, Mr (*JO*.II.vii). The name of this curate combines a suggestion of the High Church ritualism in favour at Marygreen with the local Ridgeway.

High-Stoy (*W*; *TD*.ii,xliv; *PPP*.The Lost Pyx; *HS*.Under High-Stoy Hill), a long wooded hill on the chalk downs south of Blackmoor Vale, and west of Dogbury Gate, where the main Dorchester–Sherborne road crosses the range; the road off to Melbury Osmond (the original 'Great Hintock') passes below High Stoy. (See ***The Woodlanders***, on the shift of that novel's background further east, with High Stoy replacing Bubb Down.)

Hinnom (*FMC*.xxxvii), the valley outside Jerusalem where children were sacrificed. See **Tophet** and II Chron.xxxiii,6.

The Hintocks include the Melburys north of Evershot, and villages further east. In the first edition of *The Woodlanders* Hardy had sited Hintock House (disguised) where Melbury House stands. Serial illustrations for *GND*.1 made it clear that Melbury House was the King's Hintock Court of that story, and Hardy was afraid that the Ilchester family would be further offended if they discovered that Felice Charmond could be associated with them. In preparation for the 1896 edition he therefore shifted the woodland setting 5 m. east, from NW of Bubb Down to the High Stoy region, changing names of places, but altering the description very little indeed, and merely for topographical support. Though he told his friend Gosse in 1887 that Great Hintock was Melbury Osmond (*Letters* I,164), he made no public disclosures (cf. *Life* 432/466). Great Hintock, Little Hintock (not far to the east and largely imaginary), and Hintock House cannot be placed significantly except with reference to the original setting of *The Woodlanders*. Hardy took the name 'Hintock' from the old name for Melbury Osmond, referring to it in the MS of *W* as 'Hintock St Osmund'. For Hintock House (*W*) see **King's Hintock Court**.

hip, sloping (roofed) gable end.

hippocras, a cordial of wine flavoured with spices.

Hippocrates, a celebrated physician of ancient Greece. In his *Aphorisms* (ii.46) he states that when two pains occur simultaneously in different parts, the more violent obscures the other (*FMC*.xxix). Born on the island of Cos, he is reputed to have saved Athens from the plague, and to have died (c.361 BC) in perfect health (*HS*.In the Evening).

Hippocrene (*L*.II.vii), source of inspiration, a fountain near Mt Helicon sacred to the Muses of ancient Greece; **the blushful Hippocrene . . . Tasting of Flora** (goddess of flowers) . . . **sunburnt mirth**, from Keats, 'Ode to a Nightingale' (*G.T.*).

His Immortality (*PPP*). See **Her Immortality** and **The To-Be-Forgotten**.

His Visitor (*SC*). Emma Hardy lived at Max Gate from 1885 until her death in 1912; she was a talented painter. *softling* (arbitrary use), softly sung.

His wife . . . vine . . . fruit . . . (*TT*.ii), Psalm cxxviii,3 (Tate and Brady).

hit, direct one's course; cause to be 'smitten' with love; (singing) strike up. **hit athwart = het across**.

ho (dial.), long, pine for, care, grieve.

hob-and-nob, hobnob, be on friendly terms.

hobbed, hobnailed.

Hobbema (*FMC*.xlvi; *CM*.12.ix; *Life* 120/123–4), Dutch painter, 1638–1709.

hobble, troublesome business.

hobbledehoy, awkward, uninformed young man.

Hocbridge (*DR*.i.1,3). One would not have to go further north than Banbury or Rugby for the main buildings described, but Hocbridge as a whole is not modelled on any particular town.

the hodiernal, time-reckoning in terms of the present (to-day).

Hodge (DLa; *TD*.xviii,xxii; *PPP*.The King's Experiment), a term for the country labourer. **Hodge and Giles** (*TT*.iii) have the same generic significance.

Hoffman . . . Fontana (*RN*.IV.viii), medical authorities: Friedrich Hoffman, 1660–1742, physician to Frederick I of Prussia; Richard **Mead**, 1673–1754, physician to Queen Anne; and Felice Fontana, 1730–1805, an Italian naturalist and physiologist.

Holbein (*PBE*.v; *L*.I.iii), a portrait-painter of German origin who eventually sought work in England (1497–1543).

hold the world . . . part . . . sad one (*TM*.xxxvi), *MV*.I.i,77–9.

hole-digging (*W*.xx). It was customary to dig a hole in a grass plot and listen at noon on Old Midsummer Day, expecting the sounds heard to reveal the occupation of one's future husband.

holland, linen fabric, originally from Holland.

hollands, spirits, usually gin, from Holland.

holler after (shout after), pursue.

hollowed hand, His (*D*2.III.iii), God's; cf. Isa.xl,12.

hollow-turners, makers of hollow wooden vessels such as bowls.

holmberry, holly berry, bright red like the . . . ; **holm-tree**, the holly.

Holmstoke (*WT*4), an imaginary or composite village drawn from West and East Holme, East Stoke and Stokeford, west of Wareham. (There has been no descriptive change in the setting of the story, in which Holmstoke was substituted for Stickleford.).

holt, copse.

the Holy Hedge Farm (*D*3.VII.vi), La Haye Sainte (Fr. translated).

Holy Thursday, Ascension Day; possibly Thursday in Holy Week.

The homage of a thousand hearts . . . one (*W*.xxiv), untraced.

home of lost causes and **Beautiful city! . . . perfection** (*JO*.II.i), from Matthew Arnold's 1869 preface to his first series of *Essays in Criticism*.

home-along, on the way home, to one's home.

homeliness, plain looks; **homely**, plain-speaking, plain.

Homeric blows, fighting between Greeks and Trojans in the *Iliad*.

Homer's Cimmerian land (*RN*.I.vi), Cimmeria, described at the opening of the eleventh book of the *Odyssey* as a land where the sun never shines. **Homer's fame . . . accidents of his situation** (*RN*.III.i), read by Hardy in J. A. Symonds, *Studies of the Greek Poets*, 2nd series, 1876, p. 238. **Homer's heaven, as merry as the gods in** (*FMC*.xxiii; *LLI*.5.i), cf. the ending of the first book of the *Iliad*.

Honeymoon Time at an Inn (*MV*), based on the superstition that the breaking of a mirror spells bad luck; the Spirits play important roles in *The Dynasts*. *aftergrinds*, when the subsequent **course of love** does not run smoothly.

Honiton lace, made at Honiton in Devon (and by Emma Gifford, *S.R.*42).

The Honourable Laura (*GND*.10), written for a Christmas supplement, 1881. The names Quantock, Downstaple (Barnstaple) and Cliff-Martin (Combe Martin) indicate the north Devon coastal setting.

hontish (dial.), haughty.

hope deferred . . . heart sick (*DR*.xi.1; *CM*2.viii, *CM*3.v), Prov.xiii,12.

Horatian (*DR*.xii.1), after the Latin poet Horace; cf. *Odes* IV.xiii.

Horatio, Dorax, Falstaff (*D*1.VI.vi), characters in *Hamlet*, John Dryden's *Don Sebastian*, and (Falstaff) the two parts of *Henry the Fourth* and *The Merry Wives of Windsor*.

horehound, a medicinal herb.

'hore's-bird. See **husbird**.

horn, proclaim, blare, publish. **horn of salvation** (*D*1.II.v), Psalm xviii,2. **horn up** (of dilemmas; cf. 'the horns of a dilemma'), arise, occur. **horned man**, the Devil. **horner**, adulterer.

Horner-and-Cleeves (*W*.x; cf. *TM*.xvi), a variety of apple.

the horse and the stream . . . proverb (PRF): you may take a horse to water, but you can't make him drink.

hoss (dial.), horse; attach a horse to.

Hougomont, the Château of (*RN*.IV.v). This walled farm was an important defence point during the French attacks which preceded Napoleon's defeat by Wellington at Waterloo, 1815; cf. *D*3.VII.i,ii,iv.

The hour which might have been . . . (*LLI*.1), D. G. Rossetti, sonnet 55 in *The House of Life*.

The House of Hospitalities (*TL*), the house by the communal well on the Higher Bockhampton lane. When the Hardys participated in its hospitalities (recalled to some extent in *UGT*, though the Christmas scenes are imagined in Hardy's birthplace) it was the tranter's home. At the time of the 1841 census it was occupied by Charles Keats; he and his elder brother William (W. K., *Life* 217/227; he lived in a cottage almost opposite the Hardys) were both carriers, but, whichever was Hardy's tranter, there can be no doubt that the business was conducted from the premises where Charles lived. The tithe map of 1838 shows that he was responsible for a field on each side of the lane; cf. *Life* 92/94, where the field rented from Hardy's father may have been a third, that shown belonging to Mary Hardy on the same map. For crucial evidence see *Life* 202/211.

The House of Silence (*MV*), identified as Max Gate by Hardy. *seven ages*, *AYL*.II.vii,139–66.

house-ridding, moving from one home to another, flitting.

houses for ninety-nine years, houses privately owned but on land which is leased or rented for ninety-nine years.

How all the other passions . . . (*OMC*4.II.v ep.), *MV*.III.ii,108–10.

How are the mighty fallen (*TD*.i,liv), II Sam.i,19.

How I Built Myself a House (Orel,159–67), Hardy's first published work (*Chambers's Journal*, 18 Mar 1865); written, he says, to amuse his fellow-pupils in architecture at Blomfield's in London (*Life* 47/49–50).

How She Went to Ireland (*WW*). Dora Sigerson, wife of Clement Shorter (one of Hardy's editors), died in January 1918, and was buried in Ireland.

How should I greet thee? (*PBE*.xxvii ep.), 'After long years . . . With silence and tears'; from Byron, 'When we two parted' (*G.T.*).

How small a part of time . . . fair! (*OMC*4.II.vii ep.), Edmund Waller, 'Go, lovely Rose' (*G.T.*).

Hoxton (*DR*), an area in the NE of central London.

huddied (dial.) hid, hidden.

huff (dial.), scold, reprimand.

huffle, blow unsteadily or in gusts.

Hugo, Victor (PRF), French poet, dramatist, and novelist, 1802–85. See ***The Mayor of Casterbridge***.

Human Shows, Far Phantasies, Songs, and Trifles (1925) is very miscellaneous in its subjects, with more descriptive scenes than in Hardy's earlier volumes of poetry, some of the city, the majority rural, both with touches of humour. A few poems show little hope for the future of civilization; others emphasize an altruism that extends to all living creatures. Memories of Emma continue to renew heartaches in lilting verse, and a succession of poems near the end reveals obsession with death.

Humboldt (*TT*.vii), Friedrich Heinrich von, 1769–1859, author of *Cosmos*. Hardy had read his comment on scintillation in the tropics in R. A. Proctor's *Essays on Astronomy*, 1872.

Humboldt (*JO*.IV.iii), Wilhelm von, 1767–1835. Cf. quotations in John Stuart Mill, *On Liberty* iii.

humps and hollers (dial.), ups and downs, humps and hollows.

humstrum, thought to be like the rebeck, a forerunner of the fiddle.

the Hundred of . . . (*GND*2), an ancient subdivision of a county, having its own court or moot.

A Hundred Years Since, an uncollected poem, written by Hardy for the centenary of *The North American Review*, Feb 1915. *brass gods*, idols, false values (cf. Dan.v,4); *binding Satan fast*, cf. Rev.xx.

hungry generations (*DR*.x.4), Keats, 'Ode to a Nightingale' (*G.T.*).

hurdle-sauls (dial.), stakes to which hurdles are fastened.

A Hurried Meeting (*HS*). Hardy's first published novel created offence by suggesting this sort of thing could happen in upper-class families (cf. *DR*.iii.1 and xxi.3). *crossing South*, crossing the Equator (for South Africa?); *imp*, mock impishly (as in *W*.xx).

hurst, wooded hill.

husbird, 'hore's-bird (dial.), rascal, 'bastard'.

hussif'ry, household management, housekeeping (housewifery).

hydatids (*PBE*.xxxvii). The brain-disease of sheep, usually known as 'gid', is caused by the hydatid (cf. *MC*.xxvii).

Hyde Park (London) scenes, probably adapted from *The Poor Man and the Lady*: *PBE*.xiv; *HE*.ix; *OMC*4.II.ii,iii.

hydromel, honey and water mixed to form a kind of mead.

Hylas (*FMC*.v), a youth who was lost in Mysia (west Asia Minor) when the Argonauts landed for supplies of fresh water.

Hymen . . . Harlequin . . . (*WB*.II.xiii). Hymen, the Greek god of marriage, was usually represented crowned with flowers and carrying a burning torch; Harlequin is the mischievous clown of pantomime. **Hymen, spectre to their intended feast of** (*LLI*.3.iii), an allusion to either the ghost in the banquet-scene (*Mac*.III.iv) or the ghost of **Alonzo the Brave**.

Hymenaeus and Alexander . . . blaspheme (*TD*.xlvii), I Tim.i, 19–20.

hyperbolic curve, produced when a cone is intersected by a plane which makes a larger angle with the base than does the side of the cone.

hyperborean, of the far north.

I

I am not worthy to be called thy son (*CM*4), Luke xv,21.

I am the resurrection . . . live (*D*2.III.iv), a sentence (John xi,25) at the beginning of the C. of E. Burial Service, which announces the arrival of the funeral procession.

I can find . . . womanhood (*JO*.III.vii), Browning, 'The Worst of It'.

I find more bitter than death . . . nets (*FMC*.xxii), Eccl.vii,26.

'I look in her face' (*LLE*). Hardy looks at Emma's picture, and goes off to his study. *far-off*, cf. *LLE*.On the Tune Called the Old-Hundred-and-Fourth.

'I look into my glass' (*WP*). *Cf. Life* 251/265. The thought was transferred to *WB*: cf. II.xii (the curse of his heart not ageing), III.iv (glass . . . withering carcase).

I love you true! (*TT*.xiv), an echo of Keats, 'La Belle Dame' (*G.T.*).

I lull a fancy . . . (*PBE*.xxviii ep.), Tennyson, *In Memoriam* lxv.

'I met a man' (*MV*). *upon the sunlit seas*, cf. Ezek.xxviii,2 and Rev.iv,6. *Cockers*: Warring imperialists are compared to gambling promoters of cock-fighting (a 'main' is a match between two cocks). *mistake . . . with Saul*: Saul was rejected because he repeatedly disobeyed God's command (I Sam.xiii,xv). *malign Compeer*: Hardy accepts J. S. Mill's view that God is unable to have his way because the power of evil is too strong. *Chartered omnipotents*, rulers with great military strength who have the right to make war as they please.

'I rose and went to Rou'tor Town' (*MV*). Rou'tor, named after Row Tor, one of the highest points on Bodmin Moor, is Bodmin, Cornwall. Emma Gifford's father, who lived at Kirland near Bodmin, expressed snobbishly slanderous objections to Hardy as a future son-in-law (transferred in different terms to *PBE*.ix). Here Hardy remembers with deep feeling her loyalty to him; cf. *SC*.Beeny Cliff,3, and *LLE*.A Woman's Trust. By ironical design the stanza form is that of *SC*.'When I set out for Lyonnesse'.

'I rose up as my custom is' (*SC*). Although ghosts were said to appear on All Souls' Eve (1 Nov), in conjunction with such supernatural events as those of the final stanza, they were usually associated with All Saints' Eve or Hallowe'en (31 Oct). As in the previous poem, the wife prefers the conventional husband.

I said, if there's peace . . . (*DR*.xv.1), Thomas Moore, 'Ballad Stanzas'.

'I said to Love' (*PPP*), possibly the result of Hardy's impressionable pessimism after reading articles on the philosophy of Edouard von Hartmann, 1842–1906. Cupid is addressed; the darts, swan, and dove are his classical appurtenances.

I say, 'I'll seek her' (*TL*). A fantasy: *cockcrows* (*Ham*.I.i,147–56) suggest the imminent departure of the ghostly vision.

'I sometimes think' (*LLE*). For Florence Emily, Hardy's second wife. *sow good seed*, Matt.xiii,24; *words in the wilderness*, Matt.iii,3.

'I was the midmost' (*LLE*). *Polestar*: everything in his life revolved round her, as the earth spins on its axis, and the stars appear to turn round the Pole Star (in line with the earth's axis). *wistful . . . fain*!: everywhere people are crying out for a key to the universe and life.

'I watched a blackbird' (*WW*), based on an observation on Easter Sunday, 15 Apr 1900, which was omitted from Hardy's *Life*.

I wis (archaic), to be sure, truly.

Icen or **Icening Way** (*RN*.I.i; *MC*.xliii, the *Via*; *CM*6; *WP*.My Cicely). This Roman road took its name from the Iceni, the people of Norfolk, where it began. It had various names such as Icknield (Iknield) or Ikling (Ackling) Dyke in different regions. The main road continued to Exeter and beyond; from it vicinal ways branched off, including one from Dorchester to Weymouth. (Hardy's reference in *RN* is misleading; cf. map F.)

Icenway, Lord (*GND*5). In Hardy's Wessex map, Icenway House appears to be Herriard House, south of Basingstoke. George Purefoy Jervoise (1770–1847) of Herriard House married the daughter of Wadham Locke of Rowdeford House near Devizes, and died without issue, but Hardy's map shows Maria Heymere's home (possibly Churchill Court) SW of Bristol, as indicated in his story.

Icknield Street. See **Icen** and **ridge-way.**

Ida, many-rilled (*PBE*.xi), a mountain near Troy; cf. 'many-fountain'd Ida' in Tennyson's 'Oenone'.

Idd (dial.), Is it . . . ? **idden, idn'**, is not.

Idmouth (*CM*.12.xiv,xvii), Sidmouth, Devon.

the Idea (*W*.xviii,xx; *WB*.II.ix), the perfect form or ideal which for Plato existed only in heaven, everything on earth being an imperfect representation of ideal forms; only 'poets' (all types of creative, visionary minds) had glimpses of them (a theory held by Shelley, Hardy's favourite poet).

idolum specus (Gen.Pr.), strictly *idola specus* (Lat.), Francis Bacon's idol of the cave in *Novanum Organum* I.xxxix. This expression, based on Plato's image of the cave, where shadows are mistaken for reality (*The Republic* vii, 514A–521B), means a false notion or spectre.

If I forget . . . you forget (*W*.xxv), the last two verses of 'Two Points of View' in *Firdausi in Exile*, 1885, by Hardy's friend Edmund Gosse.

'If you had known' (*LLE*), written fifty years after Hardy and Emma were caught in the rain near Beeny Cliff; cf. **The Figure in the Scene**. *white-selvaged*, white-edged; *monument*, gravestone in Stinsford churchyard.

the *Iliad* (*JO*.I.vi). The passages given here are identical with those studied by Hardy (listed in his own copy, inscribed 1858); cf. *Life* 28/32.

ill-favoured (archaic), ugly.

image and superscription (*WB*.III.viii), Matt.xxii,20.

the imaginative reason (*L*.VI.v), so called by **a finished writer**: Matthew Arnold, near the end of 'Pagan and Medieval Religious Sentiment', *Essays in Criticism*, first series.

An Imaginative Woman (*LLI*.1). 'Found and touched up' in December 1893 (*Life* 260/276), and based on a psychological fantasy Hardy found in Weismann's *Essays on Heredity* I,457–61, this was first published in April 1894. Undoubtedly its imaginings were fanned by Hardy's love of Mrs Henniker, who lived at Southsea ('Solentsea'), opposite the Isle of Wight; he hints at her husband's connection with the army. Hardy thought this his 'best piece of prose fiction'. See **Trewe**.

Imogen by the cave of Belarius (*DR*.ix.3), *Cym*.III.vi.

***Im*-patience** on a monument (*TD*.ix), cf. *TN*.II.iv,113.

impeach, call in question. **impeachment** (*DR*.viii.2), alluding to Mrs Malaprop, 'I own the soft impeachment' in Sheridan, *The Rivals* (1775), v.iii.

impedimenta, baggage, luggage.

The Impercipient (*WP*). See **Shining Land, All's Well, inland . . . sea**. The 'O doth a bird . . . ?' analogy had been anticipated by Wordsworth in *The Excursion* iv.1083–5. Hardy's illustration shows a service in Salisbury Cathedral.

Impression-picture (*W*.ii), like those of certain French Impressionist painters who depended considerably on light-effects.

In a Eweleaze near Weatherbury (*WP*). Weatherbury and the date (cf. **Thoughts of Phena**) suggest a recollection of Tryphena Sparks. Perhaps the fictional dance of *RN*.IV.iii sprang from the same occasion. For the effect of Time's chisel, cf. *WB*.III.viii and *TL*.The Revisitation. *Thine for ever*, the opening of a C. of E. hymn.

In a Museum (*MV*), written after Hardy's visit to Exeter in 1914 or 1915 (*Life* 364/392,370/401), perhaps with this passage in mind from the beginning of the 'Equilibration' chapter in Herbert Spencer's *First Principles* (see **Spencer**): 'The impulse given by a player to a harp-string is transformed through its vibration into aerial impulses; and these, spreading on all sides, and weakening as they spread, soon cease to be perceptible, and are gradually expended in generating thermal undulations that radiate into space.' Cf. *MV*.A Kiss.

In a Whispering Gallery (*MV*). The gallery runs round the base of the dome in St Paul's Cathedral, London. The Spirit is that of St Paul (*night* is death): cf. I Cor.xv,51–5. *lacune*, empty space.

In a Wood (*WP*). The note 'From "The Woodlanders" ' which appears in some editions is inaccurate. The poem stresses a theme of the novel, and was written in 1887, when *The Woodlanders* was first published; cf. *W*.vii and **the Unfulfilled Intention**.

In Front of the Landscape (*SC*). Hardy thinks of the dead, his wife (d.1912) and parents particularly, buried in Stinsford churchyard. *a headland*, Beeny Cliff, Cornwall; *the broad brow*, Emma's (cf. *SC*.A Dream or No); *the clump*, cf. **The Dead Quire**.

In Her Precincts (*MV*). A Hardy note shows that he was thinking of the wife of Cecil Hanbury, who acquired Kingston Maurward during the 1914–18 war.

In me thou seest . . . nourished by (*WB*.III ep.), Son.73.

in posse (Lat.), potential.

In quo corriget (*JO*.II.iii), Latin (Vulgate, Psalm cxviii,9) for 'Wherewithal . . . cleanse', Psalm cxix,9.

In St Paul's a While Ago (*HS*). The MS title indicates that Hardy remembered a scene in 1869. *Beatrice and Benedick*, high-spirited lovers (as in *M.Ado*); *Jew, Damascus-bound*, cf. Acts ix,1–22; *encircling mart*, shops and business premises known as St Paul's Churchyard; *epilept enthusiast*, epileptic religious fanatic.

In shadowy thoroughfares . . . (*HE*.v), Tennyson, *In Memoriam* lxx.

In Sherborne Abbey (*HS*). Hardy's own genealogical table shows that Joseph Pitcher of Melbury Osmond eloped with and married Miss Hellier of Kay, Yeovil, in the eighteenth century. See **Sherton Abbas**.

In Tenebris (*PPP*). The MS has 'De Profundis'; these Latin titles mean 'In the darkness' and 'From the depths'. The three poems were written during the period of Hardy's deep depression after the publication of *JO*, when he realized he was losing favour in the eyes of friends, and was already condemned by his wife for manifesting his strongly critical attitude towards the Church.

I. *Epigraph,* Vulgate, Psalm ci,5; English version, Psalm cii,4, 'My heart is smitten, and withered like grass.' For 'bereavement-pain' and 'severing scene', cf. *PPP.*A Wasted Illness.

II. *Epigraph,* Vulgate, Psalm cxli,5; English version, Psalm cxlii,4. *All's well,* cf. *WP.*The Impercipient. *born out of due time,* I Cor.xv,8. *Best, First, Better, Worst* are all comparable abstractions; no autobiographical significance is intended. The linked thought may have arisen from considering a view expressed by George Eliot in *Daniel Deronda* (end of lvi): 'that thorn-pressure which must come with the crowning of the sorrowful Better, suffering because of the Worse'. That Hardy's subject is 'evolutionary optimism' is confirmed by *LLE.*Apology. The Best (the ideal, 'low-voiced'; cf. 'a delicate growth') is killed by the First, the survivals of ancient ignorance, superstition, and prejudice which cramp the enjoyment of life by 'crookedness, custom, and fear'; cf. *TL.*To Sincerity.

III. *Epigraph,* Vulgate, Psalm cxix,5–6; the English version, Psalm cxx,5–6, does not express regret for the prolongation of life, as the Latin does. *sweets . . . bitter,* cf. Rev.x,9–10.

In the British Museum (*SC*). The setting is the room housing the marbles brought from Greece (from the Parthenon ruins) by Lord Elgin. For Paul's speech on the Areopagus or Hill of Mars, see Acts xvii,16–34; cf. *PBE.*xxxvii.

In the Cemetery (*SC*), suggested probably by the removal of hundreds of graveyard coffins in London (*Life* 44–5/46–7).

In the Evening (*HS*). Frederick Treves, born in Dorchester and a friend of Hardy, rose to distinction as surgeon to the Royal family, and as an author. First President of the Society of Dorset Men in London, he was succeeded by Hardy (1908–9). The poem was written after Hardy had attended his funeral service and burial (*Life* 423,424/457). *hoar,* musty atmosphere.

In the Garden (*MV*). The sundial was at Talbothays, Mary Hardy's home. Whether the event took place (before her death) or was imagined to preserve a superstition is uncertain.

In the Marquee (*WW*), based, according to Hardy's notes, on a party at Westbourne Park Villas, where he lodged from 1863 to 1867. *getting and spending,* from Wordsworth, 'The world is too much with us' (*G.T.*).

In the morning . . . shalt see (*DR.*xi.3). Cf. **Deuteronomy, woman in.**

In the Old Theatre, Fiesole (*PPP*), near Florence; cf. *Life* 191–2/199–200. Hardy thinks of Roman coins found in Dorchester excavations.

in the scrowl . . . (*TT*.iv), Samuel Butler, *Hudibras* II.iii,429–32.

In the Servants' Quarters (*SC*). For Peter's denial of Jesus before the Crucifixion, see Mark xiv,30–72.

'In the seventies' (*MV*). *Qui deridetur . . . sicut ego*, Job xii,4, Vulgate ('I am as one mocked of his neighbour'). The poem represents the faith Emma Gifford inspired in Hardy during his early career as a novelist. For the vision, compare the boy Jude's irradiation from a glorious idea, as if from a supernatural lamp, *JO*.I.iv. *my friend*, probably Horace Moule (cf. his earlier views, *Life* 33–4/37–8); *lamp-worm*, glow-worm.

In the Vaulted Way (*TL*). The place is uncertain. The MS date 1870 suggests that the incident occurred in Cornwall at the end of Hardy's summer visit, just before his departure at Launceston, where he and Emma Gifford may have stayed with her cousins. The first published title was 'In the Crypted Way'.

in their death . . . not divided (*LLI*.8b), II Sam.i,23.

In Time of 'the Breaking of Nations' (*MV*). Life goes on much the same, despite the destiny of nations. Hardy remembered the scene of the first six lines from an observation he made at the end of the rectory garden, St Juliot, in August 1870, during the Franco-Prussian war (*Life* 78–9/81–2,378/408). For the quotation, cf. Jer.li,20.

Ina, a traditionary king of Wessex (afterwards presented as King Lear), related by Hardy to Egdon Heath (*WT*4.v; *TD*.1892 pr; *RN*.1895 pr.).

inamorato (It.), lover (masculine).

incarn, assume bodily form.

inching and pinching, by slow degrees, with difficulty.

Incrédules les plus crédules (*PBE*.xx), sceptical people are the most credulous (Pascal, *Pensées*, 816).

Indeed opine . . . very truth (*TD*.xviii), Browning, 'Easter Day' viii, in *Christmas-Eve and Easter-Day*.

indemn, indemnify.

India's coral strand (*TM*.xv), from Reginald Heber's hymn 'From Greenland's icy mountains'. For another version of the context, cf. *HS*.The Rover Come Home.

indifferentist, one who lacks religious zeal.

An Indiscretion in the Life of an Heiress (*OMC*4). This plain, economical, tragic romance was fashioned from scenes in *The Poor Man and the Lady* which had not been previously cannibalized, and published in July 1878. The general setting is vague, and the place-names are inconsistent with Hardy's Wessex plan, but the Stinsford region is clear, with Kingston Maurward House and Higher Bockhampton particularly recognisable. Egbert Mayne's disillusionment with London careerism and his return to the country are like Hardy's. The stone-laying scene (I.vii) is founded on one witnessed by Hardy at New Windsor (*Life* 48/50), and Chevron Square (II.ii) will be found in another recast passage from his first novel (*PBE*.xiv).

the Inferno, eighth chasm of (*LLI*.5.i), Malebolge, all of stone, and iron-coloured (Dante, *Inferno* xviii,1–2).

infirmity of purpose (*TM*.xi), cf. *Mac*.II.ii,52.

influent star. At one time stars were thought to influence character and destiny.

Ingenium mulicrum . . . ultro (*DR*.ix.1), 'The nature of women: when you will, they won't; when you are averse, they desire you of their own inclination'; from *Eunuchus* (IV.vii,42–3), a comedy by the Roman writer Terence.

ingress and egress (*TT*.xl). See **transit of Venus** and **external and internal contact**.

Inigo Jones (*L*.II.ii; *CM*.12.i), the first great English architect (1573–1642), notable chiefly for introducing the Palladian style (classical Roman revived by the Italian architect Palladio, 1518–80).

inions (dial.), onions.

the injured lover's hell (*FMC*.xvii), jealousy; cf. Milton, *Paradise Lost* v,449–50.

inkle, hint at, give an inkling of.

inland . . . glorious distant sea (*WP*.The Impercipient), cf. Wordsworth, 'Intimations of Immortality', 162–8 (*G.T.*).

innerds (dial.), entrails, internal parts.

The Inquiry (*TL*:At Casterbridge Fair). For Hermitage, see map C. *hurdled*, set up hurdles to enclose sheep.

Ins and Outs (*WB*.II.i; *D*1.I.iii), political ministers or parties in or out of office and power; in the government or in opposition.

The Inscription (*LLE*), suggested by one read in Hutchins and, no doubt, in Yetminster Church, relating to John Horsey (d.1531) of Clifton Maybank near Yeovil and his widowed wife. The penalty of forgoing Heaven's bliss should she marry again is fictional. *maintain the apostrophe good*, remain true to what was declared in the 'adjuration' of lines 13–14. For a more modern variant, cf. *MV*.The Memorial Brass: 186–.

Inscriptions for a Peal of Eight Bells (*HS*). This should be read as a pendant to MCR (Orel,203–17). Hardy's interest in church bells may be seen in his observations in St Peter's belfry, Dorchester, during the ringing on New Year's Eve, 1884 (*Life* 169/176). Nothing in the poem indicates any connection with this. *Peal*, a set or ring of bells tuned to each other; *canon*, cannon, the part of the bell by which it is hung.

instauration, renewal, restoration.

Instead of sweet smell . . . (*WB*.III.viii), Isa.iii,24.

Institute (*L*.I.viii), the Royal Institute of British Architects (which awarded Hardy its essay prize in 1863, *Life* 42/44,403–4/433).

insulted Nature . . . rights (*JO*.III.x), Gibbon, *Decline and Fall* xv.

Integer vitae (*TD*.xxxiv), Horace, *Odes* I.xxii, of which the first two lines are given in translation.

The Interloper (*MV*). The epigraph, added after Hardy had discussed the poem in an interview with V. H. Collins (27 Dec 1920), may have been Hardy's invention. 'Madness' is too strong a term for his wife Emma's recurrent eccentricities and contrariness. Her abnormal behaviour is recalled in Cornwall (cf. 9 Mar 1870, *Life* 75/77), at Sturminster Newton, at a fashionable dinner, and at a Max Gate celebration. *pale Form*, death (cf. Rev.vi,8); *Fourth Figure*, like the Son of God, Dan.iii,25.

Interlopers at the Knap (*WT6*). First published in May 1884, it stresses the gap between the wealth of farmers and the poverty which compelled many country people to emigrate. The climbing of the signpost to ascertain the way by night happened when Hardy's father was on his way to marry Jemima Hands at Melbury Osmond. The house had belonged to her ancestors, Childses or Swetmans (*Life* 6/10–11); cf. ii (opening) and *HS*. One Who Married Above Him.

the Interpreter's . . . well-nigh choked the Pilgrim (*W*.xxiii), at the Interpreter's house in Part I of Bunyan, *The Pilgrim's Progress*.

Intra Sepulchrum (*LLE*), 'Within the Tomb'. *tether of typic minds*, restraints of common, conventional people; *wall*, of the burial-ground; *note*, distinction.

inutile (from the French), useless, futile.

Ionic, the most important of ancient Gk. languages (before Attic).

ipsa hominis essentia (Lat.), the very essence of man.

ipso facto (Lat.), by the act itself, as a result of doing it.

the iris-bow. The association of the iris or rainbow with romantic illusion may be seen in *DR*.i.5. It is usually linked with love (*PBE*.xxxii, 'iridescence died away'; *RN*.II.iii; *TD*.xxxv, 'without irradiation'). In *W*.xvi Fitzpiers uses the 'rainbow iris' for love as a wholly subjective emotion which arises at a particular time regardless of which 'young lady' appears; the fact that it is a theory adopted by a sexual adventurer undermines his Platonic (or Shelleyan) idealism. In alliance with the artist's quest for beauty, it is entertainingly ridiculed in *WB*. Repeatedly in his fiction, but nowhere to more implicit purpose than in *FMC*, Hardy affirms that enduring love is more likely to grow when based on affection and true knowledge rather than on sudden romantic fervour. His comment of 28 Oct 1891 (*Life* 239/251) shows his detached view on the subject; it is particularly relevant to Angel Clare's idealization of Tess (cf. *TD*.xxxix ending). For the iris image and romantic love, see *PPP*.The Well-Beloved (cf. *TL*.At Waking), *MV*.Looking at a Picture on an Anniversary, *LLE*.Her Apotheosis, and *HS*.The Absolute Explains (viii–ix). As an index of illusions about nature and life, cf. *WP*.To Outer Nature, *PPP*.On a Fine Morning.

iron entered the soul (*MC*.xxxii; *L*.pr.), Psalm cv,18, in the Book of Common Prayer (C. of E.).

Isaac and Jacob, love-stories of (*HE*.xxxviii), Gen.xxiv,xxix.

Ishmaelite (*JO*.III.ii), rebel, outcast. **Ishmaelitish** (*RN*.I.i), like a wilderness; (*RN*.II.vii), like an outcast (cf. Hagar's son Ishmael, Gen.xxi,9–21).

Isis (*W*.xxix), an Egyptian divinity, mother of the sun-god; a statue of her bore an inscription, part of which read, 'My veil no one has lifted.'

Island Custom (*WB*.I.iv; native custom, I.ii), the old practice in Portland of not marrying until the woman has proved to be fertile (cf. II.xii).

Isle of Slingers (*WB*; *D*1.I.i,II.iv scene,IV.i scene), the ancient name for Portland, from its mode of defence against invaders.

Isot ma drue . . . vie (*QC* title-page). Hardy's MS title-page shows that this is quoted from Joseph Bédier's *Roman de Tristan et Iseult* (1900), 'after Gottfried of Strassburg', an early medieval poet: 'Iseult, my sweetheart and friend, in you my death, in you my life!'

Israel (*TT*.xli), Jacob, from whose sons the twelve tribes of Israel were traditionally descended; he is addressing his son Joseph, Gen.xlvi,30. **Israel** (the Israelites), **labour in Egypt** (*RN*.IV.ii; *JO*.I.iv), cf. Exod.v. **Israel in Zin** (*RN*.II.vii), Num.xx,1–5. **Israel-like, made to wander** (*D3*.I.ix), in the wilderness after deliverance from Egypt, Exod.xivff.

'It never looks like summer' (*MV*). Cf. **The Figure in the Scene**. A note on the drawing of the scene by Hardy suggests that the words of the title were Emma's at the time (22 Aug 1870); he remembered them in *DR*.xv.3. The ending alludes to her death.

It shall . . . not divine (*TL*.A Dream Question ep.), Mic.iii,6.

It's hame . . . countree! (*MC*.viii). Though four of the lines are in 'Hame, Hame, Hame' by Allan Cunningham, this probably originated from a Jacobite song by an unknown author (written, or imagined sung, by a Scottish exile after the defeat of Bonnie Prince Charlie). *Annan Water*, a river in SW Scotland.

***Ivanhoe*, the most unreal portions of** (*PBE*.xv), Scott's novel (1820).

I've lost my love . . . I sowed the seeds of love . . . (*FMC*.xxiii). The first is untraced; the second, from the song 'The Seeds of Love', possibly by Mrs F. Habergham (c. 1689).

Ivel or **Ivell** (*W*.xl; *GND*.1,6,7; *LLI*.3,4; *WP*.San Sebastian; *TL*. The Homecoming), Yeovil, Somerset (Ivel is the old name for the Yeo river). **Ivel-chester** (*TL*.A Trampwoman's Tragedy), Ilchester (also on the Yeo), north of Yeovil.

The Ivy-Wife (*WP*). Cf. the paragraph of the Unfulfilled Intention (*W*.vii), which ends, 'and the ivy slowly strangled to death the promising sapling'.

Ixion, adj; **Ixionian**. For attempting to seduce Hera, wife of Zeus, he was chained eternally to a revolving wheel in Hell (Greek mythology).

J

jack, the smaller bowl which serves as a mark for players to aim at in the game of bowls. **jack, literary**, common writer. **jacks**

(*D*1.I.ii), mechanical creatures, puppets.

Jack Ketch (*HE*.xliv), executioner of the Duke of Monmouth (1685), and notoriously barbarous to his victims; cf. *Life* 126/129.

jack-lantern, jack o' lanthorn, a flitting gleam in marshy tracts (the fen-light, *D*2.IV.viii), said to be caused by marsh gas; known also as the will-o'-the-wisp and *ignis fatuus* because it misled night-travellers, who thought it a lantern light carried by one who knew his way through marshy country.

jack-o'-clock, a mechanical human figure which appears on some church towers just before the clock strikes, and appears to be responsible for the chime. See *D*1.Fore Scene for Hardy's metaphorical application of it to mankind.

jack-o'-lent, numskull, butt (from a puppet stuffed with straw which was set up to be pelted for recreation during Lent).

Jack-rag, Jack-straw, an ordinary man, common fellow.

Jack's bean-stalk (*RN*.VI.i; *L*.III.x). In the fairy-tale it grew up overnight to reach the land of the giants; (*LLI*.6.ii), **the money-bag of the giant whom Jack slew**.

Jacob, house and lineage of (*L*.V.xi), the Chosen People, here used sarcastically of the de Stancys, cf. I Chron.xvi,13; **in Padan-Aram** (*MC*.xvii), Gen.xxviii,1–2 and xxx,25–43; **Jacob's Ladder** (*L*.V.vii; *TD*.xlviii), Gen.xxviii,10–12; **Jacob . . . Rachel** (*FMC*.xlix), Gen. xxix,4–28.

Jacobean, of the reign of James I, early seventeenth century.

Jael and Sisera (*DR*.xix.4; *PBE*.xi; *PPP*.The Respectable Burgher; *WW*.The Clasped Skeletons), Judg.iv,13–23.

jamb (arch.) the side of a door or window.

James, G. P. R. (*PBE*.xv), author of historical romances, 1801–60.

Jansen (*L*.I.iii,VI.v), Cornelis Janssen, a Dutch portrait-painter (1593–c.1664) who lived in England until 1643, and died in Amsterdam.

A January Night (*MV*). At Tooting; cf. *Life* 124/127–8.

Jaques (*CM*.12.viii), cf. *AYL*.II.v,1–12.

Jared, Mahalaleel . . . (*RN*.II.vi). These 'antediluvians' (before the Flood) include Methuselah; they each lived more than eight or nine hundred years.

Jarnvid wood (*W*.vii), an iron wood in Norse mythology; cf. Matthew Arnold, 'Balder Dead' iii,335–7.

javelin-men, men carrying spears or pikes in a sheriff's retinue and acting as the judge's escort at the assizes.

jaw (colloquial), criticize, reprimand.

Jealousy is cruel as the grave (*PBE*.xxxviii ep.), Sol.viii,6.
Jehovah . . . mercy . . . sacrifice (*W*.xvii), cf. Matt.ix,13. **Jehovah**, Yahweh, the Old Testament god of the Jews.
Jeremy Taylor . . . Newman (*JO*.IV.iii), eminent theological writers from the seventeenth to the nineteenth century, including Joseph **Butler** and Philip **Doddridge**, a Nonconformist.
Jericho, flat as (*L*.v.xii) and **Jericho shout** (*TT*.vii), Josh.vi,1–20; **(wish . . .) at Jericho**, miles away; **(blown) to Jericho**, miles off.
Jeroboam, house (i.e. family and lineage) **of** (*JO*.v.iv), ruler of the new kingdom of Israel, I Kings xii-xiv.
jerry-go-nimble (dial.), circus.
Jerusalem . . . festival (*JO*.VI.i), Christminster, with the analogy of the Passover festival followed by the Crucifixion; cf. Matt.xxvi,2ff. Model of (*JO*.II.v), see **Mount Moriah,** etc. **Jerusalem, new** (*JO*.I.iii), cf. Rev.iii,12 and xxi,2,10ff.
jest (dial.), just.
the Jesuit (*L*.III.iv), Cardinal Mazarin (1602–61), a French minister who knew how to gain and retain power.
jeune premier (Fr.), leading part (in a play) as a young lover.
Jezreel (*LLE*.Jezreel), thoughts of its Old Testament history and of the town's capture by General Allenby in the 1914–18 war; see *Letters* v,282–3 and (for its site) **Panthera**; *Tishbite*, I Kings xxi,17–29; *drove furiously*, Jehu, II Kings ix,20; *Tyrian woman* (from Tyre or Sidon? cf. I Kings xvi,31), see II Kings ix,30–7, on the death of Jezebel; *'Is it peace?'*, II Kings ix,18.
jib-door (*D2*.II.ii), a door flush with, and indistinguishable from, the wall in which it stands (cf. *HE*.xlvi).
jill, girl, lass, wench; **Jill**, any common or ordinary girl; **Jill-o'-the-Wisp** (*WB*.II.i), elusive creature (cf. 'will-o'-the-wisp').
jim-crack, gimcrack; mechanical contrivance.
jine (local pronunciation), join. **jints**, (local pronunciation), joints.
jineral man (dial.), servant with general responsibilities, handyman.
A Jingle on the Times. This satirical poem (uncollected) was written in December 1914 in aid of the Arts Fund, at a time of heavy fighting in France and Belgium.
jinks (usually 'high jinks'), frolics, pranks.
Job, as poor as (*HE*.Sequel), cf. Job i,21 (after losing his wealth); **Job . . . covenant . . . maid** (*RN*.VI.iii), Job xxxi,1; **Job . . . curse . . . birth** (*MC*.xii,xl; *PPP*.The Respectable Burgher), Job iii,1–3; **Job, patience of** (*JO*.v.ii), despite degradation, depression, and

provocation he retains his faith; **Job said . . . younger . . . derision** (*JO*.I.ii), Job xxx,1.

John Barleycorn, personification of the corn from which malted liquors such as whisky are made; cf. Burns's ballad 'John Barleycorn'.

John of Gaunt (1340–99), Duke of Lancaster and son of Edward III (*GND*2); his name indicates his birthplace (Ghent, in Belgium).

John the Baptist (*RN*.III.ii), Matt.iii.

Johnson, Dr Samuel (1709–84). Boswell describes his great coat (*FMC*.i) as wide, with pockets almost large enough to hold the two folio volumes of his dictionary. He was a student at Pembroke College, Oxford (*JO*.VI.ix).

join up (dial.), mend, heal.

jonnick (dial.), honest, agreeable.

Joseph Andrews (PRF), a novel by Henry Fielding (1742) which begins as a burlesque of the virtuous heroine of Richardson's *Pamela*.

Joseph, brethren at the avowal of (*MC*.xix), when Joseph in Egypt, after becoming Pharoah's overseer, reveals himself to the brothers who had sold him to the Ishmaelites, Gen.xlv,3 and xxxvii; **the chief butler did not remember Joseph** (PRF), Gen.xl,23; **Joseph the dreamer** (*JO*.IV.i), cf. Gen.xxxvii,5–10; **who knew not Joseph** (*TT*.xli; *WB*.III.viii), those of the succeeding generation, Exod.i,8.

Josephus, a history of the Jews by Flavius Josephus, a Jew of the first century AD.

Joshua's . . . moon (*PPP*.Zermatt: To the Matterhorn), Josh.x,12–14.

Joshua's trumpets (*PPP*.The Respectable Burgher). See **Jericho**.

jot or tittle (PRF), the smallest trace, Matt.v,18.

Jötuns (*MC*.xi, *CM*6), giants in Norse mythology.

journeyman, employee (paid by the day; cf. Fr. *journée*).

Journeys end in lovers meeting (*PBE*.xi ep.), *TN*.II.iii,42, from the song 'O mistress mine' (*G.T.* 'Carpe Diem').

Jove, another name for Jupiter, chief of the Roman gods; he wielded thunderbolts, and engaged in countless amours (*L*.I.xv).

jowl, cheek, face (side view).

jown (dial.), damn. **Jown it** (from 'Drown it'? Cf. **Chok it all!**).

joy in heaven (over this repentant sinner, *MC*.xl), Luke xv,7.

Joyous Gard (*QC*.xix), the estate given by King Arthur to Sir Lancelot for defending the Queen's honour; cf. *QC*.i.

Joys of Memory (*MV*). The 'certain day' may be 7 March, when Hardy began his first journey to St Juliot, but this was hardly spring; cf. *SC*.'When I set out for Lyonnesse'.

Jubilate (*MV*). The title refers to the opening of Psalm c ('O be joyful'). The MS 'Mellstock Ridge' confirms that the scene for this fantasy is Stinsford churchyard. *Urim and Thummin*, objects worn on the Jewish high priest's breastplate for divining God's will (cf. Exod.xxviii,15–21,30); *Eden New*, a hymn tune; *in Little-Ease*, on earth (cf. *WP*.Friends Beyond).

The Jubilee of a Magazine (*SC*), the golden jubilee of *The Cornhill Magazine*, where the poem appeared in January 1910. Hardy refers to the new cover-design by Godfrey Sykes; for his thought, cf. *Life* 389/–. *seedlip*, a box or basket for carrying corn to be sown by hand; *steel-roped plough*, drawn up and down by two traction-engines, one at each end of the field.

Judah (*D2*.III.ii), rebellious and threatened by prophets; cf. the headings of Isa.i, and Jer.xiii,9,19.

Judas Iscariot, the disciple who betrayed Jesus; contrasting with John (*FMC*.i); and the trial of his master (*RN*.v.i). See Matt.xxvi,14ff and xxvii,1–5.

Jude. See **Fawley**.

Jude the Obscure originated from a suicidal story which came to Hardy in April 1888, on a young man 'who could not go to Oxford' (*Life* 207–8/216). It developed on the educational side after the news of his cousin Tryphena's death in March 1890 (see the preface). Later a worsening of his own marital relations changed the bias of the novel, giving it a contrasting emphasis between the more spiritual and the physical when he became infatuated with Mrs Henniker. In preparation for his work Hardy visited training-colleges for teachers in 1891, Whitelands giving him an impression of girls as the weaker sex, the other being Stockwell where Tryphena had been trained. (Hardy's main impressions came from his sisters' teacher-training experiences at Salisbury, Kate feeling so hostile that she did not mind if Tom published 'how badly we were used'. The period Hardy gives for the story is 1860–70. In October 1892 he visited Great Fawley ('Marygreen'); in June 1893, Oxford ('Christminster'). See *Life* 207–8/216, 224/234, 235/246–7, 236–7/248, 250–1/265, 257/272–3, 433/467. The novel did not get under way, after a change in the opening, until 1894; and, like *Tess*, it was hampered by the preparation of two versions, one emasculated for serialization.

The title for this was first 'The Simpletons', then 'Hearts Resurgent'. The novel was not finished until March 1895, appearing in book form on 1 November (post-dated 1896; cf. *Life* 269–70/286–8). The Calvary or Crucifixion theme, recurrently stressed in the concluding stages, explains 'Christminster'. The distant 'New Jerusalem' (suggested by Rebekah Owen) proves delusive; merged with Tennyson's Camelot symbolism (in *Idylls of the King*), it opposes light and music and idealism to sensuality which is imaged in porcine terms. The tragic irony of bells and music, one Sue episode (after wading through the river), and features of Father Time, were suggested by Sarah Grand's *The Heavenly Twins*, which Hardy read soon after its appearance in 1893. Mrs Henniker's High Church imperviousness to Hardy's radical religious views provided his major satirical thrust; he conceived Sue as the intellectually enfranchised woman (*Letters* II,23–4), but tragedy overwhelms her (partly through hereditary factors culminating in Father Time), destroys her reason, and makes her a fearful victim to superstitious Church orthodoxy. Jude remains stronger in the crisis, but he is deluded into thinking that his marriage with Sue is sanctified by nature. Their affinities are exceptional, but they are physically incompatible. By sexual submission to Jude (initiated by jealousy) Sue sins against her nature or instinct; emotionally distraught by the loss of her children, she thinks she has sinned against God. The heterodox views which she and Jude share on marriage and community responsibility for children (v.iii) may have occurred to Hardy as desiderata, but at the time they were those of simpletons, as he knew. Bitter experience made him think of matrimony as an 'iron contract', sanctified by the Church with licence to love 'on the premises'; it revived the Swinburnian dream of Greek joyousness (v.v). Hardy's critical charge is against an unenlightened Church, represented at its darkest in Christminster, with police acting as regulators of the law. Living reality is found outside the walls of an Establishment which judges by the letter or rubric, and is befogged by Tractarian supernaturalism. For the bishop who burnt his copy of *Jude*, and the lady who, 'having shuddered at the book' in a review (*JO*.ps. to pr), wished to make Hardy's acquaintance, see *Life* 277–8/294–5 and 279–81/296–8.

judges across the Atlantic (*MC*.pr), Rebekah Owen and her sister, two Americans who came to England (where they settled) and cultivated Hardy's friendship for a period. Rebekah's plea for the restoration of most of xliv (which occurred in the 1895 edition) was supported by her friend Miss Drisler in New York (Carl J. Weber, *Hardy and the Lady from Madison Square*, Waterville, Maine, 1952, pp. 33,59,64–6,86,110).

Judgment, judgment (the day of), the day of the final reckoning before God; cf. Matt.x,15 and xxv,31–46.

Juggernaut (*FMC*.xl), an unrelenting threat of death (like the Juggernaut, the enormous chariot of Krishna, beneath the wheels of which fanatical Hindu worshippers were said to seek salvation by death).

Julian, Christopher (*HE*). His forename shows Hardy's sympathy with this minor hero; it was the name his parents first thought of giving Hardy.

Julian the Apostate (*JO*.II.iii), a Roman emperor of the fourth century who gave up his Christianity and tried to re-establish paganism; **the chapter dealing with** his **reign** is the 23rd of Gibbon's *Decline and Fall*. In the quotation which follows Swinburne uses the dying words attributed to him, 'Vicisti Galilaee'.

Juliet (*HE*.xviii), cf. *RJ*.II.i,93–106.

Jumping-jack, Jumping-jill, puppets, toy figures (of man, woman) manipulated by strings. The **Jumping Jill** of *WB*.II.i is directed by the goddess (Lat. *Dea*) Aphrodite.

jumps (noun, dial.), stays.

junk, lump, chunk.

junketing, feasting, merrymaking.

Juno, queen of heaven in Roman mythology. **Juno's bird . . . Argus eyes** (*MC*.xlii), the peacock. Argus had a hundred eyes, of which only two ever slept. When he was slain, Juno placed his eyes in the peacock's tail.

jury (with reference to parts of ships), temporary, makeshift.

Justice . . . balances . . . wanting (*FMC*.lv), Dan.v,27.

justify the ways . . . men (*HE*.ii), cf. Milton, *Paradise Lost* i,26.

Justin Martyr . . . Jerome (on baptism, *L*.I.vii): **Justin Martyr**, one of the Fathers of the Church, martyred about the year 165; **Irenaeus**, one of the Greek Christian Church, a missionary bishop of the second century ('For he came to save all in his own person; all, I say, who through him are reborn in God, *infants*, very young boys, boys, and youths'); **Wall**, theologian, 1647–1728; **Tertullian**, Carthaginian theologian, c.160–220;

Cyprian, Bishop of Carthage in the third century; **Naziansen**, St Gregory of Naziansus in Cappadocia, bishop and theologian of the fourth century; **Chrysostom**, made Archbishop of Constantinople in 398; **Jerome**, the most learned and eloquent of the Latin Fathers of the Church (see **St Jerome**).

juties (abnormal pronunciation) duties.

juvinals, juveniles.

K

Kalpe (*D*1.II.i), Calpe, the classical name for Gibraltar.

Kamtschatka, eastern Siberia, on the other side of the world.

Karnac, avenues of (*MC*.xx), columns among the ruins of Karnak, part of ancient Thebes, Egypt.

Kaytes (*UGT*.I.ii), Keats (local pronunciation). A Keats family (with a tranter business) lived below the Hardys during the period of the novel; see **The House of Hospitalities**.

keacorn (dial.), windpipe, throat.

Keats and **too happy happiness** (*FMC*.xxiii), John Keats (1795–1821), 'Ode to a Nightingale' (*G.T.*); house where he died (*WB*.III.i); where buried, see **Rome: At the Pyramid of Cestius . . . .** See also **At a House in Hampstead** and **At Lulworth Cove a Century Back**.

Kedar, **tents of** (*DR*.xiv,4), Sol.i,5.

ken (archaic), know; sight, viewing-distance, gaze, knowledge, understanding.

Ken, Bishop (1637–1711), the 'saintly author' and 'gentle-voiced prelate' (*JO*.II.i). See **Barthélémon at Vauxhall** and **The Chapel-Organist**.

Kenilworth (PRF, where Hardy says that 'no historian's Queen Elizabeth was ever so perfectly a woman' as the fictitious queen of Scott's novel).

kennel, gutter.

Kennetbridge (*JO*), Newbury, on the Kennet river, Berkshire.

kern (vb.), set (of fruit, after pollination).
kerseymere, twilled fine woollen cloth.
ketch, a strongly built two-masted vessel.
kex (dial.), dry hollow stalk of cow-parsnip or cow-parsley.
kick up Bob's a dying, make a great to-do or fuss.
kidney, sort, class, nature.
King Arthur . . . sons (*UGT*.IV.ii), a miller, a weaver, and a tailor. See *Letters* I,198–9.
The king called down . . . (*RN*.I.iii), from the ballad known variously as 'Queen Eleanor's Confession', 'Earl Marshall', and 'The Jovial Crew'.
King Edward 'the Martyr' (*JO*.IV.i), assassinated at Corfe Castle in 978, and buried at Shaftesbury.
King George's watering-Place (*WT*2), Weymouth, where George III often resided in the summer.
King Lemuel (*TD*.xxxix), Prov.xxxi, on the virtuous woman.
King Norman's day (*TD*.iv). Durbeyfield's memory is confused; he means that his ancestors go back as far as the 'renowned knight who came from Normandy with William the Conqueror' (*TD*.i) in 1066.
Kingcreech. See **Kingscreech**, which seems more probable by derivation and from its adoption in F. E. Hardy's limited edition (though both forms occur in the MS copy and the first published version; cf. **Old Mrs Chundle**).
The King's Experiment (*PPP*). For a parallel which Hardy must have known (cf. *Life* 327/351), see George Crabbe's 'The Lover's Journey', which begins

> It is the Soul that sees: the outward eyes
> Present the object, but the Mind descries.

King Doom: cf. **Doom and She**.
King's Hintock (*WT*6; *GND*.1; *TD*.xix,liv; *CM*.10; PPP.Her Late Husband), Melbury Osmond, to which Hardy's mother's family belonged. Some of his ancestors, the Swetmans (associated with a very dubious tradition concerning the Duke of Monmouth), had lived at Townsend, on the Melbury Park side of the village, the grand fictional name of which arises from its proximity to Melbury House ('King's Hintock Court').
King's Hintock Court (*W*.xix; *GND*.1; *CN*.10; *TL*.Autumn in King's Hintock Park), Melbury House, situated in a large park 13 m.

NW of Dorchester. Founded mainly in the sixteenth century, it belonged to the Strangways. One of their heirs by marriage, Stephen Fox (see **Reynard** and **Dornell, Betty**), gained the King's favour, and became the first Earl of Ilchester. See **the Hintocks**.

A King's Soliloquy (*SC*). Hardy watched Edward VII's funeral procession in May 1910 (*Life* 350/377). *book and bell*, ritual; the medieval phrase 'bell and book' alluded to the Mass. *That*, the Immanent Will.

King's Stag (*TL*.A Trampwoman's Tragedy; *HS*.A Last Journey), the old inn and hamlet in Blackmoor Vale, $4\frac{1}{2}$ m. WSW of Sturminster Newton. The name recalls the semi-legendary story (*TD*.ii) which gave the Vale the name of the Forest of White Hart.

Kingsbere (*FMC*.1; *RN*.I.v; *TM*.xxvi,xxvii; *TD*, where **sub-Greenhill** means below **Greenhill**; *PPP*.The Well-Beloved), Bere Regis, where King John often stayed. Part of the manor estate passed into the hands of descendants of the Turbervilles who came over at the time of the Norman Conquest. The church contains the Turberville Chapel.

Kingscreech (*OMC*.1), named from Kingston and Creech Barrow; the given distances suggest Church Knowle. See map D.

Kingston Maurward House (*UGT*.I.iv, 'the Manor'; *MV*.An Anniversary, In Her Precincts; *HS*.The Harvest-Supper). See **Knapwater House** and **Tollamore**; for 'The Harvest-Supper' cf. *Life* 19–20/24–5 and *FMC*.xxxvi. Kingston Park extended north to the Puddletown road, and a path from Stinsford to Higher Bockhampton crossed it.

kip (dial.), keep.

kit (*MC*.xxxix), small fiddle.

Kitto, Dr (deaf). Hardy gained his information (*RN*.II.i) from Herbert Spencer's *Principles of Biology*, 1864.

Kleber, General (*L*.v.i), Kléber, a commander in the French army during the Revolution and under Napoleon; born at Strasbourg (Germ. Strassburg) in 1753.

knap, a hillock.

Knapwater House (*DR*), Kingston Maurward House, Stinsford. Hardy's name gives its setting, on a hill above a lake. Lora Grey, the last of the Greys who had lived at the old Tudor manor house near the farm, married George Pitt, who had the new manor built, and ruined himself (according to tradition) having it faced with stone, because George III regretted it was built in brick; see **Enckworth Court**.

knee-naps, leather pads worn over the knees by thatchers.

Kneller, a portrait-painter of German origin (c.1649–1723) who came to England (*PBE*.v; **Sir Godfrey**, *L*.I.iii,VI.v).

Knight, Henry (*PBE*). There were many Knights related to the Hardys at Stinsford in the eighteenth century. In his professional role, he may owe something to Horace Moule, Hardy's friend and adviser, but in some respects he is not unlike Hardy; his portrait at thirty (xiii) resembles Hardy's at the same age, and the reading of the church-lesson (xix) is autobiographical. In his illusory expectation of innocence in the loved one, he bears some resemblance to Angel Clare.

Knights Hospitallers (*TD*.i), military monks of the order of St John of Jerusalem, who cared for pilgrims in the Holy Land.

knit hands and beat the ground (*D*2.IV.vi), Milton, *Comus*,143.

knock about, rove from place to place. **knock in**, consume.

Knollingwood Hall (*GND*2), St Giles's House, Wimborne St Giles, near Cranborne (Knowlton and Knoll Hill are near).

Knollsea (*HE*), Swanage, where the Hardys lived in 1875–6.

knop, bud, protuberance, knob.

knot, problem, knotty question. 'The Knot there's no Untying' (*UGT*.v.i title; *FMC*.xxiv), from Campbell's poem 'How delicious is the winning' (*G.T.*).

Knox, John (c.1513–72), Scottish Calvinist reformer (*L*.I.iv); addressing Mary Queen of Scots (*FMC*.xxvi).

Kranion (Gk.), 'the place of a skull' (*TL*.Panthera; *LLE*.The Wood Fire), Golgotha. For this and the Crucifixion, see Matt.xxvii, 33–8.

L

La Belle Dame sans Merci (*PBE*.vii,xxxi), pacing steed . . . love thee true: see the poem by Keats with this title (*G.T.*).

la jalousie rétrospective (*CM*.12.xvii), jealousy in retrospect.

labour of love (*GND*3), I Thess.i,3.

Lachesis, a Greek fate who spun the thread of life.

lackaday, careless, indifferent, lackadaisical.

The Lacking Sense (*PPP*). Cf. Nature 'red in tooth and claw' (Tennyson, *In Memoriam* lvi). *Waddon Vale*, south of the chalk hills running west from Ridgeway to Portesham (map G). *weaves . . . world-webs*, linking cause and effect throughout the universe, including 'the great web of human doings' (*W*.iii). *plods dead-reckoning on*, in a blind, automatic process.

Lackland, John (*LLI*.8 Introduction, prologues, and conclusion; cf. *LLE*.Welcome Home). Named after King John (surnamed Lackland), he is an uprooted person, with no land or country which is any longer his home. Hardy probably had in mind White Lackington, which is part of his 'Longpuddle'.

Lady Day, Old Style (DLa; *TD*.xlii,li–ii). Lady Day, the feast of the Annunciation (i.e. of the conception of Jesus, announced by the angel Gabriel to the virgin Mary, Luke i,26–33) has always been on 25 March, nine months before Christmas. Farmers kept to the old calendar by making the operative day when recently engaged employees started work with them Lady Day, Old Style, i.e. 6 April. See **Old Style**.

The Lady Icenway (*GND*5). See **Icenway, Lord**.

The Lady in the Furs (*WW*). First published as 'The Lady in the Christmas Furs' when city shops were displaying them for sale (4 Dec 1926). Hardy's altruism extended to all life, and the irony for him was that goods derived from slaughter were fashionable gifts at the season which proclaims peace on earth.

Lady Mottisfont (*GND*4). Ashley Down and Mottisfont Priory, north of Romsey, Hampshire, supplied Sir Ashley Mottisfont's name. Deansleigh is Broadlands (formerly home of Lord Palmerston), 1 m. south of Romsey; Fernell Hall is most probably Embley (once the home of Florence Nightingale), 2 m. to the west. For the Contessa, cf. *Life* 194–5/202–3.

The Lady Penelope (*GND*8) relates to Wolfeton House, in the parish of Charminster near Dorchester, and the marriages of Lady Penelope Darcy; see **Drenghard**. Her second husband was Sir John Gage; her third, Sir William Hervey.

Lady Susan (1743–1827). Daughter of the first Earl of Ilchester (see **Reynard**), she created a scandal when she eloped in 1764 with the handsome Irish comedian William O'Brien (1738–1815), whom she met at Holland House in London. After a period in

America and elsewhere, they retired to Stinsford House, where Hardy's father recalled seeing her. Hardy's grandfather constructed the vault for the interment of both in Stinsford Church. See *Life* 9/13–14,163–4/170,250/264; *WP*.Friends Beyond; *TL*.The Noble Lady's Tale.

Lady Teazle . . . (*PBE*.xvii), Sheridan, *The School for Scandal* IV.iii.

Lady Vi (*HS*). This satire of the upper classes is typical of Hardy's early fiction; cf. *Life* 61–2/62–3, on *The Poor Man and the Lady*, a scene from which, in Rotten Row, was adapted to *PBE*.xiv. Here the satire combines with condemnation of blood-sports, big-game hunting in Africa and India, fox-hunting at home. *Vi*, Violet; *wend*, change of direction.

lady-chapel, a chapel to our Lady (the Virgin Mary) attached to a large church or cathedral.

Lambeth, part of central London, on the south side of the Thames; (*CM*.12.xii) Lambeth Palace, residence of the Archbishop of Canterbury, head of the Anglican Church.

Lambing Corner (*CM7*), towards the upper end of Clatford Bottom in the downs 2 m. west of Marlborough and north of the Bristol road.

Lambing-Down Gate (*FMC*.viii), probably on the hills north of Puddletown.

lamiger (dial.), cripple.

Lammas, Lammas-tide, 1 August, an early C. of E. harvest festival day.

lammicken, lammocken (dial.), ungainly, slouching, clumsy.

lanch, lanchet. See **lynchet**.

land of darkness . . . (*DR*.xiv.3), Job x,22.

Landwehr (Germ.), men called up for military service only in war-time.

Langdon (*TD*.xiii). Richard Langdon (d.1803) was a cathedral organist and hymn-tune composer. His only composition to attain wide circulation was a double chant in F major. (Whereas a single chant is a tune for one verse of a psalm, a double chant is for two.) Hardy gave Mrs Gertrude Bugler a copy of what appears to be only the first part of it, inscribing it 'Langdon in F'. It is in the major key, and she found in an old hymnal that it was sung to Psalm xxv (metrical version), the opening words of which fit Tess's situation perfectly; 'To God in whom I trust, I lift my heart and voice; O let me not be put to shame, Nor let my foes rejoice. Those who on thee rely, Let no disgrace attend;

Be that the shameful lot of such As wilfully offend.'

langterloo (*W*.x), an early form of loo, a gambling card-game.

Laocoön (*MC*.xii; *JO*.II.vii), the Trojan priest who was squeezed to death by sea-serpents, after attempting to save his children from them; his struggle, the subject of a famous sculpture in the Vatican, is described in the second book of the *Aeneid*.

A Laodicean appeared in monthly instalments from December 1880 to December 1881. Thirteen chapters were concluded by October 1880 when Hardy fell ill; the remainder was dictated to Mrs Hardy and completed in May 1881, at Upper Tooting. From a historical novel (*TM*) Hardy had turned to a modern subject, the clash of old and new values in an age of science and industrial technology, of aristocratic effeteness and enterprising plutocracy. With an architect as hero (affording him ample opportunity to draw from his own professional background), he develops a love-story which turns on intrigue and travelogues, the latter based on holidays in Rhineland, Holland, and Normandy (*Life* 110/113–14,120–1/124,138–9/142–3). Paedobaptismal arguments and the garden-party at Stancy Castle are also recollections (*Life* 29–30/33–5,128/131). Again (as in *TM*), though briefly, Hardy resorted to plagiarism: the offending passage, on Sir William de Stancy as a horse-racing 'star' (I.v), was subsequently revised, reduced, and veiled with dialect; his old aristocartic platitudes were influenced by those of **Gracian**. Whatever the merits of the story in which the heroine is attractively presented and suspense is sustained, its humour is thin and limited; its central theme fails to infuse the novel as a whole. 'Transitional' in the opening paragraph provides a key, illustrated by the utilitarian design of the redbrick Nonconformist chapel in contrast with the splendours of Gothic art, by aptly named Power's feat of engineering, the railway tunnel, and Stancy Castle. Hardy finds romance in 'science, steam, and travel' (I.xii; cf. *LLE*.After a Romantic Day; his thoughts in this direction may have been stimulated by the opening paragraph of George Eliot's *Daniel Deronda*, Book III); he illustrates it in his description of the telegraph wire (I.ii). Tradition and modern trends create Paula's indecisiveness or Laodiceanism; in the same way architecture and poetry, art and science, present a dichotomy which Hardy feels must be integrated. To achieve such integration of the emotional life and the intellectual, of the romantic past and contemporary technology, one needs to develop what Arnold calls the **imaginative reason.**

Laodicean lukewarmness (*UGT*.II.iv; *FMC*.i; *L*.title), Rev.iii, 13–15; verses 15–17 quoted, *L*.I.ii.

Laon and Cythna (*JO*.IV.iv), the hero and heroine lovers in Shelley's *The Revolt of Islam*.

larry, noisy celebration, lark, commotion, disturbance.

The Last Chrysanthemum (*PPP*). *retrocede*, recede, draw back. *Great Face*, the Creator or First Cause, masked by, or immanent in, Nature.

Last Day luridness, (*TD*.xxxiv), the end of the world (Zeph.i,14–18) and the day of judgment (John xii,48).

the last infirmity of (a) noble mind (*DR*.ii.4; *HE*.xxxvi), desire of fame, cf. Milton, 'Lycidas',71 (*G.T.*).

The Last Leaf (*HS*), a fancy woven round the memory of Emma Hardy's death (27 Nov 1912).

The Last Performance (*MV*). See **Lost Love**.

The Last Signal (*MV*). See **Barnes**. The path Hardy follows is from Max Gate to Conygar Hill. The funeral procession is from the rectory on the Wareham road; afterwards it would turn off along a by-road 'athwart the land' beyond the hill-slope to Barnes's church at Winterborne Came. Hardy was on his way to the funeral service (11 Oct 1886).

Last Supper (*D*3.III.i), of Jesus and his disciples, Luke xxii,14ff.

Last Words to a Dumb Friend (*LLE*). This was the cat Snowdove, killed on the railway below Max Gate not long before the lines were written.

Late Lyrics and Earlier (1922). This volume is notable for its preface, in which Hardy defends himself against the charge of pessimism. The first paragraph of this *apologia* gives a chronological summary of the poems, and Hardy is right, though severe, in admitting that the former freshness of his poetry – not evident at the outset – is 'now unattainable'; the general level is still high, but a slight decline is felt. A lighter note is supplied in songs on general subjects. Recollections of Emma are still prominent, and the main source of his inspiration.

Latimer, Will (*WT*7.v–vii), the actual name of such an officer, according to Hardy, who thought he was buried at Osmington (3 m. NE of Weymouth).

Latin cross, with the lower limb longer than the others.

laugh . . . to scorn (*DR*.xiii.8), Job xxii,19, and *Mac*.IV.i,79.

Laura (*WB*.I.vii). See **Petrarch** for the allusion.

Lausanne (*PPP*). See *Life* 294–5/312–13, where Hardy quotes the passage from Milton's *The Doctrine and Discipline of Divorce* which gave him the last two lines. He could appreciate Edward Gibbon's elegant sarcasms at the expense of the fifth-century Christian Church in chapters 15–16 of *The Decline and Fall of the Roman Empire*, 1776–88.

lave, washing; wash, bale or draw water.

Laveleye, Émile de (DLa), a Belgian Socialist writer, 1822–92.

layers-out, those who prepare a body for burial.

Lazarus coming from the tomb (*RN*.v.ix), John xi,1–44. The description was suggested by **Sebastiano** del Piombo's picture.

lazy-tongs (*L*.v.ii), a complicated mechanism with many pairs of levers crossing scissor-fashion, for picking up objects at a distance.

Le Chant du Départ (*D*1.III.iii), The Departure Song (Fr.).

Le point du jour . . . (*R*N.IV.ii). Clym Yeobright sings a song he learnt in Paris, on dawn: the cheerfulness it brings to nature, and the sorrow it causes the shepherd when he leaves his loved one. The song is from Étienne's comic opera *Gulistan*, 1805, which was revived in 1844.

Lead, kindly light . . . (*FMC*.lvi), J. H. Newman's hymn; cf. *Life* 274–5/290–1.

leaden-eyed despairs (*DR*.iii.2), Keats, 'Ode to a Nightingale' (*G.T.*).

leading-strings, for holding children when they learn to walk.

leads, strips of lead on rather flat roofs; leaden milk-pans.

Leahs . . . Rachel (the desired one: *TD*.xxiii), cf. Gen.xxix.

Leave thou thy sister . . . (*TD*.xxvii), Tennyson, *In Memoriam* xxxiii.

A Leaving (*HS*). Emma Hardy's hearse leaves Max Gate (30 Nov 1912); the 'journey afar' implies death.

leaze, meadow-land. **leazings**, bundles of gleaned corn.

Leddenton (*JO*.IV.iv), Gillingham, 4 m. NW of Shaftesbury. The fictional name is from the neighbouring Leddon river, a tributary of the Stour; the actual name is given to the schoolmaster.

leer, **leery**, empty, hungry, exhausted, faint.

leetle (local pronunciation), little.

Leghorn hat, plaited with straw from Leghorn, Italy.

legitimate (drama: *HE*.xxii), traditional, normal, as opposed to the drama of illegal theatres in the eighteenth century.

leg-wood, consisting of tree branches.

Leicesters, a hornless, long-woolled breed of sheep.

Leipzig (*WP*). For the battle, see *D*3.III.i-v, where six stanzas of the poem are included. The One is Napoleon, the three ('trine') are the allied forces of Russia, Prussia, and Austria. *prow*, valiant; *swords to ploughshares*, cf. Isa.ii,3–4; *prime*, period of highest excellence; *Elster-Strom*, the river Elster.

Leland, John (*RN*.I.i; *GND*5), English antiquary (c.1506–52) and author of *The Itinerary*, an account of tours in England. Hardy's quotation of the phrase Leland used to describe Newton St Loe near Bath (SE of Bristol) may have appealed to an antiquarian audience, but was not intended to locate Heymere House (see the Wessex map).

Lely, Sir Peter (*PBE*.v; *HE*.xxxviii; *L*.I.iii,VI.v; *GND*6; *JO*.III.ii), a Dutch portrait-painter (1618–80) who made his reputation in London.

Lemprière . . . Scarron . . . Bible (*JO*.III.iv). Sue had broadened her mind by resorting to the classical dictionary compiled by the British scholar John Lemprière (1788), and by reading freely in the Latin poets Catullus, Martial, and Juvenal, the Greek writer Lucian, Jacobean plays by the collaborators Beaumont and Fletcher, stories by the Italian writer Boccaccio (1313-75; author of *The Decameron*), scandals in descriptions of the Valois court by Pierre de Bourdeilles, Seigneur de Brantome (c.1530–1614), works by the French writer Paul Scarron (1610–60), and by the eighteenth-century English novelists Defoe, Sterne, Smollett, and Fielding, as well as Shakespeare and the Bible.

lerret, boat for heavy seas.

Let a beast . . . king's mess (*PBE*.ix), *Ham*.v.ii,86–7.

Let not your heart be troubled . . . Nazarene (*TD*.xxxix), said by Jesus of Nazareth, John xiv,27.

Let the day perish . . . born (*JO*.v.iii,VI.xi), Job iii,3ff.

Let there be light (*RN*.I.iii), Gen.i,3.

Let Your Light so Shine (*FMC*.viii), words (from Matt.v,16) used by the priest to initiate the offertory during the Communion service.

let-alone, disposed to give in or 'knuckle under'.

letter in the candle (*TM*.xii), indicated by a spark in the wick, according to popular superstition.

The letter killeth (*JO*.title-page,VI.viii), II Cor.iii,6.

lettre-de-cachet (Fr.), ('sealed letter', originally a warrant signed by the king of France), fiat, peremptory summons.

The Levelled Churchyard (*PPP*). While living at Wimborne, Hardy probably heard stories of what happened to graves when major restoration of the Minster took place in 1855–7; cf. MCR (Orel,207–8). The ending imitates the Church Litany.

Leveller, the grim (*FMC*.xlii), Death, from 'Death the Leveller', a lyric in a masque by James Shirley, 1659 (*G.T.*).

Levite . . . Bethlehem . . . Gibeah (*PBE*.xix), Judg.xix.

Levitical passing-by (*LLE*.Apology), in the parable of the good Samaritan, Luke x,32.

lew, lewth, shelter from wind and rain.

Lew-Everard (*TD*.xxxiv), West Stafford; the name is taken from Lewill Mill by the Frome on one side, and Frome Everard, the old name of Stafford House, on the other.

Lewgate (*UGT*.I.i; *LLI*.7 and 8 Introduction), the upper end of Higher Bockhampton, near the heath; the name was suggested, but not adopted, for the Hardy's home there. 'Lew' indicates 'sheltered'; 'gate', road or lane.

Lewsdon (i.e. Lewesdon) **Hill**; see **Molly Gone**.

Leyden jar, electric condenser invented at Leyden in Holland.

Liberty Hall (*GND*9), a place free or open to all comers.

libration, state of balance or equipoise.

Libyan bay . . . Trojans (*WT*5.iv), Virgil, *Aeneid* i,157ff.

Liddell and Scott (*WW*). H. G. Liddell and R. S. Scott compiled *A Greek–English Lexicon*, 1843, making use of work by the German lexicographer Franz Passow. Greek names given by Hardy are letters of the Greek alphabet; the words printed in Greek are the two first and the last in Liddell and Scott's work. *College living*: after being head of Westminster, Liddell became Dean of Christ Church, Oxford, in 1855. James *Donnegan* compiled the Greek–English dictionary of 1826.

lief, gladly, willingly; **liefer**, rather, sooner.

liege, loyal; **liegely**, faithfully; **liegeness**, loyalty.

Life Laughs Onward (*MV*). Hardy remembers a visit to Plymouth in search of places connected with his first wife's childhood, daisies (her favourite flower) in Stinsford churchyard where she is now buried, and the terrace above the river by their home at Sturminster Newton (revisited 1916, *Life* 373/403).

life-holders (liviers) **. . . lives dropped . . . property fell** (DLa; *OMC*4; *W*.xiv; *TD; LLI*.8i), labourers whose cottages and gardens were leased by the lord of the manor for three generations or lives. This lease was renewable by agreement, but often 'fell in' when the tenant of the third generation died ('the lives dropped').

Life's Little Ironies (1894) contained *WT*2 and *WT*3 (replaced by 'An Imaginative Woman' in 1912). Mature stories, some powerfully anti-clerical, contrast with a number of light anecdotes in 'A Few Crusted Characters'.

the light . . . days (*HE*.i), Thomas Moore, 'Oft, in the stilly night' (*G.T.*).

A Light Snow-Fall after Frost (*HS*). The Hardys lived at Surbiton (London, SW) during the winter of 1874–5 (*Life* 101/104,105/108).

like a tired child . . . placid mind (*HE*.xxvii end). Cf. the last verse of Shelley's 'Stanzas Written in Dejection, near Naples' (*G.T.*).

Like some fair tree . . . (*DR*.xii.1), Psalm i,3 (metrical version).

Like the laughter of the fool, thorns crackling (*WT*1), Eccl.vii,6.

liker (dial.), more likely.

Lilith, the first wife of Adam, according to Rabbinical writings.

Lilliputian (*PBE*.xx; *FMC*.xxiv), diminutive, as in Lilliput; see Part I of Swift's *Gulliver's Travels* (1726).

lily her name connoted (*JO*.VI.v), i.e. the name Susanna (as in the new Testament and the Apocrypha).

limber, the detachable forepart of a gun-carriage; **limber up**, connect these two parts, in order to move an army gun.

limber, limberish, frail, lacking resistance.

Limbo (*RN*.I.iii), the first circle of Hell in *The Divine Comedy* by 'the sublime Florentine' Dante (said to have been the favourite book of Hardy's mother). It contains the spirits of those who were denied the grace of baptism and Christianity; 'souls of mighty worth' is from H. F. Cary's translation. The common meaning is oblivion or the place of forgotten things (*TT*.v).

lime . . . wings, catch, snare (from the old practice of smearing branches with sticky lime to catch birds; cf. *UGT*.III.iii).

Lines (*WP*). Lady Jeune (a distant relative of Mrs Hardy) was a rich hostess with whom Hardy often stayed in London; she never met a more modest man, she wrote. For the American actress Ada Rehan and the poem, see *Life* 211/219–20,228/238–9. *Nature's quandary*, see *HS*.Discouragement. *Vitalized without option*, brought into life without choice (cf. *TD*.iii, near the end).

lines . . . fallen . . . places (*L*.1896 pr; *WB*.III.vii), Psalm xvi,6.

Lines to a Movement in Mozart's E-Flat Symphony (*MV*). The MS 'Minuet' for 'Movement' is confirmed, *Letters* v,237. The reminiscences seem to be of Florence Dugdale/Hardy, in the Lake District with Hardy and his brother in 1911 (cf. **The Coronation**) and at Aldeburgh, Suffolk, earlier or later; and of

Emma Gifford at St Juliot (cf. **By the Runic Stone** and *LLE*.The Dream is – Which?).

lingered and wandered on . . . die (MCR), Wordsworth, 'Inside of King's College Chapel, Cambridge' (*G.T.*).

linhay, lean-to building, shed.

linkman, attendant holding a light.

linnit, lint (used for tinder); **to linnit**, to pieces.

the Lion, the Virgin (*TT*.viii), two signs of the Zodiac; **lion-and-unicorn**, the Royal coat of arms (on which they appear); **the Lion's Rump** (*TT*.xli), Signal Hill or Table Mountain.

lip, say to oneself, murmur, utter.

lirruping (dial.), lazy, slovenly.

Lisbon earthquake . . . French terror . . . St Domingo burlesque (*D*1.I.i), events causing great loss of life: the earthquake in 1755; guillotining during the French Revolution, especially from 1792 to 1794; ruthless attempts by French forces in 1801 to suppress the insurgents of St Domingo (in the West Indies) who had gained their freedom under Toussaint l'Ouverture.

list, thick layer of inedible bread; please; desire, inclination (also **listing**); listen, listen to. **'list**, enlist.

little finger . . . loins (*HE*.Sequel; *TD*.lii), I Kings xii,10.

The little less . . . worlds away (*TD*.xxxv), Browning, 'By the Fire-side'.

a little more . . . too much (*L*.III.ix), *1.H4*.III.ii,72–3.

The Little Old Table (*LLE*). Probably bought second-hand by Hardy's mother when he began to study seriously, and possibly the one in the Hardy Room at the Dorset County Museum. Cf. *Life* 120–1/123–4 on 'the beauty of association'.

little toilette (*W*.xix, from the French), removal of hair from around the neck before an execution.

Little Trianon. See **Petit Trianon**.

liven (dial.), living; enliven.

liveried, in uniform.

liviers. See **life-holders**.

Livy, Tacitus . . . Euripides . . . Antoninus (*JO*.I.vi). All these are classical (Greek or Roman) authors; see a classical dictionary and **Aurelius**.

The Lizard, a quatrain contributed by Hardy to *The Book of Baby Pets* by Florence Dugdale (Mrs Hardy), 1915.

LL.D., Doctor of Laws.

lobby-wicket, a small door in the entrance-enclosure.

Locals, local **militia** men.
lock, bundle.
locum tenens (Lat.), a temporary deputy in a professional post.
locus standi (Lat.), 'place of standing', recognised or accepted (respectable) position.
Lodge, Nashe, or Greene (*L*.II.vii), lyrical Elizabethan poets.
The Lodging-House Fuchsias (*WW*). Mrs Masters was the wife of the captain with whom the Hardys lodged at Swanage when *HE* was completed; cf. *Life* 107–8/110–11 and *HE*.xxxi, where her husband and garden are recalled, it seems, in 'Captain Flower'.
logan-stone, rocking-stone, a large boulder left delicately balanced by natural processes.
Logs on the Hearth (*MV*). Hardy's sister Mary, the playmate of his early years, died on 24 Nov 1915.
Loke the Malicious (*W*.iii), an evil Norse god who cut off the hair of Thor's wife.
Lonely Days (*LLE*), inspired very possibly by a passage in a diary kept at Max Gate by Emma Hardy; Hardy forgot her birthdays sometimes. She returned to Plymouth, where she spent her childhood, to attend her father's funeral. *forespent*, spent (there) earlier.
Long tears . . . sad delight (*W*.xl), Swinburne, 'A Ballad of Life'.
Long-Ash Lane (*WT*6; *GND*.1; *TD*.xliv,xlv; *CM*4), part of the Dorchester–Yeovil road (Roman originally) from Grimstone to Holywell.
long-dog, greyhound.
long-headed, shrewd, far-seeing.
long-hundred, six score (i.e. 120).
Longpuddle (*UGT*; *LLI*.8; *HS*.The Sexton at Longpuddle), suggested by the Piddle or Puddle valley, running through Piddletrenthide and Piddlehinton to Puddletown. Upper Longpuddle is distinguished from Lower Longpuddle or Weatherbury (*FMC*.vii), the extensive parish of Puddletown, which includes the 'Longpuddle' area around Waterston House and Druce Farm (map A).
Looking Across (*MV*), from below Max Gate across the Frome valley to Stinsford, where Hardy's father (d.1892), mother (d.1904), first wife (d.1912), and sister Mary (d.24 Nov 1915) are buried. The poem was occasioned by Mary's funeral.
Looking at a Picture on an Anniversary (*MV*). Hardy looks at the picture of his first wife (d.27 Nov 1912); the MS gives 'March

1913'. On the anniversay of their first meeting (7 Mar 1870, which he has in mind: *Life* 74/77) he had returned to Cornwall (*Life* 361/389).

Looking Back, an uncollected poem in the MS of *TL*, its place being taken in the published volume by 'In the Vaulted Way'.

Lord Amherst's wart, in Gainsborough's painting; **Bennet Earl of Arlington's nose-scar**, in the portrait 'after Sir Peter Lely' (*L*.III.i).

Lord Angelo of Vienna (*TT*.vi), *MM*.II.iv,1–4.

the Lord Chancellor, the highest judicial functionary in England.

The Lord look'd . . . tower (*TT*.ii), Psalm liii,2 (metrical version).

Lord Lyttelton, the second (*RN*.II.vi), Thomas, son of 'the wicked Lord Lyttelton', died three days after being warned of his death in a dream (1779);

the Lord Mayor's Show, an annual occasion of great pageantry, with a banquet at the Guildhall, in honour of London's first citizen.

Lord-Quantock-Arms Hotel (*L*), the Luttrell Arms, Dunster, Somerset, its fictional name indicating the proximity of the Quantock Hills.

Lord's (*LLI*.2.iii), the new ground (now famous) prepared by Thomas Lord and opened in 1814, at St John's Wood, London, for the Marylebone Cricket Club (the M.C.C.).

Lord's anointment (*PBE*.xxvi). Cf. I Kings i,34 and Psalm xlv,7.

Lord's doing . . . marvellous . . . eyes (*D*3.VII.v), Psalm cxviii,23.

lord and ladies (*TD*.xix), 'buds' or flower-heads of the cuckoo-pint. The children's game of opening the spathe or hood to see if the spike is pale or purple, a lady or a lord, is recalled.

Lorna the Second (*WW*). A disappointed lover of the first Lorna, daughter of Hardy's friend Bosworth Smith of Bingham Melcombe, Dorset (cf. *Life* 342/369), married her daughter Lorna in July 1927.

Lornton Inn (*GND*2), Horton Inn, on the Cranborne–Wimborne road; **Lornton Copse** (*TT*.ii) is near.

lost and was found (*WB*.II.vi), cf. Luke xv,24.

Lost Love (*SC*), a memory of Emma at Max Gate; cf *MV*.The Last Performance and *Life* 359/386–7.

The Lost Pyx (*PPP*). For Cernel Abbey see **Abbot's Cernel** and map C; the second abbey, north of Blackmore Vale, is at Sherborne. The pyx is a vessel containing the host or sacramental bread, regarded as the body of Christ. Cross-in-hand is of cardinal importance in *TD*, where two other traditions relating to it are given (xlv).

Lot, land of (*TM*.x), the plain of Jordan, Gen.xiii,10.

Lothario or Juan (*TT*.i), handsome deceivers of women (from Nicholas Rowe's play *The Fair Penitent*, 1703, and Byron's *Don Juan*).

lotus-eaters, inhabitants of a land who eat the fruit of the lotos, which induces a dreamlike forgetfulness of cares and responsibilities (cf. *Odyssey* ix, and Tennyson's 'The Lotos-Eaters').

lotus-headed (arch.), with a capital of ancient Egyptian design, like their water-lily.

Louisa (Louie), Louisa Harding, buried near Emma Hardy (*HS*.Louie). See **Transformations, The Passer-By, To Louisa in the Lane.**

louring, gloomy, threatening; gloomy appearances, threats, worries.

Love in a Village, The Maid of the Mill (*FMC*.xliv), comic operas by Isaac Bickerstaffe, 1762 and 1765.

Love is a sowre delight . . . (*DR*.iii.2), Thomas Watson, *The Passionate Centurie of Love* (1582), sonnet 18.

Love is not love . . . alteration finds (*DR*.xi.4), Son.116 (*G.T.*).

love of women, surpass (*TT*.xxxv), cf. II Sam.i,26.

love . . . strong as death . . . (*FMC*.lvi), Sol.viii,6–7.

Love talks . . . dearer love (*W*.xlv), *MM*.III.ii,140–1.

Love the Monopolist (*MV*). Based on a memory of leaving Emma Gifford at Launceston in 1870 or 1871 (cf. *Life* 72/75,78/81,85/87).

Love was in the next degree (*PBE*.xix ep.), Dryden, 'Alexander's Feast',76 (*G.T.*).

love-making (*TD*), courtship, kissing, embracing (cf. *W*.xxxix; *WB*.II.xii,xiii).

Love's Labour's Lost (*L*.III.vi–viii), early play by Shakespeare; quotations from II.i (13–14,90–1) and v.ii (347–8); gags from *RJ*.I.v (91–4,101–5).

Love's passions . . . wintry sky (*G.T.*). See **Bright reason**.

lover's love (*TT*.xli), Donne, 'A Valediction'. For the sentiment here expressed, cf. the ending of *FMC*.lvi.

Lucifer, fallen from heaven (*OMC*3.iii), the rebel archangel known as Satan; passages quoted from Isa.xiv,10–23. The expression 'proud as Lucifer' is misunderstood by rustics, who think it refers to a **lucifer** match (*DR*.v.1; *FMC*.vi,xxii).

Lucifer, the Morning Star, the planet Venus.

Lucina, the Roman goddess who presided over childbirth.

lug, drag, pull, (colloquial) bring.

Lulwind Cove (*DR*.ii.4; *FMC*.xlvii,xlviii; *WT*2,7; *D*1.II.v), Lulworth Cove, 9 m. east of Weymouth (cf. *LLE*.At Lulworth Cove a Century Back).

lumber, useless (like pieces of old timber or furniture).

lumper (dial.) stumble along, walk heavily or with difficulty.

Lumsdon (*JO*), Cumnor, a village near Oxford.

lunge, a long rope used in horse-breaking (taming).

Lunnon (DLa), London, as pronounced by a rustic.

lustrum, period of five years (from an ancient Roman rite).

Luxellian, Lord (*PBE*), named after a saint associated with Cornwall, and particularly from 'Luxulian', the name of a village SW of Lostwithiel, not far from the original of Endelstow House (cf. **Endelstow**). His daughters are named after Hardy's sisters.

Lycaonians staring at Paul (*JO*.VI.i), Acts xiv,6–18.

Lydia Languish (*RN*.II.vi), in R. B. Sheridan's *The Rivals*, 1775; Harriet Mellon, who later played the part, became Duchess of St Albans.

Lying Awake (*WW*). Hardy sees the Morning Star (the planet Venus) and the tips of the beeches in front of Max Gate, then thinks of the meadow behind the house, and (beyond this) of members of his family buried at Stinsford on the other side of the Frome valley.

lynchet, flinty outcrop, or a similar piece of land which has to be left uncultivated, in a ploughed field.

lynes (a local mispronunciation), loins.

Lyonnesse (*PBE*.xv; *SC*.'When I set out for Lyonnesse', 'I found her out there'; *LLE*.Meditations on a Holiday; *QC*). This romantic name, associated with Arthurian legend and the Cornish coast, had been revived by Tennyson's 'Morte d'Arthur'. **Lyonesse** (*sic*), **Isles of** (*CM*.11), the Scilly Isles; Giant's Town is Hugh Town on St Mary's.

Lysippus (*WB*.II.iii), a sculptor of c.325 BC who explained his excellence by saying that, unlike his predecessors who represented men in their natural form, he represented them as they *appeared*.

M

Macaulay, T. B. (*OMC2*; *PBE*.x), author, 1800–59. He was responsible for many reforms when legal adviser to the Supreme Council of India, 1834–8.

Macbeth, phantoms before (*PBE*.xxii), *Mac*.I.iii.

Machiavellian (*L*.I.v), astute, clever. Machiavelli (1469–1527), an Italian stateman misrepresented chiefly by the clergy, was the founder of political science; his most renowned work is *The Prince*.

machinery, supernatural (*DR*.viii.1), gods and goddesses who direct the actions of mortals in classical epics (cf. the *Iliad* and the *Aeneid*).

madder, reddish.

madness lies that way (*LLE*.Apology), *KL*.III.iv,21.

Madonna della Sedia (*PBE*.i), painting by Raphael. See **Raffaelle**.

Maenades (*RN*.I.iii), women of wild appearance and demeanour, like the Bacchantes (priestesses of the Greek god Bacchus).

Magdalen (*PBE*.xxvii, Guido's picture in the N.G.; *TD*.xx), Mary Magdalene, a devoted supporter of Jesus (cf. Mark xv,40–7, xvi,1–9) and traditionally a fallen woman who repented (cf. the chapter-headings of Luke vii). See **Guido** and **Resurrection**.

Magellan, clouds of (*TT*.xl), galaxies named after the Portuguese navigator (c.1480–1521) who described them in detail.

Magi (*L*.IV.iii), the wise men and the star, Matt.ii,1–12.

Magnificat (*D*.After Scene footnote), cf. Luke i,46–55, especially 52, from the Greek version of which Hardy took his title 'The Dynasts'.

magpie all alone. Such a sight was considered unlucky.

The Maid of Keinton Mandeville (*LLE*), a recollection of her singing at a Sturminster concert (K. M. is in Somerset. See **Should he upbraid**).

the Maid of Neidpath (*L*.v.v), cf. Scott's poem (*G.T.*) with this title ('Her welcome, spoke in faltering tone, Lost in his courser's prancing').

maid . . . ornaments . . . bride her attire (*UGT*.v.i), Jer.ii,32.

Maiden's Blush . . . Provence . . . Crimson Tuscany (*FMC*.iii), varieties of roses, from pink to red.

The maiden's mouth . . . head (*TD*.xlii), Swinburne, 'Fragoletta'.

Mai-Dun (Maidon) Castle (*TM*.xxvi; *MC*.xliii; *CM*6; *WP*.The Alarm, My Cicely; *TL*.After the Club-Dance) Maiden Castle, a vast prehistoric earthwork or fortress SW of Dorchester; it was the capital of a British tribe, the Durotriges, before the Roman occupation. According to Hardy, whose information came from Hutchins, it is ' "the Castle of the Great Hill", said to be the Dunium of Ptolemy' (the astronomer and geographer, c.90–168 AD).

Mail, Michael (*UGT*; *TL*.The Rash Bride, The Dead Quire; *MV*.The Choirmaster's Burial; *LLE*.The Country Wedding; *HS*.Winter Night in Woodland, The Paphian Ball). Whatever his delineation may owe to any member of the Stinsford instrumental choir (from what Hardy heard at home), he suggests legendary tradition as much as fiction. Like William Dewy and others, he used to tell the story of the Chalk-Newton choir (*CM*4).

mal à propos (Fr.), inappropriately.

Malbrook, a popular French nursery ditty in the eighteenth century, after the Duke of Marlborough's Netherland victories; sung to the tune of 'For he's a jolly good fellow'; cf. *D*3.I.i.

Malchus' ear (*PPP*.The Respectable Burgher), John xviii,10.

malic, from apples.

Maltese cross (*TD*.xiv), like the cross of the Knights of Malta, the arms narrowing towards the centre.

Malthusian (*TD*.v), like T. R. Malthus, 1766–1834, who maintained that population would outgrow food-production.

'Mameluke' sleeves, spencer with (*TM*.xxv), short jacket with sleeves and deep cuffs, after the style in Paris.

mammet (dial.), doll, puppet.

Mammon led them on . . . (*HE*.xxvii), Milton, *Paradise Lost* i,678–80.

mampus (dial.), crowd.

A Man (*PPP*). H. of M. remains unknown; he was most probably an employee of the firm engaged about 1850 in demolishing the Elizabethan house of the Trenchards (remains of which can still be seen) at the junction of Glyde Path Road (Shirehall Lane; cf. *Life* 352/379) and High West Street, Dorchester, close by Hardy's home, 1883–5. For the title, cf. the letter which Ethelberta burns, *HE*.ix. *bay*, space between two pilasters; *quoin, cove,* see **Rome: Building a New Street . . .** ; *backed his tools,* put them on his back; *close*, quarrel; *rude*, little educated, unpolished.

Man Friday (*L*.II.i). See **Robinson Crusoe**.

Man that is born . . . one stay (*D*2.III.iv), words spoken by the priest or chaplain just before the body is lowered into the grave, C. of E. service (words from Job xiv,1–2).

'A man was drawing near to me' (*LLE*), Emma Gifford, as Hardy was finishing his first journey to St Juliot; see map E. (There was no railway then to Otterham; he was driven from Launceston). *legends, ghosts*, cf. *S.R.*39–41,51–2. *pharos-fire*, cf. **The Wind's Prophecy**.

The Man Who Forgot (*MV*). The fiction contains a memory of the summer-house in the rectory garden when Hardy visited St Juliot before marriage; it was no longer there, it seems, when he returned in 1913; cf. *MV*.Where They Lived. The rectory still stands.

The Man with a Past (*MV*). Hardy thinks of the blows that befell Emma: some mental affliction, unhappiness in marriage, final illness and death. Only the last afflicted him (in retrospect) as it ought.

the Manche (*D*1.I.ii), the English Channel (Fr.).

mandrake (*DR*.xii.6; *PPP*.The Mother Mourns), a plant that assumes symbolical meaning for Hardy, suggestive of both decay and adversity, from Shelley's 'The Sensitive Plant', where it springs up with other loathsome weeds when the garden is ruined by winter. The superstition that it shrieked when wrenched out of the ground was common.

mandy (dial.), saucy, cheeky.

mane, mean; **maned**, meant (dial).

mangling (colloquial), the process of being decided or settled.

Manila, from Manila in the Philippines.

man-jack, every, each and all (with reference to common people).

manna, food divinely or miraculously provided (as it was for the Israelites in the wilderness, Exod.xvi,4–15).

Manston (*DR*). In naming him Aeneas and his mother (Miss Aldclyffe) Cytherea, another name for Venus, Hardy offered a Virgilian clue to their hidden relationship. Cf. ***Talibus incusat***.

mansum infra manerium suum (*PBE*.v), the dwelling-place within his manorial property.

mantle of Elijah (*LLI*.1), I Kings xix,16,19.

man-trap (*W*), nineteenth-century mechanism for catching poachers.

many a slip. Cf. the proverb 'There's many a slip 'twixt cup and lip.'

many a voice . . . delight (*DR*.iii.2), Shelley, 'Stanzas Written in Dejection, near Naples' (*G.T.*).

many-chevroned, with numerous zigzag mouldings.

maphrotight, a rustic version of 'hermaphrodite'.

Marathon (*PBE*.xxxvii), near Athens, celebrated for the victory there of a relatively small Athenian army against the Persians, 490 BC.

The Marble Tablet (*LLE*). It was designed by Hardy, and placed in St Juliot Church in memory of Emma Hardy (cf. *Life* 361/389,373/403–4).

The Marble-Streeted Town (*LLE*). The title is taken from Emma Hardy's description of Plymouth (*S.R.*10), which Hardy had recently read. She lived there in her youth; cf. **The West-of-Wessex Girl**. For the queried dates of the MS (1914,1913) cf. *Life* 361/389,364/392.

The Marchioness of Stonehenge (*GND*3), first published as 'The Lady Caroline' in December 1890; associated with Wilton House, near Salisbury, the Avon river, and Stonehenge (the last two supplying titles of lords in the story).

Marian (*TD*), a dairymaid, 'one of the few portraits from life' in Hardy's works; he taught her at Stinsford Sunday School (*Life* 25/30).

market-nitch (dial.), market-day fill of liquor.

Markton (*L*), Dunster, west Somerset.

Marlborough (*FMC*.lvii), John Churchill (1650–1722, made Duke of Marlborough). He scored several victories, mainly against the French, in the War of the Spanish Succession, notably at Blenheim (1704), then, a few years later, in the Netherlands; cf. **Malbrook**.

Marlbury Downs (*CM*7; *SC*.The Sacrilege), Marlborough Downs, Wiltshire.

Marlott (*TD*), Marnhull, in the Vale of Blackmoor, north of Sturminster.

marnels (dial.), marbles.

Mars, the classical god of war. **Mars Hill** (*PBE*.xxxvii; *LLE*.Apology): see **In the British Museum**.

Marshcombe Bottom (*W*.xxxv), originally Tutcombe Bottom (Stutcombe Bottom, about $\frac{1}{2}$ m. SW of Melbury House), a swampy hollow (referred to in xix) which was 'popularly supposed to be haunted by the spirits of the fratricides exorcised from Hintock House'.

Marshwood (*W*.xlv), Middlemarsh (map C).

martel (dial.). See **mortal**.

Martin, Mrs (*TT*), the hero's maternal grandmother, probably drawn to some extent from Hardy's paternal grandmother at Higher Bockhampton.

Martinez (*PBE*.ix), port wine from the firm of Martinez, Jones, Gassiat & Co.; '40 (1840) is the year of vintage.

Martinmas, St Martin's Day, 11 November. **Martinmas summer**, a late, or Indian, summer; used figuratively, *MC*.xiv.

Martock (*HS*.On Martock Moor), in south Somerset, to the west of Yeovil. The MS title was 'On Durnover Moor'; see **Durnover**.

marvellous boy (*W*.xxv), Thomas Chatterton, the young poet who commited suicide in 1770, so described by Wordsworth in 'Resolution and Independence'.

Mary Stuart (*FMC*.xx; *RN*.IV.v). Mary Queen of Scots (1542–87), suspected of being a threat to Queen Elizabeth, lived in several English 'prisons', finally at Fotheringhay, where she was beheaded. Her **Puritan visitors** (*DR*.xi.4), from Scotland; after the death of her husband, the king of France, she was urgently required in Scotland, of which realm she had been queen since she was a week old.

Marygreen (*JO*), Fawley, Berkshire; named after Hardy's paternal grandmother (née Mary Head), who spent her childhood there (*Life* 420/453), and the extensive village green; probably also with the memory of his sister Mary, who took him there in 1864. The new church was opened in 1866. For Hardy's visit when preparing *JO*, see *Life* 250–1/265.

Marys, the two (*TD*.xliii). cf. Mark xv,40–7.

mash-tub, a large container for brewing, vat.

masque, play; **masquing**, dance for which facial masks are worn, appearance in a play (from the early seventeenth-century masque).

Master John Horseleigh, Knight (*CM*9; pub. 1893). The story, which opens as if originally designed for *GND*, arose from discrepancies which Hardy found in the marriages of Sir John Horsey of Clifton Maybank (near Yeovil), the description of which (and the initiating evidence) was found in Hutchins.

masterly inaction (MCR), 'masterly inactivity' in the first section of *Vindiciae Gallicae* by Sir James Mackintosh (1791).

Matthew . . . grind to powder (*FMC*.xxxiii), Matt.xxi,42–4.

Matthew, Mark, Luke, and John, bless the bed . . . (*RN*.I.iii), a common version of the opening of 'A Cradle in the Dark' by Thomas Ady (1655).

maul down (dial.), lift or pull down.

mawn-basket (dial), large round two-handled wicker basket.

Max Gate, Hardy's house at Dorchester. It was completed in 1885, and named to preserve local history. Not far away, on the opposite side of the road, had stood the cottage of the toll-gate keeper Mack; his turnpike gate was known as Mack's Gate (cf. *D*1.II.v). The relatedness of several poems to Max Gate is indicated under their separate titles.

Mayfair (*HE*; *HS*.A Poor Man and a Lady), one of the fashionable parts of West London; see **At Mayfair Lodgings**.

maying, a May-Day (or spring) celebration or outing.

Mayne brick (DLa), bricks made at Broadmayne, $3\frac{1}{2}$ m. SE of Dorchester.

Mayne, Egbert (*OMC*4). The name is a modification of 'Will Strong', that of the architect hero of *The Poor Man and the Lady* (both variants of 'Hardy'). It has been suggested that the name came from Sir Richard Mayne, the Police Commissioner who took strong measures to preserve the peace during a working-class rally organized by the Reform League in 1866. The offices of the League were below Blomfield's, where Hardy worked at the time. He had heard J. S. Mill address a London crowd during his 1865 electioneering; and Strong addresses a crowd of working-class men in Trafalgar Square. Mayne is a schoolmaster with Strong's radical sentiments.

The Mayor of Casterbridge was written largely in 1884, after Hardy's removal to Dorchester (June 1883). Though he had given it great thought, it was written with many interruptions, and not concluded until April 1885. It was published in May 1886, about the time its weekly serialization on both sides of the Atlantic (2 Jan to 15 May 1886) ended. The novel is characterized by its continuous succession of dramatic scenes (even more climaxes being engineered for the serial version). In it Hardy gave himself space to create a community at various levels, though it was published with misgiving, 'because the lack of gentry . . . made it uninteresting'). He develops a background, familiar to him from boyhood, in depth, and with detail much enlarged by reading of local events such as wife-sales and skimmington-rides in copies of *The Dorset County Chronicle*, some of them more than half a century old. Hardy changes local chronology (as he does the site of his original for Lucetta's house) for artistic ends (cf. **Royal personage**), but is near the mark when he attributes the beginning of the *Casterbridge* story to 1850 (*Life* 351/378). *The Mayor* is remarkable among Hardy novels for the subordination of the love-element, for having a town as its main setting, and for the stress placed on character in the destiny of his greatest hero. Henchard derives more from literature than from life; he and a number of episodes owe much to the developmental analysis of Oedipus in Sophocles' play by J. A. Symonds in *Studies of the Greek Poets* (from which Hardy noted that 'Sophocles made it clear that the characters of men constitute their fatality'), to Saul in the Old Testament (his love of music, moodiness, jealousy) and his opposition to David, to scenes in *The Mill on the Floss* and *King Lear*, and, more remarkably, to Hugo's *Les Misérables* (details of which are given in my *Thomas Hardy: Art and Thought*, London, 1977, pp. 183–5). All Hardy's borrowings are imaginatively transmuted in the Wessex setting. His attitude to characters from poor homes is changing; they still supply comic relief, but they are more sympathetically treated. The most moving speeches, on the deaths of Mrs Newson and Henchard, are in the vernacular; Elizabeth-Jane may present the Hardy point of view at the end (like Sophocles' at the end of his *Oedipus Rex*), but Whittle shows more humanity (loving-kindness) than anyone. The novel presents change and progress, but finally seems to dramatize the question of what the latter is worth without the spirit of charity; Whittle points ahead to Marty South and Tess Durbeyfield.

maypole (cf. *RN*.VI.i), a high pole, brightly painted in spiral stripes, and wreathed with flowers, round which merrymakers danced on May Day.

Me and Not Me (*W*.vi). This subjective or transcendental idea of the world, which includes the 'rainbow iris' or iris-bow view of love (*W*.xvi), derives from Thomas Carlyle's essay 'Novalis', where he makes reference to the 'far-famed *Ich* and *Nicht-Ich*' (I and Not-I) theory of the German philosopher J. G. Fichte, 1762–1814, a forerunner of existentialism.

'Me', no other god but . . . neighbour's wife (*DR*.xvii.1), a play on the first, and a reference to the tenth, commandment (cf. Exod.xx,3,17).

mead, alcoholic liquor made from fermenting honey and water.

meaner beauties of the night (*MC*.xxv), from Sir Henry Wotton, 1568–1639, 'On his Mistress, the Queen of Bohemia' (*G.T.*).

med (dial.), may, might; cf. **mid**.

meditate . . . Muse . . . Amaryllis (*DR*.iii.2), Milton, 'Lycidas' (*G.T.*).

Meditations on a Holiday (*LLE*). Hardy thinks of Cornwall ('Lyonnesse') with Tintagel and its Tristram and Iseult associations (cf. *QC*), Stratford-upon-Avon (Shakespeare, 'the Swan of Avon'), Lakeland (Wordsworth), Scotland (Burns and Scott, author of the Waverley novels), and London (the poet Shelley's elopement with Mary Godwin from Skinner Street, accompanied by Claire Clairmont; cf. *Life* 17/22,42/44,304/327). *lawns Elysian*, the Elysian fields or meadows, always bright and refreshing, the abode of the virtuous after death in the underworld of Greek mythology; *behoove*, behove, befit.

mee dear, my dear (as pronounced locally).

meekness . . . long-suffering . . . endurance (*TD*.xxxiii), aspects of Christian charity; cf. I Cor.xiii,4–7, Col.iii,12, and Gal.v,22–3.

meet, afford.

A Meeting with Despair (*WP*). 'Egdon Heath' was erased from the MS; cf. *RN*.I.i.

meetinger (dial.), chapel-goer, Nonconformist.

meine Liebliche (*WT*3.iii), my darling (Germ.).

Melancholy ('like Melancholy herself'). See **forgetting . . . .**

The Melancholy Hussar (WT3). Evidence for the shooting of the deserters (buried in Bincombe churchyard) appears in Hardy's research notes for *TM*; cf. *Life* 116/119, 27 July 1877. First published in January 1890, the story was included in *LLI* (see the 1896 preface – Orel,30 – for 'Phyllis'); it was transferred to *WT* in 1912.

melancholy ruins . . . (*WB*.I.i), Shelley, *Prometheus Unbound* IV, 288–9.

Melbury, George (*W*). The surname indicates the locality where he lives: see **the Hintocks**.

Melbury, Grace (*W*), a girl whose natural inclinations are warped by 'the veneer of artificiality' in her fashionable education (a kind of snobbishness that becomes cruel in *LLI*.2). See *Life* 220/230–1 for Hardy's comment on her future.

Melchester (*FMC*.x,xli; *HE*; *TT*; *GND*.1,2; *LLI*.5,8h; *JO*), Salisbury. Places of interest include the Cathedral and its Close, the White

Hart and the Red Lion, the training-college for teachers, and the church of St Thomas. **Old Melchester** (*LLI*.5.iii), Old Sarum, 2 m. north, site of the ancient city, surrounded by Norman earthworks.

meliorism (*LLE*.Apology), the doctrine that the world can be improved by human effort. Hardy maintained that he was a meliorist, not a pessimist (*Life* 387/420), but believed in facing the truth (cf. *PPP*.In Tenebris II, and Gen.Pr.). The 1914–18 war and post-war events made him realize that he had appeared too optimistic at the end of *The Dynasts*, though it expresses a yearning rather than a conviction (cf. *Life* 453–4/491–2). He could sometimes express the view that it was better not to be born (not a suicidal one), but, deep down, his meliorism persisted (cf. HS.Compassion); it was rooted in Christian principles which made him hope that charity would persist when Churches failed (cf. *JO*.VI.iv and *LLE*.Apology).

Melius fuerat non scribere (*TD*.1912 pr.), Latin: 'Better had it not been written' (i.e. the subtitle of *TD*, 'A Pure Woman').

Mellstock (*UGT* and numerous other references), Stinsford, Higher Bockhampton and Lower Bockhampton. Between Stinsford Church and the latter (with its school and post office) is Kingston Maurward House; a wooded path below this and its lake continues from Church Way to the bridge at Lower Bockhampton ('Lower Mellstock') over the main Frome stream. The road north from this point crosses the Tincleton road at Bockhampton ('Mellstock') Cross; its continuation to the Dorchester–Puddletown road is Cuckoo Lane. From this a narrow road leads NE through Higher Bockhampton ('Upper Mellstock'); beyond the Hardy birthplace is Puddletown Heath. In the opposite direction, from Cuckoo Lane, a short lane is followed by a cross-country path, the lower part of which crosses the eweleaze which is part of Kingston Park (cf. *Life* 84/507), a route often followed by the Hardys to Stinsford Church. See map A.

Mellstock Quire . . . verse elsewhere (*UGT*.1912 pr.). cf. *WP*.Friends Beyond; *TL*.A Church Romance, The Rash Bride, The Dead Quire; (later than 1912) *LLE*.The Country Wedding; *HS*.Winter Night in Woodland, The Paphian Ball. See also *Life* 8–14/12–19.

Melodious birds sing madrigals (*PBE*.iii ep), Marlowe, 'The Passionate Shepherd to his Love' (*G.T.*).

Melpomene, the Greek muse of tragedy.

Melport (*OMC*4.I.viii), Weymouth, formerly known as Melcombe Regis.

The Memorial Brass: 186– (*MV*). See **The Inscription**.

Memories of Church Restoration (Orel,203–18), a paper prepared by Hardy for the annual meeting of the Society for the Protection of Ancient Buildings, London, June 1906 (cf. *Life* 331/356).

Men may love . . . longest (*PBE*.xxxviii), cf. *TN*.II.iv,32–4.

menny (*JO*.VI.ii), many; cf. **Malthusian** and 'overpopulation' (*LLI*.5.i).

Mephistopheles (*WB*.III.ii), the Devil to whom Faust sold his soul (*HE*.xxxix; *L*.II.v); he wore a red cloak (*RN*.I.ix). See **Goethe**.

Mercury (or Hermes), messenger of the classical gods.

mercury . . . falling, i.e. in a barometer.

A Mere Interlude (*CM*.11; 1885) combines Wessex names with actual: St Michael's Mount; Mousehole and St Clement's Isle; Falmouth. The climax of chance whereby the heroine lies between her two husbands, one sleeping, the other dead, is followed by comic surprise and an agreeable ending.

meridional, running south (i.e. a line of longitude).

mésalliance, marriage with a socially inferior person.

Messiah (*OMC*4.II.ii), Handel's oratorio, first performed in 1742.

mete (vb.), measure; **meted**, regular, at measured intervals.

metheglin, spiced mead.

meum* and *tuum (Lat.), mine and thine.

mew, place of confinement.

mews, seamews, seagulls.

Michaelmas, 29 September, the feast of St Michael.

mid, middle; (dial.) may, might.

the Middle Sea (*WP*.Leipzig), the Mediterranean.

Middle-Age Enthusiasms (*WP*), addressed to Hardy's sister Mary, his boyhood companion (Henry, the next in the family, was ten years younger than M.). They shared many interests, and were temperamentally akin; see *Life* 371/401–2.

Middleton Abbey (*W*.xxvii–xxix; *OMC*3), Milton Abbas, 10 m. NE of Dorchester. See **The Doctor's Legend**.

middle-watch (nautical), from midnight to 4 a.m.

Midnight on Beechen, 187– (*HS*). Hardy climbed Beechen Cliff for a view of Bath when Emma was staying there in June 1873 (*Life* 93/96).

Midnight on the Great Western (*MV*). Perhaps Hardy, travelling to or from London, had seen such a boy; cf. Little Father Time,

JO.v.iii, 'In the down train . . .'. Here he seems to symbolize life's journey as Hardy saw it: third-class, from the unknown to the unknown.

the Midnight Review (*RN*.II.vi), a poem by the Austrian writer J. C. von Zedlitz (1790–1862), in which Napoleon's dead soldiers are raised from the dead by a spectral drummer.

Midsummer Eve. Many age-old superstitions grew up in connection with this time, especially on love and marriage. If certain rites were performed on the evening of 23 June (5 July, **Old Style**), one's future spouse, or the phantom of the beloved (alive or departed) would appear that night; cf. *UGT*.I.viii; *W*.xx; *JO*.III.viii; *MV*.On a Midsummer Eve (where three superstitions are given).

miff (dial.), slight quarrel, tiff.

Milan (*CM3*.ix; *PPP*.The Bridge of Lodi; *D1*.I.vi), visited by Hardy in April 1887. Afterwards he believed he thought of Napoleon's coronation scene for *The Dynasts* while he was on the cathedral roof (*Life* 195/203).

militia, enlisted soldiers, trained periodically and subject to compulsory military service whenever required.

Mill, J. S. (*JO*.IV.iii), quotation from *On Liberty* (1859), a treatise which Hardy held in high esteem. His 'cures for despair' included Mill on 'individuality'; cf. *Life* 58/59,330/355–6 and **Utilitarianism**.

miller-moth (cf. *RN*.IV.vii; *LLI*.8c; *JO*.IV.vi), associated with death or the soul (in old superstition).

Millpond St Jude's (*FMC*.viii; *TD*.i), most probably Milborne St Andrew, though the maltster's (or Hardy's) direction is wrong.

Millpool (*GND*6), Milborne Port, near Sherborne.

mill-tail, stream immediately below the mill-wheel (**mill-head**, above it).

Milton! . . . thee (*HE*.xxvii), Wordsworth, 'London, 1802' (*G.T.*).

Miltonic . . . Cromwellian (DLa; *TD*.xviii), cf. Gray's 'Elegy Written in a Country Churchyard', 59–60 (*G.T.*).

Milton's monument (MCR). A floor plaque in St Giles's, Cripplegate, London, indicates approximately where Milton is buried. For Hardy's interest in the memorial bust set up in the 1860s, see *HE*.xxvii.

Milton's Satan . . . Paradise (*FMC*.ii), *Paradise Lost* iv,131ff.

milts, spleens (prepared for food, *TM*.xvi).

mind, remember.

Minden (*TM*.xxvi), in Germany; here in 1759 the English and

Hanoverian army had defeated the French.

Mine own familiar friend (*PBE*.xxv ep.), Psalm xli,9.

Minerva, goddess of wisdom (cf. Elizabeth-Jane, *MC*.xx,xlv); said to have invented the flute, which she threw away when Juno and Venus ridiculed her because it distorted her features (*FMC*.viii).

ministering angel (*HE*.xxiv), *Ham*.v.i,235.

minney (dial.), minnow.

the Mint (*PBE*.xxix; *TD*.v; *JO*.VI.vii), the Royal Mint (formerly near the Tower, east London), where British money is coined.

The Minute Before Meeting (*TL*). Probably Hardy's thoughts before meeting Emma Gifford in May 1871 (*Life* 85/87). The ironical juxtaposition with 'He Abjures Love' is characteristic.

miracle of . . . the sick of the palsy (*PBE*.xx), Matt.viii,5–13.

Miraculous Draught of Fishes (*RN*.v.ii), Luke v,1–11.

Miranda-like curiosity (*PBE*.i), cf. *Tem*.I.ii,33–5.

mischty (dial.), mischief.

miserable, of all women most (*HE*.xxiii), cf. I Cor.xv,19.

Miserere Mei (*D*2.v.ii), Have mercy upon me (from the Vulgate, e.g. Psalm vi,3; English version, vi,2).

misprise, misunderstanding, false estimate of the position.

misprision, error, misunderstanding; scorn.

The Missed Train (*HS*). Probably a recollection of what happened to Hardy on one of his return journeys, after visiting Emma Gifford in Cornwall.

Mistover Knap (*RN*; *LLI*.7). In his copy of *RN* Hardy vaguely identified it as 'Troytown'; see **Roy-Town**. The novel gives directions which suggest that it is approximately north of Blooms-End and in a line from Higher Bockhampton to Troy Town. This position is supported by *LLI*.7. The neighbouring pool was suggested by Greenhill Pond.

mixen, midden, manure-heap, dunghill.

mizzel (dial.), hurry off, 'be off'.

The Mock Wife (*HS*). For the trial of Mary Channing, see Orel,228–9, and the reference to her barbarous death in Maumbury Rings, Dorchester, in *MC*.xi. Whether's Hardy's story of her husband's death is traditional or fictional is uncertain.

modden (dial.), must not.

Modern Painters (*CM*3.iv) by John Ruskin, five vols., pub. 1843–60.

modus vivendi (Lat.), working arrangement or way of settling difficulties between two parties.

moil, toil, drudgery, turmoil.

Moivre (*L*.II.i), Abraham Demoivre, French mathematician, 1667–1754. *The Doctrine of Chances* (1718) was translated into English.

mollia tempora fandi (*TT*.xxxviii), favourable occasions for speaking; cf. Virgil, *Aeneid* iv,293–4.

Molly Gone (*MV*), recollections of Hardy's sister Mary (d.1915): in the garden at their birthplace, on outings, and at Talbothays, West Stafford, where she lived with Henry and Kate in her later years. The town by the sea is Weymouth; Montacute Crest is west of Yeovil, and Corton Hill, north of Sherborne; Lewesdon Hill is west of Beaminster. See **Monmouth** for Sedgemoor, and cf. *WW*.The Musing Maiden (an early poem) for the final (eye-meetings) thought.

mollyhorning (of uncertain origin), idling, with little to do.

mollyish (dial.), soft, yielding, weak.

moment-hand, second-hand of a watch.

Moments of Vision (1917) maintains a generally high level. Most of the poems were written during the early years of the 1914–18 war, and so many were related to Hardy's past, especially with Emma, that he felt embarrassed by their publication at a time when people seemed to have little value in 'this nonchalant universe' (*Life* 378/409). Lyricism is to the fore, and the poetry of ordinary life (e.g. 'In a Waiting-Room') is notable. Philosophy produces some interestingly inventive symbolism; its general tone is less despondent, and less confidently aggressive, than in the past. War poems contain some patriotic appeals which were written at the request of the Government.

mommet (dial.), odd figure, guy.

mon ami (Fr.), my friend.

Mon cher . . . est perdu (Fr. *D*3.I.iii), My dear . . . is lost.

Monism, the theory that God and nature (the universe), mind and matter, are indivisible. Hardy's Immanent Will sets him among the monists; cf. **Xenophanes**. **Monistic theory of the Universe** (*D*.pr.), the doctrine that it is governed by one universal God or Being.

monitor (*JO*.IV.vi). The term was commonly used for 'pupil-teacher'; strictly, a monitor was an assistant who could be used as such only up to the age of seventeen, in a school where no teacher was qualified to instruct and train pupil-teachers.

Monk (*L*.I.i), either Edwin (1819–1900) or William (1823–89). Both were active in the Anglican music revival, and both, editors of hymn-books, the latter being best known as editor of *Hymns Ancient and Modern*, and composer of music for 'Abide with me' and other hymns. See **Apostrophe . . . .**

Monksbury (*LLI.*8g), Abbotsbury. As Hardy had used 'Abbotsea' only once, about ten years earlier, in 'Abbotsea Beach' (*TM.*xxvi), he probably did not notice the inconsistency.

Monmouth, the Duke of. After his defeat at the battle of Sedgemoor (Somerset) in 1685, this claimant to the English throne fled. Hardy's interest was reinforced by a family tradition that he took refuge at Melbury Osmond (cf. *Life* 6/10–11 and *CM.*10). Evidence concerning his capture on Shag's Heath, near Horton and Holt (where he was brought before Justice Etterick), probably came to Hardy from his friend Horace Moule; cf. *HS.*At Shag's Heath.

monstrari digito (Lat. *PBE.*i), being pointed at, receiving attention from (Persius, *Satires* i,28).

Mont St Michel (*PBE.*xxxvii; *TT.*iv), a steep rocky island off the coast of Normandy.

Montagues and Capulets (*WB.*I.v,vi,viii), the feuding families in *RJ*.

monthly rose, the 'Common Blush' China rose, so called because it continues to bloom for a long period.

Montislope House (*CM*9), Montacute House near Yeovil.

Montmartre (*CM*8; *D*3.IV.iii) in the north of Paris.

the monument (*TM.*xii), the memorial tower to Admiral Hardy on Black Down.

the Monument (How I Built Myself a House), a pillar 200 feet high, commemorating the Great Fire of London in 1666.

The Monument-Maker (*HS*). For the reality upon which this fantasy is based (with a genuine sense of guilt), cf. *LLE.*The Marble Tablet and *Life* 361/389–90,373/403–4. *planet . . . height*, and (according to astrology) most influential (here deemed auspicious).

moon . . . her so-called inconstancy (*WB.*III.ii), cf. Shelley, 'To the Moon'; . . . **sisterly divinity**, Diana, goddess of the moon.

Moore, George. In *Conversations in Ebury Street* (vi,vii) Moore disparaged Hardy's writings, and wrote contemptuously of his style. J. M. Murry came to his rescue in *The Adelphi*, Apr 1914. Hardy himself attempted no reply until he was on his death-bed; his brief lines end with the thought that, if dustbins were heaped on Moore (as he deserved), they would not reach 'The apex of his self-conceit'.

Moorish arch, curved like a horse-shoe.
mops and brooms, to be all, to be upset, out of sorts.
Mordecai . . . Jair (*PPP.*The Respectable Burgher), Esther ii,5–7.
more sinned against than sinning (*TD.*xxxv), *KL.*III.ii,59–60.
Moreford (*LLI.*7; *WP.*The Slow Nature), Moreton, in the Frome valley.
the Morning Hymn (*TD.*xiii), 'Awake, my soul, and with the sun' by Bishop Ken; cf. *Life* 10/16 and **Barthélémon**.
Moroni (*UGT.*II.ii), Italian painter (c.1525–78); Hardy alludes to his 'Portrait of a Tailor' (N.G.).
morrow, morning.
mortal, extremely great, mighty; individual, single; person, thing.
Morton (*FMC.*xxi), his tragic face after the battle of Shrewsbury, 2.*H4.*I.i,60ff.
Mosaic law: 'Burning . . . strife' (*FMC.*xliii), an inaccurate recollection of Exod.xxi,25.
Moses' face . . . Mount (*W.*ix; *MV.*'I met a man'; *LLE.*She Who Saw Not), face shining on Mount Sinai, Exod.xxxiv,29; **Moses in Horeb** (*FMC.*xxviii), Exod.xvii,6; **meek as Moses** (*TT.*xxvii), Num.xii,3; **Moses, on the Lord's rage when censured by his creatures** (*TL.*A Dream Question), cf. Deut.i,27–37; **Moses . . . Pharaoh** (*FMC.*xx), Exod.x,24–8; **Moses: 'Then shall the man . . . woman shall bear her iniquity** (*JO.*v.viii), Num.v,31.
mossel (dial.), bit, morsel.
moth, once associated with the soul of the dead (cf. *WP.*Friends Beyond; *MV.*Something Tapped); see **miller-moth**.
the moth frets the garment (*WB.*III.viii), Job xiii,28.
The Moth-Signal (*SC*). See *RN.*IV.iv and, for the tumulus and the second man near Clym and Eustacia's house, IV.v (where the trees are firs).
the Mother, Nature; see **At a Bridal**. The classical term 'Magna Mater' (Great Mother) was applied to such daughters of the Earth and Sky as Rhea and Cybele, who were associated with natural fruitfulness.
mother . . . crowned . . . heart (*RN.*VI.iv), Sol.iii,11.
The Mother Mourns (*PPP*). Cf. **the Mother** and *Life* 163/169. *needle-thicks*, tufts of needles on the pine trees; *a Creature . . . so excelling*, see **the Unfulfilled Intention**; *soul-shell*, the body (for the thought, cf. *Life* 218/227: 7 Apr 1889); *popinjay*, a name applied to the green woodpecker; *rank*, rebellious.
The Mother of the Months (*W.*xxxiv), the moon, from the first

chorus of Swinburne's *Atalanta in Calydon*.

Moule, Horace (1832–73). Of 'the seven brethren' (*Life* 412/445), sons of the Revd Henry Moule, vicar of Fordington for a long period, he was the one with whom Hardy was most familiar during his early career. He was a classical scholar who initially failed to obtain a degree at Oxford and Cambridge, owing, it is said, to mathematical shortcomings. He was devoted to music, and Hardy thought he showed distinct poetical promise. He appealed to Hardy's aspirations, discussed contemporary thought with him, gave him books, including *The Golden Treasury* and a translation of Goethe's *Faust*, but advised him to keep to architecture rather than study classical literature in preparation for a university career. He remains an enigmatic figure; at Salisbury in 1860 one of his private pupils saw clearly that he was a heavy drinker. He was often in London, supporting himself by journalism, particularly for *The Saturday Review*. In 1865 he succeeded his brother Charles as a teacher at Marlborough College, retaining this position until the end of 1868, though he was already subject to depression, bouts of drinking, and suicidal tendencies. (Years later Hardy intimated to his second wife that Horace was implicated with a girl of dubious morality in Fordington, who became pregnant and was sent to Australia; cf. **The Place on the Map**.) Moule's academic success was won at Cambridge, where he was awarded the Hulsean Prize for his *Christian Oratory* in 1858, and where, after taking his B.A. in 1867, he received his M.A. in 1873. His reviews of *DR* and *UGT* were belated, but helped, the first especially, to give Hardy the encouragement he needed. In July 1872 a post had been found for him as a Poor Law inspector for East Anglia. His suicide at Queens', his Cambridge college, in September 1873, was probably due to the deepening depression which set in when his fiancée broke off their engagement. Horace Moule's 'tutorial' role and his reviewing contributed to the portrait of Henry Knight (*PBE*); his alcoholism, to Jude. Cf. *Life* 32–4/37–8,84/86,87/89–90,93/95–6,96/98; *WP*.A Confession to a Friend in Trouble; see also **An Experience**, **Standing by the Mantelpiece**, **Before My Friend Arrived**, **The Five Students**.

Mount Moriah, etc. (model of Jerusalem, *JO*.II.v): **Moriah**, site of the Temple; **Valley of Jehoshaphat**, on the eastern side of the city; **City of Zion**, the 'Upper City', in the SE of Jerusalem; **Calvary**, a hill north of the city, the scene of the Crucifixion (here introducing the figurative theme of the tragedy); **the Mount of Olives**, scene of Christ's agony before the Crucifixion, east of the Valley of Jehoshaphat.

Mount Sinai (*JO*.I.iv), where Moses received the Commandments from God.

mountains . . . groves (*TD*.xlvi), associated respectively with the worship of God and with pagan religious rites.

mountains, She had . . . moved . . . (*HE*.xxxi), cf. I Cor.xiii,2.

mouster, to be stirring or on the move (from 'muster').

Mrs Elizabeth Montagu (*W*.xxxvi), a society writer, first of the 'blue-stockings', 1720–1800.

Mulotters, mispronunciation of 'mulattos'.

Multimammia (*MC*.xlv; *TL*.By the Barrows). See **Diana**.

multiplying eye (*FMC*.xlii), cf. Burns, 'Death and Doctor Hornbook',12–24.

multum-in-parvo (Lat.), much in little (applied to a pocket-knife which has a number of blades and other accessories).

mumbudgeting (dial.), creeping up silently, taking by surprise.

mumm, act (in the usual sense), perform in dumb-show. **mumming** (*D*.pr.): Hardy implies no more than acting; 'technicalities' refers to the use of such stage terms as 'Act' and 'Scene'. See **Christmas mummers**.

mun (dial.), must.

Munditiae, et ornatus, et cultus (*PBE*.xxviii), Elegance, adornment, and stylish dress; from the history of the Roman empire by Livy (59 BC–17 AD), XXXIV.vii,9.

the murder (is out), the secret.

Murillo (*OMC*4.II.i; *D*3.II.iii), Spanish painter, 1617–82.

Murmurs in the Gloom (*LLE*). Written when the outbreak of the Boer War (cf. *PPP*.War Poems) was imminent. *ensample* (archaic), example; *smooth no waters*, cf. **'And there was a great calm'**; *breathing threats and slaughters*, like Saul, afterwards St Paul, Acts ix,1; *frowardly*, in the wrong direction; *vawardly*, onwards, to progress ('vaward', the archaic form of 'vanguard').

murrey-coloured, mulberry-coloured, reddish.

Muscovy (*D*1.I.v, etc.), Russia.

Music drew an angel down (*TT*.viii), cf. the last line of Dryden's 'Alexander's Feast' (*G.T.*) and his 'Song for Saint Cecilia's Day' (*G.T.*).

Music in a Snowy Street (*HS*). Hardy's description of 'a somewhat similar scene' in Dorchester on 26 Apr 1884 is rather misleading (cf. *Life* 165/171). The listener remembers tunes from France after the victorious Napoleonic era, and even earlier, from the pre-Revolutionary period of Marie Antoinette and her husband Louis XVI (both guillotined in 1793).

Music, sphere-descended . . . (*DR*.xii,1), Collins, 'The Passions' (*G.T.*).

The Musical Box (*MV*). Millgate notes (192–3) that the singular pronouns of the main narrative were plurals in the MS, as if the Hardys were returning and their servant Jane came out. (Was she waiting 'high-expectant' for her lover? Cf. **Overlooking the River Stour**.) This personal question is not crucial, for the poem centres in the spirit which sings; it is not a person ('Thus did it sing . . . As she came to listen for me without'). The spirit remains concealed and unheard; it is what the tune of the musical box conveyed in retrospect. Hardy knows that the happiness he and Emma shared at Sturminster Newton was not to last (cf. *LLE*.The Two Years' Idyll).

The Musing Maiden (*WW*). Hardy may have been thinking of Eliza Nicholls (Millgate, 94), a London friend, when she was at home at Findon (west Sussex), on the Channel side of the South Downs. For his concluding fancy, cf. *MV*.Molly Gone.

mustard-seed, grain of (*DR*.xix.2; *FMC*.xlix), Matt.xiii,31–2.

Muzio gambit (*PBE*.vii), opening moves perfected by the seventeenth-century Italian chess-master Muzio.

My Cicely (*WP*). A narrative in fictional disguise, as of the eighteenth century, written most probably after Hardy had cycled with his brother Henry to Exeter, and on to the grave of their cousin Tryphena (née Sparks; cf. **Thoughts of Phena**) at Topsham, where he learned that she often served behind the bar at her husband's hotel. The rider from London (its Baals or false gods recalling Clym Yeobright's view of Paris, *RN*.III.ii) follows the Roman road (the **Icen** way), past historic places: Basing House (near Basingstoke, long besieged by Parliamentary forces during the Civil War), Salisbury Cathedral (Poore, its first bishop), and downland where tumuli mark the burial-places of ancient chieftains; then via Blandford Forum with its slow river, past Weatherbury Castle (an ancient hill-fortification; see **Rings-Hills-Speer**). Beyond Dorchester he passes the gibbet (shown in Hardy's illustration), the circle of nine stones near Winterbourne Abbas, then above the Bride tributaries on his left, and past Eggardon Hill with its ancient earthworks to the right.

Eventually, after crossing the Axe and Otter rivers, he reaches Exeter. For other places, see **Mai-Dun**, etc.

My Mind to me a Kingdom is (*RN*.III.i title), the opening line of a poem by Sir John Dyer, c. 1545–1607.

'My spirit will not haunt the mound' (*SC*). Ghosts were supposed to haunt the places they loved in life, a view which makes Hardy think that he will not find Emma in the form of a spirit (her 'curious air') by her grave at Stinsford but, if he still cares for her (she says), in Cornwall, wherever they were happy together.

myrmidons, assistants, employees (originally the soldiers who supported Achilles in the war of the Greeks against Troy).

myrtle, a plant sacred to Venus (cf. *DR*.xvi.4; *PBE*.xxx).

N

'n, him, it.

nab, catch, seize. **nabs**, self-consequential fellow.

nabob, one who returned with great wealth from India (strictly, an Indian governor).

Naboth (*DR*.xx.2), I Kings xxi,15–21.

nadir, down, at one's feet (a point opposite the zenith).

nail't wi' Scripture (*PBE*.xvii), Burns, 'Death and Doctor Hornbook'.

Nain widow's only heir (*PPP*.The Respectable Burgher), raised from the dead, Luke vii,11–15.

name it all, damn it all; **why the name**, why, in God's name (or 'why the devil'; cf. 'what the name').

nameless, unutterably shameful.

nammet, break for a meal by farm-labourers.

Naomi . . . Ruth (*HE*.x; 'Let me find favour . . . handmaid', *PBE*.xxx), Ruth i and ii,13.

Napoleon (*FMC*.v), almost certainly a reference to Haydon's picture of him on the island of St Helena in the south Atlantic, where he was kept in British custody after his defeat at Waterloo.

Napoleon el chico (*D2*.II.vi), 'the little man', a description by Spaniards of Joseph Bonaparte, after he had been made King of Spain in 1808 by his brother Napoleon. See **Bonaparte**.

Narrobourne (*LLI*.4), one of the Coker villages, south of Yeovil.

Nasmyth hammer, a steam-hammer invented by James Nasmyth in 1839.

natant, swimming, floating.

nater (dial.), nature.

nath (Cornish), puffin.

Nathan tones (*MC*.xxx), when David is accused of arranging Uriah's death, so that he can marry his wife Bathsheba; see II Sam.xii,7.

Nation!, **'nation**, damnation, damnably. **what the nation**, what the devil.

the nation . . . dwells in the cottage (*WB*.II.i), from a speech by John Bright the Radical in 1858.

National School. Before elementary education in England was made compulsory for all in 1870, a large and growing number of voluntary schools had been organized by the National Society for children's education according to C. of E. principles; they continued to function side by side with State elementary schools after 1870. Only the most able pupils reached the Sixth and Seventh standards, the highest levels of attainment within the system.

natomy, **'natomy**, bodily frame, skeleton (for anatomical study).

natty, smart, spruce, fine.

naturalism (CEF), a view of life in which only natural and environmental factors are considered to affect human destiny; such determinism eliminates the possibilities of spiritual forces and free will.

nature is fine in love . . . (*W*.xlv), *Ham*.IV.v,158–9.

Nature's holy plan (*TD*.iii), quoted from Wordsworth's 'Lines Written in Early Spring' (*G.T.*).

Nature's Questioning (*WP*). Cf. *Life* 409/440. The broken key of Hardy's accompanying sketch denotes not only an insoluble problem but 'a dreadful bodement' (omen or presage, Earth's 'old glooms and pains' continuing). For the Wessex superstition, see *FMC*.xxxiii, and with the opening verse cf. Hardy's second note for 30 May 1877 (*Life* 114/117).

navarchy (*D1*.v.i), naval command or commanders.

navvy, labourer employed in excavating for canals, roads, etc.

Nazareth, good thing out of (*TD*.xxxix), John i,46.
Nazarite . . . razor (*L*.I.i), Num.vi,1–5.
Near Lanivet, 1872 (*MV*). 'Literally true', Hardy told Mrs Henniker; the signpost, he recorded, stood at the old road south to St Austell (see map E). It stood at one of two neighbouring T-junctions forming, as he remembered it, crossroads, about 1 m. east of Lanivet, near which, at St Benet's Abbey, Emma was staying with the Serjeants (cf. *Life* 91/93 and *S.R.*43–5).
near-foot-afore, the left front foot.
neat, without dilution. **neat(s)**, oxen.
Nebo (*RN*.I.iii), the mountain from which Moses viewed the Promised Land, Deut.xxxii,49–50.
Nebuchadnezzar's dream (*RN*.II.iii), Dan.iv; **Nebuchadnezzar's furnace** (*L*.VI.ii; *JO*.I.iii; *PPP*.The Respectable Burgher), Dan.iii,8–25; **isolate a Nebuchadnezzar** (*WT*.1), cf. Dan.iv,28–33.
Nec Deus intersit (*D*1.I.iii), neither should a god intervene (Lat.), from Horace (*Ars Poetica*, 191).
Neckar (*L*.V.vii; *W*.xxvii), Rhineland river; cf. *Life* 110/113.
necrophobist, one who is morbidly fearful of corpses or skeletons.
Neitan's Kieve (*QC*.xi), St Nectan's Kieve, an impressive waterfall 2 m. east of Tintagel; sketched by Hardy in October 1871.
neither length nor breadth . . . divide (*JO*.IV.v), Rom.viii,38–9.
Nelson . . . Saul (*D*3.VII.ix). Napoleon wishes he had been killed in battle (at Waterloo) as Nelson had been off Cape Trafalgar, King Harold of England at Hastings (1066), Hector at Troy, Cyrus the Younger at Cunaxa (401 BC), and Saul against the Philistines (I Sam.xxxi,1–6).
Nelson's flag-captain at Trafalgar and his **birthplace** (*D*.pr.), Captain (later Admiral Sir) Thomas Hardy of Portesham, near Weymouth.
Nemesis (classical), retributive fate.
neo-Georgian (*LLE*.Apology), new Georgian, in the reign of George V, 1910–36. For Hardy the true Georgian period was from 1714 to 1830, when the first four Hanoverian Georges reigned in succession.
Neptune . . . primaries (*GND*9), like Neptune, then thought to be the most remote of the planets revolving round the sun.
nescience, nescientness, lack of awareness.
nesh, delicate, sickly.
Nether-Moynton, Nether Mynton (*DR*.xiii.2; *TM*.ix,xxvi; *WT*7), Owermoigne, 6 m. SE of Dorchester (map D).

Nettlecombe-Tout (*TM*.xii; *TD*.ii,iv,xlii), a prominent hill ('tout' means 'lookout') in the chalky 'elevated dorsal line' south of the Blackmoor Vale.

Neutral Tones (*WP*). For the situation (not the setting) and the imagery, cf. the last verse of Shelley's 'When the lamp is shattered': 'Bright reason will mock thee, Like the sun from a wintry sky . . . Leave thee naked to laughter, When leaves fall and cold winds come.' Cf. 'negative beauty of tragic tone', *TD*.xlv.

New Jerusalem (*HE*.xxxi; *JO*.I.iii), cf. Rev.xxi (by St John, 'the Apocalyptic writer').

New Light (*L*.I.vii,IV.iii), a person holding, as he thinks, advanced and enlightened views, especially in religion; cf. 'modern lights' (*JO*.III.i).

New lords new laws (*FMC*.viii), an old English proverb.

New Year's Day, Old Style (*W*.xix), 25 March; it was changed to 1 January in 1752. See **Old Style** for the September change that year.

A New Year's Eve in War Time (*MV*). The horsemen galloped past Max Gate precisely at midnight, at the year's end (*Letters* v,199). *gable-cock*, weathercock above the gable; *Young Unknown*, New Year; *Death astride*, cf. Rev.vi,8.

The Newcomer's Wife (*SC*). *crabs upon his face*: this suggests Weymouth harbour (cf. *WB*.I.vii).

new-kerned (of apples, *D*3.VII.i), recently formed or set.

Newland Buckton (*W*.xxix), Buckland Newton, 3 m. east of High Stoy; about a mile further east the road from Milton Abbas crosses the Lydden stream not far from its source.

new wine in old bottles (*JO*.III.iv), Matt.ix,17.

news-bell, a singing in the ear which was thought to herald bad news.

Newton, Isaac (*TT*.xxxvi), a mathematician, best known for his work on light and gravitation (1642–1727).

Ney (*PPP*.The Sick Battle-God), an important figure in *The Dynasts*. After winning glory under Napoleon, Marshal Ney submitted to Louis XVIII in 1814. When Napoleon escaped from Elba, he rejoined him and fought valiantly to the end; he was tried and executed in 1815.

niaiseries (from the French), silly things (said).

the Nicene creed (*FMC*.i; *JO*.II.vii), based on the agreement reached by the bishops at the Council of Nicaea (with Constantine the Great), and emphasizing the consubstantiality of Christ and God the Father; it is used in the C. of E. communion service. For the Apostles' creed, see the 'Morning Prayer' service.

Nicholas or **Nick**, the Devil.

Niflheim (*W*.xiii), the underworld of Norse mythology, where the unfulfilled, not the heroes, dwell after death.

nigger performance, minstrel show in which whites with blackened hands and faces sing plantation songs in the manner of American negroes.

the night cometh (Gen.Pr.), death, John ix,4.

Night in the Old Home (*TL*), the Hardys', at Higher Bockhampton.

A Night in November (*LLE*), probably written on the anniversary of Emma Hardy's death. Perhaps she knows he loves her.

A Night of Questionings (*HS*). *All Souls'*, cf. **'I rose up as my custom is'**; *years . . . locusts*, Joel ii,25; *circuiteer*, the wind that moves circuitously; *Different as dyes although*, despite colour-differences in decoration;. *Comorin . . . Horn . . . Wrath*, southern point of India, of South America, and the NW corner of Scotland. *Ardennes*, hills in SE Belgium; a line from this region to Dover cuts across some of the major British battlefields in the 1914–18 war against Germany. *knave*, cause by knavery; *white cap your adorning*, when hanged or 'stretched'; *lovely . . . true*, cf. **Things true, lovely**.

night wisps in bogland. See **jack-lantern**.

night-hawk (**night-jar**). Its 'scurr' or 'whirr' is used sarcastically rather like a comment by the Spirit Sinister: *PBE*.xxiv; *RN*.IV.vii; *W*.xx; *HS*.A Hurried Meeting.

A Nightmare, and the Next Thing (*WW*). Hardy thinks of his approaching death; cf. **Christmastide**.

night-rail, **nighty-rail**, night-dress.

Night-Time in Mid-Fall (*HS*). The reference to witches (flying on their broomsticks, according to superstition) suggests Hallowe'en (cf. **'I rose up . . .'**). *storm-strid*, with the storm striding across.

Nijni Novgorod (*FMC*.1), now Gorky, in central Russia (U.S.S.R.), once famous for its August–September fair.

nimb, **nimbus**, halo, investing light or atmosphere. **nimbi**, the Latin plural of 'nimbus', the bright or golden disk (aureole) traditionally surrounding the head of a saint.

Nine-Barrow Down (*HE*.xxxi). See map D.

Nineveh (*HE*.xxiv). See **Sennacherib**.

nipperkin, small measure of liquor.

nitch, bundle, load.

no bird sang (*RN*.III.v), cf. Keats, 'La Belle Dame sans Merci' (*G.T.*).

no enemy but winter . . . weather (*DR*.v.2), *AYL*.II.v,7–8 (*G.T.*).

No more of me you knew, my love (*PBE*.vii ep.), from the song 'A weary lot is thine, fair maid' in Scott's *Rokeby* III.xxviii (*G.T.*).

No Song no Supper (*TM*.xxx), a comic opera by Stephen Storace, 1763–96.

Noah (*UGT*.II.vi,v.i; FMC.ii,xlii), Gen.vi–viii.

nobbiest (slang), smartest, most elegant.

nobble, hobble, potter.

noble citizen of old Greece . . . burnt . . . (*TT*.xiv), from Valerius Maximus, *Facta et Dicta Memorabilia* III.3.

The Noble Lady's Story (*TL*). The story is imaginary; see **Lady Susan**. *grey hall*, Stinsford House; *semblant*, resembling (her).

Nobody Comes (*HS*). The scene is outside Max Gate, as Hardy anxiously awaits his wife Florence's return after her operation in London.

Noe, Noë (*PPP*.By the Earth's Corpse), Noah; see above. **eating and drinking as in the days of** (*TM*.xxvi), Matt.xxiv,37–9.

Nollekens, Joseph (*PBE*.iv), English sculptor, 1737–1823; reference to his bust of William Pitt (the Younger, 1759–1806; cf. **Shockerwick**).

Non illa . . . Minervae . . . manus (*DR*.xix.1), Virgil, *Aeneid* vii,805–6: her woman's hands were unaccustomed to Minerva's distaff and baskets of wool.

***non lucendo* principles** (*FMC*.xli), of contrariety, from the Latin *lucus a non lucendo* (the wood is so called because it gives no light).

nonce, for the, for a particular purpose or occasion (as in *Ham*.IV.vii,160), for the time being; **the nonce** (*MV*.The Musical Box), the present.

(one) nook . . . the retreat . . . of other geniuses from a distance (*WB*.1912 pr.), the prison on Portland for convicts.

Noon . . . darkness . . . ninth hour (*PPP*.Zermatt: To the Matterhorn), until 3 p.m. at the Crucifixion (cf. Mark xv,33).

Norcombe Hill (*FMC*). As the Beaminster road below Toller Down runs through a spur of this hill, it must lie north of Toller Whelme and Westcombe coppice (which helps to supply its name; see map C). Hardy was interested in this region because some of his ancestors owned much land at Toller Whelme (*Life*

5/9,214/223–4). Perhaps this name is slightly disguised in 'Tewnell Mill', which probably indicates the old mill at Hooke.

Normal School, a name (from the French) given for a time to a training-college for teachers.

Normandy and **northern France** (*PBE*.xxxvii; *HE*.xxxiii–v; *L*.v.x,VI.i–iii). Henry Knight visits Amiens, Ardennes Abbey, Laon, Noyon, Rheims, Chartres, Coutances, Vezelay, Sens (places which Hardy visited imaginatively when studying architectural sketches in William Nesfield's *Specimens of Medieval Architecture*, 1862, one of the architectural prizes he won in 1863), and the church of St Ouen in Rouen. Ethelberta and her pursuant admirers travel by train from Cherbourg to Bayeux, Caen, and Rouen (where the Hardys spent part of their honeymoon before going on to Paris). Another pursuit takes Paula Power to Normandy in search of George Somerset; before finding him at Étretat, she visits Cherbourg, Lisieux, Caen and [Le] Havre; she had previously stayed at Amiens. Cf. the Hardys' 1880 holiday, *Life* 138–9/142–3.

Normandy pippin, a kind of apple, originally 'Norman's pippin'.

North Star, the Pole Star (Polaris).

Northern, no'thern, ignorant, uncertain, stupid (person).

Northern Lights, the Aurora Borealis.

Not boskiest bow'r . . . (*W*.title-page ep.), written by Hardy in August 1895 (*Letters* II,85) from his own experience, and in keeping with the dominant mood of the novel. See ***The Woodlanders***.

Not in utter nakedness . . . we come (*TD*.li), Wordsworth, 'Intimations of Immortality',63–4 (*G.T.*).

Not Known (*WW*). The MS deletion reads '1914: After reading criticism'; cf. *WW*.A Poet's Thought.

'Not only I' (*HS*). Emma Hardy in her grave. *lively red*, cf. *SC*.'I found her out there'; *Call*, when the dead are raised.

not willingly let die (*W*.xlv), from Milton, *Reason of Church Government*.

'Nothing matters much' (*HS*), in memory of Judge B. F. Lock, a native of Dorchester who died in 1922 at Bridlington, Yorkshire.

Notitiam . . . crevit amor (*JO*.II ep.), Ovid, *Metamorphoses* iv,59–60: Proximity brought acquaintance and first developments; love grew with time.

nott, hornless.

Novalis (*MC*.xvii), German romantic poet, 1772–1801. Hardy most probably first noticed his statement that character is fate in George Eliot's *The Mill on the Floss* VI.vi; cf. *D2*.VI.vi.

Now, if Time knows . . . (*WB*.I ep.) from 'Wishes to his (supposed) Mistresse' by Richard Crashaw, 1612–49 (*G.T.*); cf. *MV*.'I said and sang her excellence'.

Nubian Almeh (*WB*.II.vi), black dancing-girl from Nubia (a region south of Egypt).

nullo cultu (*DR*.i.3), with no conscious cultivation (Virgil, *Eclogues* iv,18).

Number One (*WT6*.i), self, self-interest.

nunch, lunch, nuncheon.

nunnywatch, fix, predicament (looking like a ninny from not knowing what to do).

Nuttlebury (*TD*.xxxvii,1), Hazelbury Bryan in Blackmoor Vale, little more than 2 m. NW of Bulbarrow Hill.

Nymphean, glamorizing; classical nymphs were semi-divine.

O

O come in . . . dew (*W*.xx), a sexual invitation, from an old ballad, well known in various parts of England.

O daughter of Babylon . . . (*PBE*.xxxiii ep.), Psalm cxxxvii,8.

O foolish Galatians . . . you? (*TD*.xliv), Gal.iii,1.

O ghastly glories of saints (*JO*.III.iv), Swinburne, 'Hymn to Proserpine'; cf. **Thou hast conquered, O pale Galilean**.

O last regret . . . die (*PBE*.xxxv), Tennyson, *In Memoriam*, lxxviii.

O Lord, be thou my helper! (*LLI*.4.iii), Psalm xxx,10.

O love, who bewailest . . . (*PBE*.iii), Shelley, 'When the lamp . . .' (*G.T.*).

O Nannie (*MC*.viii), a song in Percy's *Reliques of English Poetry*, 1765.

O that 'twere possible (*LLE*.Apology), Tennyson, *Maud* II.iv,1.

O what a tangled web . . . deceive! (*CM3*.vii), Scott, *Marmion* VI.xvii.

O, what hast thou . . . away! (*DR*.xii.1), tr. from Horace, *Odes* IV.xiii.

O ye Sun and Moon . . . magnify Him for ever! (*TD*.xvi), from the Benedicite, commonly part of the C. of E. Morning Prayer service at the time.

Oak, Gabriel (*FMC*). Both names indicate strength of character, 'Gabriel', the strength of God; Oak owes something to Adam Bede, but his name probably derives from the oak image in an earlier story by George Eliot, 'Mr Gilfil's Love-Story': 'a noble tree. The heart of him was sound, the grain was of the finest'; the main trunk of his nature, like Oak's, remained true to 'a first and only love'.

Oakbury Fitzpiers (*W*.viii,xxiii). The name was suggested by Okeford Fitzpaine SE of Sturminster Newton, but the village seems to be nearer to High Stoy. (The hill 'like a great whale' is Dungeon Hill.)

Oaker's Wood (*UGT*.v.i), on the heath, 2 m. east of Tincleton.

An oath for confirmation . . . strife (*TT*.iii), Heb.vi,16.

object-glass (*TT*.v; *JO*.VI.i), the telescope lens, or combination of lenses, nearest the object viewed.

The Obliterate Tomb (*SC*). The story may have been generated from Hardy's resolve to look for the Gifford tombs at Plymouth ('the western city') in 1913 (on his way to Cornwall), and from what Emma Hardy had reported on the family vault (*Life* 360/387). *hackered*, uttered with chattering teeth; *shards*, fragments of stone.

obstinate questionings, blank misgivings (*LLE*.Apology), Wordsworth, 'Intimations of Immortality', 140ff. (*G.T.*).

occupation . . . gone (*DR*.xii.7; *JO*.IV.vi), *Oth*.III.iii,361.

od, 'Od, the beginning of an oath, originally 'God . . . '; the usual meaning is 'damn it' or 'damn me'. **'Od's blood, Od zounds**, old oaths (by the blood or wounds of the crucified Jesus).

Oedipus (*RN*.v.ii), a son of Laius, King of Thebes; destined (according to Greek legend) unwittingly to murder his father and marry his mother. He tore out his eyes when he discovered the truth.

Oenone (*TT*.xxxvii), the nymph of Mt Ida who married Paris, son of Priam, King of Troy; he forsook her for Helen of Sparta, thereby bringing total ruin to his country, as Oenone had prophesied. The quotation is from Tennyson's 'Oenone',15–16.

off or **off-side**, the right side of a vehicle, the driver or leader of the horse(s) being on the left.

Offenbach (*L*.II.ii), a German-Jewish composer (1819–80), notable for his comic opera in Paris.

ogees, mouldings or designs in rounds and hollows.

ogive, pointed arch.

Oh, for my sake . . . provide (*OMC*4.I.iv ep.), Son.111.

Old Christmas Day (*DR*.xii.8–9), 6 January; see **Old Style**. Friday was considered to be an unlucky day.

Old Eccl'iastes (*UGT*.II.ii), the writer of Ecclesiastes (cf. Eccl.i,12–14).

Old Excursions (*MV*), written with Emma in mind. All names of places except Casterbridge are actual. For Cerne, see **Abbot's Cernel**; Sydling, **Broad Sidlinch**.

old feller, the Devil (old Harry, old Nick, or old gentleman).

Old Furniture (*MV*). Cf. **all a-sheenen**. The MS has 'My father's' for 'As whilom' (l.22). *nut*, bridge.

Old Hundred-and-Thirteenth Psalm (*DR*.x.3). Ironically this is a song of praise to God; see **the Wold Hundredth**. Hardy had probably heard it chimed at Plymouth (cf. *SC*.Places and *S.R*.11–12,70–1).

An Old Likeness (*LLE*), the picture of Rosamund Tomson, possibly in a copy of her poems which she sent Hardy in 1891 (cf. Millgate,297, and *Letters* I.248). *fancy*, love; *blight-time*, old age.

Old Mortality (MCR). Sir Walter Scott's *Old Mortality* (1816) took its title from the name acquired by the itinerant whose mission was to keep fresh, with his chisel, the inscriptions on the tombs of the Scottish Convanters who had died for their faith.

Old Mrs Chundle (*OMC*1), based on a story which Hardy heard from Henry Moule, Curator of the Dorset County Museum; written 'about 1888–90'. Florence Hardy had it published at Philadelphia in the *Ladies' Home Journal* (Feb 1929) and, the same year, in a limited edition (New York). Moule, a painter himself, suggested the sketching curate in this entertaining but critically telling presentation of the Church.

The Old Neighbour and the New (*LLE*). The visit may have been imaginary. Hardy was thinking of William Barnes at Came rectory, though he died in October; see **The Last Signal**.

The old order changeth (*L*.pr; *TD*.lii), Tennyson, 'Morte d'Arthur',240.

The Old Ship (*TM*.xxvi), a predecessor of the Ship inn opposite where the road from Sutton Poyntz enters Preston ('Creston', map G).

Old Style. The Julian calendar had been proved inaccurate in its estimate of the length of the year for a long period, before its successor, the Gregorian calendar (New Style) was adopted in England in 1752, when the day following 2 September was made 14 September; hence the cry, 'Give us back our eleven days'. The difference was changed to 12 days after 1800, and to 13 after 1900. Various practices continued for a period in the nineteenth century according to the Old Style Calendar. For **Old-Midsummer Eve** and **Old Lady-Day**, see **Midsummer Eve** and **Lady Day**.

Oldham, Mr (*CM*4). His original was Charles Redlynch Fox-Strangways, brother of the Earl of Ilchester. He died in 1836 at Maiden Newton (**Chalk-Newton**), where he had been rector for many years.

Oliver Grumble (*TD*.iii), i.e. Oliver Cromwell, leader of the Roundhead army and ruler of Britain after the Civil War, 1642–51.

Olympian, goddess-like (*L*.II.vii). **Olympian . . . Pharaohs** (*TD*.xvi), of Greek gods and goddesses (who lived on Mt Olympus), Alexander the Great, Julius Caesar, or rulers of Egypt in its early magnificence.

Olympus (*FMC*.x), a mountain in Greece, so high the ancients believed the gods dwelt on its summit, which reached the heavens.

On a Discovered Curl of Hair (*LLE*), given by Hardy's wife Emma, now dead, in Cornwall before their marriage.

On a Fine Morning (*PPP*). See **To Outer Nature**.

On a Heath (*MV*). The heath and distant 'town-shine' suggest 'Egdon' (near Hardy's birthplace) and Dorchester. 'All that was bright of me' recalls *MV*.'In the seventies'. Hardy, in one of his regretful retrospective moods (cf. **The Opportunity**), may have remembered a rendezvous with Cassie Pole, a lady's maid at Kingston Maurward House, not long before he met Emma Gifford for the first time; cf. **At Rushy-Pond** and **At Mayfair Lodgings**. *nigh*, in time.

on a poet's lips, sleeping (*LLI*.1), Shelley, *Prometheus Unbound* I,737 (*G.T.* 'The Poet's Dream').

On an Invitation to the United States (*PPP*). Though invited several times, Hardy never visited the States. The poem underlines his attachment to Time's changes, the historical past, in a familiar environment (a strong feature of *MC* and several poems in *WP*).

emprize, enterprise.

on end, on-end (for), ready, set, intent on.

On One who Lived and Died where he was Born (*LLE*). Though he changed the date of his death for artistic unity, Hardy had his father in mind: he died in his birthplace in his eighty-first year; he was 'wealth-wantless', with no business ambition (*Life* 21/25–6,247/261,248/262).

On Stinsford Hill at Midnight (*LLE*), based on Hardy's experience, 4 Feb 1894 (*Life* 262/278).

On Sturminster Foot-Bridge (*MV*). Hardy added '(Onomatopoeic)' because a critical reviewer (Robert Lynd, cf. *Letters* v,318–19) had missed his intended effects; see *Life* 301/323–4,390/422. *eyot-withies*, willows on the island in the river; *she*, Emma Hardy (cf. **Without, Not Within Her**).

On the Belgian Expatriation (*MV*). Germany's invasion of Belgium at the beginning of the 1914–18 war had forced many Belgians to take refuge in England. *Land of Chimes*, Belgium, famous for its carillons.

On the Doorstep, grimly realistic, the only one of twelve poems first printed in *The Fortnightly Review*, Apr 1911, which Hardy did not collect; see **Satires of Circumstance**. (*MV*.On the Doorstep contains a memory of Emma Hardy at Max Gate.)

On the Esplanade (*HS*), a Weymouth scene, recollected, like *HS*.Singing Lovers, from 1869 (*Life* 63–4/65–6); based on a description in *DR*.iii.2, and an old superstition (see **Midsummer Eve**). *In its overblow*, after fully blooming.

On the Portrait of a Woman about to be Hanged (*HS*), written three days before Edith Thompson was hanged for the murder of her husband. Her love story and letters had created much sympathy in the press. *Clytaemnestra*, in classical legend, like Mrs Thompson, contrived her husband's murder with her lover's assistance; cf. Hardy's comment (*Life* 221/231, where he has Tess in mind), alluding to the sacrifice of their daughter by Clytemnestra's husband as an extenuating factor.

On the Tune Called the Old-Hundred-and-Fourth (*LLE*). 'Old' signifies the tune for the psalm in the hymnal version by Sternhold and Hopkins, which preceded the Tate and Brady metrical psalms. Thomas Ravenscroft's setting to Psalm civ was published in 1621.

On the Western Circuit (*LLI*.5) was bowdlerized for publication at the end of 1891. Mrs Harnham is named after Harnham Bridge at Salisbury and Constable's picture of Salisbury from Harnham Hill.

On thy cold . . . sea (*PBE*.xxi ep.), Tennyson, 'Break, break, break'.

Once at Swanage (*HS*). Hardy and Emma lived there in 1875–6 (cf. *Life* 108/111, 'Evening' note). The second verse, contrasting with the 'weirdsome' spell of the first, illustrates Hardy's propensity to make poetry out of what T. S. Eliot describes as 'the unexplored resources of the unpoetical'; cf. *Life* 114/117–18.

ondrew, came on, drew on (in time).

One hope . . . smother (*DR*.ii.4), Shelley, 'One word . . . profaned' (*G.T.*).

One on her youth . . . giant size (*DR*.xx.2), adapted from Dryden's translation of Virgil, *Aeneid* v,430–1.

One shape of many names (*WB*.title-page and II.i), Shelley, *The Revolt of Islam* I.xxvii.

One We Knew (*TL*). Mary (née Head) Hardy, Hardy's paternal grandmother, who had lived at Fawley, Berkshire (the Marygreen of *JO*) in her early years. She married Hardy's grandfather in 1799 (two years before they occupied their new home at Higher Bockhampton), was widowed in 1837, and continued to live with Hardy's parents until her death in 1857: cf. 'Domicilium' (*Life* 4/8–9) and *Life* 215/224,420/453. *maypole*, cf. *RN*.VI.i; *death . . . France*, Louis XVI, guillotined in January 1793 (cf. *RN*.II.i); *warlike preparations*, cf. **The Alarm**; *gibbet, neighbouring town*, either on the road to Wantage or near Dorchester (cf. *JO*.I.xi and **My Cicely**).

One Who Married Above Him (*HS*). The sycamore tree with its steps, and the house with its mullioned windows and stone quarried at Hamdon Hill (west of Yeovil) indicate the house at 'Townsend', Melbury Osmond, where some of Hardy's maternal ancestors, the Childs or Childses, once lived (cf. *Life* 6/10, and the first paragraph of *WT6*.ii). *whimmed*, followed her whim; *Bollen*, a name given elsewhere (*W*.vi) to a farmer in the same neighbourhood; *graytime . . . sere*, winter to summer and autumn.

onetime, formerly.

oneyer, a rare one, unusual person.

onriddle (local pronunciation), unriddle, fathom, explain.

ooser (*RN*.IV.vi; *GND*.1), grotesque mask with opening jaws, surmounted with a cow's hair and horns; worn to frighten people.

Oozewood (*CM9*), Ringwood, on the Avon, 15 m. south of

Salisbury.

ophicleide, a strong wind-instrument, developed from the serpent.

The Opportunity (*LLE*). Hardy with hindsight thought Helen Paterson (who illustrated the serial edition of FMC, and whom he first met in May 1874) one of his 'lost prizes' (cf. *Letters* III,218); she married William Allingham (cf. *Life* 101/103). Both subject and metre are like those of Browning's 'Youth and Art'.

or ever, before. **Or ever the silver cord . . .** (*PBE*.xxvi), Eccl.xii,6.

orange-flower and the sad cypress (*CM*.12.xi), the first associated with marriage, the second with death, as in *TN*.II.iv,50–1.

orbit, course (as of a heavenly body, determined by 'unalterable law').

orchet (dial.), orchard.

orders, styles of architecture.

ordinary, a meal regularly provided at a fixed price.

ordinates (*D*.pr.). Hardy's geometrical reference is not very helpful; by a series of them he alludes to co-ordinated scenes.

Orion (*FMC*.ii; *D*3.I.xi; *TL*.Shut Out That Moon; *MV*.Before Marching and After), a prominent constellation in the late autumn and winter sky (northern), seen by the ancient Greeks as the mighty hunter Orion, with belt and sword, his club raised to meet the onslaught of Taurus, the Bull.

os femoris (Lat.), thigh-bone.

Osmanlee to Hekla's mound (*D*2.VI.vii), Turkey to Mt Hekla in Iceland.

ostent, either wonder or appearance.

Ostium . . . (*TD*.lii), Entrance to the tomb of the ancient d'Urberville family.

Othello . . . his Ancient (*HE*.vii), his standard-bearer Iago, who contrives his master's tragedy in Shakespeare's *Othello*.

ounce pennies (*MC*.xviii), minted for private trading, and heavier than ordinary pence. Used to ensure that the eyelids of the dead remained closed; if left open, it was feared that another death in the family would soon follow.

Our Exploits at West Poley (*OMC*6), a cautionary tale for boys. In November 1883 it was sent to a Boston editor, who received a revised copy which he failed to publish; eventually the proprietor of the firm gave it to his son-in-law, editor of *The Household*, where it was serialized from November 1892 to April 1893.

Our house, my sovereign liege . . . (DLa), *1.H4*.I.iii,10–13.

Our Old Friend Dualism (*WW*). See **Monism** and **Dualism**. Hardy's title comes from his letter to Dr Saleeby (*Life* 369–70/399–400; the poem was probably written after reading this letter while he and Florence were preparing Hardy's *Life*. *Protean*, assuming various forms, as did the Greek sea-god Proteus; *Spinoza* (1632–77), a Dutch philosopher and outstanding monist. Among the dualists are the French philosopher Henri Bergson (1859–1941) and the American psychologist William James (1842–1910). *flamens*, priests (Roman), theologians who believe in God the Creator outside his creation (unlike Hardy's Immanent Will).

out, go (or come) out, recede.

outleant, stretched or laid out, lying there; cf. its use in both *PPP*.The Darkling Thrush and *MV*.Honeymoon Time at an Inn. (Whether such fabrication of language is justified is doubtful; cf. **out**, **outshrill**.)

outshade, shadow forth, hint at.

outshape, give form to, develop, become, assume proportions.

outshow, display, manifest.

outshrill, cry out.

Outside the Window (*SC*), suggested possibly by Mr Lightfoot's sketch of Miss Amory near the end of Thackeray's *Pendennis* lx.

outstand, stand out, be prominent.

outstep, exceed; out-of-the-way.

outwrought, worked out, fully developed.

Over the Coffin (*SC*). *patriarchs*, a reference to Old Testament rulers of families or tribes, e.g. Abraham, Isaac, and Jacob.

overborne, overcome, broken in spirit.

Overcombe (*TM*; *D*1.v.vii), a village below Bincombe Down, composite in its features, being drawn from Sutton Poyntz (further east, with its mill and pond), and from Upwey (the mill particularly); cf. *Letters* III,285. The church is Bincombe Church.

overget, overcome.

overlook, cast an evil eye on, bewitch.

Overlooking the River Stour (*MV*). The MS '1877' after the title gives the 'wet June' when the Hardys lived at Riverside Villa, Sturminster Newton. The poem, like the two which follow it, may have been prompted by his 1916 visit (cf. *Life* 373/403; 111–12/114–15,119/122). As the Sturminster period was the Hardys' 'happiest time' together (cf. *Life* 118/122 and *LLE*.A Two-Years' Idyll), Millgate (191–2) is probably right in thinking that what Hardy did not notice within the house was the pregnancy of their servant Jane; see 13 Aug 1877 (*Life* 116/119).

over-right, opposite, in front of.

Ovid . . . 'Video . . . sequor' (*MC*.xxx), Latin poet, 43 BC–17 AD: 'I see and approve better things, but follow worse', from *Metamorphoses* vii,20–1.

Owlscombe (*TD*.xxi). See **Conjurors**.

The Oxen (*MV*), based on a common superstition, which Hardy heard from his mother; he includes it in *TD*.xvii. The barton stood in the hollow at the Cuckoo Lane end of the Higher Bockhampton lane.

Oxford (*PBE*; *TT*; *LLI*.2). All Souls College suggested All Angels. For other references, see **Christminster**.

Oxwell (*TM*), Poxwell, a village 5 m. NE of Weymouth. Oxwell Hall is Poxwell Manor.

P

packet, packet-boat, a vessel carrying goods, mail, and passengers.

paean (vb.), hymn, sing in praise of.

Paedobaptists (*L*.I.vi–vii; cf. *Life* 29–30/33–5), believers in the baptism of children, as opposed to Baptists, who believed in adult baptism.

the Pagan moralist (*TD*.xxxix). See **Aurelius**.

A Pair of Blue Eyes (1873), the first of Hardy's novels to appear with his name on the title-page, took its title from the song in Sheridan's *The School for Scandal*, III.iii. Though in externals it presents features from the Cornwall and Emma Gifford he knew, including the readiness of her father (*S.R.*18) and Elfride's to quote Latin, and bases the class-distinction aspect of its theme on parallels with the Gifford and Hardy families, it is more remarkable for its departures from actuality than from adherence to it. The emotional side of Hardy's nature (more feminine than male, xxxviii), and his observation that snubbing begins in women when domineering ceases in the man (xxvii) reflect autobiographical truth; other observations based on the Hardy–

Emma relationship were undoubtedly included besides the paraphrase from one of her letters, 'I must take you as I do the Bible . . . in a lump, by simple faith' (xix). The communal authenticity which enriches the dialogue in *UGT* is succeeded by authorial invention, often tediously spun out or forced in the early stages of the novel. Only when the plot is complicated by Knight's falling in love with Elfride does tension begin. His hectoring character and the weak immaturity of Elfride and Stephen have as little appeal as the heightening of the jealousy motif from *UGT*. Most peculiar in Knight, it reaches its climax when he finds he is betrayed by his romantic illusions, rejects Elfride, and leaves the country, foreshadowing Angel Clare. Both are rigidly inhuman in their crises; for both the woman is 'dead and buried'. Such is 'the chance of things', in the complex of which, as in *Tess*, the principal characters are the dominant factor. Knight's harrowing experience before his hair-breadth escape from death originated from Leslie Stephen's 'A Bad Five Minutes in the Alps' (*Fraser's Magazine*, Nov 1872), but any resemblances are far outweighed by striking differences between imaginative, exciting narrative and prolonged, studious philosophizing. Interesting incorporations include the Rotten Row scene (xiv) from *The Poor Man and the Lady*, an imaginative reconstruction and transfer of a Stinsford vault-scene (cf. xxvii and *Life* 9/14), and a chapter (xxix) based on Hardy's voyage from London to Plymouth, for Cornwall, in 1872 (*Life* 91/93). 'O love . . . the frailest . . . bier!' (iii), substituted for lines which include the original title 'A Winning Tongue Had He', epitomizes the plot, with its recurrent reminders of entombment and death. Coincidence is most daring at the conclusion, which, verging on the comic in its preliminary phases, provides one of the most moving and successful of Hardy's tragic endings. He wisely refused to change it for one more cheerful.

pair-royal. See **raffle**.

pale, palings, fence, boundary.

pale death . . . poor . . . kings . . . foot (*TT*.xli), Horace, *Odes* I.iv.

Palestine, skill used up in (*TD*.xix), during the Crusades.

Paley and Butler (*JO*.III.i), William Paley's *Evidences of Christianity*, 1794 (cf. *LLI*.4.ii) and Joseph Butler's *Analogy of Religion*, 1736.

Palissy (*TT*.v), a sixteenth-century French potter who endured years of poverty before he succeeded in making enamels.

Palladian, a style of architecture adopted in mansions of the seventeenth and eighteenth centuries, after Palladio (1518–80), an Italian who imitated the ancient Roman style.

Palladour. See **Shaston**.

Palmerston, Lord (DLa: dirt is only matter in the wrong place), an eminent statesman who died in 1865, after being a member of several British cabinets.

Pan pipes (*CM*.11.vii), an early musical instrument ascribed to Pan, comprising a series of reeds graduated in length to produce a musical scale.

Pandemonium (*TD*.xlviii; *CM*.12.xv), the abode of all the demons, and the capital of Milton's hell in *Paradise Lost*.

Panglossians. Voltaire (1694–1778), French free-thinker and satirist, uses Pangloss in *Candide* as the exponent of the optimistic theology that 'all is for the best in this best of all possible worlds' (*LLE*.Apology); cf. the conclusion of *GND*.1. The reference to the Lisbon earthquake of 1755 in *D*1.I.i should be read in the light of *Candide* v.

Pans . . . Priapus (*TD*.x). When Syrinx was pursued by the satyr Pan, the gods of classical mythology changed her into a reed; similarly Lotis was changed into a tree when Priapus tried to violate her.

Pantheistic, expressing belief in a universal God or Spirit.

Panthera (*TL*). Following the Higher Criticism, Hardy produces (with cautionary touches) a rational version of the birth of Jesus. He had found references to the story, and various forms of it, in Bellamy's 1660 translation of Origen's *Contra Celsum; The Talmud*, the Jewish collection of civil and religious law, doctrine and ritual, with reference to Scripture; *Sepher Toldoth Jeschu*, a medieval pseudo-history bent on discrediting Christianity; fragments of lost apocryphal gospels; David Strauss's *Das Leben Jesu* (1837) translated by the writer who became 'George Eliot'; and Ernst Haeckel's *Die Welträtsel* (1899), *The Riddle of the Universe* in translation. Hardy was encouraged to print his poem by J. B. Bury, Regius Professor of Modern History at Cambridge. *Pax Romana*, peace preserved by Roman power; *Cappadocian*, from Cappadocia, a large mountainous area in Asia Minor (central modern Turkey); *Calvaria*, Calvary (Luke xxiii,33) a hill north of Jerusalem; *Calabria*, in southern Italy; *Jezreel*, a city between the plain of Esdraelon and the Jezreel valley, north of Mt Gilboa and south of the town of Nain; *Tabor*, a mountain SW of Lake Galilee; *Nazareth*, where Mary, the mother of Jesus, lived; *Pyrrhic*, an armed dance originating in Greece; *temple . . . raze it*, cf. Mark xiv,58 and John ii,18–21; *naysaying*, denying, refusing; *Fors Fortuna!* (ironical: he means *luckless* fortune or chance); *He . . . hazardry*, a version of 'He that hath wife and children hath given hostages to fortune' (Francis Bacon, 'Of Marriage and Single Life'); *Procurator*, Roman governor (Pontius Pilate, procurator of Judaea and Samaria, AD 26–36); *Mauretania, Numidia*, in north Africa (Morocco and Algeria roughly); *Parthia*, a mountainous region (NE Iran); *Son of Saturn*, Jove; *the Three*, the Fates (cf. **distaff . . .**).

pap-and-daisy . . . verse (*DR*.ii.3), the pretty-pretty or sentimental verse of poetasters.

The Paphian Ball (*HS*). For 'While shepherds watched' and its miraculous effect, cf. **The Dead Quire**; for a choir which does the reverse in church, see *LLI*.8f. *Paphian*, devoted to Venus (see **Paphos**). *Rejoice, ye tenants*, another Christmas carol or hymn.

Paphos, in Cyprus, once noted for its lascivious worship of Aphrodite or Venus, goddess of love and beauty.

Par nobile fratrum (*D2*.I.vii), noble pair of brothers: Horace, *Satires* II.iii,243.

Paradox (*HS*). This poem on his sister Mary (d.1915) shows how much Hardy's thoughts on immortality had changed; cf. **He Prefers Her Earthly**.

parallelepipedon (a geometrical term), an object the six sides of which are parallelograms, each opposite pair being parallel.

Paramaribo (*GND*5), in Dutch Guiana (now Surinam), South America.

pari passu (Lat.), step by step with, at the same time as.

parian (*RN*.I.vi), a new kind of porcelain used for figure-modelling, and named after white statuary marble from the Greek island of Paros (cf. *RN*.III.iii, a detail in the Greek aspect of the novel).

Paris (*TT*.xxxvii; *WB*.II.vii; *WW*.The Clasped Skeletons), son of Priam, King of Troy. Appointed by the gods to choose the most beautiful of the goddesses Hera, Pallas, and Aphrodite (Juno, Minerva, and Venus), he chose Aphrodite, who promised him the most beautiful woman in the world. He deserted Oenone, and married Helen, wife of Menelaus, King of Sparta. So began the Trojan War.

parish clerk, a parishioner appointed to assist the clergyman, especially with responses during church services.

parle, talk, conversation.

Parliament artillery forces (*L.*I.ix; *GND7*), against the Royalists in the civil war during the reign of Charles I.

Parrett Down (*PBE.*v), near Tresparrett (map E).

parsley-bed (*WB.*III.iii), hinting at pregnancy (originally, the mother's womb).

Parthenon (*JO.*III.iii), the temple to Pallas Athena on the Acropolis, Athens; Hardy had seen fragments of its frieze in the British Museum.

Parthians, and Medes . . . Mesopotamia (*CM2.*iii), Acts ii,9.

partie carrée (Fr. 'square party'), party of four, foursome.

pas de charge (*D3.*VII.viii), at the double (Fr.).

Pascal, Blaise (French mathematician and philosopher, 1623–62): 'La dignité de la pensée' (the dignity of thought) quoted in CEF; Hardy had noted this expression in an article on Schopenhauer in the *Revue des Deux Mondes*, 1 Oct 1886. Quotation from the preface to *Pensées* in *TD.*xviii: The more intellectual one is, the more original people one finds. Ordinary persons find no difference between people.

pas-de-deux (Fr.), a dance or figure for two persons.

passados (fencing), forward thrusts.

passed into silence (*JO.*II.i), cf. Psalm cxv,17.

passée (Fr.), past her prime.

The Passer-By (*LLE*). Hardy indulges the fancy that Louisa Harding (d.1913; cf. **Transformations**) remained single ('my fate') for his sake.

passing, surpassing; surpassingly, exceedingly.

passion's slave (*TD.*xxxv), *Ham.*III.ii,70.

Passover (*LLE.*The Wood Fire), an annual Jewish feast, associated with the Paschal lamb, to commemorate both the sparing of the Israelites in Egypt, when the first-born of Egyptian families were slain, and their consequent freedom (Exod.xi–xiii).

Pastoral Symphony (*DR.*viii.4), probably that in Handel's oratorio *The Messiah* (rather than Beethoven's).

The Pat of Butter (*HS*), based on the memory of an agricultural show, held perhaps when the Hardys lived at Yeovil in the summer of 1876. The Yeo valley (*Lea* indicating pasture-land) is near, as is the stream running by the Coker villages. Kingcomb is much further south (map C), and Netherhay, south of Crewkerne.

Paths of Former Time (*MV*), recollections of walks with Emma in the Frome valley below Max Gate.

patristic, pertaining to the Fathers (early Christian Church leaders).
patroon (archaic), patron.
pattens, 'overshoes' supported on iron frames to protect ordinary shoes from mud or water.
Paul the Apostle (careless about outward things, *RN*.IV.vi), cf. Phil.iv,6; **of Tarsus** (*TD*.xxv), in Asia Minor (where he was born); **Pauliad** (*TD*.xxv), a work relative to Paul.
Paul-and-Virginia life (*TM*.xxv), of idyllic love as in the novel *Paul et Virginie* by Bernadin de St Pierre, 1788 (a translation of which Hardy received from his mother when he was a young boy, *Life* 16/21); cf. *JO*.IV.iv.
pay to the uttermost farthing (*TD*.xxxiv), Matt.v,26.
Pay . . . vowed . . . not pay (*TT*.iii), Eccl.v,4–5.
The Peace Peal (*HS*), rung in Dorchester at the end of the 1914–18 war; *Gothic bower*, nest in a church-tower of Gothic design.
The Peasant's Confession (*WP*). Hardy's story is a surmise (cf. *Life* 298/317). He had bought Adolphe Thiers's *Histoire du Consulat et de l'Empire* in preparation for *The Dynasts*, where the Waterloo battle is presented in considerable detail. The passage quoted from Thiers indicates that if the officer sent by Napoleon had reached Marshal Grouchy there would have been no question. He did not, however, as Grouchy maintained all his life, and it has never been known whether he was captured by, or went over to, the enemy.
Pebble-bank (*WB*). See **Chesil Bank** and map H.
peckle (dial.), pickle.
The Pedestrian (*MV*), at Colehill, probably when Hardy lived near at Wimborne Minster, 1881–3. *Nox venit* (Lat.), the night cometh (death), John ix,4; *beaver*, hat of beaver fur; *Schopenhauer, Kant, Hegel*, German nineteenth-century philosophers; *fountained Muses*, see **Helicon**.
Pegasus, Square of, four bright stars which form almost a square (beyond Cassiopeia from the Pole Star).
Pelham (PRF), a highly successful early novel (1828) by Edward Bulwer, afterwards Lord Lytton.
pelican in the wilderness (*FMC*.ix), Psalm cii,6.
Pembroke table, with end-leaves which can be dropped.
pend, depend on it, be the outcome, be in store for.
***penetralia* of the temple** (*TM*.xxxiii), the inner sanctuary, holy of holies.
The pennie's the jewel that beautifies a' (*PBE*.xxxvi ep.), Burns,

'There's a youth in this city'.

Penny, Robert (*UGT*; *HS*.Winter Night in Woodland), based on Robert Reason and his shop at Lower Bockhampton; cf. *Life* 92/95,394/427,428–9/462. He died in 1819, long before the period of *UGT*.

Penpethy (*HS*.Green Slates). Here, on his first visit to Cornwall, Hardy travelled with Emma Gifford and her married sister to inspect slates for church-restoration at St Juliot (*Life* 75/77).

Pensa molto, parla poco (It.), Think much; speak little.

pension (Fr.), boarding-house.

Pensioner, a Chelsea Pensioner, a veteran handicapped by war-injuries and rewarded for gallant service by being made an inmate of Chelsea Hospital; for Hardy's interest in this institution, cf. *Life* 78/81,106/109,111/114.

pent, enclosed, buried.

Pentecost, talk like the day of (*TT*.i), cf. Acts ii,1–13.

Pentelic (marble), white, from Mt Pentelicus near Athens.

pent-roof, single roof on a lean-to shed.

Pen-Tyre (*QC*.v), headland SW of Tintagel, north Cornwall.

Pen-zephyr (*CM*.11), Penzance, south Cornwall.

Periclean (CEF), relating to the period of Pericles, the great Greek statesman and orator of the fifth century BC, when Greek drama flourished.

Peripatetic school (*W*.vii). As the Athenian philosopher Aristotle taught his students while they walked in the gardens of the Lyceum, they were known as Peripatetics.

Perpendicular, the final Gothic style of English architecture from the late fourteenth to the sixteenth century, its traceried windows characterized by vertical mullions which reach upwards to their **architraves**.

A perplexing and ticklish possession is a daughter (*W*.xii), from the surviving fragments of comedies by Menander, the Greek poet, c.343–291 BC.

personalty, personal possessions.

perspective toys (*MC*.xxix), fashionable early in the nineteenth century, and presenting views of buildings in three-dimensional form.

Perugino (*RN*.II.iv; *WB*.III.viii), Italian painter, c.1445–1523.

Peter at the cock-crow (*OMC*.1; *SC*.In the Servants' Quarters), John xviii,15–27.

Peter the Great (*TD*.xix), emperor of Russia. Determined to make his country a great naval power, he worked in Dutch and British shipyards in 1697–8.

Peter's Finger (*MC*.xxxvi), a corruption of 'Peter ad Vincula' (Peter in chains; cf. Acts xii,1–11), name of an inn at Lytchett Minster, Dorset.

Petherwin (*HE*). Hardy took this name for his Ethelberta family from a village near Launceston, Cornwall.

Petit Trianon, a small palace in the grounds of Versailles.

petite mort (Fr.), momentary faintness.

petits soins (Fr.), little attentions.

Petrarch (*RN*.III.iv), Italian poet (1304–74), whose idealizing passion for Laura inspired most of his lyrical verse.

Petrick, Timothy (*GND*6), Peter Walter of Stalbridge House (NW of Sturminster Newton), who died in 1745 at the age of 83. His grandson died in 1753.

The petty done . . . vast! (Gen.Pr.), Browning, 'The Last Ride Together'.

phaeton, light four-wheeled open carriage.

phantasmagoria, exhibition of optical illusions; a shifting and changing external scene.

phantastry, fantastic show, a fantast's vision.

phantom of delight . . . daily food (*FMC*.xlix), Wordsworth, 'She was a phantom of delight' (*G.T.*).

Pharaoh, baker, butler (*DR*.v.1; *TM*.xvii), Gen.xl. **Pharaoh's chariots** (*MC*.xxxvii), Exod.xiv,5–9,23–5.

pharisaical . . . not as . . . (*FMC*.xxii), Luke xviii,11.

phasm, phantom, lifeless or unreal image, anything visionary.

Pheidias (*RN*.III.i), the supreme sculptor of ancient Athens. **Pheidias . . . William of Wykeham** (*L*.III.v), all eminent builders: the sculptor **Pheidias** connected with the splendour of Athens in the fifth century BC, **Ictinus** and **Callicrates** being contemporary Athenian architects; **Chersiphron**, designer of the temple of Diana at Ephesus; **Vitruvius**, a Roman architect of the first century AD; **Wilars of Cambray**, a French architect of the thirteenth century; **William of Wykeham** (1324–1404), a great builder who became Bishop of Winchester, founded New College, Oxford, and Winchester School, and transformed the nave of Winchester Cathedral.

Phelipson, Richard (*CM*9), Richard Phelips of Montacute House near Yeovil; (one of the same family appears in *GND*.1).

Philistine's greaves of brass (*RN*.I.iii), Goliath's leg armour, I

Sam.xvii,6; **Philistines be upon us** (*FMC*.ix), cf. Judg.xvi,4–21; **uncircumcized Philistines** (*L*.v.xi), enemies (cf. I Sam.xvii,26).

philosoph, philosopher. **philosopheme**, philosophy.

the philosopher's stone (*D*1.II.i), a hypothetical substance sought by medieval philosophers because they thought it would turn all baser metals into gold.

A Philosophical Fantasy (*WW*). Hardy makes fun of a God conceived in man's own image, since the Immanent Will had never been aware of man's existence, is unethical, and motivated to no purpose. *life-shotten*, exhausted of vitality; *confections*, creations; *limned*, pictured in the Old Testament as an irascible god, quick to punish; *'blind force persisting'*, an idea usually associated with the German philosopher Schopenhauer (1788–1860) and familiar reading to Hardy in contemporary journals; *unlisting*, heedless.

Phoebe . . . Diana! (*JO*.I.v), the opening lines of Horace's 'Carmen Saeculare', addressing the sun (Phoebus) and the moon (Diana, goddess of chastity).

Phoebus, a name given to **Apollo**.

phosphor, light-giving, phosphorescent; **Phosphor**, the Morning Star.

photosphere, luminous envelope (like that around the sun or a star).

phylactery (*PBE*.xiv), an inscribed roll (in medieval art), usually proceeding from the mouth to indicate what is said.

Picard (*L*.v.x), of Picardy, the old name for a province in northern France, with Amiens as its capital.

Piccadilly (*OMC*4.II.ii; *DR*.vii.3; *WB*.II.xiii; *LLE*.The Woman I Met), part of central London.

pick out (in painting), make distinct.

pickers (*TM*.xxvii), used to clear musket-vents, or pick cartridges.

pick-thong, a kind of apple.

picter (dial.), picture.

pier, pillar.

pig . . . washed . . . wallowing . . . mire (*JO*.VI.iii), II Pet.ii,22.

pile, stake.

the pilgrim's Eternal City (*L*.pr.), the Celestial City or heavenly Jerusalem of *The Pilgrim's Progress* by John Bunyan, 1628–88.

pillar of a cloud (*TD*.x,1), Exod.xiii,14–22.

Pilsdon Pen, a high hill in west Dorset (visited by Hardy in September 1885: *Letters* I,136 and V,111).

The Pine Planters (*TL*). For the fictional scene and the thought that it was better not to be born (suggested while Hardy was planting trees to provide shelter for his new house Max Gate; cf. *Life* 173/509), see W.viii.

Pine-Avon, Mrs Nichola (*WB*). Her eyes are 'round, inquiring, luminous' (II.ii), like those of Lady Portsmouth's daughter, Lady Catherine Milnes-Gaskell (*Life* –/209).

pinion, hipped end of a building (i.e. a sloping roofed gable).

The Pink Frock (*MV*), based on Lady Yarborough and her deceased uncle (*Life* 264/281). *accordion-pleated*, pleated like an accordion.

pink in (of the day), draw in, close; (of daylight) diminish.

pinner (dial.), pinafore, apron and bib.

pins (colloquial), legs.

Piombo (*PPP*.The Respectable Burgher). See **Sebastiano**.

Pipe Rolls, annual records of the royal revenue and exchequer.

pis aller, last resort, what one accepts when one can't do better.

pitch-halfpenny (*GND*.II.ii), using halfpennies in the game of **pitch-and-toss** (*FMC*.vi). In this each player tosses a coin; the one nearest the mark then tosses all the coins and pockets all those that fall head up; the next nearest does the same with the remainder, and so on.

pith, spirit, essential quality, main strength; **pith and pulse** (*D3*.VI.vi), the strongest and most vital section.

Pitt Diamond (*RN*.III.vii). When he obtained the diamond named after him, Thomas Pitt, an East India merchant and governor of Madras, sent it to England, it is said, in his son's shoe.

The Pity of It (*MV*). Hardy gives surviving Anglo-Saxon expressions which he had heard in the country, proving the kinship of Germans and English, then (1915) at war; cf. ''Ch woll' (*W*.xvii).

pixy-led, led astray, as if by pixies.

The Place on the Map (*SC*), another projection of **The Christening** theme, probably suggested by the knowledge that Hardy's friend Horace Moule, who taught at Marlborough from 1865 to 1868, was the father of an illegitimate child. The MS title is 'A Poor Schoolmaster's Story'.

Places (*SC*). The references are to Plymouth (*the Three Towns*, Plymouth, Stonehouse, Devonport) and Boscastle. See **Old Hundred-and-Thirteenth Psalm**. *Saint Andrew's*, where Emma was baptized; *beneaped*, to no purpose (like a ship grounded by the neap tide).

plain, complain.

A Plaint to Man (*SC*). MS title, 'The Plaint of a Puppet'. *deicide*, cf. *SC*.God's Funeral and the last verses of Swinburne's 'Hertha' (*Songs of Sunrise*, 1871); *loving-kindness*, see **Altruism**.

Plaistow Marshes (*D*1.v.v), north of Thames docks to the east of London.

plannards (dial.), planets.

Plato's Socrates. 'What is wisdom?' (*RN*.III.ii), asked by Socrates in Plato's *Theaetetus*.

play upon him . . . instrument (*MC*.xxxviii), *Ham*.III.ii,360–3.

pleasing anxious beings (*JO*.v.v), cf. Gray's 'Elegy',86 (*G.T.*).

pleasure girdled about with pain (*TD*.xxv), Swinburne, *Atalanta in Calydon*, fourth chorus.

Pleiads, the Pleiades, a constellation of seven stars, which appear small and dim near Aldebaran.

Plena Timoris (Lat. title of a poem in *HS*), Full of Fear.

plenus rimarum (*DR*.xiv.3), 'full of chinks', unable to keep things to himself; from *Eunuchus* (I.i,25), one of the comedies of the Roman playwright Terence, c.190–159 BC.

plim (dial.), rise, swell.

plinth, projecting part of a wall immediately above the ground; **plinthstone**, square base of a column.

plock (dial.), block.

plough, let go the (*TD*.xlvii); **put my hand to . . . back** (*HE*.xxiv). Cf. Luke ix,62.

Plutarchian heroes (*D*3.IV.iv), in the lives of the Greek historian Plutarch (c.46–120 AD): **Brutus**, defeated at Philippi, committed suicide; **Themistocles**, the Athenian hero after the naval battle of Salamis against the Persians, became ostracized; **Cato** 'the Younger', a Stoic philosopher, committed suicide when the forces he had espoused against Julius Caesar were finally defeated; **Mark Antony**, ruler of the eastern part of the Roman empire (which he neglected for Cleopatra), committed suicide after defeat in the battle of Actium.

Plutonic master (*TD*.xlvii), Pluto himself, god of the Greek underworld or hell.

poachest, jailest (dial.), most disreputable (poaching, gaol).

Poems of 1912–13 (*SC*), inspired by the death of Emma Hardy on 27 Nov 1912, Hardy's return to places in Cornwall they had visited when they were in love, and a stay at Plymouth, where she had spent her early years. In the 1915 edition the last three poems were transferred to the group from the 'Lyrics and Reveries' of *SC*. See *Life* 359–61/386–9. (Notes on some of these poems are given separately.)

Poems of Pilgrimage (*PPP*). For Hardy's visits to Italy and Switzerland, 1887 and 1897, see *Life* 187/194ff and 292–5/310–13. (Notes on some of the poems are given under their titles.)

Poems of the Past and the Present (1901). Hardy's second volume of poetry opens with two groups, first on the Boer War, then on European visits. Acting on Matthew Arnold's maxim that great poetry implies the application of ideas to life, he then presents a gloomy Darwinian series of poems on Nature and the First Cause, followed by a substantial miscellany in which brighter moods are far outweighed by depressing poems with wintry overtones; see **frost**. Not surprisingly Hardy chose to end the volume on a more hopeful note, but it does little to counterbalance the iteration of poems which are bleak in both philosophical and personal outlook.

A Poet (*SC*). First intended as the final poem in the volume, it pays tribute to Hardy's two wives. Emma's encouragement did much to maintain Hardy's will to succeed as a writer. The poem was written a few months after his second marriage.

Poet of Liberty . . . great Dissector of Melancholy (*JO*.VI.ix), Shelley and Robert Burton (1577–1640), author of *The Anatomy of Melancholy*.

Polaris, the Pole Star (directly over the North Pole).

pole-wound (*D*3.IV.vi), caused by a carriage-pole (shaft; cf. *TD*.xxiii).

politesse du coeur (Fr.), genuine or heartfelt civility.

poll, top of the head.

Polly Peachum (*RN*.II.vi), heroine of John Gay's *The Beggar's Opera*, 1728. Miss Fenton, who played the part initially, became Duchess of Bolton.

pomace, pommy, the crushed apples or 'cheese' in cider-making.

Pommery. See **Pummery**.

Pomona (*W*.xxv), Roman goddess of fruit trees.

pomped, rode in pomp.

Pompeian, of Pompeii, buried by an eruption of Mt Vesuvius in 79 AD.

Pompey and Caesar (*D*2.VI.vii), two rival rulers of the Roman empire.

Pontius Pilate, at the trial of Jesus (*PPP*.The Respectable Burgher),

Matt.xxvii,11ff; 'What is truth?' (*RN*.III.ii), John xviii,38.

pony-shay (dial.), pony chaise, a light open carriage.

A Poor Man and a Lady (*HS*). See below. *fan*, wing; *town campaigns*, social engagements in town (i.e. in London), as if she sought to impress.

The Poor Man and the Lady. Written from the late summer of 1867 to January 1868, and revised by June 1868, at Higher Bockhampton, Hardy's first novel was originally subtitled 'A Story with no Plot, Containing some original verses'. It was inspired largely by 'a passion for reforming the world', its socialist satire including the upper classes, 'modern Christianity, church-restoration, and political and domestic morals in general'; its style aped Defoe's 'affected simplicity'. John Morley, Macmillan's reader, noted 'queer cleverness and hard sarcasm', but liked 'the opening pictures of the Christmas Eve in the tranter's house'. Advising for the publishers Chapman and Hall, George Meredith was responsible for the complicated plot connections of Hardy's next novel, *Desperate Remedies*. *The Poor Man and the Lady* remained unpublished, and the MS was eventually destroyed. Some of the material was used for the Knapwater setting and winter scenes in *DR*; the Christmas scenes were improved in *UGT*; the Rotten Row scene was adapted to *PBE* (cf. also Chevron Square, *OMC*4.II.ii,iii and *PBE*.xiv); and some of the satire probably entered *HE*. Some of its episodes (and radical views) contributed to 'An Indiscretion in the Life of an Heiress', 1878; another is preserved in *HS*.A Poor Man and a Lady. Hardy's later appraisals of the novel varied widely; he described it in December 1910 as 'the most original thing (for its date)' he had ever written. See *Life* 56–64/57–66, *Letters* IV,130, and **Mayne.**

Poor wounded name . . . lodge thee (*TD*.title-page), *TGV*.I.ii, 114–15.

poppet, puppet, doll, dear (addressed to a child).

popplestones, pebbles, shingle.

poppling, bubbling, brewing (a plot).

poppy . . . mandragora (*WT*5.iii; *W*.xxxvi), soporifics, *Oth*. III.iii,334–7.

poppy-head, the carved finial at the end of a pew.

A Popular Personage at Home (*HS*). Wessex was Florence Hardy's terrier. The emphasis is on 'at Home'; he attacked most strangers. See *Life* 434–5/469–70 and *WW*.Dead 'Wessex' the Dog to the

Household.

populous solitude (*RN*.I.vii), Byron, *Childe Harold* III.ci,cii.

porker, pig.

Port-Bredy (*MC*; *WT*4.ix, *WT*5; *TD*.xli; *LLI*.8d), Bridport, named after the river Brit which runs through the town; Hardy's name is from the river on its eastern side, the Bride, formerly the Bredy. St Mary's Church and the Black Bull Hotel are actual. The description of West Bay, to the south, as 'a little haven, seemingly a beginning made by Nature herself of a perfect harbour . . . famous', is a paraphrase of Holinshed's description in Hutchins.

the Porte (*D*2.I.viii), the Ottoman or Turkish Government.

Portingal (*D*1.v.v). Portugal is meant.

Portland (*TM*.xxxiv; *PPP*.The Souls of the Slain). See map H and **Isle of Slingers**. **Portland Roads** (*TM*.xxx), sheltered water north of Portland where ships could lie at anchor.

Po'sham (*TM*.xxxiii; cf. *D*1.v.iv), Portesham, where Captain Hardy (afterwards Admiral Sir Thomas) lived. See **Black'on**.

Positivism, Positivist. The Positivists did not attach importance to an unknowable other-life beyond life on earth. Taking their ideas from the French philosopher Auguste Comte (1798–1857), they urged the improvement of the lot of humanity as a whole through education and science, above all through creating 'the religion of humanity', a fervent will for altruistic endeavour in the cause of social justice and amelioration. Like George Eliot, Hardy sympathized greatly with this nineteenth-century creed. Cf. *Life* 146/150–1,332–3/358–9,376/407, *LLE*.Apology, and **Altruism**.

Possest beyond the Muse's painting (*DR*.v.3), William Collins, 'The Passions',6 (*G.T.*).

post hoc (*W*.xi), from the Latin *post hoc, ergo propter hoc*: after this, therefore on account of it.

postern-gate, entrance at the back (or side) of a building.

pot-housey (slang), vulgar, characteristic of an ale-house.

pot-walloper (from boiling one's pot), householder with a vote.

Poulkowa (*TT*.xxxviii), near Leningrad; it had a large astronomical transit instrument in 1838.

pourparlers (Fr.), preliminary discussions.

poussette, dance round and round with linked hands.

Poussin, Nicholas (*FMC*.xxii), French painter, 1594–1665.

poverty . . . consented . . . beaten (*JO*.VI.i), *RJ*.v.i,75.

Power, Paula (*L*). The surname alludes to the crucial importance of the new industrial 'aristocracy' in the national economy.

Praxitelean, by Praxiteles, a great sculptor of ancient Greece.

prebendary . . . diocesan (*L*.VI.iv), canon . . . bishop of the diocese.

precisian, one who is rigidly precise in observances.

prédilection d'artiste (Fr.), artistic preference (*L*.I.xiv). For the essay from which Hardy took the phrase, see **Wertherism of the uncultivated**; Hillebrand attributes it to A. W. Schlegel.

Premonitions (*HS*). They are connected with the death of Betty Privett's husband; see *LLI*.8c.

prepense, premeditated, deliberate.

President of the Immortals, in Aeschylean phrase (*TD*.lix), *Prometheus Bound*, 169; cf. *Life* 243–4/256–7. The view is quite inconsistent with Hardy's, which is more accurately reflected at the end of *TD*.xi; 'sport' recalls the *King Lear* quotation in the 1892 preface.

press, hurry; **prest**, hurried.

Prester John, a legendary priest and king, later identified as the legendary king of Ethiopia. The story (*MC*.xix) is from Ariosto's *Orlando Furioso* XXXIII.cvi–cviii.

Priddle, Retty (*TD*). In naming her, Hardy thought of poorer descendants of the aristocratic Paridelles; cf. Nanny Priddle (*GND*.1) and *Life* 202/211, 3 Sep.

primâ-facie (Lat.), based on first impressions.

prime, age of perfection, the first (primitive) era; excellent; (vb.) supply, load, trim. **the Prime**, the Prime Mover or First Cause; **primest**, best.

primum mobile. Beyond the concentric spheres of the Ptolemaic or pre-Copernican universe was the outer, the *primum mobile*, which imparted motion to all of them; hence its use in *TD*.xlvii as the Prime Mover or First Cause responsible for Tess's suffering, which is represented in the main action of the chapter, and is summed up in 'once victim, always victim'. In *TT*.xxxiv the term means 'prime cause'.

Prince of Darkness (*WT*.1; suggested in *CM*.12), the Devil, *KL*.III.iv,139; cf. 'Beelzebub the prince of devils', Matt.xii,24.

Princess Ida (*MC*.xx). It is in fact the hero prince who writes 'in such a hand', Tennyson, *The Princess* I,233–4.

Prinny (*D2*.IV.vii), a familiar name for the dissolute Prince of Wales, who became Prince Regent in 1810 and George IV in 1820.

Prisoners' base, a game for two groups with two bases, the object being to capture as many of the 'enemy' as possible; a player in the middle is chased by one of the other side, who is then pursued by one from the other.

Pro – Pre – (*W*.xxxv), Prometheus who, for bringing fire from the sun to the earth, was chained to a rock in the Caucasus at the behest of Zeus, his liver to be gnawn, without diminution, by a vulture for 30,000 years.

pro tem (Lat. *pro tempore*), for the time being.

pro-cathedral, a church which is used as a cathedral.

A Procession of Dead Days (*LLE*). The first three relate to Hardy's first visit to Cornwall, and falling in love with Emma Gifford; the next alludes to their engagement; the fifth, to their marriage. the sixth, to unhappiness in marriage; the seventh, to Emma Hardy's death. *I did not know*, cf. *Life* 359–60/386–7; *thrums*, tufts of ivy flowers (the ivy, an evergreen, has been traditionally associated with death and immortality); *third hour*, from 8 to 9 a.m., when Emma died, with a Crucifixion overtone (cf. Mark xv,25 and **Near Lanivet**).

prodigal's favourite . . . (*PBE*.xxii), Wordsworth, 'The Small Celandine' (*G.T.*).

professor of the tongue (*MC*.pr.), Sir George Douglas, a Scottish writer (not professor) whose friendship with Hardy began in 1881, when Sir George was visiting his brother, who studied land-agency at Wimborne.

The Profitable Reading of Fiction (Orel,110–25), written for *The Forum*, New York, where it appeared in March 1888.

proh pudor! (Lat.), for shame!

projick (dial.), project, plan; prodigy.

Promethean (*RN*.I.iii), like that of Prometheus; cf. **Pro – Pre –** .

prophet on the top of Peor (*TD*.xl), Balaam, Num.xxiii,27–xxiv,10.

The Prophetess (*WW*), Emma Gifford; the song, by Edward Hoffman, seems to be alluded to in *MV*.The Change.

Prophet's chamber (*MC*.xxxii), II Kings iv,10.

prophet's gourd (*TD*.lv), Jon.iv,10.

propylaea (Gk. 'before the gate'), gateway.

Proskenion (*D*1.II.i), proscenium, stage, spectacle (Gk.).

The Prospect (*HS*). After Emma's death and burial, Hardy wishes to join her. For the garden party 'last July', see *Life* 359/386.

Prospero . . . Ariel (*CM*.12.viii), cf. *Tem*.I.ii,189ff.

Protean ability, to change appearance, like the classical sea-god

Proteus.

Proud Songsters (*WW*). Cf. *TD*.xx, opening.

Prout, Samuel (*W*.v), English painter, 1783–1852.

prow, valiant.

Psalm of Asaph (*W*.xxxv), Psalm lxxiii; see verses 14–15.

Psyche, the Greek personification of the soul.

Ptolemaic System (*TT*.vii), the pre-Copernican, in which the earth was thought to be central to the universe.

Publicans . . . Pharisees (*TD*.xliv). Cf. Luke vii,34 and xi,43–4.

pucker, confusion, state of agitation.

Puck-like . . . Hermia . . . Demetrius (*TT*.xxxix), *MND*: Puck's mismating affects Lysander and Helena; Demetrius is already in love with Hermia.

Puff . . . Lord Burleigh's nod (*PBE*.xiv), the interpreter at the rehearsal of his own play; he finds profound meaning in the silent impersonator of Queen Elizabeth's minister, who makes his exit, shaking his head (Sheridan, *The Critic* III.i, a play referred to by the Prince of Wales, *D*2.II.iii).

Pugin, Augustus (*HE*.xxxviii; *L*.I.i), English architect (1812–52), who did much to revive the Gothic style in England; in *JO*.v.vi he is contrasted with Christopher Wren (1632–1723), whose churches, notably in London after the Great Fire, were built in the classical style.

pugree (cf. 'puggree', an Indian turban), a scarf of thin muslin or silk wound round the crown of a sun-helmet, and falling down behind to shade the neck.

pulse-glass, an instrument which, when held, registers the pulsing of the blood.

pulsion, propulsion, impelling influence.

Pummery (*MC*.xvi; *WP*.The Burghers, The Dance at the Phoenix, My Cicely; *TL*.The Curate's Kindness; *HS*.A Sheep Fair, The Flight on Durnover Moor), the local name for Poundbury Camp, which may have been fortified by the Romans. This hill overlooks the Frome river, immediately NW of Dorchester.

pummy. See **pomace**.

Punchinello, Punch of the puppet-shows, introduced from the Continent during the Restoration period. For the diversion of the spectators he was often associated with kings and people of high degree. Here (*TT*.xxxix), and in the reference to Puck which follows, the role of the Mephistophelean Louis Glanville is hinted at.

pupil-teacher, young elementary-school teacher, receiving tuition for his/her lessons from the head in out-of-school hours, and hoping to qualify for college-training.
pur sang (Fr.), of pure blood, genuine.
Purbeck, from the Isle of Purbeck (map D).
purblinking (dial.), dull, dim.
Purchess, Jems (James: *D*1.II.v), perhaps the actual surname; cf. *Life* 162/168.
A Pure Woman (*TD*.title-page), suggested perhaps by the 'pure womanly' of Thomas Hood's 'The Bridge of Sighs' (*G.T.*), though it has a different significance.
Purification Day. See **Candlemas**.
the purple light and **bloom** (*DR*.III.2; *PBE*.iv; *W*.xxiv) of love: Gray, 'The Progress of Poesy', 41 (*G.T.*).
Pusey, Edward (1800–82), an Oxford Tractarian; he began *The Oxford Library of the Fathers* in 1836 (*LLI*.4.ii).
Puss-in-the-Corner (MCR), a children's game in which one player surplus to the number of recognised places attempts to gain one when the others change positions.
put, a card game rather like nap.
put upon, victimized, exploited.
putlogs, pieces of strong timber for supporting scaffold-boards.
put-to, tried, distressed.
The Puzzled Game-Birds (*PPP*), entitled 'The Battue' in the 1912 edition; cf. *WP*.She, to Him I,10.
pyle, baker's long-handled shovel for placing loaves in large ovens or extracting them when baked.
Pyramus and Thisbe (*UGT*.I.vi), *MND*.v.

Q

Quae finis . . . poenas luam (*PBE*.vii, translated later in the chapter), Horace, *Epodes* xvii,36–7; see xii for Swancourt's thoughts.

quag, mess.
quantities (*JO*.v.viii), lengths of vowels or syllables.
quare (dial.), queer.
quarrenden, a red early apple.
quarries, small diamond-shaped window-panes.
quarten, about four pounds.
quarter, eight bushels (a full sack).
quarter-jack, a mechanical human figure, striking each quarter-hour.
Quartershot (*JO*.v.v,vii), Aldershot (Hardy's name suggests an army centre).
quat (dial.), squat, stoop.
Quatre Bras (*L*.v.ix), a preliminary battle to Waterloo. For the battle, and the ball in Brussels, see *D*3.VI.ii–vi.
Queen Caroline to her Guests (*HS*). Some sympathy is expressed for Caroline the princess in *D*2.VI.vi,vii and *D*3.II.iv,III.viii, but it is more evident here. She was the wife of the notorious Prince Regent. When he came to the throne in 1820, she returned to the Continent, where she had lived indiscreetly. She was refused entrance at his coronation, and committed suicide three weeks later.
Queen Charlotte (*TM*.xxi; cf. xii. *D*1.II.iv), wife of George III.
Queen of Love (*RN*.II.vi), Venus. See **Aeneas**.
Queen of Night (*RN*.I.vii title), the name of a character in *The Magic Flute* (opera with music by Mozart).
Queen of Sheba (*TD*.xix), her visit to Solomon, I Kings x,1–13.
Queen, Shall be his (*TT*.vii), suggested by a line in Tennyson's 'The Beggar Maid'.
Queen Scheherazade (*RN*.II.iii), the *raconteuse* of wonderful tales in *The Arabian Nights*.
Queen's Scholar, a pupil-teacher who was awarded a maintenance grant for a training-college. Named after Queen Victoria, such scholarships were awarded on the results of annual examinations. They were instituted in 1846; in 1856 they were made available to all who were recommended by the colleges, not just pupil-teachers; some time after 1863 they were abolished. The term 'Queen's Scholar' was subsequently applied to anyone who passed the training-college entrance examination.
A Question of Marriage (*WW*). This originated from Lady Waldegrave's answer to Robert Browning's marriage-proposal (*Letters* II,144): 'We dine our poets . . . but we do not marry

them'.

queue (Fr. tail), pigtail; follow, dog.

quick, quicken, vitalize. **the quick**, the living (people).

Quid Hic Agis? (*MV*). The title is from I Kings xix,9, Vulgate ('What doest thou here?') All three references to the story of Elijah are related to Hardy's wife Emma and the church at St Juliot, the first to August 1870 (when she may have played the harmonium across the aisle), the second to August 1872 (when he read the lesson; cf. *Life* 156–7/162 and *PBE*.xix), the third to Hardy's memorial to Emma in the church, and his feeling during the war, like Elijah's 'O Lord, take away my life . . . I, even I only, am left'. *sands*, the sands of Time. The poem was first published in August 1916, when Hardy knew that the memorial tablet he had ordered had been erected (*Life* 361/389,373/403–4).

The Quiet Woman (*RN*; *LLI*.7). The original inn (facing Puddletown Heath from the Stinsford–Tincleton road) was called the Travellers' Rest (cf. *LLE*.Weathers). Its site is occupied by Duck Farm buildings.

quieted by hope (DLa), slopes into a darkness not . . . ; the negative of Browning's *Sordello* i,370.

Quin, James (1693–1766), the leading actor in England; he died at Bath. See **Shockerwick House**.

quire, choir (Hardy usually concentrates on the instrumentalists).

quirk, follow sudden inclinations.

quiz, make fun of, gaze inquiringly at, pry into, examine closely; an eccentric person; quizzing, banter.

quoin, corner.

quondam, former, at one time.

Quoniam Tu fecisti (*LLE*.After Reading Psalms XXXIX, XL, etc). References to the Vulgate below are followed by those to the common English version:

> Because Thou didst it, xxxviii, 10 = xxxix,9.
> Thou hast led me, lx,3 = lxi,2, where it is omitted.
> Thou hast upheld me, xl,13 = xli,12.
> Thou hast made my days, xxxviii,6 = xxxix,5.
> O Lord, Thou hast known, xxxix,10 = xl,9.
> Whom hast Thou chosen? lxiv,5 = lxv,4.

Quos ego (*DR*.ix.6), Whom I (Lat.), indicative of menace and anger which are restrained (cf. Neptune in Virgil, *Aeneid* i,135).

R

the Race, a dangerous area of waters where 'two seas' meet near Portland Bill; see map H.

race . . . swift . . . strong (*LLI*.8 Introduction), Eccl.ix.11.

rack, torment.

racket, exciting occasion; **rackety**, noisy, boisterous.

rackless (dial.), careless, heedless, reckless.

Raffaelle, or Raphael (*RN*.II.iv; *L*.I.ii,VI.v; the infant John the Baptist in the 'Garvagh Madonna', acquired by the N.G. in 1865, *TT*.i; *WT*5.ii), Italian painter, 1483–1520.

raffle, a gambling game with three dice. An equal pair is higher than a throw of three different numbers, and a **pair-royal**, a throw of three equal numbers, higher still; the highest is 'a raffle of aces'.

raft (dial.), rouse, upset.

Rain on the Grave (*SC*). *S.R.* had reminded Hardy that daisies had been Emma's earliest memory. 'I am longing to see daisies again, I love them', she wrote in March 1902.

Rainbarrows, three neighbouring tumuli on Puddletown Heath about $\frac{1}{2}$ m. SE of Hardy's birthplace. The most prominent is the **Rainbarrow** of *RN* (cf. *TM*.pr. – 'beacon-hill' – and xii,xxvi; *D*1.II.v, *D*3.v.vi; *WP*.The Alarm; TL.By the Barrows; *HS*.The Sheep-Boy, The Paphian Ball). The Roman road ran north of them, past Stinsford, and through Dorchester.

the rainbow, a sign of blessing, from God's blessing after the Flood (Gen.viii,21–ix,17). **rainbow iris**: see **iris-bow**.

raison d'être (Fr. reason for existence), key, justification.

Rake-Hell Muses (*LLE*). *rake-hell*, rake (the MS has 'seducer'), thorough scoundrel; *intermell*, mixture (of gladness and sorrow); *ell*, a short length (just over a metre).

rale (local pronunciation), real.

Raleigh, Walter, etc. (*JO*.VI.ix). **Raleigh**, Elizabethan courtier and navigator, was a student at Oriel College, Oxford; John **Wycliffe** (c.1329–84), Church reformer, was for a short period Master of Balliol; William **Harvey** (1578–1657), physician and Warden of Merton College, Oxford; Richard **Hooker** (1554–1600), theologian, fellow of Corpus Christi, Oxford; Matthew **Arnold**; and writers of 'Tracts for the Times' (supporters of the High Church or 'Oxford Movement' begun by J. H. Newman; see **Tractarian**).

Rama . . . innocents . . . Herod (*MV*.Then and Now), Matt.ii,12–18.

The Rambler (*TL*). *SC*.In Front of the Landscape,49–66, and *SC*.Self-Unconscious may throw light on Hardy's thought. The personal associations of place, which grow with time, have much greater significance than such places had, or have, in the present. The reference to constellated daisies and cuckoos, then to nature eloquent with love divine, suggests that Hardy's poem developed from his disagreement with Wordsworth's view of his own youth (when 'every common sight' seemed invested in celestial splendour).

rames (dial.), skeleton, carcass, remains.

randy, randyvoo (dial.), party, celebration, merrymaking.

rantipole (dial.), noisy, wild.

The Rash Bride (*TL*). *Woolcomb, Swetman*, cf. map C and *Life* 214–15/223–4; the Swetmans were related to Hardy's maternal grandmother (*Life* 6–7/10–11). Michael, see **Mail**; *old bass player*, see **Dewy, William**.

rashness of those parents (*JO*.VI.ii), Adam and Eve, an allusion to the Fall in Milton, *Paradise Lost* ix,780.

Rasselas. At the end of the sixth chapter of this novel by Samuel Johnson (1759) the inventor attempts his first flight, and falls immediately into a lake after leaping from a promontory. His wings are useless in the air, but sustain him in the water (*RN*.IV.ii). A reader who seeks 'didactic reflection' will find 'large lumps' in this novel (PRF).

the Ratcatcher's Daughter, a popular street-ballad in the nineteenth century.

ratch (for 'reach'), extend, stretch.

rathe (archaic), soon, early. **ratheness**, eagerness. **rathe-ripes**, apples which ripen early.

rat-tailed (of a horse), the tail having little or no hair.

The Raven (*JO*.II.vi), a reciter's poem (by Edgar Allan Poe).

rawmil, made from raw (unskimmed or creamy) milk.

ray (dial.), dress, array.

raze . . . written troubles . . . brain (*WT*.1), *Mac*.v.iii,42.

read, mark, learn (*OMC*4.I.iii; **and inwardly digest**, *JO*.II.ii), from the collect for the second Sunday in Advent (see the Book of Common Prayer).

ready writer (*LLI*.8g), Psalm xlv,1.

realty, real property or estate.

The Recalcitrants (*SC*). This title had been chosen for *JO*; cf. *TL*.The Conformers. *brazen god*, false god, idol (cf. Dan.v,4).

recent poet (*MC*.xiv), Tennyson, alluding to 'Tears, idle tears, I know not what they mean' (*The Princess* iv,21); 'recent' was added in the 1895 edition, after the poet's death in 1892.

re'ch, sail on a reach (i.e. a run on one tack).

reck, care, consider. **reck'd not . . . rede**: see **steep**.

the Red King's Castle (*WB*), Rufus Castle, Portland. Tradition holds that it was built by William II (reigned 1087–1100); see **Rufus**.

redan, a salient earthwork defence with two faces forming an angle.

redding, red ochre, used for marking sheep.

redingote grise (*D*3.v.iii), grey frock-coat (Fr.).

Redrutin (*CM*.11.vi), Redruth, Cornwall.

reductio ad absurdum (Lat.), example carried to an absurd extreme.

reed shaken with the wind (*DR*.xiii.1), Matt.xi,7.

reed-drawing, method of obtaining the best straw from sheaves of corn, particularly for thatching stacks of corn (*TD*.xliii; cf. the use of 'reed-sheaves' in *FMC*.xxxvii).

The Re-Enactment (*SC*), a fiction woven around the rectory at St Juliot and Hardy's memory of Emma (*same gown*, cf. *Life* 69/71,78/81; *brown* hair, cf. *SC*.A Dream or No; *piano*, *PBE*.iii). They are 'the predestined sorrowers' (cf. *LLE*.'Where three roads joined').

A Refusal (*HS*). In July 1924 a petition signed by leading statesmen and writers, including Hardy, for a memorial to Byron in Westminster Abbey, on the centenary of his death, was rejected on the grounds of his dissolute life and licentious verse. *dict*, teaching; *Philistian*, Philistine, materialistic; *horner*, adulterer; *name mere*, mere inscription; *gablet*, gabled niche. Shelley and Swinburne, both condemned by the conventional, were Hardy's favourite poets.

regrater, middleman, intermediary.

The Rejected Member's Wife (*TL*), *the balcony*, at the County Hall, High West Street, Dorchester, when the previous M.P., Colonel Brymer of Ilsington House, Puddletown, lost his seat in the

January 1906 election.

relieving officer, official responsible for poor-relief.

reliveing, renewal of lease by life-holders.

Rembrandt (*FMC*.l; *RN*.II.vi; *L*.I.xv), Dutch painter (1606–69), his work characterized by chiaroscuro.

Remembrance Day (*JO*.VI.i), Commemoration Day at Oxford; attended by Hardy in 1893 (*Life* 257/272–3).

Reminiscences of a Dancing Man (*TL*). One MS suggests it was written in 1895, after Hardy and his wife had visited Almack's (*Life* 274/289). For reminiscences cf. *Life* 42–3/45 (Almack's, 'sometime' – i.e. formerly + Willis's) and 34/38–9,43/45 (Argyle and Cremorne). *jaunty jills*, lively young women; *Jullien* (1812–60), a French conductor who had helped to popularize music in London (cf. *Life* 123/126–7); *doth moue*, grimaces at.

remnant not yet cut off (*PBE*.xiv), cf. Isa.xiv,22.

removing . . . things . . . remain (*TD*.xviii; *LLE*.Apology), Heb.xii,27.

Render unto Caesar (*WT7*.iv,vii), Mark xii,17.

rendlewood (*W*.xxxvii), oak branches stripped of bark.

repeater, a watch that strikes the hour.

repoussé, beaten on the reverse side to give ornamental relief.

reprise, reprisal, retaliation.

Resurrection . . . Magdalen (*TD*.xx), John xx,1–18; see **Magdalen**.

Retty's Phases (*HS*). *Retty*, a common form of 'Henrietta'; *Vale*, the valley of the shadow of death (Psalm xxiii).

The Return of the Native (twelve monthly instalments in *Belgravia*, 1878) was begun early in 1877 at Sturminster Newton, after a Christmas visit to Higher Bockhampton and 'Egdon Heath' (*Life* 113/116). Difficulties with publishers and editors (including Leslie Stephen, who feared that the developing situation would be 'dangerous' for serial readers) made Hardy revise the first fifteen chapters, probably giving greater emphasis to its Hellenic theme, after reading Matthew Arnold's 'Pagan and Medieval Religious Sentiment'. (Seven of the revised chapters were ready in August.) Arnold's reference to Heine and 'the brilliant whirl of Paris' may have determined the choice of Eustacia's goal, but Pater's essay on Winckelmann had a deeper influence. Besides nourishing the antithesis (deeply rooted for Hardy in Swinburne) between pagan or Hellenic enjoyment of life and the fever and fret of modernity, between hedonistic Eustacia and altruistic Clym, it suggested the fire and dancing of I.iii. Pater regarded such pagan ritual as an 'anodyne' against 'the law which makes life sombre for the vast majority of mankind', a view which informs the opening chapter on Egdon. By overloading Eustacia with Greek and other associations, especially in the Queen of Night chapter, Hardy attempts a grandeur which her role cannot sustain; the reference to her as Clym's 'Olympian girl' rings false, and her assumption that she deserves a Saul or a Bonaparte in his place indicates authorial misjudgment as much as romantic illusion. The tragedy depends on two possibilities which can hardly suspend disbelief: Mrs Yeobright's inexplicit questioning about the guineas which is nothing less than an insult to Eustacia, and the coincidental murmuring of 'Mother' which leads the latter to think that Clym has opened the door to her. Nevertheless the tragic ending (v.iii reinforced with some theatrical language from Webster's *The White Devil*, IV.ii) is excitingly managed and movingly told, so much so that the happy ending may seem *de trop* at first. Hardy's explanation that it was a serial requirement is hardly adequate, for it satisfies some legitimate expectations, and completes (conceptually, at least) the artistic unity of the novel, pagan celebrations and a Rainbarrow scene by day counterbalancing those in darkness at the beginning. Clym is unfitted for the May-day festivities, and his sermons have little meaning for poor people without the amenities of life. His mother-fixation raises the question whether Hardy, who had disappointed his mother by giving up a career in a capital city, and (more than is known perhaps at this stage of his life) probably in the choice of his wife, put more into this novel than he or Emma realized. By stressing the insignificance of the protagonists, heath images of ephemeral insect life and of geological time give the tragedy a Darwinian dimension, especially in the pitiless circumstances of Mrs Yeobright's death. The fire of the dispassionate sun is natural, unlike the fire and blaze which symbolize Eustacia's passion and rebelliousness against fate. Her local reputation as a witch is confirmed for the superstitious Susan Nonsuch on hearing from her son how she had looked through a window at Mrs Yeobright. Like Clym's blindness, scenes at the well and during the eclipse have a more obvious symbolism than that of the plantation in the storm (III.vi), an active Egdon expression of Hardy's modern view of life compared with the ancient and more natural. The rustic characters in chorus may or may not equal those of *FMC*, but the tragedy is more strongly developed, and *RN* undoubtedly marks a surge forward in the kind of fiction which was to appeal most to Hardy as a philosopher of life.

Revalley (*TM*.xxi), a common English pronunciation of 'Reveille', the early morning military trumpet-call.

Revelations, end of (*PBE*.xxiii), end of the world, formerly linked with 'kingdom come' (the coming of the new heaven and earth of Revelation).

Reveller's (*W*.xxviii), **Revellers** (*W*.xlv) **Inn**, Revels Inn, now a farm-house, once a coach-inn, on the old Sherborne and Bristol road NE of Dogbury Hill.

Revett and Stuart (*L*.I.i), authors of *The Antiquities of Athens* (1762), which helped to revive Greek architectural style in England.

Revised Code (*TD*.iii). The Code or regulations for elementary schools, teachers, and training was frequently amended from 1846 to the 1870 period, when elementary State schools became obligatory wherever voluntary schools could not provide the required education for all; the main changes came with the Revised Code of 1862.

The Revisitation (*TL*), first published as 'Time's Laughingstocks, A Summer Romance'. The old barrack is at Dorchester; Milton Woods, near Milton Abbas; Dole Hill, to the north of Puddletown. For other places, see map A and **Waterston**. *Sarsen stone*, a large stone from which the surrounding chalk has been washed away in the course of time (from 'Saracen', because such stones were associated with pagan rites); *fief*, inherited land. *Time's transforming chisel*, cf. *WP*.In a Eweleaze . . . . *Love is lame at fifty years*, cf. the lovers at the end of *CM*2.

Reynard, Stephen (*GND*.1), Stephen Fox of Farley, near Salisbury, who married Elizabeth Horner in 1736, prospered at the court of George II, and became Lord Ilchester in 1741 and Earl of Ilchester in 1756.

Reynolds, Sir Joshua (*OMC*4.II.i; *HE*.xxxviii; *L*.I.iii; *WT*5.v; *JO*.III.ii; *D*1.VI.vi; *Life* 216–17/226), English painter, 1723–92.

Rhadamanthus, a judge in the Greek underworld of the dead.

ribstone-pippin, a variety of dessert apple.

Richter, J. P. F. (*RN*.I.vii), German novelist and humorist (1763–1825) who wrote under the name of 'Jean Paul'.

Rickman, Thomas (*L*.I.xi), author of *Styles of Architecture in England*, 1817.

The Riddle (*MV*), Emma Gifford in Cornwall, and Emma Hardy (facing east, sunrise symbolizing the Resurrection) in her grave.

Riddles of death Thebes never knew (*D*.pr), Shelley, *Hellas*,1083.

Ridgeway, Ridge-way (*UGT*; TM; *WT*3; *D*1.I.i,II.iv,IV.i; *WP*.The Alarm; *MV*.Great Things, Old Excursions). The first is the old road crossing the downs between Dorchester and Weymouth; *CM*.1 shows that it crossed the second, 'the old Ridge-way', running 'at right angles' on the downs (map G).

ridge-way, Ridge-way, Ridgeway (*JO*), on the downs south of Wantage (map I). Although it has been marked 'Icknield Way' on various maps, and Hardy says it was 'the Icknield Street and original Roman road through the district' (I.iii), some believe that the Roman route was a little to the north, below the downs.

riding-lights, lights of ships at anchor.

Ridley, burning of (*JO*.VI.vi). See **Christminster**.

right ascensions and declinations (*TT*.vi), co-ordinates which, corresponding to lines of longitude and latitude, give the position of heavenly bodies.

Rimsmoor Pond (*RN*.IV.vi), not far SE of 'Alderworth'; **Oker's Pool** is further along this route, near Oaker's Wood.

The Ring (*MC*.xi), Maumbury, or Maumbury Rings; see **Casterbridge**.

ring bells backward. Church bells were rung backward (in the reverse of the usual order) as an alarm-signal.

Rings-Hill Speer (*TT*). Though the tower was suggested by a more impressive one in Charborough Park, 4 m. west of Wimborne, its site is that of the memorial obelisk on Weatherbury Castle, a wooded hill ringed with earthworks south of Milborne St Andrew and 3 m. ENE of 'Weatherbury'.

Ringsworth (*DR*.iii.2; *WT*7.iv), the cliffs of Ringstead Bay, east of Weymouth Bay.

rithe (living too), fast, wildly (dial.).

River of Life . . . Evangelist (*TD*.xvi), Rev.xxii,1, seen by John, the reputed author of the fourth gospel (New Testament).

road to dusty death (DLa; *TD*.xviii), cf. *Mac*.v.v,23.

The Roast Beef of Old England (*MC*.v), a popular song: words by Henry Fielding (1731) set to music by Richard Leveridge (d.1758).

robed . . . beheld her not (*WB*.II.ix), Shelley, 'Epipyschidion', 199–200.

Robinson Crusoe, hero of a popular adventure story by Daniel Defoe (1719), originating from the experiences of Alexander Selkirk, who had been put ashore on the uninhabited island of

Juan Fernandez. Crusoe is shipwrecked, and manages alone by ingenuity until his island is visited by cannibals; his life is saved by the poor savage Friday, who becomes his servant; an English ship rescues him. Gabriel Oak owns a copy of the book (*FMC*.viii); as solitary as Robinson Crusoe, *DR*.v.1; Crusoe's first shot, *PBE*.xii; Crusoe after seeing the print of a man's foot in the sand (the first sign of the cannibals), *L*.II.iv; his inability to drag the large boat he had built down to the water, *TT*.ix, *JO*.II.vi; the returned Crusoe of the hour, *MC*.xlv; Crusoe's island, *W*.xix; losing a day during his illness (he had slept through it, and wakened two days later), *WB*.III.viii.

Rochefoucauld, La (*MC*.xv), French writer (1613–80) best remembered for his *Réflexions* or *Maximes*, no. 289 of which is referred to: 'La simplicité affectée est une imposture délicate.'

Rocher des Doms (*D*3.IV.vi scene). This rocky site (now a park) near Notre Dame des Doms, the cathedral at Avignon, ends precipitously above the Rhone and affords extensive views.

rock, clean, remove the 'fur' from inside a kettle.

rod in pickle, punishment in store.

Rogers . . . Tomline (examples of contented mediocrity, *RN*.III.ii): Samuel **Rogers**, 1763–1855, poet; Benjamin **West**, 1738–1820, an American painter who lived in England; Lord **North**, 1733–92, George III's prime minister when the American colonies were lost; Sir George **Tomline**, 1750–1827, a friend of the younger Pitt; he tutored him at Cambridge, and became his secretary (cf. *D*1.VI.viii); after being Dean of St Paul's and, for a long period, Bishop of Lincoln, he became Bishop of Winchester.

the Rogue's March (*MC*.xxxiii), played in the British army when a soldier was dismissed in disgrace.

Roman (nose), with a distinct bridge.

Roman Catholic young man (*LLE*.Apology), J. M. Hone on Hardy's poetry in *The London Mercury*, Feb 1922. Edmund Gosse, reviewing *LLE* in *The Sunday Times*, 28 May 1922, had made light of this 'knowing reviewer'.

Roman cement, made from chalk or clay with lime, sand, and water.

Roman Forum (*CM*6), an open space in ancient Rome for spectacular State occasions.

The Roman Gravemounds (*SC*), based on the loss of Hardy's 'study cat' Kitsy in November 1910, and the discovery of Roman graves at Max Gate when it was being built (cf. Orel,191–4).

The Roman Road (*TL*). It ran across Puddletown Heath ('He'th in *TL*.By the Barrows, and elsewhere), and south of Hardy's birthplace in the Dorchester direction. Hardy remembers childhood walks with his mother.

Romance (blood), of Roman origin.

The Romantic Adventures of a Milkmaid (*CM*.12; hastily written about the turn of the year 1882–3), a fantasy combining the fairy tale with the real, and a Cinderella-like episode with Mephistophelean elements; for the Prince of Darkness suggestions, cf. the final lines of *TL*.Reminiscences of a Dancing Man. Hardy had thought of ending with Marjorie accompanying the Baron, never to return, on the yacht that disappears as if in Arthurian romance; he adopted the reunion of wife and husband to suit magazine requirements. As the story was conceived in a world radically different from that of *TD*, Hardy changed its setting for inclusion in *CM*; originally it was chiefly at Stickleford in the Swenn (Frome) valley, and at Casterbridge, Winford Hill being Stinsford Hill, and the Baron departing from a little cove (recognisably Lulworth) flanked by 'miniature pillars of Hercules'. See **Chillington Wood**.

Rome (*WB*.III.i), the steps above the Piazza di Spagna, leading up to the Trinità de' Monti church, and houses where Shelley lived and Keats died.

Rome: At the Pyramid of Cestius (*PPP*). The irony is that little is known of Cestius, whose grand pyramidal tomb (cf. Shelley's *Adonais* l) guides the visitor to the humbler graves of the 'two matchless singers', Keats and Shelley.

Rome: Building a New Street . . . (*PPP*). *Outskeleton*, present in skeleton form; *metope*, square space of stone between triglyphs in the frieze; *gnome*, maxim; *cove and quoin*, architectural features where (a) wall and ceiling, (b) walls, meet.

Rome: On the Palatine (*PPP*). On this, the largest of Rome's seven hills, Roman emperors and aristocracy had lived. Hardy visits the ruins of the temple of Jupiter Victor, the dining-room of Livia, wife of the emperor Augustus, with its decorated walls, then (via the Crypto-Portico route) the remains of the emperor Caligula's palace, where he hears waltz strains by the Viennese composer Strauss; cf. *Life* 189/196.

Rome. The Vatican: Sala delle Muse (*PPP*), the hall devoted to the nine classical muses; see **Helicon**, and cf. *Life* 189/196,299–300/320–1.

Romney, George (*OMC*4.II.i; *L*.VI.v), English portrait-painter, 1734–1802.

rood-screen (MCR), a carved screen of wood or stone, surmounted by a rood or cross, beneath the chancel arch, and dividing the nave of the church from the choir.

rookery, cluster of tenements densely populated by the poor.

Rookington Park (*HE*.viii), Heron Court and its wooded park, NE of Bournemouth.

rooted melancholy . . . ministry can reach (*TT*.xli), cf. *Mac*.V.iii, 40–1.

Rosa, Salvator (*L*.VI.v), Italian painter, 1615–73.

Rosalind, **played with the perfection of** (*GND*.1), in *AYL*. **Rosalind's exclamation** (*MC*.xxxiii), *AYL*.III.v,57–8.

Rosaline (*WB*.I.viii), whom Romeo loved before falling in love with Juliet, *RJ*.I.ii,82–4. The views which follow were Hardy's when he thought of a novel *Time against Two, Life* 164/171.

Rossini (*WB*.II.xi), Italian operatic composer, 1792–1868.

rote, habit, routine; **in (by) rote**, mechanically.

rouge-et-noir (*MC*.x), red and black (cf. v, rich complexion verging on swarthiness, black eye), suggested by the title of Stendhal's novel *Le Rouge et le Noir*, 1831.

round robin, petition or protest with signatures arranged in a circle, so that nobody can be accused of being the ringleader.

the round world . . . therein (*D*1.II.v), Psalm xcviii,8.

Rousseau (of Wildeve, *RN*.III.vi), a man who tends to live in his subjective world, a prey to his emotions and imagination, like the French writer Jean Jacques Rousseau, 1712–78.

rout, once a fashionable word for a party.

The Rover Come Home (*HS*), written from a passage on Bob Loveday, who returns with an increased resemblance to his mother (*TM*.xv). *Canso Cape to Horn*, Nova Scotia to the southern point of South America; *Comorin . . . Behring's Strait*, the southern point of India to the passage between Asia and Alaska.

Row (Rotten Row), **Boulevard**, **Rialto**, **Prado** (*PBE*.xiv), in London, Paris, Venice, Madrid.

Royal personage, visit of a (*MC*.pr and xxxvii). Albert, Prince Consort of England, visited Dorchester in 1849 *en route* for Weymouth, beyond which he laid the foundation-stone of the breakwater which created the Portland naval base. (Hardy's chronology is deliberately confused: the railway, for example, reached Dorchester in 1847; the archway leading to North Square was demolished in 1848, and the museum (xxii) was not opened in a back street – Trinity Street – until 1851.)

Royal Society (*TT*.ix), incorporated by Charles II in 1662 for the promotion of the physical sciences.

Royal unicorn, on the coat-of-arms of the British royal family.

Royal-tower'd Thame (*JO*.v.iv), the last words of Milton's 'At a Vacation Exercise'; the reference is to the Thames near Windsor Castle.

Roy-Town, Troy Town, a small hamlet on the Dorchester road west of Puddletown, once important (Hardy suggests) for its old coach-inn (the 'Buck's Head', *FMC*.xlii; *CM*2.vi).

rozum (dial.), quaint saying, odd or eccentric person. **rozum away**, work away with [his] bow (from 'rosin'?).

rub (archaic), difficulty. See **What sport . . . .**

Rubens (*OMC*4.II.i; *PBE*.i; *WB*.II.vii, goddesses in his 'Judgment of Paris': Aphrodite or Venus, Juno, and Minerva), Flemish painter, 1577–1640.

Rubicon, decisive step, act of committal (Caesar's crossing of the Rubicon river into Gaul was tantamount to a declaration of war).

ruck, common sort, general run.

Rufus (Lat. 'red'), the name applied to red-haired Festus Derriman (*TM*.v), after William the Red (or Rufus), son of William the Conqueror.

rule-of-three, a deduction based on three given numbers, the first being in the same ratio to the second as the third is to the required number; cf. **He Revisits His First School**.

rum, strange, queer.

rummer, large drinking-glass.

running dimension, measurements set out in columns.

rush . . . angels tread (of fools, *W*.xxxvii), Pope, *Essay on Criticism*,625.

rushing . . . mighty wind (*D*3.II.iv, final description), Acts ii,2.

Rushy-Pond (*WT*4.vii; *CM*2.vi probably; *HS*.At Rushy-Pond, The Paphian Ball), on the heath, about ¼ m. SE of Hardy's birthplace; by it old roads, one following the Roman, met.

Ruskin College (*JO*.ps. to pr.), a residential college at Oxford for adult education; founded in 1899.

Russia duck, untwilled linen, originally from Russia.

rusty (colloquial), rough, rude, surly.

Ruth (Book of), sublime words (*FMC*.xiii), Ruth i,16.

Ruysdael (*FMC*.xlvi), Dutch landscape-painter, c.1628–82.

S

Sabaoth (*D*3.VII.viii), armies (Hebrew plural).

Sacerdotalism (*JO*.VII.iii), the doctrine or belief that priests are invested with divine or supernatural gifts by virtue of their ordination.

sacrarium (*MC*.ii), the sanctuary of the church, the part which surrounds the altar or communion table.

'Sacred to the memory' (*LLE*), the first words of the inscription Hardy prepared for his sister Mary's tombstone at Stinsford.

The Sacrilege (*SC*). *Dunkery Tor*, Dunkery Beacon (1707 ft.), Exmoor (**Exon Wild, Exon Moor**); *Priddy*, a village in the Mendips, once famous for its fair. The cathedral must be at Wells, near the Mendip Hills.

St Aldhelm's (St Alban's) Head (*TM*.xii,xxx; *WT*3.ii; *D*1.IV.i scene; *HS*.Days to Recollect). On this high headland, 4 m. south of Corfe Castle, a chapel was built to St Aldhelm, first bishop of Sherborne.

St Anthony's temptation (*TT*.viii). Religious paintings of this third-century Egyptian anchorite depict his tempters or devils as beasts.

Saint Augustine (*TD*.xv), a convert to Christianity who became perhaps the most influential of the Christian 'Fathers' (d.430). The irony of the quotation is that it reflects Hardy's views but not St Augustine's faith. Philosophical reflections in the latter's *Confessions* suggest the thought at a number of points; cf. VII.v, VIII.ix, XI.xxix.

St Cleeve, Swithin (*TT*). The name derives from Swithin Cleves, a seventeenth-century rector of Rampisham (NW of Maiden Newton); Hardy probably became interested in the history of the church when he worked for John Hicks, who was engaged in its restoration in 1859 (Purdy,43,293).

St George (*DR*.xviii.2; cf. *PBE*.xii), the legendary slayer of the dragon, and patron-saint of England.

St Helen's (*D*2.II.v, ships from Portsmouth), at the eastern end of the Isle of Wight.

St Heliers (*WB*.III.vii), St Helier, a town in Jersey.

St Jerome (*L*.I.vii), a Christian ascetic and scholar (c.342–420) who studied in Rome. 'If an offence come out of the truth, better is it that the offence come than that the truth be concealed' (*TD*.1891 pr.).

St John (*FMC*.i), the disciple whom Jesus loved.

St John Long (*FMC*.xxii), a London quack (1798–1834) who became a fashionable consultant for rheumatism and consumption; he died of the latter, without recourse to the treatment he prescribed for others.

St Launce's (*PBE*; *SC*.St Launce's Revisited; *MV*.Love the Monopolist), Launceston, Cornwall, where Hardy's train-journeys ended when he visited Emma Gifford, who had relatives there.

St Lazarus (*RN*.IV.iii), the patron saint of lepers or lazars (cf. Luke xvi,19–25), who carried a rattle to warn people of their approach.

St Martin's Day, 11 November (Martinmas).

St – St Mary Magdalen (*JO*.II.iii). See **Magdalen** for Sue's hesitation.

St Michael's Mount (*CM*.11.iii), a steep crag in Mount's Bay near Penzance, surmounted by a castle and a priory which belonged to the Benedictine abbey of St Michel (*TT*.iv) across the Channel.

St Peter (*JO*.II.iii), a disciple of Jesus who became a leading missionary in the foundation of the Christian Church.

Saint Sebastian (*RN*.V.viii), a Christian martyr (d.288) who, after being shot with arrows, was beaten to death.

St Stephen . . . Heaven opened (*JO*.IV.i), Acts vii,54–60.

St Swithin, bishop of Winchester in the ninth century. His reburial in the new cathedral, due on 15 July 971, was delayed by heavy rains. Hence the superstition that if it rains on that day (St Swithin's) it will rain for forty days (cf. *TM*.xvii; *CM*.12.viii).

St Thomas's, 21 December, a day dedicated to this apostle.

St Valentine's Day, 14 February, celebrated the martyrdom of two Valentines, a priest and a bishop of the early Christian Church. It is merely by chance that this anniversary coincided with the centuries-old custom of sending love-tokens or missives (often anonymously).

St Vitus's dance, a nervous disease characterized by involuntary jerking of the muscles.

Saint-Simonian (*FMC*.viii), after Saint-Simon, 1760–1825, founder of French socialism.

sakes, for Heaven's sake.

Salamanca (*D3*.I.iii), in Spain, where Wellesley (afterwards Duke of Wellington) defeated the French in 1812. Death of Colonel Sir Martin Jones at the moment of victory (*HE*.iv).

Sallaert, c.1590–1657, and **Van Alsloot**, c.1570–1626, were Flemish landscape-painters (*RN*.III.iii; *TD*.xvi).

salle à manger (Fr.), dining-room.

sallies, thick woollen grips on bell-ropes.

the *Salon* (*CM*3), the annual exhibition in Paris of work by living artists.

Salon-Carré (*D*2.v.viii), the 'Square Room' (once a drawing-room) in the Louvre Palace.

Samaria, the woman of (*D*1.VI.vii), John iv,5–19.

Samson: blinded after being enticed by Delilah (*L*.II.v; *JO*.I.vii,xi); pin and web (*TT*.xxx); shaking himself (*TD*.xxxvii); shorn (*MC*.xliv; *JO*.VI.vii). See Judg.xvi,1–21.

San Sebastian (*WP*). Hardy took the hint for the poem, a crime against a girl of seventeen, and other details from W. F. P. Napier's account of the storming of this fortified town in his *History of the War in the Peninsula*. *blink your bays*, ignore your successes; *fauss'bray . . . . hornwork*, all part of the defences. For the unscientific idea that 'we shape our offspring's guise From fancy', cf. **An Imaginative Woman**. *Sergeant M——*: the MS gives 'died 184–'; see **Pensioner**.

sanct, holy, sacred.

Sand, George (*CM*.12.xvii; *LLE*.An Ancient to Ancients), pseudonym of a prolific French woman novelist, 1804–76.

Sandbourne (*HE*; *TD*; *WB*; *JO*.III.iv,v.vii), Bournemouth.

sang froid (Fr.), coolness, cold blood.

sanguine clarus (Lat.), distinguished in blood, blue-blooded.

sans tarriance (archaic), without delay.

Sapphic (*WB*.II.vi), characteristic of the Greek poetess Sappho (born c.600 BC). **Sapphic Fragment** (*PPP*): for Hardy's comments on the original and Swinburne's translation, see *Life* 287/305, where there is a reference to the 'Thee, too, the years shall cover' lines in 'Anactoria' (*Poems and Ballads*, 1866). **sapphics**, in a metre used by Sappho; cf. Swinburne's example in the volume just mentioned.

Sappho (*RN*.I.vi); quoted in H. T. Wharton's translation, 1885 (*JO*.III.ep). **Sappho . . . Phaon** (*HE*.ii). Both were beautiful, and lived on the island of Delphos; legend has it that the boatman Phaon's disdain caused Sappho to throw herself into the sea; cf. *SC*.A Singer Asleep,vi–viii.

sappy, simpleton.
sarpless, surplice.
sartin, certain.
Satan . . . Ithuriel's spear (*RN*.II.vii), Milton, *Paradise Lost* iv,799–819; **Satan . . . to and fro on the earth** (*HE*.xxiv; *L*.II.v), Job i,7.
Satanic School (*HE*.xxxvi), an expression first used by the Poet Laureate Southey in 1821 against Byron, Shelley, and other writers deemed to be impious or immoral in their works.
Satires of Circumstance (*SC*). All fifteen of these ironical sketches were dated 1910 in the MS. When eleven of them were published in April 1911, Hardy informed Mrs Henniker that they were written from notes he had made twenty years earlier, and then found more suitable for verse than for prose. The incongruity of these verses with 'Poems of 1912–13', and their republication in *SC* after the opening of the First World War made him wish he could suppress them; cf. *Life* 367/396–7. Subsequently he thought it appropriate to transfer them from their place in the 'Lyrics and Reveries' section (not far removed from 'Poems of 1912–13') to the end of the volume. Notes on some are given separately.
Satires of Circumstance (1914). The first edition was to have ended with 'Exeunt Omnes' and 'A Poet's Epitaph' (as if Hardy had thought it might be his last volume). 'Men Who March Away', written soon after the outbreak of the 1914–18 war, was added as a postscript while the volume was being printed; (it was transferred to *MV* in 1919). *SC* consists almost entirely of relatively recent poems, reaching by and large a higher level than Hardy had previously attained, especially in 'Poems of 1912–13', the most genuine love-elegy in the English language. The slighter, generally shallow, 'Satires of Circumstance' (above) were included because Hardy felt they would be expected after their publication in *The Fortnightly Review* more than three and a half years earlier.
Saul: at his **reception by Samuel** (*MC*.xxvi), I Sam.ix,24; **Endor and Samuel** (*MV*.Apostrophe to an Old Psalm Tune), I Sam.xxviii,4–25; **mistake I made with** (*MV*.'I met a man'), cf. I Sam.xv,xxviii; his **death** (*D*2.VI.vii, *D*3.VII.ix), I Sam.xxxi,1–6.
Saul (*CM*5.v), oratorio by Handel, 1739. See **Dead March**.
Saunders, Ezekiel (*UGT*.II.vi,v.i). There was a clockmaker named Thomas Saunders in High East Street, Dorchester, in 1851.
saur (local pronunciation, *WB*.II.xi), sir.
Save his own soul he hath no star (*JO*.II ep; cf. *L*.IV.iii and *Life*

56/58,345/372), Swinburne, 'Prelude', *Songs before Sunrise*, 1871.
saved as by fire (*JO*.VI.v), I Cor.iii,15.
says (dial.), sayings, things said.
Saxon, belonging to the period immediately preceding the Norman conquest of England (1066).
scallops, stringy parts of fat which cannot be made into lard.
scammish (dial.), awkward, rough, untidy.
scantling, remnant, small piece.
scath, harm, loss, misfortune. **scathe** (vb.), damage, hurt.
Scherzando (mus.), in a light, playful manner.
Scheveningen (*RN*.I.i; *L*.v.ix), significant as an expression of Hardy's view of life. For his visit to this place, and his impressions, cf. *Life* 110/113,120–1/123–4.
schiedam, Schiedam, gin, named after the place of its manufacture in Holland. For Owlett (*CM*5.iv) and smuggling, cf. *WT*7.
Schiller (1759–1805), German playwright, poet, and historian; see **Cunigonde**. A translation of this letters to Goethe appeared in 1877; Hardy quotes from them on 'the inner Necessity and Truth' of artistic presentation (*TD*.1892 pr.). *PPP*.After Schiller is his translation of the first stanza of 'Ritter Toggenburg'.
Schleiermacher (*W*.xix), German theologian and philospher, 1768–1834.
Schönbrunn (*D*3.v.iv), the imperial palace on the outskirts of Vienna.
Schopenhauer (*LLE*.Apology), a pessimistic German philosopher (1788–1860), with whose ideas Hardy became familiar from reading acticles in journals, after his basic views had been formed chiefly by such English writers as Charles Darwin, J. S. Mill, and Herbert Spencer. His influence on Hardy has been exaggerated. **Schopenhauer and Leopardi**, the pessimistic Italian poet, 1798–1837 (*TD*.xxv).
The Schreckhorn (*SC*). The poem occurred to Hardy in Switzerland, when gazing at the peak in 1897 (*Life* 293/311). Leslie Stephen, who, as editor of *The Cornhill*, accepted *FMC* and *HE* for serialization, was the first to climb the Schreckhorn (1861). Hardy, who thought Stephen's philosophy influenced him 'more than that of any other contemporary', was chosen to witness his renunciation of Holy Orders in 1875. For the thought of the sestet, cf. *SC*.'My spirit will not haunt the mound'.
Schwarzwald, the Black Forest in SW Germany.
Schwarzwasser (Germ. 'Black Water', *MC*.xix). There was a river

of this name in East Prussia.

Schwilgué (*L.*v.i), German mechanician and clockmaker, 1776–1856.

The Science of Fiction (Orel,134–8), first published in *The New Review* of April 1891.

sconced, ensconced, screened, sheltered.

a score (*JO.*I.x), for every twenty pounds (in weight).

scot-and-lot, paying a tax of that name to a municipal corporation.

scotch, gash and render harmless for a while.

Scotland-yard, gentlemen from, police detective from Scotland Yard, headquarters of the Metropolitan (London) Police.

Scott, the witching pen of (*LLE.*An Ancient to Ancients), Sir Walter Scott, poet and novelist (who became known as 'the Wizard of the North'), 1771–1832 (as of three other novelists: Edward Bulwer–Lytton, 1803–73, and two French writers, Alexandre Dumas, 1802–70, and George Sand, 1804–76). Sir Walter is 'Scott the First' (MCR).

Scott, Sir George **Gilbert** ('Scott the Second', MCR), the leading architect during a period of Gothic revival in the nineteenth century. He founded the Society for the Protection of Ancient Buildings, at a meeting of which MCR was read.

scram (dial.), puny, emaciated; **scrammed**, numbed.

screech-owl (*JO.*VI.v). Cf. its association with a shroud (*MND.*v.i, 365–7).

screw, worn-out or broken-down horse.

scrimp (dial.), economize. **scrimped up**, screwed up.

Scrimpton (*LLI.*8d), Frampton, near Maiden Newton. The hunting parson of the story was modelled on the Revd William Butler, a friend of the Prince Regent; he became vicar of Frampton in 1800 and died in 1843.

Scripture, him who can cite (*HE.*vii), the Devil.(*MV.*I.iii,93).

scroff (dial.), odds and ends, rubbish, bits of dead wood.

Scrounch it all!, an exclamation of disgust (cf. 'Hang it all!').

scrub (dial.), insignificant person.

Scutari (*CM*5), on the Bosporus; here Florence Nightingale took charge of a hospital for soldiers wounded in the Crimean War.

Scyllaeo-Charybdean position, a dilemma (from the classical legend of the dangerous passage between Italy and Sicily, with Scylla changed into rocks on one side, and Charybdis, a whirlpool, on the other).

Scythian, of Scythia, part of ancient Russia (cf. *D*3.I.viii).

The Sea Fight (*HS*). Hardy was a friend of the vicar of Stinsford and his wife Mrs Cowley, sister of Captain Prowse, who went down with his ship on 31 May 1916 in the battle of Jutland, against the German fleet.

sea of troubles (*W*.iv), *Ham*.III.i,59.

seamy, greasy, fat and perspiring.

Seasoning justice with mercy (*DR*.xv.3), *MV*.IV.i,192.

Sebastiano del Piombo (*JO*.III.ix; *WB*.III.viii), Italian painter, c.1485–1547. Hardy saw his 'Raising of Lazarus' in the N.G.

A Second Attempt (*HS*). The MS date of composition 'About 1900' and the opening lines show that Hardy had been recalling life with Emma from 1870.

Second Invasion (*PBE*.xxxvii), of Greece by the Persians. Defeated at Marathon in 490 BC, they resumed the war in 480 BC, with defeat in the pass of Thermopylae and in the sea-battle of Salamis.

The Second Night (*LLE*). Possibly Hardy thought of his cousin Tryphena Sparks, who had taught in Plymouth, and of his wife Emma, whose girlhood was spent there, when he wrote this star-sparked romantic ballad. His interest in the locality was based on the knowledge (from *S.R.*9) that Emma had enjoyed excursions from West Pier across Plymouth Sound to Cremyll, and (most probably) that Napoleon, while a prisoner there on board *The Northumberland* – *en route* for St Helena – had wished to land and walk on Mount Edgcumbe near Cremyll.

The Second Visit (*WW*). Hardy and Emma walked along the river to the mill when they lived at Sturminster Newton, 1876–8. The revisit with Florence could have been in 1916, 1921, or 1922 (*Life* 373/403,413/446,415/449).

Secretum meum mihi (*LLE*.Her Apotheosis), Vulgate, Isa.xxiv,16: 'My secret to me' (marginal note in the English Bible).

sedile (Lat., *PBE*.xxxi), seat, like one of the 'sedilia' or recessed seats (usually three together, for the clergy) in the south wall of the chancel.

see the nakedness of the land (*HE*.xxv), cf. Gen.xlii,9.

seed (dial. vb.), saw, seen.

seed-lip, basket or box for carrying corn to be sown manually.

Seeing the Moon Rise (*WW*). Hardy remembers walks with his wife Florence to the tumulus overlooking the Frome valley (by the road from Max Gate towards Lower Bockhampton) to see the moon rising over Puddletown Heath.

seise, acquire legal possession. **seised of**, possessing.
Seize . . ., a mild oath (probably from 'The Devil seize . . . ').
self-humiliation to the very bass-string (*W*.xlii), *1.H4*.II.iv,4.
The Selfsame Song (*LLE*), title from Keats, 'Ode to a Nightingale' (*G.T.*).
Self-Unconscious (*SC*). Hardy thinks of what he did not realize in Cornwall before his marriage. See map E for Bossiney. *specious plans*, unrelated to what 'mattered' most between him and Emma Gifford; *all that mattered*, including Emma; *God, the elf*, described in *WT*5.viii as the 'whimsical God . . . blind Circumstance'; *thing . . . loomed . . . immortal mien*, probably Love (the expression is grandiosely vague).
The Self-Unseeing (*PPP*). Hardy's recollection of his happy boyhood self at Higher Bockhampton, when the front door gave direct access to the living-room. He thinks of his father, his death in 1892, and his own ecstasy when he danced to his father's violin (*Life* 15/19).
semi-Norman arches (*TT*.xi), transitional between the rounded Norman and the pointed Gothic.
seneschal, an official to whom domestic arrangements in a nobleman's house were entrusted, steward.
sengreen, houseleek.
se'night (archaic dial.), a week (seven nights).
Senlac and Crecy, clothyard shafts at (*WT*1), arrows (a yard long) in the battles on Senlac Hill (Hastings), 1066, and at Crecy (in France), 1346.
Sennacherib, King of Assyria (his capital Nineveh on the upper Tigris): (*HE*.xxiv) Hezekiah . . . Lachish (in Judah), cf. II Kings xviii,13–14; destruction of his host (*RN*.v.vii), II Kings xix,35–6.
sensitive plant (*JO*.VI.iii), an allusion to Shelley's poem 'The Sensitive Plant', where it thrives in an atmosphere of love and beauty and delight, but is killed by the winter in which loathsome things thrive.
sensual hind who . . . lived carelessly with his wife through the days of his vanity (*JO*.III.i), cf. Eccl.ix,9.
Sentimental Journey (*W*.viii,ix), alluding to Laurence Sterne's *A Sentimental Journey* (through France and Italy), 1768, with a hint of the transience and shallowness of Mrs Charmond's impressions.
Sept, Rouge, Impair, et Manque (Fr.), seven, red, odd, and fall short or miss (the result announced by the croupier after spinning

the roulette wheel, *L*.IV.iv).

sere, old age; withered, aged. **the sere and yellow leaf** (*WT*.1), declining age; cf. *Mac*.v.iii,23. **sereward**, towards decay.

The Sergeant's Song (*WP*). Though written in 1878, only verses 1 and 4 appeared in the serial and first edition of *TM* (v), 2 and 3 being added for the 1881 edition. 1803 indicates the year of preparation against an invasion of England by Napoleon, though the novel suggests 1804.

Sermon on the Mount (*DR*.xii.1; *RN*.VI.iv; *TD*.xlvi), Matt.v–vii; and **meek men** (*FMC*.xxxiii), Matt.v,5.

sermons in stones (*TD*.xxiii), *AYL*.II.i,17.

the serpent hisses . . . birds sing (*TD*.xii), cf. R of L,871.

Servant David (*MC*.xxxiii). Many of the psalms are ascribed to David, who is repeatedly described in the Old Testament as God's servant.

servant, ox, . . . wife (*TD*.1892 pr.), tenth commandment, Exod.xx,17.

servants of corruption . . . (*TD*.xlvi), II Pet.ii,18–22.

Seven of the Wain (Waggon), seven stars forming **Charles's Wain**.

the Seven Sleepers (*MC*.ii), seven Christian youths of Ephesus who, according to legend, fled during the Diocletian persecution of AD 250 to a cave, where they slept some two hundred years. According to the Koran, they had a dog who was admitted to heaven by Mahomet for having remained loyally on guard during this period.

seven sorrows (*W*.xv), an allusion to those of the Virgin Mary, the 'Notre Dame des sept douleurs' of Swinburne's 'Dolores', which Hardy knew from *Poems and Ballads*, 1866.

seven thunders (*TD*.xlvii; *D*1.II.v), Rev.x,3–4.

The Seven Times (*LLE*). Hardy's *Life* (74–98/77–100) shows six visits to Emma Gifford in Cornwall, the fourth in August 1872 (91/93). The tryst before his *journey's end* (cf. **journeys end**) could hardly refer to their meeting in Bath (93–4/6); perhaps he met Emma at Launceston late in 1873, when they were planning marriage (cf. 97/100). The seventh visit took place after her death.

the seventh (of the Ten Commandments), 'Thou shalt not commit adultery.'

Sexajessamine Sunday (*FMC*.xv). Sexagesima Sunday, eight Sundays (literally sixty days) before Easter, is meant.

shadder (rustic pronunciation), shadow (of her true self, *DR*.viii.3); **shaddery**, shadowy, uncertain.

the shade from his own soul upthrown (*MC*.xliv), Shelley, *The Revolt of Islam* VIII.vi.

Shadow of Death (*PBE*.xviii), Psalm xxiii,4.

The Shadow on the Stone (*MV*). For the Druid stone in Max Gate garden, see *Life* 223–4/245. The last line, with reference to the vision of Emma's spirit, recalls the classical story of Orpheus and Eurydice (emerging from Pluto's abode of the dead).

the shadowy third (*JO*.IV.v), Browning, 'By the Fire-side'.

Shadrach, Meshach, Abednego (*FMC*.lii), Dan.iii.

Shadwater Weir (*RN*.v.ix). The original, in the Frome meadows, more than a mile from its fictional location, has only nine hatches. In his youth, Hardy had seen a body recovered from the pool below the weir, and thought at first it was a girl; *RN* developed from this recollection. The name may be intended to suggest 'the shadow of death'.

shail (dial.), shuffle, walk inelegantly.

Shakeforest Towers (*CM7*), Clatford Hall, on the southern side of the Bristol road, a few miles west of Marlborough; the name was suggested by Savernake Forest, SE of the town. On the other side of the road a lane leads to 'Lambing Corner' and the 'Druidical trilithon'.

Shallow and Silence (*MC*.xxviii), foolish country justices, *2.H4*.III.ii.

The Shambles (*PBE*.xxix), east of Portland Bill (map H).

Shapes . . . hideously multiplied (*JO*.v.iv), Shelley, *The Revolt of Islam* iii.xxiii.

shardful, enough to fill a fragment of a cup.

sharper than a serpent's tooth (to have a thankless child, *GND*3), *KL*.I.iv,228–9.

Shaston, Shastonbury (*TD*; *JO*; *TL*.The Vampirine Fair), the ancient hill-town of Shaftesbury, which overlooks the Vale of Blackmoor. It was called Caer Pallador by the British, and 'Mount Paladur' by Geoffrey of Monmouth; locally it is known as Shaston. 'Grove's Place' ('Old Grove Place'), the schools, and Trinity Church, Bimport Street, and Abbey Walk are easily identifiable; the 'old Church' is St Peter's. Little remains of the abbey, and 'Castle Green' is the sole reminder of the castle.

shawm, a medieval instrument of the oboe class.

She at His Funeral (*WP*). Hardy's sketch shows Stinsford Church; the poem is dated 1873. (Horace Moule was buried at Fordington.)

She called to her lover . . . foggy dew (*RN*.VI.iv). For this mildly bawdy ballad, cf. **O come in . . . dew**.

She moved . . . stream (*W*.xvi), Shelley, *The Revolt of Islam* II.xxiii.

'She opened the door' (*HS*): what Emma did for Hardy, and means to him.

She Revisits Alone the Church of Her Marriage (*LLE*). Whether it was actual or imaginary, Hardy presents Emma's return to St Peter's, Paddington, where they were married (*Life* 101/103; cf. K. Phelps, *The Wormwood Cup*, Padstow, 1975, p. 41.

She shall follow . . . lovers . . . (*HE*.xxxv; *TD*.xlvii), Hos.ii,7.

She, to Him (*WP*). Hardy stated that the four sonnets are to be regarded as one poem; they were part of 'a much larger number which perished'. Attempts (never wholly convincing) to identify the hill in Hardy's sketch (Blackdown with the monument to Admiral Hardy, or the cliff-top with Clavell Tower above Kimmeridge Bay) are an irrelevance, since it is a symbol of life's hill with the setting sun; the woman is ageing. If any person *suggested* the sequence, it could have been Mrs Julia Augusta Martin (cf. *Life* 41/43,18–20/23–5,102/104–5). The second sonnet was paraphrased in *DR*.xiii.4. Sportsman Time who 'rears his brood to kill' is a precursor of *PPP*.The Puzzled Game-Birds, which was entitled 'The Battue' in the Wessex Edition of 1912.

She was active . . . nothing at all (*OMC*4.I.ii. ep.), Browning, 'The Flight of the Duchess' viii.

She Would Welcome Old Tribulations, an uncollected poem, based possibly on one of Emma Hardy's recollections.

sheen, shine, light; **sheened** (dial.), shone; **sheenen**, shining.

The Sheep-Boy (*HS*). The scene is below the three Rainbarrow tumuli; the sea-mist comes up over the downs near Poxwell (Oxwell). *Draäts-Hollow*, its heather in full bloom, is named after the winds (draughts) it attracts; *Kite Hill* is south of Puddletown. *Israelite*: Hardy seems to assume the cloud was raised by Moses; see **pillar of a cloud**.

sheer, clear, defined.

Shelley, Percy Bysshe, the poet (1792–1822): pencillings . . . ideas in the rough, like Shelley's scraps (*LLI*.1); habit of sailing paper-boats (*LLE*.Apology); his house in Rome (*WB*.III.i). When his ashes were buried in the Protestant Cemetery, Rome, the attempt was made to bury his son's remains beside him, as he wished, but they could not be found (MCR).

Shelley, Timothy (*D*1.I.iii scene), father of Hardy's favourite poet.

Shelley's Skylark (*PPP*). Shelley's 'To a Skylark' was written at

Leghorn. Hardy's poem was inspired more by Browning's 'Memorabilia'.

Sheol's lair (*PPP*.The Respectable Burgher; *LLE*.On the Tune Called the Old Hundred-and-Fourth), the dark Hebrew underworld of the dead.

Sherborne Abbey (MCR). See **Sherton Abbas**.

sherd, potsherd, shard, fragment of broken earthenware.

Sheridan, R. B., playwright and parliamentarian, 1751–1816. His **renowned Begum speech** (*RN*.I.v): Sheridan's reputation as a parliamentarian (cf. *D*1.I.iii) began during the impeachment of Warren Hastings; in this he made a great speech accusing him, when Governor-General of India, of extorting money from Indian princesses ('begums'). His romantic comedy *The Rivals* (*CM*8); *The Critic* (*D*2.III.iii). See also *D*2.IV.vii,V.iv.

Sherton Abbas (*W*), Sherborne, north Dorset. Its abbey (cf.xxxviii,xxxix) is 'the Abbey north of Blackmore Vale' (*PPP*.The Lost Pyx). The 'Earl of Wessex' is the Digby Hotel (old, xxv; new, xlviii); Hardy takes licence with local chronology in his Wessex fiction, the railway reaching Sherborne in 1860, before the period of *W* (see **Vic.**). **Sherton Castle** (*W*.xxiii; cf. *GND*7 and *CM*9), ruins of a stronghold belonging to the Digby family.

shet (dial.), shut; **shetters**, shutters.

Shimei, who cursed David (*FMC*.xxxiii), II Sam.xvi,5–13.

Shiner, Farmer (*UGT*). As 'Shinar' (his original name in *UGT*), he is twice mentioned in *MC* (xiii,xvii).

shingled, in or pertaining to boards or thin planks.

Shining Land (*WP*.The Impercipient), the abode of the Shining Ones, Christian exemplars who live 'upon the borders of heaven', where the sun shines night and day (Part I of *The Pilgrim's Progress* by Bunyan).

The Ship (*UGT*.III.ii), an inn on the old section of Ridgeway, just above its lower junction with the new, and east of Upwey.

Shockerwick House (*D*1.VI.vi), 4 m. NE of Bath. Hardy seems to have deliberately included the 'Roll up that map' story of Pitt before his death at his home in Putney. In 1902 he told Sir George Douglas he had been staying in Bath 'close to where Pitt was living when he received the news of Austerlitz that is said to have killed him' (*Letters* III,41). He learned this address from R. E. Peach's *Historic Houses of Bath*, where he also read that Pitt was on a visit to Shockerwick when the news came. Hardy seems to have overlooked the fact that the Mr Wiltshire who told the story was a boy when, in the absence of his father, he was showing Pitt the portrait of the comedian Quin as the galloping courier arrived with news of the allies' defeat at Austerlitz.

shoon (archaic plural form), shoes.

Shortening Days at the Homestead (*HS*). The scene may be in Blackmoor Vale ('Pomona's plain'; cf. *W*.xxv). *pollard*, their sprouting branches lopped off periodically, making their trunks develop broad heads; *embossed*, capped, crowned (from 'boss' in architecture).

The Shortest Way with the Dissenters (*HE*.ix), a pamphlet by Daniel Defoe (1702), for which he was fined, pilloried, and imprisoned.

shotten, that have been spawned; worthless, good-for-nothing.

Shottsford Forum, Blandford Forum, a town 16 m. NE of Dorchester.

Should auld acquaintance . . . (*PBE*.xxiii ep.), Burns, 'Auld Lang Syne'.

Should he upbraid, a song by Henry Bishop (1786–1855), knighted in 1842), which Hardy heard at Sturminster Newton in 1877 (*Life* 118/122); included in *PBE* after his wife's death.

shovel-hat, a stiff broad-brimmed hat turned up at the sides.

shrammed (dial.) numbed, stiff with cold.

shroff. See **scroff**.

Shut Out That Moon (*TL*), a deeply personal poem, expressing the death of love which was to affect Hardy's relations with his first wife until her death in 1912; cf. *TL*.The Dead Man Walking, and *HS*.The Absolute Explains vii–viii. *the Lady's Chair*, Cassiopeia, one of four constellations mentioned.

Sic diis . . . placet (*D*3.VII.ix), a common classical point of view (cf. *TD* ending), which Hardy clearly finds outdated.

sich (dial.) such.

Sicilian Mariners' Hymn, the old chimes of St Peter's, Dorchester (*MC*.iv; *TL*.After the Fair; MV.The Chimes), after R. Merrick's setting of Psalm xix.

sicklied o'er . . . pale cast (*PBE*.xiii; *JO*.VI.xi), *Ham*.III.i,85.

sickness-or-health. In the C. of E. marriage-service, each partner vows to take the other 'for richer or poorer; in sickness and in health'.

Siddim, slime pits of (*FMC*.vi), Gen.xiv,3,10.

Siddons, Mrs Sarah (*RN*.I.vi), a great tragic actress, 1751–1831.

siffle (from Fr. *siffler*), a hissing or whistling sound.
sigh gratis (*TD*.xxviii), *Ham*.II.ii,319.
signal-redoubt (*D3*.III.vi), fortified position for signallers.
signis auroque rigentes (*PBE*.xii), stiff with gold brocade, from Virgil's description of Helen of Troy's robe, *Aeneid* i,648.
A Sign-Seeker (*WP*). *subtrude*, steal in or under; *weigh the sun*, from Tennyson's 'Locksley Hall' (186); *the general word*, the Logos or the Creator (cf. John i,1); *As vouchsafed*, Hardy's previous 'Vouchsafed to' may be clearer. In later poems, after losing his wife and his sister Mary, he was less positive on the subject of death.
A silence . . . tears (*OMC4*.II.vii), Shelley, *The Revolt of Islam* VI.xxxi.
Silences (*WW*). Hardy's birthplace was empty and neglected when he visited it in May 1922; 'often when he left he said that he would go there no more' (*Life* 415/449; cf. *WW*.Concerning His Old Home).
Sileni (*TD*.x), drunken companions. The classical demi-god Silenus usually appears intoxicated, riding on an ass. **Silenus ('worthy toper old') . . . Chromis and Mnasylus** (*FMC*.xxiii), Virgil, *Eclogues* vi.
siller tags, silver lace-tags.
silver string of a violin (*MC*.xvi) and **the small**, strings for (1) the lowest notes (2) the highest.
Silverthorn (*CM*.12), Silverton, in the Exe valley, Devon (previously Stickleford; cf. **The Romantic Adventures . . .**).
sin . . . damnation . . . parlous case (*TD*.xl), cf. *AYL*.III.ii,36–40.
Since Love will needs . . . patiently (*WB*.II ep.), the opening lines of an untitled poem by Sir Thomas Wyatt, 1503–42.
sine prole (DLa), without offspring (Lat.). **Sine Prole** (*HS*). The title applies to Hardy himself. For the origin of the metre, see *Life* 306/329. *Unlike Jahveh's nation*, the Israelites, who, continually overrun, looked forward to being as numerous as the stars in heaven and the sands on the seashore (Gen.xxii,17; *Jahveh*, **Jehovah**, their god).
A Singer Asleep (*SC*). Swinburne's revolt against the Victorian Church in favour of Greek joyousness appealed strongly to Hardy from 1866 onwards, if not earlier. The poem was begun at Bonchurch, on the south coast of the Isle of Wight, where Swinburne was buried. *ness*, headland; *fulth*, fullness; *far morning . . . classic guise*, an allusion (as the next lines suggest) to the first series of *Poems and Ballads*, 1866, rather than to *Atalanta in*

Calydon, 1865 (both of which Hardy seems to have in mind in *Letters* II,158); *Lesbian . . . Leucadian*, see **Sappho**; *hydrosphere*, waters around the earth; *orts*, fragments.

single-stick, a kind of fencing.

Sir Joshua: see **Reynolds**.

Sir Peter . . . Godfrey . . . Joshua . . . Thomas (*L*.I.iii). See **Lely**, **Kneller**, **Reynolds**; Sir Thomas Lawrence (1769–1830) was a distinguished portrait-painter.

Sirius or **the Dog Star** (*FMC*.ii), the brightest of the stars.

Sisera: see **Jael**.

six (*JO*.III.iii), six pennyworth. **The Six Boards** (*HS*), the sides and ends of a coffin. **six-eighted**, played in 6/8 time.

six-handed reels (*RN*.I.iii,II.v), dances for two lines of three dancers, the interweaving reel figure being danced along the lines of three.

six-hands-round (*UGT*.I.viii). The dance with which this opens is 'The College Hornpipe', the only one Hardy could remember beginning with six-hands-round (Orel,254), a sequence in which only the top three couples take part.

skeer (local pronunciation), scare.

skeleton-closet, a private source of shame which people prefer to keep secret; cf. 'skeleton in the cupboard'. **skeleton-drill**, drill done by a small number of men for the instruction of officers.

skellington, skillenton, illiterate forms of 'skeleton'.

skimmer, beat with a skimming-ladle. **skimmer-cake**, cake baked on a metal skimming-ladle.

skimmington-ride, skimmity-ride (*WP*.The Bride-Night Fire; *RN*.I.v; *MC*.xxxvi,xxxix), described by J. S. Udal as 'a kind of matrimonial lynch law or pillory intended for those in a lower class of life who, in certain glaring particulars, may have transgressed their marital duties'. The name probably arose from the skimming-ladle used to beat the effigy of the offender during the organized processional demonstration.

skip . . . hare . . . counsel (*TT*.xxiv), *MV*.I.ii,17.

skit, restive horse.

skitty-boots, heavy hobnailed boots reaching high above the ankle.

skiver (dial.), fasten with a skewer, truss.

Skrymer, Skrymir, a Norse giant who snored like thunder.

the skull at the banquet (*RN*.VI.iv). See **Alonzo the Brave**.

slack (dial.), impudence, cheek.

slack-twisted (dial.), lazy, spineless, shiftless.

slap (have a slap at), attempt, effort, 'go' (dial.).

slat (dial.), pounding, splintering.

sleep of the spinning-top (*JO*.II.vi), Carlyle, *Sartor Resartus* iii; cf. 'as humming-tops sleep', *UGT*.I.viii.

Sleeping-Green (*L*.I.ii). The name for this imaginary village in Somerset comes from that of a village north of Wareham, Dorset.

slent (dial.), shattered.

Sleswig (*RN*.I.vii), Schleswig, a region south of Denmark from which came some of the Anglo-Saxon invaders of England.

slim-faced, slim-looking (dial.), sly, crafty.

slittering (dial.), skipping, never at rest.

slop, outer protective garment; spill, sag over.

Slough (miry ground, bog) **of Despond** (DLa; *GND*6). Christian falls into it at the outset of his journey (Part I, *The Pilgrim's Progress* by Bunyan).

slow-coach, colloquial term applied to one who is slow to act.

slummocky, dirty, slovenly.

slur in music (*UGT*.I.vii; *HE*.xxxiii), a bow-shaped line over two or more notes that are to be played or sung smoothly and connectedly.

Slyre, Lane of (*TL*.The Revisitation), Slyres Lane; see map A. The carrier of *LLI*.8 follows this road only a short distance; see **A Few Crusted Characters**.)

smack-and-coddle, kiss-and cuddle.

small, of low alcoholic content.

small deer (cf. *KL*.III.iv,134), of little worth.

Smeaton, John, 1724–94 (*PBE*.xvii), designer of the Eddystone Lighthouse (see xi for its location).

Smith, Adam (*PBE*.x) refers to pin-making, which required eighteen operations in manufacture, in support of his argument for specialization or division of labour, in his main work *The Wealth of Nations*, 1776.

Smith, John (*PBE*). Though he and Hardy's father were master-masons, the likeness seems to end there (*Life* 73/76). The scene in which he and his workmen prepare for the interment of Lady Luxellian was imagined (a version of the Lady Susan story being incorporated) from all Hardy knew about the construction of a vault in Stinsford Church for the latter and her husband (*Life* 9/14).

Smith, Stephen (*PBE*). See *Life* 73–4/76. Hardy gave him the surname of the architect who employed him in London when he was writing the novel.

smock, smock-frock, knee-length outer garment formerly worn by farm-labourers.

smoke-jack, a mechanism which uses the flow of air or draught in the chimney to turn the roasting-spit.

the smoothly shaven historian . . . Christianity (*JO*.II.i): see **Gibbon**.

snacks (dial.): **go snacks with**, marry (go shares with).

Snail-Creep (*UGT*.IV.i), a path through the wood by Hardy's birthplace to the Puddletown road and Grey's Wood beyond (map A).

snap, snack, a hasty meal or 'bite'.

snapdragon, a game, usually played at Christmas, in which raisins are snatched from a bowl of burning brandy.

snapper (dial), a sudden, short spell of severe weather.

sniche (dial.), stingy, grasping, greedy.

sniff and snaff, sniffing (dial.), a courting agreement (from 'to say "sniff" if another say "snaff" ').

snipe (dial.), mean or contemptible person.

snoach (dial.), snuffle, snore.

snock (dial), knock, crash.

snoff (dial.) snuff or burnt end of candle-wick.

Snow in the Suburbs (*HS*). The MS title ran 'Snow at Upper Tooting' (where the Hardys lived, 1878–81).

So I soberly . . . end (*OMC*4.I.v ep.), Browning, 'Instans Tyrannus'.

So like, so very like . . . day to day (*DR*.xii.5; *CM*2.viii), Wordsworth, 'Elegiac Stanzas: Suggested by a Picture of Peele Castle'.

So true a fool is love (*DR*.xii.7), Son.57.

So Various (*WW*). The title, from the sketch of Zimri in Dryden's *Absalom and Achitophel* (I,545), points to contrasting qualities Hardy found retrospectively in himself.

sock (dial.), sigh loudly. **the sock,** the stage (strictly comedy, from *soccus*, the low shoe worn by Roman actors in comedy).

Socratic εἰρωνεία (*W*.xvi), the irony of Socrates in Plato's dialogues, especially in his way of putting questions to establish the truth.

sodger (old rustic pronunciation), soldier.

Sodom and Gomorrah (*DR*.ix.4; *TT*.xvi; *LLI*.8f), wicked cities destroyed by fire from heaven, Gen.xviii,20 and xix,24–9.

soft torments . . . distresses (*TD*.iii), untraced.

a Soho or Bloomsbury Street, fashionable parts of London.
soi-disant (Fr.), self-styled, assumed (name).
sojer; see **sodger**.
solatium, money paid as a solace.
The soldier-saints . . . (*JO*.IV.v), Browning, 'The Statue and the Bust'.
Solentsea (*HE*.ii; *LLI*.1), Southsea, near Portsmouth; the Solent separates it from the Isle of Wight.
sol-fa, sing note by note, using *do, re, mi, fa, so, la, ti* for the notes of the major scale (C, D, E, F, G, A, B).
solicitus timor (*MC*.xlii), anxious fear, Ovid, *Heroides* i,12.
Solomon (son of David) . . . All is vanity (*TD*.xli), Eccl.i,1–2. **Solomon's mines** (*SC*.The Elopement), proverbial, from the abundance of gold in Solomon's temple (cf. I Kings vi,21–2). **Solomon's Song**, the theological interpretation of its chapter-headings (*JO*.III.iv; *PPP*.The Respectable Burgher). **Solomon's temple** (*MC*.xiv), cf. I Kings vi; its **magnificent pillars** (*TD*.iv), probably a reference to Solomon's house, I Kings vii,6.
solve, cause the dissolution of.
Somers, Alfred (*WB*), probably modelled to some degree on the landscape-painter Alfred Parsons, whom Hardy took to 'Budmouth' (*Life* 217/226,229/239).
Somerset, George (*L*). Hero of a story set principally in Somerset, he recalls Hardy as a young architect, with an interest in arguments for and against paedobaptism (*Life* 29–30/33–5), and as one who attached more importance to poetry, theology, and the reorganization of society than to his profession.
'Something tapped' (*MV*), based on the folklore superstition (here with reference to Emma Hardy) that the soul of the dead could take the form of a moth; cf. *LLI*.8c.
The Something that Saved Him (*MV*), Hardy's recovery from 'In Tenebris' moods. Cf. the opening with that of Psalm lxix; the ending recalls the setting and conclusion of Browning's 'Childe Roland to the Dark Tower Came'. *cit and clown*, city-dweller and countryman.
sommat, sommit (dial.), something.
son, only . . . widow (*LLI*.8g), Luke vii,12.
Song from Heine (*PPP*), 'Die Heimkehr' in the *Buch der Lieder*.
Song of Hope (*PPP*). *null*, cancel; *hueing*, becoming colourful. For the broken viol-strings, cf. *PPP*.The Darkling Thrush.
Song to an Old Burden (*HS*). Hardy thinks of dancing in boyhood

at Higher Bockhampton to his father's music (*Life* 15/19), and of happiness with Emma during courtship in Cornwall. The old burden or motif emerges at the end (cf. *MV*.Looking Across); the cello-player is Hardy's grandfather, buried at Stinsford.

The Son's Veto (*LLI*.2), an earnest of Hardy's indignation at the unChristianity of the Church in *JO*; first pub. in December 1891. For the after-midnight scene of traffic to Covent Garden, cf. *Life* 210/219.

sooth, truth.

Sophoclean (*W*.i), 'dramas of a grandeur and unity' like those of the Greek dramatist Sophocles (of the fifth century BC), whose surviving plays include *Antigone* and *Oedipus Rex*. For the rural drama Hardy had in mind, *FMC* and *TD* might be considered in addition to *W*.

Sophocles . . . the Will 'the gods' . . . shame (Spirit of the Pities, *D*1.v.iv), *Trachiniae*,1266–72; cf. *Life* 284–5/302,383/414.

Sortes Sanctorum (*FMC*.xiii, Lat.), divination by Holy Writ.

so's (souls), good people (a rustic form of addressing friends).

sotto voce (It.), to oneself, in a subdued voice.

sou, a French coin of little value.

sough, sigh,

The Souls of the Slain (*PPP*), first pub. in April 1900 with a note which indicated Hardy's view that Portland was an appropriate place for a bird following the 'great circle' through South Africa and Great Britain to alight. See map H for the Race. *mighty-vanned*, large-winged; *lovely and true*, see **true . . . good report**; *Pentecost Wind*, cf. Acts ii,1–4.

A Sound in the Night (*LLE*). Woodsford Castle, in the Frome valley, dates back to Edward III's reign; Hardy's father did restoration work there (*Life* 27/31). The nine-hatches weir from which Shadwater Weir (*RN*.v.ix) originated was not far off. The name of the farm (from Wyrdesford, the ford of fate, i.e. Rocky Shallow, according to J. O. Bailey) may have suggested the story. *coupled*, married.

The Sound of Her, a macabre poem (which remained uncollected) describing the creaking as Emma Hardy's coffin-lid was screwed down. Hardy was persuaded to exclude it from *MV*; he substituted 'The Tree and the Lady'.

South, Robert (1634–1716), a divine who wrote pungent anti-Puritan sermons (*GND*3; quoted, *TD*.xiii).

Southern cause (*W*.xxi), in the American Civil War, 1861–5.

southing, southward course.

sowers . . . wayside . . . thorns (*MC*.xxiv), Matt.xiii,3–9. **sow tares** (evil), cf.Matt.xiii,24–30. **sown the wind . . . whirlwind** (*TT*.xxxvii), Hos.viii,7.

Spaddleholt Farm (*JO*.I.viii). The name derives from two villages in the 'Marygreen' country: Chaddlesworth, SSE of Fawley, and Sparsholt, west of Wantage (map I).

spade-guinea, English gold coin worth 21 shillings and minted from 1787 to 1799, bearing a shield which resembled a pointed spade.

sparrowgrass, asparagus (once a common mispronunciation of it).

spatters, spatterdashes, leggings, gaiters.

spawls, chippings or fragments of stone.

spear-bed, bed of reeds.

the *Spectator*, essays, mainly by Addison and Steele, which appeared daily for public entertainment and edification from March 1711 to December 1712.

The Spectre of the Real, the title of the story Hardy helped Mrs Henniker to write in the autumn of 1893, when he had *JO* in mind. He was responsible for most of the planning: she, for most of the writing, though Hardy touches (including quotation) and impressions, in addition to rather stock situations, are noticeable. He modified the ending, revised with this change in mind, and provided the published title. His direction and advice did not lead to success; the unfavourable criticism the story received when it appeared under joint authorship, with others by Mrs Henniker, in *In Scarlet and Grey*, 1896, arose from intrinsic weaknesses as much as from prejudice against the author of *JO*.

spectre-thin (*DR*.xiii.3), Keats, 'Ode to a Nightingale' (*G.T.*).

spell, interpret, understand.

The Spell of the Rose (*SC*). The manor-hall is a thin disguise; Max Gate is the setting. Emma Hardy planted a rose a few weeks before her death. (On 28 Dec 1918 Hardy writes that it has grown luxuriantly, and Emma would be pleased to know he tended it.)

A Spellbound Palace (*HS*). In the spell created by the fountain's flow ('lapse'), the figures of Henry VIII and Cardinal Wolsey (who built Hampton Court by the Thames near Twickenham, and presented it to the King in 1526) are seen clear ('Sheer') in the sunshine.

spencer, close-fitting jacket.

Spencer (Herbert, evolutionary philosopher, 1820–1903). His 'paralyzing thought' (Gen.Pr.) is given at the close of his autobiography of 1904. His scientific thinking had a profound effect on Hardy, who wrote in 1893 (*Letters* II,24–5) that Spencer's *First Principles* (1862) 'acts, or used to act, upon me as a sort of patent expander when I had been particularly narrowed down by the events of life'. In this work, which nourished his idea of an Ultimate indifferent to human fate, he probably met the expression 'First Cause' for the first time.

Spenserian (*DR*.xiii.3), alluding to the 'Ephithalamion' and 'Prothalamion' of the Elizabethan poet Edmund Spenser.

spet (dial.), spit; **spetten**, spitting.

Sphinx-like (*HE*.xxvii), inscrutable, enigmatic.

spigot on her escutcheon (*HE*.xxxv), her being a butler's daughter.

Spinoza (*W*.xvi; *JO*.I.xi). See **Our Old Friend Dualism** and *Letters* I,261–2.

The spirit moved them (*RN*.I.vi), suggested perhaps by Gen.i,2. The wind in the Scriptures can express the 'spirit'; cf. John iii,8, 'The wind bloweth where it listeth . . . Spirit', and Acts ii,4, where the Holy Ghost comes as 'a rushing mighty wind'.

A spirit passed . . . (*MV*.The Clock of the Years), Job iv,15.

spirit . . . poured . . . prophesy (*HE*.xxv), Joel ii,28.

Spirits from the vasty deep, call up (*OMC*5), *1.H4*.III.i,53.

spit-and-dab, made of mud, plaster, or rough mortar.

A Spot (*PPP*). The two are Hardy and Emma Gifford in their happy courtship days; the glen is the Valency valley.

spouse in your pocket, make a, save your money by remaining single.

sprawl, energy, activity.

sprigged-laylock (rustic pronunciation, *LLI*.7), embroidered with sprigs of lilac blossom; cf. 'sprig-muslin' (*LLE*.Weathers).

Springham (*TM*.ix), Warmwell, NE of Poxwell.

Springrove, Edward (*DR*). Despite Hardy's disclaimer, he is in some respects like him: of rather humble origin, an architect, and a poet who knew Shakespeare 'to the vey dregs of the footnotes'. The cider-making and some of the Budworth scenes are based on Hardy's experience, the first at home, the second at Weymouth.

spud, narrow curved spade for digging up weeds; dig or prise up.

squail (dial.), fling, throw.

squat (dial.). strike, flatten, crush.

squench (dial.), quench.

Squire Hooper (*WW*). Hardy's interest in Edward Hooper's hospitality at his home near Cranborne, and the manner of his death (in 1795, at the age of ninety-four), at Hurn Court, Hampshire, derived from Hutchins.

Squire Petrick's Lady (*GND*6). See **Petrick, Timothy**.

Stacie's Hotel (*TM*.xxvi), on the site of the Royal Hotel, Weymouth; its Assembly Rooms were opened in 1776. Hardy seems to regard the two hotels as one; cf.**The Ballad of Love's Skeleton**.

staddle, framework, supported by staddle-stones, on which corn is stacked or a granary built.

stag of ten, a stag with ten antlers.

Stagfoot Lane (*W*.iv; *TD*), Hartfoot Lane, a village in the hill country between Nettlecombe Tout and Bulbarrow. The MS indicates Fox Inn, Stagfoot Lane, as the scene for *TL*.The Man He Killed.

stale, flat . . . (*UGT*.III.iii; *TM*.xxxvi; *CM*2.iii), *Ham*.I.ii,133.

staling (by custom, *HE*.xxiv), cf. *AC*.II.ii,239 and *WW*.The Bad Example.

stalled ox (*UGT*.v.i), hatred, Prov.xv,17.

Stancy Castle (*L*). Though Hardy's Wessex map and some details of the twelfth-century war between Stephen and Matilda serve to identify it with Dunster Castle, it is Hardy's invention. Many details relative to the history of Corfe Castle were transferred from Hutchins, as were phrases from his historical account of Sherborne Castle. A passage on payments to workmen was prepared from similar entries in Hutchings. Hardy saw almost all the paintings at Kingston Lacy in 1878 (*Life* 122/125). As there is no evidence that he ever visited Dunster, and Dunster Castle still stands, his topographical caveat in the 1912 ps. is especially pertinent.

standing, stall.

Standing by the Mantelpiece (*WW*). Based on Hardy's last impressions of his friend Horace Mosley Moule, at Queens' College, Cambridge (*Life* 93/96). After teaching at Marlborough, he became a local government inspector. His intemperance and fits of depression caused his fiancée to break their engagement. It is to her, at this point, that he is imagined speaking. The candle-wax shroud, suggested by Hardy's visit to King's College Chapel, Cambridge (*Life* 93/96,141/145), has the ominous significance of an old popular superstition. Moule committed suicide at Queens' in September 1873 (*Life* 96/98). *wintertime* is

symbolic; *drape*, drapery in the form of a shroud.
stand-to, come round, show sense.
stanhope, an open, one-seated vehicle (first made for a Stanhope).
Stannidge, Mr (*MC*). The actual name of the landlord of the Three Mariners in 1851 was Standish.
stap (local pronunciation), step.
the star in the east (*WT*6.ii), Matt.ii,9.
a Star-Chamber matter (*LLE*.Apology), cause for rigorous censure or prosecution (from the name of the Prerogative Court at Westminster which worked for the Crown, and endangered individual liberty; abolished in 1641).
stark, completely; bare, desolate.
starry sky, silence . . . of (*HE*.xxv), from the conclusion of Wordsworth's 'Song at the Feast of Brougham Castle'.
stars in their courses (*L*.I.ii), Judg.v,20.
Start, Start Point, on the south Devon coast.
starving (dial.), freezing or frozen.
The Statue and the Bust (*DR*.iii.2), 'one of Browning's finest poems' (*Life* 192/200; cf. 199/207–8).
status quo (Lat., 'state in which'), former state.
Staunton and Morphy (*PBE*.xviii), chess experts, the first being the author of the *Chess Praxis*, 1860, the second world champion in 1858.
steading, farm outbuilding.
steep and thorny way (*FMC*.xxix; 'reck'd not her own rede', ignored her own advice or counsel), *Ham*.I.iii,46–51.
steer (variant of 'stir'?). See **stoor**.
Stephen, stoning of (*TT*.ii), Acts vi,9–15 and vii,54–60; and the Council (*W*.xxxvii), Acts vi,15.
stepping-stone to higher things (*TT*.xxviii), Tennyson, *In Memoriam* i.
Sterne . . . speak . . . good of the dead (*DR*.xi.1), Laurence Sterne (1713–68), an eccentric clergyman, author of *Tristram Shandy*; cf. ***Sentimental Journey***. The statement occurs in Sterne's letter of 30 Jan 1760, in which he disputes the wisdom of the old maxim *De mortuis nil nisi bonum*.
Stickleford, Tincleton, 4 m. east of Stinsford.
Stiėvenard's 'Lectures Françaises' (*WB*.III.v), a textbook of French readings (used by Hardy in London, *Life* 49/52).
Still quiring . . . cherubim (*L*.I.ii), *MV*.v.i,62.
still sad music of humanity (SF), Wordsworth, 'Lines Composed

. . . above Tintern Abbey',91.

still small voice. See **Elijah . . . fire from heaven**.

stillicide, dripping of water.

stitching (colloquial), getting married.

stiver, coin of low value (orginally Dutch).

stock (*UGT*.v.i), swarm of bees.

stocks, a wooden structure which used to stand in each parish, usually near the churchyard; it was designed to clamp the feet of offenders as they sat, exposed to the public, for periods which varied according to their misdeeds.

stocks and stones (*GND*4), blocks of wood and stone; cf. Milton's sonnet 'On the Late Massacre in Piedmont' (*G.T.*).

Stoke-Barehills (*JO*.v.v,vii), Basingstoke, Hampshire.

the stomach's sake, drops for (*HE*.xxxiii), cf. I Tim.v,23.

Stonehenge (similes in *TM*.xxvi and *MC*.xxxiii; *TD*.lviii; *SC*.Channel Firing), a megalithic monument once thought to have been a Druidic temple, near Amesbury, north of Salisbury. Originally its outer circle of stones supported a rim of horizontal stones; parallel to this ran an inner circle of smaller stones. Within this stood five trilithons, forming a horseshoe, with an inner horseshoe of smaller stones. At the centre was a flat stone, thought to have been an altar, the Stone of Sacrifice. The fact that from this, at the summer solstice, the sun may be seen rising over the isolated Sun (or Hele) Stone has suggested, as Hardy indicates, that Stonehenge was once a temple for pagan heliolatry. If he did not rule out the traditional Druidic associations of Stonehenge, the Tess scene is linked with her sacrifice to Alec in the Chase (v and xi).

stooded (dial.), stationary, stuck.

stoor (dial.), to-do, crisis, disturbance.

stopt-diapason, soft or muffled organ tone.

Store of ladies . . . bright eyes . . . influence (*GND* title-page, pr., and 4), Milton, 'L'Allegro',121–2 (*G.T.*).

storied, celebrated in history.

stound, astound, stun.

Stour (*JO*.IV.iv; *MV*.Overlooking the River Stour, On Sturminster Foot-Bridge) a river flowing through Gillingham, Sturminster Newton, Blandford, and near Wimborne.

Stourcastle (*TD*.ii,iv,xvi; *D*3.II.i,v.vi), Sturminster Newton; little is left of the ancient castle. Cf. **The To-Be-Forgotten**.

Strafford (*RN*.I.vii,IV.iv), Thomas Wentworth (1593–1641) who, after being lord-lieutenant of Ireland, became principal adviser to Charles I, and was made Earl of Strafford. Impeached by the king's enemies, he defended himself most ably; his execution was a travesty of justice.

strakes, sections of iron forming the rim of a cart-wheel.

The Stranger's Song (*WP*). Hardy's story 'The Three Strangers' (*WT*.1) was dramatized as 'The Three Wayfarers', and staged in London, with the producer Charles Charrington as the hangman, in June 1893.

strappen (for 'strapping'), strongly built, sturdy.

Stratleigh (*PBE*.xi,xii), Bude (on the north coast of Cornwall), named from the neighbouring town of Stratton.

strawberry-tree, a species of the arbutus shrub, named from the appearance of its fruit.

strawmote, a single straw.

Street of Wells (*WB*), Fortune's Well, Portland; described in *TM*.xxxiv.

strent (dial.), slit, rent.

Strenuus Miles, vel Potator (Lat.), an energetic soldier or, rather, drinker (*GND*8).

striae (*CM*6), ridges.

string-course, a projecting ornamental layer of brick or stone.

strook (dial.), struck, astonished.

stubbard, an early codling apple.

stud (dial.), quandary, 'brown study'; **studding**, lost to the world.

stump bedstead, bed without posts. **stumpy**, heavy-footed.

stunpole, stunpoll (dial.), blockhead.

stuns: put the stuns upon (dial.), weigh down, check.

Stygian shore (*OMC*6.i), of the river Styx in the underworld of Greek mythology.

The Subalterns (*PPP*). *freeze*: see **frost**. *shorn one*, an ironical reminder of the proverb 'God tempers the wind to the shorn lamb'. *North*, the north wind. *ark*, body; cf. **tabernacle**: as the body is the 'soul-shell' (*PPP*.The Mother Mourns), so the Ark contained the Covenant between Yahweh and his people, which was later kept in the holiest part of the Tabernacle.

subdued . . . worked in (*W*.ii; *JO*.III.i), Son.111 ('like the dyer's hand').

the sublime, From . . . to the ridiculous . . . but a step! (*D*3.I.xii). The thought came to Napoleon from Tom Paine's *The Age of Reason*. Hardy translates Napoleon's remark to De Pradt, the

Polish ambassador, after the retreat from Moscow in 1812.

such a kind of gain-giving . . . (*TT*.xxxviii), *Ham*.v.ii, 207–8.

such stuff as dreams are made on. See **We are such stuff**.

Sudarium of St Veronica (*W*.xxxvi), the towel which, according to tradition, Veronica gave Jesus to wipe his face as he carried his cross to Calvary, and which bore an image of his face when he returned it.

suffereth long and is kind (*SC*.Wessex Heights); **suffereth . . . thinketh no evil** (*MV*.The Blinded Bird; *LLE*.Surview). See I Cor.xiii,1–13 for all the virtues of Charity, and cf. **Apostolic Charity** and Tess.

Suffer-little-children argument (*L*.I.vii), Matt.xix,14.

suisse (Fr.), church beadle or hall porter.

Sully-Prudhomme, French poet, 1839–1907 (hearing a penal sentence in the fiat 'You shall be born', *TD*.xxxvi); 'fiat' implies no choice for the children (cf. *TD*.iii).

summa genera (SF), the highest or most important types or qualities.

summer's farewell, a variety of Michaelmas Daisy.

sumple (dial.), soft, supple.

sun . . . just . . . unjust (*TD*.xix), Matt.v,45.

The Sun on the Bookcase (*SC*). Written in 1870, or 1872 (MS deletion), at Higher Bockhampton, it seems, with Emma Gifford in mind.

A Sunday Morning Tragedy (*TL*). Hardy wished to present the subject first as a play. Two sketches for this exist, 'Birthwort', the title of one, indicating the herb fatally used. After being rejected by *The Fortnightly Review*, the poem was accepted by Ford Madox Hueffer for his new publication *The English Review* (Dec 1908). *Pydel Vale*: see **Longpuddle**. Hermann Lea states that the banns were called in Piddlehinton Church. *loved too well*, cf. 'not wisely, but too well', *Oth*.v.ii,347; *picotee*, an attractively edged carnation (this term of endearment is the name of the second heroine in *HE*).

The Sun's Last Look . . . Girl (*LLE*), Mary Hardy, d. 24 Nov 1915.

The Sunshade (*MV*). It was found either when Hardy visited Swanage in 1916 (*Life* 373/403) or when he and Emma lived there, 1875–6.

The Supplanter (*PPP*). The original MS title was 'At the Cemetery Lodge'; for 'the Field of Tombs' see **Her Death and After**.

suppressio veri (Lat.), suppression of the truth.

surrogate, bishop's deputy, with power to issue licences for marriage without banns, fifteen days' residence in the parish where the ceremony was to take place being nominally required.

Surview (*LLE*). Epigraph: Vulgate, Psalm cxviii,59; English version, Psalm cxix,59, 'I thought on my ways' (cf. 'Birthday notes', *Life* 405/435). The poem alludes to Phil.iv,8 and I Cor.xiii,1–13.

Swaffham tinker (*RN*.II.iii), the fifteenth-century pedlar John Chapman, who, according to legend, dreamed that if he went to London he would hear something to his advantage. There he met a man who had dreamt of a treasure under the pear tree belonging to John Chapman of Swaffham (in Norfolk). On his return, the pedlar found this buried treasure.

the Swan (*TT*.iv), Cygnus, one of the northern constellations.

swealed (dial.), burnt, scorched.

Sweet-and-Twenty (*PBE*.iii), cf. 'O mistress mine' (*G.T.*), *TN*.II.iii.

sweet-oil-and-hartshorn, olive oil, probably, and an aqueous solution of ammonia (ammonia was once obtained from hartshorn).

Swenn, the name for the Frome river in the original versions of 'The Romantic Adventures of a Milkmaid' and 'The Withered Arm'.

swim into his ken (*PBE*.xxiii), Keats, 'On First Looking into Chapman's Homer' (*G.T.*).

swingel, cudgel, flail (cf. *Life* 443/477–8).

swipes (dial.), thin or weak beer.

Swoln with wind . . . drew (*FMC*.xxi), Milton, 'Lycidas',126 (*G.T.*).

the sword of the Lord and of Gideon (*W*.xiv), Judg.vii,15–22.

Sylvania Castle (*WB*), Pennsylvania Castle, a mansion (later a hotel) built in 1800, at George III's suggestion, in a dell above the Cove of Church Hope, Portland (map H).

symboliste . . . décadent (*LLI*.1). Hardy had read an article on Symbolists and Décadents in contemporary French literature in *Revue des Deux Mondes*, 1 Nov 1888.

Symonds (PRF), John Addington Symonds, 1840–93, a scholarly writer whose main work was on the Renaissance in Italy. See ***The Mayor of Casterbridge***.

T

tabernacle, the body as a (*HE*.xxxix; *TD*.xlv; *WB*.I.ii,III.vii title; *TL*.New Year's Eve), II. Cor.v,1–4.

table, writing-tablet (as in *Ham*.I.v,98). **the Table**, the Communion Table. **the Table of the Law** (*TT*.xi), the ten commandments (see below) displayed in order, here in the customary two tables, the first (1–4) indicating duties to God, the second (5–10), to one's neighbour. ***table d'hôte*** (Fr.), a common table for guests at a hotel.

Tableaux Vivants (*D*3.v.ii scene), live motionless representations.

tacker-haired (dial.), with wiry black hair (tacker: shoemaker's thread).

taedium vitae (Lat.), ennui.

tailing, light and inferior corn.

Taine, H. A. (1828–93), a distinguished French writer: quoted on the subject of 'photographic fiction' (PRF), from his *History of English Literature*; his ridicule in *Notes on England* of clothing worn by the urban poor (DLa).

Take, O take those lips away (*TD*.ix), *MM*.IV.i,1–6 (*G.T.*).

take the current . . . served (*TM*.xxxvi; *L*.III.iii,v.iv), *JC*.IV.iii,221.

Taking Thought (*DR*.i.3), for the morrow, Matt.vi,24–34.

Talavera . . . Vittoria (*TM*.xii), victories in Spain against Napoleon, followed by the invasion of France (Toulouse, 1814), finally Waterloo (1815). See *D*2.IV.iv for the battle of Talavera, and *D*3.II.i-iii for that of Vittoria.

Talbothays (*TD*), named from the farm owned by Hardy's father at West Stafford (cf. *Life* 6/10 for the historical origin of the name). It was imagined some three or four miles (by road) to the east of Stinsford Church, from 'several dairies in Frome Valley (combined)', Hardy wrote.

tale (archaic), number.

tale that is told (*JO*.v.v), Psalm xc,9. **tale told by an idiot** (*TD*.liv), *Mac*.v.v,26–7.

'Talian iron, Italian iron, a hollow cylindrical heater used for fluting and crimping laces, frills, etc.

Talibus incusat (*DR*.xi.1), In such terms he complains (Virgil,

Aeneid i,410, at the end of a conversation between Aeneas and his mother Venus).

tall-boys, tall chimney-pots.

tallet, loft.

Talleyrand (1754–1834), a French statesman and skilful diplomatist, who held office during the Revolution, was minister for foreign affairs under Napoleon, turned against him, dictated the terms of his deposition, and was minister for foreign affairs under his successor Louis XVIII (*TM*.xviii); a cool, calculating person (*CM*.12.vii).

Tamerlane's trumpet (*MC*.xxxiv). The army of this Tartar conqueror (1336–1406) carried trumpets seven feet long.

tangent and parallax (*TT*.xl). The main reason for studying the transit of Venus was to determine the scale of the solar system; for this it was necessary to make observations from widely separated points on the earth. The results were expressed in terms of the solar parallax; in calculating this, trigonometrical functions such as the tangent could be used at several points.

Tannhäuser (*W*.xxviii), a legendary German minstrel who lived seven years with Venus. (Swinburne's poem 'Laus Veneris', 1866, is based on this tradition.)

Tantalus (*RN*.I.ix), a king in classical legend who was punished by being placed up to the chin in a river which receded when he tried to drink; he was tantalized similarly by a bough laden with fruit above his head.

Tantrum Clangley (*UGT*.v.ii), an imaginary village, named after its percussion band.

Tarentines . . . State (*DR*.i.3), indolent citizens of Tarentum, a port in south Italy, subjugated by Rome in the third century BC.

Targan Bay, Pentargon Bay, Cornwall (map E).

Tarrying Bridegroom (*WW*). Cf. Matt.xxv,5 for the title, and *UGT*.v.i for a more light-hearted treatment of the subject. *shalloon*, woollen dress.

Tartarean (*RN*.I.iv), dark like Tartarus in the classical hell.

tass, cup, small goblet.

tasset, a kilt of armour-plating.

Tate-and-Brady, the metrical psalms. Versified by Nahum Tate and Nicholas Brady, and authorized in 1696, they were sung as hymns until the second half of the nineteenth century; cf. *MV*.Afternoon Service at Mellstock.

taters, **taties**, potatoes.

tay (old pronunciation), tea.

Taylor, Jeremy (1613–67), an English divine whose sermons and passages from *Holy Living* and *Holy Dying* provide splendid examples of his eloquent and harmonious prose. Thinking of one's death and the day of it (*TD*.xv). Jude destroys his theological and ethical works (*JO*.IV.iii), including writings by Taylor, Joseph Butler (1692–1752), Philip Doddridge (1702–51), William Paley (1743–1805), Edward Pusey (1800–82), and John Henry Newman (1801–90).

Te Deum. Cf. the translation in the C. of E. 'Morning Prayer' service.

tear her smock (*RN*.I.iii), lose her reputation (virginity? Cf. 'tear your gown' in Jane Austen's *Mansfield Park* x).

tear on, race away. **tear-brass** (dial.), rowdy, boisterous.

The tearful . . . dawn (*DR*.ix.3), Tennyson, 'A Dream of Fair Women',74.

teave (dial.), get worked up, struggle, toil.

teen, sorrow.

teetotum, a toy that could be spun like a top.

tell (archaic), count.

Temp. Guliel. IV (Lat.), during William IV's reign, 1830–7 (*WW*.The Catching Ballet of the Wedding Clothes).

Tempe, Vale of . . . Thule (*RN*.I.i), a beautiful valley in Thessaly, northern Greece, compared with bleak northernmost territories; cf. **Ultima Thule**. The vale is below Mt Olympus, on which lived the gods and goddesses of ancient Greek mythology (*W*.v).

template, a shaped piece of wood or metal used for accurate design in carving or moulding; a horizontal support beam for building.

'tempted (*TT*.i), attempted (i.e. before her parents' marriage).

tempted unto seventy times seven (*JO*.II.iv), Matt.xviii,21–2.

the Ten Commandments, from Exod.xx,1–17, as numbered in the Book of Common Prayer (see 'The Catechism') and commonly displayed in churches (cf. *JO*.v.vi). On 'the crash of broken commandments' and tragedy (CEF): the first and third relate to the one God, and not taking his name in vain; the sixth relates to murder (Hardy's 'as much as necessary' includes war); the seventh to adultery (cf. *TT*.xi); the ninth to false testimony; the tenth, 'Thou shalt not covet thy neighbour's house . . . ', is alluded to in 'How I Built Myself a House' (Orel,162).

Ten Years Since (*HS*), i.e. after Emma Hardy's death. *lofts*, the attics at Max Gate which she had converted into her own flat, where she died.

Terburg (*FMC*.ix), Terborch, a Dutch painter, 1617–81.

term, statue or bust representing the upper part of the body, like that of the Roman god Terminus.

terrene, on earth, terrestrial; stretch of country, land.

the Terrible Ten (*FMC*.xxvi), the Ten Commandments (above).

Tertiary Age (*D*1.I.vi), the third geological phase of stratification, during which the human being is supposed to have come into existence.

Tess of the d'Urbervilles, begun in the autumn of 1888, was not published until 1891, after being held up in its early stages as a serial, and eventually transferred to another publisher for emasculated serialization. The story originated from a Dorchester reminder of the steady impoverishment of noble families (*Letters* I,258), the 'down, down, down' which had affected Hardy's own (*Life* 214–15/223–4; *TD*.xix). Aspects of the plot had been anticipated in *DR*, one being hinted at in the 'Too Late, Beloved' title (from Shelley, 'Epipsychidion',131–2) which Hardy had contemplated. The subject of rape had been suggested most probably by the youthful misfortune of his paternal grandmother; the domestic christening scene, by the baptism conducted by his maternal grandmother (Millgate,294). Though an afterthought, the subtitle 'A Pure Woman' gives point to a theme presenting a heroine whose intentions are always good but whom destiny repeatedly victimizes, ruining 'her every and only chance' (xxv). Hardy's novel is implicitly critical of the traditional *dénouement* in Shakespeare's *The Rape of Lucrece* and Richardson's *Clarissa*: the heroine does not seek refuge in death after being dishonoured; the 'determination to enjoy' (xv–xvi; *Life* 213/222) prevails, but the harvest of consequence defeats her ('Once victim, always victim'), as the threshing-scene (xlvii) illustrates. This symbolism, with the First Cause or Prime Mover inseparable from the action, is successful, but the attempt to introduce the blind Mother (Nature) in the bedroom scene (ix; cf. *PPP*.The Bullfinches) is a relative failure. This is preceded by a garden scene where Alec d'Urberville's springing over the wall stresses his Satanic role (cf. *Paradise Lost* iv,178–83), accentuated recurringly in smoke or smoking (v,x,xii), finally in conjunction with a traditional reminder of hell-fire (l). Contrasting with these are the Eden-like days of happiness between Tess and Angel (xx,xxvii), each worshipping the other, with 'hardly a touch of earth' in their love. Angel's immature idealization of Tess has tragic consequences, the analysis of which (end of xxxix) should be related to Hardy's comment of 28 Oct 1891 (*Life* 239/251), which applies also to the pursuit of the Idea in *W* and *WB*. More than once Hardy shows a Swinburnian preference for Greek or pagan joyousness, but his related remarks on conventional prejudice (xiii,xiv,xv) are an inartistic intrusion; they are untrue to Tess and her world, and an apt testimony to the truth of D. H. Lawrence's maxim 'Never trust the artist. Trust the tale.' The recurrent red and blood motif is evident; card-playing references (vii,x,lvi) have a dubious significance. Like the heroine in Scott's *The Bride of Lammermoor*, Tess's mind gives way when she is tricked by her lover's late return; she kills the situation (*Life* 221/231) in a less romantic and appealing fashion. Harmony of summer, autumn, and winter settings with events contributes significantly, but the psychology of miniature pictorial scenes is more subtle. Vision ranges from near to far, from the subjectively and objectively realized to the philosophical. The poet's presence is continually felt, and weight of thought is communciated in numerous apt references and quotations, Biblical particularly. The hopeful ending recalls that of *Paradise Lost*; the figurative reference to the President of the Immortals' sport with Tess gives a view held by **Aeschylus**, but completely at variance with Hardy's directing belief in a First Cause which is indifferent to human fate (cf. *Life* 243–4/256–7).

tester, bed-canopy.

tête-à-tête, en, in private, without the company of a third person.

Τετέλεσται (*FMC*.xliii), 'It is finished' (Gk.), the last words of Christ on the Cross, John xix,30.

Tetuphenay, T. (*JO*.II.vi). The name, from the Greek 'to have struck', anticipates the 'hard slap'. Hardy had Benjamin Jowett, Master of Balliol, in mind, and there is evidence which indicates that Tetuphenay's letter may have been based on one Hardy received from Jowett.

teuny (dial.), weak, undersized.

Teute and Pole (*D3*.I.iii), Germany and Poland (Teutons and Poles).

That Moment (*HS*). It seems that Hardy remembers hurtful words from Emma for which, afterwards, he thought she was not responsible.

That never would become that wife . . . amiss (*TD*.xxxii), from the ballad 'The Boy and the Mantle'. The boy comes to King Arthur's court with the magic mantle that only the pure can wear; when Queen Guinevere tries it, it turns to shreds and changes colour.

That which . . . deep . . . out? (*PBE*.xix), Eccl.vii,24.

that willing suspension . . . poetic faith (*D*.pr.), Coleridge, *Biographia Literaria* xiv.

That-it-may-please-Thees (*TD*.xxiii), Litany intercessions (C. of E.).

theäs oon (dial.), this one.

Theban family woe (*LLI*.4.i), particularly relating to Oedipus, son of Laius, king of ancient Thebes (in Greece).

Then fancy shapes . . . (*PBE*.xvi ep.), Tennyson, *In Memoriam* lxxx.

Then I said in my heart . . . (*OMC*4.II.iv ep.), Eccl.ii,15.

Then shall the man . . . iniquity (*JO*.v.viii), Num.v,31.

Theomachist (Gk.), one who struggles against God (*DR*.viii.4).

There are two who decline . . . (*JO*.VI ep.), Browning, 'Too Late' x.

There is nothing either good or bad . . . (*TT*.xvi), *Ham*.II.ii,248–50.

'There seemed a strangeness' (*HS*). The revelation of God's purpose and the coming of his kingdom are imagined; 'phantasy' indicates Hardy's scepticism. *Men have not heard . . . seen . . .*, cf. I Cor.ii,9; *glass . . . face to face*, I Cor.xiii,12.

There was a being . . . (*JO*.IV.v), Shelley, 'Epipsychidion', 190–1,21–2.

There was a sound of revelry by night (*JO*.II.vi), from Byron's description of the eve of Waterloo (*Childe Harold* III.xxxi).

Thermidorean (*TD*.xxiv), very hot. Thermidor was the midsummer month in the French Revolutionary calendar.

Thermopylae and Salamis. See **Second Invasion**.

thesmothete (*FMC*.x), one who lays down the law (a name given to some of the chief magistrates in ancient Athens).

Thessalonians and the chronology of the New Testament (*JO*.III.iv).

'They are great trees', lines recalling the Avenue, Wimborne, where the Hardys lived, 1881–83; included in Hardy's *Life* (386/416).

They that go down to the sea. See **go down**.

They Would Not Come (*LLE*). When Hardy revisited St Juliot after his wife's death, the ghosts of the past (specifically Emma Gifford and her brother-in-law the Revd Caddell Holder) were not recalled. *lectioned*, read from the lectionary (those portions of

Scripture appointed for Church services); *wisps*, will o' the wisps (lights from marsh-gas, thought to be spirits) which misled night wanderers in marshy localities.

Thick-coming fancies (*L.*v.xiii), *Mac.*v.iii,38.

thief in the night (*FMC.*x), I Thess.v,2.

The Thieves Who Couldn't Help Sneezing (*OMC*5), Hardy's amusingly satisfying Christmas story for children; pub. by *The Illustrated London News* in *Father Christmas*, Dec 1877.

thik (dial.), this, that. **thik oon**, this one.

thill (of a horse), in the shafts.

thimble-and-button, a term of contempt (originally applied to tailors).

thimble-rigger, a swindler in a game played with three thimbles and a pea.

The Thing Unplanned (*HS*). The meadow-rills, bridge, and thatched post-office (not the ridge) suggest Lower Bockhampton. Possibly the poem relates to Hardy's early infatuation with Mrs Henniker; if so, the 'thing better' was the continuation of their correspondence and friendship, which lasted until her death early in 1923.

Things true, lovely, of good report (*TD.*xxxi; *PPP.*The Souls of the Slain, The To-Be-Forgotten; *LLE.*Surview; A Jingle on the Times), Phil.iv,8.

The Third Kissing-Gate (*WW*). From the avenued road out of Dorchester, the girl walks through the first gateway and along the meadows on the north side of the Frome, following the path to Stinsford (eventually below the garden wall of Stinsford House) until, near a small waterfall, she reaches the third kissing-gate (which gives access to the path leading below Kingston Maurward to Lower Bockhampton; see map A). A kissing-gate swings within fencing which partially encloses it on either side, allowing only one person to pass through at a time.

thirtingill (dial.), wrong-headed, perverse.

thirtover (dial.), contrary, cross, obstinate.

This is the chief thing . . . perturbed (*TD.*xxxix). See **Aurelius**.

This Summer and Last (*HS*): 'yester-summer' alludes to an early one when Emma's 'corn-coloured hair' was 'abundant in its coils' (*Life* 73/76).

thistles for figs (*RN.*IV.vi), cf. Matt.vii,16.

Thomas, Sir (*CM.*10), Sir Thomas Strangways of Melbury House.

Thor and Woden, Norse gods worshipped in Anglo-Saxon England

(*RN*.I.iii). Thor, son of Woden, and god of war, produced thunder when he wielded his hammer (*FMC*.xv; *CM*6).

Thorncombe (*TL*.She Hears the Storm), a wood near Hardy's birthplace. He is most probably thinking of his mother after his father's death.

thorny crown (*TD*.xxiii), cf. the crown of thorns, Matt.xxvii,29.

thorough, through; thoroughly. **thorough-bass**, the bass part only, with figures to indicate the accompanying chords and harmonies.

Thou fool . . . required of thee! (*TD*.xxvi), Luke xii,20.

Thou hast been my hope . . . tower . . . enemy (*PBE*.xxxi), Psalm lxi,3 (Common Prayer version; the fact that this is part of the C. of E. marriage-service increases the irony).

Thou hast conquered, O pale Galilean . . . (*JO*.II.iii), Jesus of Nazareth in Galilee; from Swinburne, 'Hymn to Proserpine' (*Poems and Ballads*, 1866), on the Victorian conflict between Christian asceticism and 'Hellenic' joyousness. See **Julian the Apostate**.

Thou shalt be – Nothing (*PPP*.Sapphic Fragment ep.), from Edward FitzGerald's *Rubáiyát* of Omar Khayyám (xlvii).

Thou shalt not commit (adultery, *TD*.xii), Exod.xx,14.

Thou wilt not utter . . . (*PBE*.xi), cf. *1.H4*.II.iii,108–9.

Though an unconnected course of adventure . . . more required . . . than . . . reality (*DR*.title-page), Scott, Introduction to *The Monastery*.

Though I give my body . . . nothing (*JO*.VI.vi), I Cor.xiii,3.

Though this has come upon us . . . way (*UGT*.IV.v), Psalm xliv,17–18.

thought, a **parasite**, a **disease of the flesh** (*RN*.II.vi), cf. *Ham*.III.i,85. Hardy was influenced by Pater's essay on Winckelmann, which maintains that realization of the Hellenic ideal life discredits our world and makes thought *fret the flesh*.

thought to the morrow, give (DLa), cf. Matt.vi,34.

Thought's the slave of life . . . time's fool (Gen.Pr.), *1.H4*.v.iv,81.

Thoughts from Sophocles, one of Hardy's uncollected poems, a free rendering of a chorus (ll.1200–50) in Sophocles' *Oedipus at Colonos* which emphasizes the ills of old age, and maintains that nothing offered by life equals 'the good of knowing no birth at all'.

Thoughts of Phena (*WP*). For the circumstances in which this poem was begun, in March 1890, a few days before the death of Hardy's cousin Tryphena, see *Life* 224/234. They became friendly after his return from London in 1867, before she left Puddletown at the end of 1869 to begin her teacher-training in London at the age of eighteen. See **My Cicely** and ***The Well-Beloved***; for 'my lost prize', cf. **The Opportunity**. Hardy's illustration shows a shrouded body of a woman laid on a sofa, the original of which was given Hardy by his mother and kept at Max Gate (Basil Willey, *Cambridge and Other Memories*, London, 1968, p. 54).

thoughts . . . tears (*PBE*.i), Wordsworth, 'Intimations of Immortality' (*G.T.*).

thousand things lawful . . . expedient (*L*.IV.i), cf. I Cor.vi,12.

thread-the-needle, a children's game, all joining hands, the player at the end of the 'string' passing between the last two at the other end, the rest following.

The Three Strangers (*WT*.1), the best of Hardy's short stories in conception; first pub. in March 1883; dramatized at Barrie's suggestion for production in London (June 1893) as *The Three Wayfarers*.

three-cunning (dial.), knowing, secretive.

thrid, thread, make one's way through intricacies, understand the deviousness of.

throned along the sea (*WB*.III.iv). Cf. **Dundagel**.

Throope Corner (*RN*.IV.iii), at the crossroads south of Throop and to the east of 'Alderworth' (map D).

throughly, thoroughly (Biblical; cf. Matt.iii,12).

thunder, lightning, rain (*DR*.viii.4), a presage of evil, *Mac*.I.i,2.

A Thunderstorm in Town (*SC*). See **Henniker, Mrs** and Hardy's letters to her while they were in London, June–July 1893.

thwart, contrary, adverse; misfortune, setback.

Thy aerial part . . . body (*JO*.v ep.), from George Long's translation (1862) of the *Meditations* of Marcus Aurelius Antoninus. See **Aurelius**.

tickle, touch-and-go (cf. a 'ticklish' situation).

tidden, 'tidn (dial.), it isn't.

tide of affairs (*L*.III.vii), cf. *JC*.IV.iii,216.

tide-times, holidays (coinciding with Church feasts, e.g. Easter-tide).

tightener (colloquial), exercise that is physically bracing.

till death us do part (*JO*.VI.vi), from the C. of E. marriage-service.

tilt, canopy of a cart or carriage.

Time, like a stream (*DR*.xii.6,xiii.4; *UGT*.IV.vii; *TM*.i; *CM*2.viii). Cf. the words of a popular old C. of E. hymn: 'Time, like an ever-rolling stream, Bears all its sons away.'

Time and I against any two (*L*.III.iv), said by Mazarin (1602–61), cardinal and minister of France; cf. ***The Well-Beloved***.

Time . . . own grey style (*MC*.xlii), Shelley, 'Epipsychidion',55.

time to embrace . . . (*TD*.xxiii), **time to laugh** (*RN*.III.vii; cf. 'A man would never laugh . . . ', *Life* 112/116), Eccl.iii,4–5.

Time's Laughingstocks (1909). The title derives from Tennyson, *The Princess* iv,496. Although the volume contains a number of poems voicing bitter disillusionment with life and love, they are more than counterbalanced by verses on ancestors dear to Hardy (particularly his mother), boyhood memories, and outward-looking narrative poems and dramatic monologues. Some brief returns to the Unfulfilled Intention theme are offset by lighter verse and a marked increase in lyrical deftness.

Time's revenges. See **whirligig of time**.

Timing Her (*MV*). Hardy looked forward to visits by the young Lalage Acland, daughter of the Curator of Dorset County Museum, when she brought notes and documents from her father to Max Gate.

Timon, isolate a (*WT*.1), cf. Shakespeare's *TA*. When he loses his wealth, Timon discovers that his friends have been self-seeking flatterers; be becomes a misanthrope, and leaves the haunts of men.

Timothy (*TT*.xxix). The Timothy to whom Paul sent his two epistles seems to have been in charge of the Church at Ephesus; hence 'prototype'.

Timothy Titus Philemon (*TM*.xxii), names of three to whom consecutive epistles (as arranged in the New Testament) were sent by Paul (cf. *TD*.xxv).

tine (dial.), close, shut.

ting, produce a ringing sound (to induce bees to swarm).

Tintagel Castle (setting for *QC*), on the coast of north Cornwall (map E), not far from St Juliot; cf. *Life* 78/81.

Tintinhull (*TL*.The Flirt's Tragedy; *LLE*.Vagg Hollow), a village with a manor-house, 4 m. NW of Yeovil.

Tintoretto (*L*.VI.v), a Venetian painter, 1518–94.

tipstaff, officer, executor (carrying a metal-tipped staff).

tirailleurs (Fr.), sharp-shooters, usually drawn from the infantry, who skirmish independently.

tire-woman, woman who assists at her lady's toilet, lady's maid.

'Tis She . . . character (*DR*.x.4), cf. **Now, if Time knows**.

Tishbite . . . talking . . . pursuing . . . journey . . . sleeping . . . awaked (*TD*.xi), Elijah, I Kings xviii,27 (cf. xvii,1).

tisty-tosty (dial.), plump, round (like the cowslip ball made by children for a game in which their husbands, or the latter's occupations, were foretold).

the tithe question (*TT*.xxv). Originally one-tenth of its produce was paid for the use of Church land; in 1836 this tithe was commuted to a rent charge, although the question remained unsettled in some parts of the country.

tithe-paying . . . cummin (*DR*.xii.6), Matt.xxiii,23.

Titian (*L*.VI.v; *MC*.xxii; *WB*.III.viii), an Italian painter (c.1490–1576) who dominated Venetian art during its peak period. The key movement in *MC*, 'throwing her arm above her brow' (or head), may be seen in several Titian pictures, three in London: 'Bacchus and Ariadne' (N.G.), 'Perseus and Andromeda' (Wallace Collection); best of all in 'Lucretia' (Hampton Court Palace).

Tivworthy (*CM*.12.x), Tiverton, a town in the Exe valley, Devon.

To a Bridegroom, an uncollected abridgment of verses written in 1866, asking whether, through the vicissitudes of time and chance, the bridegroom will observe his vows (C. of E. marriage-service) 'to love and to cherish, till death us do part'.

To a Lady (*WP*), Rebekah Owen, an American lady who had been friendly with Hardy and was critical of *JO*; cf. Carl J. Weber, *Hardy and the Lady from Madison Square*, Waterville, Maine, 1952, pp. 111–16.

To a Lady Playing and Singing in the Morning (*LLE*). As often occurs in Hardy's poetry, imagination weaves a subject round something from his life. The last two lines imply regret that he had not found enough time for Emma's singing during their marriage.

To a Motherless Child (*WP*). The idea may have sprung from Tennyson's 'Locksley Hall',91–2. *Dame*, see **At a Bridal**; *mechanic artistry*, blind, mechanical activity (cf. the first words of the Spirit of the Years in *D*1.Fore Scene).

To a Sea-Cliff (*HS*). Durlston Head is near Swanage (cf. *Life* 108/111). *sword*, a symbol of division between a married pair (from Meredith, *Modern Love* i).

To a T, exactly and wholly.

To a Tree in London (*WW*). Cf. *PBE*.xiii and **Bede's Inn**.

To an Impersonator of Rosalind (*TD*), Mrs Scott-Siddons (most probably the actress of the next sonnet) at the Haymarket

Theatre, London. *'very, very Rosalind'*, *AYL*.IV.i,63.

To an Unborn Pauper Child (*PPP*). Hardy's MS bore the note ' "She must go to the Union-house to have her baby." *Casterbridge Petty Sessions*.' Cf. Fanny Robin, FMC.xxxix–xlii. *Doomsters*, cf. *WP*.Hap and 'Wrongers' in *TL*.After the Last Breath. *Travails and teens*, heavy labours and sorrows. *wold*, open, exposed country.

To be thus . . . safely thus (*HE*.xxxi), *Mac*.III.i,47–8.

To C. F. H. (*HS*). Hardy's gift to his godchild Caroline Fox Hanbury of Kingston Maurward House in September 1921 was a copy of this poem in a silver box (*Life* 414/448).

To everything . . . season (*L*.I.xv; *LLI*.8d), Eccl.iii,1.

To Lizbie Browne (*PPP*), Elizabeth Bishop (*Life* 25–6/30,206/214).

To Louisa in the Lane (*WW*). See **Transformations** and *LLE*.The Passer-By. The hollow in the lane is on the way from Stinsford to Bockhampton Cross (cf. Hollow Hill, *UGT*.I.i).

To make you sorry . . . in nothing (*PBE*.xvii), cf. II Cor.vii,9.

To Meet, or Otherwise (*SC*). Written to Miss Dugdale, and first printed in December 1913; she and Hardy were married the following February. *Cimmerian*, gloomy (classical).

To My Father's Violin (*MV*). *Nether Glooms, Mournful Meads*, 'a Virgilian reminiscence of mine of Acheron and the Shades' (*Life* 410/440; cf. *Aeneid* vi). *eff-holes*, f-shaped holes; *purflings*, decorative inlay of (e.g.) ivory and mother-of-pearl.

To Outer Nature (*WP*). The radiance lost by Darwinian disillusionment (Darkness-overtaken) is centred in the rainbow image (Iris-hued embowment), originally a symbol of God's blessing (Gen.ix,8–17); cf. *PPP*.On a Fine Morning. See ***The Woodlanders***.

To Please His Wife (*LLI*.6). Cf. *LLE*.The Sailor's Mother. 'Jolliffe' commemorates a famous citizen of Poole, who captured a French privateer in 1694; his memorial tablet is in St James's Church; the Town Cellar (iii) is also actual.

To set . . . heaven (*PBE*.xxix), Robert Pollok, *The Course of Time* (1827).

To Shakespeare (*MV*), written to mark the tercentenary of Shakespeare's death, at the invitation of Professor Gollancz, King's College, London, for his edition of *A Book of Homage to Shakespeare*. *tower*, of Stratford Church reflected in the Avon river; *published . . . passing-bell*, one stroke for each year of his life.

To sorrow . . . (*RN*.title-page), Keats's ode, *Endymion* iv,146ff.

To that last nothing . . . (*PBE*.xxvi ep.), Tennyson, 'The Two Voices',333.

toadsmeat (cf. 'toad-cheese', 'toadstool'), a poisonous fungus.

The To-Be-Forgotten (*PPP*). The MS shows that Hardy imagined the action in All Saints churchyard, Casterbridge (Dorchester), then in the churchyard at Stourcastle (Sturminster Newton); it dates the poem 'Feb. 9, 1899' (cf. the date of *PPP*.His Immortality). See **Things true . . . report**.

Tobit, the mishap of (*TT*.xxxix). He was blinded by droppings (faeces) of sparrows; see the Book of Tobit (ii) in the Apocrypha.

togs (colloquial), clothes.

toil (dial.), set a trap, snare; (noun) snare, grip, inescapable trouble.

Tolchurch (*DR*), Tolpuddle, 2 m. east of Puddletown.

told (*D*3.VI.vi). His days are 'numbered' or concluded; see **tale**.

tole (dial.), entice, draw.

Tolerance (*SC*), on the relationship that developed between Hardy and his first wife.

Tollamore (*OMC*4), Stinsford and the Bockhampton district. **Tollamore House**, Kingston Maurward House.

Toller Down (*TL*.The Homecoming; cf. *FMC*.ii). See map C.

Tom Jones, Henry Fielding's greatest novel, 1749: not altogether an example of superior artistic form (PRF).

Tombless . . . remembrance (*PPP*.Sapphic Fragment ep.), *H5*.I.ii,229.

Tom-rig, Tom-straw, an ordinary man, common fellow.

Toneborough (*L*; *GND*.10; *LLI*.3), Taunton (Somerset) on the Tone river. The Vale of Taunton Deane to the NW is the **Toneborough Deane** of *SC*.The Sacrilege.

a tongue with a tang (DLa), a sharp tongue, *Tem*.II.ii,48.

tongues of fire (*JO*.IV.vi), cf. **cloven tongues.**

Too rash . . . lightning (*WB*.I.viii), *RJ*.II.ii,118–19.

Toogood, Parson Billy (*LLI*.8d). See **Scrimpton** and Hardy's 1896 preface to *LLI* (Orel,30–1).

Tophet (*FMC*.xxvi; *WT*5.iii; *TD*.xlvii; *TL*.The Flirt's Tragedy), a place near Jerusalem which became synonymous with hell from the sacrificial burning of children there to the god Molech; cf. Jer.vii,31–4.

topper (dial.), blow, blow on the head; topple, overthrow.

tops, high hunting-boots with uppers of white or light-coloured leather.

Tor-upon-Sea (*CM*.11.i), Torquay, Devon.

totties (dial.), feet (usually of little children).

touch, touch-down in the game of rugby. **touch of nature** (DLa), 'One touch . . . makes the whole world kin', *TC*.III.iii,175. **touching the spot** (*JO*.1912 ps. to pr.), raising a sensitive issue, touching a sore spot (as *Jude* clearly did with the reviewer for *The Athenaeum*, 23 Nov 1895).

touchwood, soft white substance into which wood is converted by fungi; named from its readiness to burn.

tournure (Fr.), shape and bearing, general appearance.

touse (dial.) battering.

tout (dial.), hill (from 'look-out').

tout ensemble (Fr.), general appearance or effect.

Towards the lodestar . . . owlet light (*OMC*4.II.ii ep.; *W*.xxviii), Shelley, 'Epipsychidion',219–21.

Tower of Babel (*JO*.I.iii), Gen.xi,1–9.

to-year, this year.

Tra deri . . . nouvelle (*TT*.xxviii), 'It's an old story', the refrain of a contemporary French song.

Tractarian (*TD*.xxvii), very High Church, influenced by *Tracts for the Times*, the voice of the Oxford Movement (*JO*.II.i,III.iv,VI.ix).

trading o't to (*FMC*.viii), going (treading).

A Tradition of Eighteen Hundred and Four (*WT*2), Hardy's story of a nocturnal reconnaissance by Napoleon to the south coast of England. First pub. in *Harper's Christmas*, 1882, it became a tradition (*Life* 391–2/424–5). For the narrator's name, cf. *Life* 116/119 (27 July 1877). See ***Wessex Tales***.

Trafalgar line-of-battle ships (*W*.iii; cf. *D*1.v.i), the British fleet before the battle off Cape Trafalgar in October 1805.

A Tragedy of Two Ambitions (*LLI*.4), completed in the summer of 1888 (*Life* 213/222), recalls 'A Son's Veto' in its implicit denunciation of false social values in the Church. The stick turned tree (an external sign of implanted and undying guilt) was suggested by the Bockhampton tradition of a carter's whip-handle which grew into a willow tree after he had been drowned in Heedless William's Pond (map F).

A Trampwoman's Tragedy (*TL*). Hardy thought this his most successful poem (*Life* 311–12/335). Though it had been rejected by *The Cornhill Magazine* (*Life* 317–18/341), he told his publisher in 1910 that such stories were popular, and that he could write them with ease. It was written after a bicycle journey over Polden Hill (past Marshal's Elm) to Glastonbury; the circumstances had been known to Hardy for many years, and the woman's name was Mary Ann Taylor (*Letters* III,83). For the Somerset places, see Hardy's map of Wessex. *Lone inns*: see **King's Stag**; Windwhistle, west of Crewkerne; The Horse, at Middlemarsh, on the Dorchester–Sherborne road; The Hut, Long Bredy Hill, on the Dorchester–Bridport road; Wynyard's Gap, on the Crewkerne road, north of Beaminster. *Marshwood*, on the Dorset–Devon border SW of Crewkerne; *Ivel-chester*, Ilchester; *Blue Jimmy* (his story was written, with Hardy's assistance, by Florence Dugdale; cf. Purdy,314. The 'neighbour' of the note was father of the William Keats whom the boy Hardy knew at Higher Bockhampton.) *last fling*, when hanged on 25 Apr 1827; *Glaston*, Glastonbury; *Western Moor*, Sedgemoor.

trangleys (dial.), toys, playthings, bits of apparatus.

transformation scene (*HE*.v), a scene disclosed in a pantomine.

Transformations (*MV*). The yew stands in Stinsford churchyard near the Hardy graves. For the girl whose friendship Hardy wished to cultivate, cf. *Life* 26/30,502 and *HS*.Louie. (His late evidence may seem a little self-contradictory, one statement being that he met her during his Dorset visits from London up to his 23rd or 24th year.) Louisa Harding lived near Stinsford Church, her father being a fairly rich farmer who discouraged her friendship with young Hardy. This attitude and her being sent to a boarding-school for young ladies may have promoted the poor-man-and-the-lady theme in Hardy's earlier fiction, and provided an idea for *The Woodlanders*.

transit of Venus (*TT*.xxix), the passage of the planet across the sun.

Transition-Norman (MCR), style of architecture about the end of the twelfth century, developing from the Norman to the Early English.

trant (vb.), trade as a tranter, a carrier who transported goods for other people, especially on market-days.

Trantridge (*TD*), Pentridge, NNW of Chaseborough. (*LLI*.8h), Tarrant Hinton, on the Salisbury–Blandford road 7 m. SW of Pentridge; **Tranton** in the serialized version is no doubt what Hardy intended for the latter.

traps (slang), articles, belongings.

trate (local pronunciation), treat.

the Travailler (*D*1.Fore Scene), one in travail, labouring to bring forth (a better world. Nature, however, is subject to the Immanent

Will; cf. *PPP*.Doom and She, The Subalterns).

travel, trouble ('travail' is meant).

treadmill, formerly an instrument of punishment in prisons.

treble-bob, ring the treble bell in a succession of peal-changes.

The Tree (*PPP*). *gnarl*, knotty protuberance on a tree. *Fiord* (in Norway) and *Strom . . . Fleuve* (German . . . French), river.

The Tree and the Lady (*MV*). Emma Hardy at Max Gate. *greenth*, greenness, verdure; *Nor'lights*, the Northern Lights or Aurora Borealis.

tree of knowledge (*JO*.I.iii), of good and evil, Gen.ii,9.

treen (archaic plural), trees.

trendle (dial.), large circular bowl for making dough.

trew (local pronunciation), true.

Trewe, Robert (*LLI*.1). The name suggests an actual counterpart: he is drawn considerably from the poet Dante Gabriel Rossetti, and the idealization of his Lady in *The House of Life*. 'Severed Lives' was suggested by 'Severed Selves', and Hardy quotes the opening lines of 'Stillborn Love' (sonnets xl and lv in that series). He alludes to W. R. Buchanan's attack on Rossetti in 'The Fleshly School of Poetry' (1871), and bases his description on Holman Hunt's portrait of Rossetti and the 'slouched hat' of his later years.

Trewthen, Baptista (*CM*.11). The surname seems typically Cornish (cf. 'Trewen', *PBE*.xxxvi); the Christian name suggests a strictly religious upbringing.

trifles light as air (*L*.III.xi), *Oth*.III.iii,326.

trilithon, two standing stones with a third resting on them.

Trilobites (*PBE*.xxii), one of many varieties of extinct animals with three-lobed bodies.

trim, adjust (sails); outfit, dress, appearance.

trimming (dial.), excellent, gratifying, great.

the Trine, the Trinity: the Father, the Son, and the Holy Ghost of Christian theology.

Tringham, Parson (*TD*), named after the Revd Charles Bingham, rector of Melcombe Bingham (near Hartfoot Lane) from 1842 to 1881, and a keen antiquarian. His history of the d'Urbervilles (*TD*.i) is from Hutchins.

Trink-halle (Germ.), spa pump-room, where medicinal waters are drunk.

triolet, an eight-line poem in which the first two lines set up all the rhymes, the first line recurring in the 4th and 7th, the second in the 8th.

triple-bob-major. Such a peal would require eight bells; Hardy's bell-ringing here (*DR*.Sequel) is based on what he knew of the six-bell peal at Fordington.

tristful (Fr. *triste*), sad.

triumph of the crowd . . . hero . . . few (CEF), a thought copied from an article in the *Revue des Deux Mondes*, 15 May 1886.

Troglodytean, secluded, living apart (like cave-dwellers).

Trojan women . . . Carthage (*WB*.III.vii), Virgil, *Aeneid* i,479–82.

trouvaille (Fr.), lucky find or discovery.

trow, believe, suppose; believe in.

Troy (*PBE*.iii), destroyed by fire as a result of Paris's love of Helen.

Troy, Francis (*FMC*), named from Troy Town ('Roy Town', map A). Hardy's uncle John Sharpe, at one time a soldier, had some of Troy's dashing qualities; see **Everdene, Bathsheba**.

trucks, a light two-wheeled handcart (strictly, the wheels).

true . . . and of good report (*TD*.xxxi), Phil.iv,8.

Trufal (*CM*.11), Truro, Cornwall.

Trumpet, final (cf. **trump**, *D*2.v.viii), when the dead are raised, I Cor.xv,52.

The Trumpet-Major (serialized month by month throughout 1880 in *Good Words*) was written at Upper Tooting; it was probably begun in the spring of 1879, Hardy offering it early in June to Blackwood as 'a cheerful story, without views or opinions . . . intended to wind up happily', evidently in reaction to not very favourable reviews of *RN*. It was the kind of serial, with George III 'just round the corner' (*Life* 127/131), which Leslie Stephen would have welcomed. Hardy's copious research for it, at the British Museum and, orally, in Dorset, set him on the road to *The Dynasts* (*Letters* III,286); evidence of it, on a variety of subjects, is clear throughout the novel, which gives an impression of diligence and studied particularity rather than of spontaneity and inspiration. The author's main object is to entertain; his attitude is often Thackerayan in its comic detachment; from the nautical Bob Loveday to minor background figures, the character-tendency is towards the type; the Derriman episodes incline to the farcical. The general humour appears artificial rather than indigenous. Once the story is under way, a close succession of incidents, events, and ingeniously contrived situations maintains interest, but it is limited by want of a great action and greatness of character, by a vacillating heroine and a shy, self-immolating hero. Festus and his uncle are a foil to the ordinariness of life which Hardy deliberately preferred to the grand events of historical novels (the 'Big Bow-wow' strain which Walter Scott contrasted with Jane Austen's exquisite perceptions of her familiar world). Hardy's deeper touches arise from involving characters in a background fraught with unknown destiny (old Cornick and Anne, for example, watching the *Victory* out of sight). His sense of Time, recurrently stressed from the opening mill-scene onwards, gives an added dimension to his historical scale, after-events adding interest to little things such as the volunteers' pikes (xxiii), or creating poignant effects, notably in Stanner's death (v), and the silencing of the trumpet-major, on bloody battlefields in Spain. The chronology at the end of the novel (which covers a period from 1804 to 1808) could be clearer; the invasion alarm was shifted from 1804 to 1805 for fictional gain. The sulphurous spring near which Anne, after strolling through Radipole (serial version), meets George III was probably at Nottington (where a 'spa-house' was built in 1830). The drilling-scene (cf. the preface) led to a charge of plagiarism, Hardy overlooking Gifford's acknowledgement of a source which was ultimately American. The vane (ii) has a proleptic value with respect to the heroine. Hardy's notes and sketches for the novel are included in R. H. Taylor's *The Personal Notebooks of Thomas Hardy*, London, 1978.

Truth like a bastard . . . birth (*PPP*.Lausanne: In Gibbon's Old Garden), from Milton, introductory address to *The Doctrine and Discipline of Divorce*; cf. *Life* 294/312n.

A Tryst at an Ancient Earthwork (*CM*6; written early in 1885). Notable for its impressions of Maiden Castle and its suggestion of dishonesty in a local archaeologist (cf. Millgate,244–5). Its 1893 publication in England made Hardy anxious lest it was thought that the character in question was 'drawn from a local man, still living, though . . . meant for nobody in particular'.

Tuileries . . . Louvre (*RN*.III.iv). These Parisian buildings date from the sixteenth century, the first a royal palace adjacent to the Louvre. It was destroyed by fire during the Commune uprising of 1871; the Louvre is the national museum and art gallery.

turk, Turk. The word is used to intensify expression, or as an oath like 'the devil', from traditional Christian antipathy to Ottomans.

Turk's-head brush, a round long-handled brush.

turmit-head (mispronunciation), idiot, fathead (head like a turnip).

turned . . . wickedness . . . soul alive (*TD*.xlv), cf. Ezek.xviii,27.

Turner, J. M. W. (*OMC*4.II.i; *PBE*.xiii; *FMC*.v; *Life* 185/192,216/225–6,329/354), English painter, 1775–1851.

Turner of the Wheel (*D*1.Fore Scene), the Immanent Will and the universe; cf. **primum mobile**.

The Turnip-Hoer (*HS*). *Terminus*, the Roman god of limits and boundaries; *Southernshire* (invented); *hoe*, hoer; *Dook*, a rural pronunciation of 'Duke'; *Ike*, a familiar form of 'Isaac'.

turnip-lantern, hollowed-out turnip with a burning candle inside; used on Hallow-e'en, initially to represent a bogy.

turnpike-road, a main road with toll-gates at intervals where charges were made for the upkeep of the road; the toll-gate keeper lived at the **turnpike-house**; **turnpike bonds** (*W*.iii) could be bought by investors who hoped that turnpike-roads would be profitable.

Turpin (*FMC*.1), a highwayman, partnering Tom King (whom he accidentally shot when on the point of arrest in 1737); he was caught and hanged at York. His legendary ride to York on Black Bess derives from Harrison Ainsworth's novel *Rookwood*, 1834.

Tuscan, the plainest of the classical orders of architecture (cf. **the Five Orders**); the early Renaissance Florentine school of painting.

Tussaud, shining, waxwork; cf. *MV*.At Madame Tussaud's . . . .

Tutcombe Bottom (*W*.iv), Stutcombe Bottom, a marshy hollow about $\frac{1}{2}$ m. SW of Melbury House.

twaddn' (dial.), it was not.

twanking, twanky (dial.), complaining, peevish, mournful.

'Twas on . . . winter's day (*PBE*.ii ep.), an Irish ballad, the 'old thing' originally of iii (cf. **Should he upbraid**).

twenties, small, cheap candles, twenty to the pound (weight).

twenty-five want a crown, five shillings less than £25.

the Twins (*TT*.iv), Gemini, a sign of the Zodiac containing Castor and Pollux, the stars after which it is named.

twit, twyte (dial.), tease, taunt, reproach.

twitched the robe . . . draped (*JO*.III.iv), Browning, 'Too Late' ix.

two-and-thirty winds (*TT*.xvi), blowing from all directions (the points of the compass).

The Two Houses (*LLE*). Cf. *W*.iv, par. 4, and *LLE*.A House with a History. *upfetched*, brought up; *inbe*, dwell (be in).

The Two Men (*WP*). The MS has the title 'The World's Verdict: A Morality-rime'. The poem is a bitter comment on the efforts of an idealist like Clym Yeobright, and the ending recalls the 'Vanity of vanities . . . all is vanity' of Eccl.i,2. The higher aim, 'to mend the mortal loft And sweeten sorrow' links this poem with the next.

Two on a Tower (1882). Hardy's interest in an astronomical subject for a novel probably began soon after he settled at Wimborne. On the first night there (25 June 1881) he saw Tebbutt's Comet (*Life* 149/154; alluded to in *TT*.xii). The tower in Charborough Park (with memories of Henry Moule's telescope on the tower of Fordington Church) suggested fictional possibilities, and he visited Greenwich Observatory late in 1881 (cf. *Life* 151/155–6 and *Letters* I,96). His undertaking in January 1882 to provide an eight-part serial for the American *Atlantic Monthly* was encouraged by prospective public interest in the second transit of Venus at the end of the year, after its occurrence in December 1874. The work was completed, rather hurriedly at times, by mid-September, appearing in book form, with little revision, at the end of October. Hardy's interest in astronomy had been stimulated in his youth by viewing with the Moules, and he made good use of R. A. Proctor's *Essays on Astronomy* (1872). He may not have kept to the calendar of celestial events, but his novel shows up-to-date knowledge, particularly in American research on variable stars. Perhaps his subject had been suggested by Maggie Tulliver's remark in *The Mill on the Floss* (II.i) on astronomers who live in high towers and hate women, because they might talk and distract attention from the stars. Hardy's ideal purpose, as outlined in the 1895 preface and adumbrated in his 1866 sonnet 'In vision I roamed', reaches imaginative achievement at scattered points, but is rarely integrated with the dramatic action. The recurrent element of chance leads to the tragic shock of the conclusion, but much of the later plot is ingeniously devoted to comic contrivance, which ends in an ill-calculated *coup d'audace* with the fooling of the Bishop by a 'Mephistophelian' whose chief concern is self-interest. The serious side of the story elevates the Positivist virtue of altruism.

The Two Rosalinds (*TL*). Altogether, this seems an improbable fiction; cf. *Life* 228/238–9 and **To an Impersonator of Rosalind** (1867). *Arden, the seasons' difference, running brooks*: *AYL*.II.i,1–18. *Orlando*: IV.i,V.iv.

the Two Tables (*JO*.V.vi), the Ten Commandments in two parts (as they were traditionally believed to be inscribed by God on the two 'tables of stone' which Moses brought down from Mt Sinai, Exod.xxxii,15–16). See **the Table of the Law**.

The Two Wives (*LLE*). Cf. 'Fellow-Townsmen' (*WT*5).

A Two-Years' Idyll (*LLE*), Hardy and Emma at Sturminster Newton, 1876–8; 'Our happiest time' (*Life* 118/122). *smart and tall*, Emma's, not Hardy's; *uplipped*, raised to the lips.

Tw–s on a . . . Gowrie (*MC*.xxiv), from 'The Lass of Gowrie', a Scottish ballad by Lady Nairne, 1776–1845.

Tycho Brahe . . . Kepler . . . Ferguson (*TT*.xxv), astronomers: Danish (1546–1601), German (1571–1630), Scottish (1710–76).

tything, tithing, small community, originally the old Anglo-Saxon district containing ten householders (a tenth part of the old 'hundred'), **tything-man**, parish constable (formerly the head of the tithing).

U

Ujiji, Unyamwesi (*TT*.x), in Tanganyika (now Tanzania), E. Africa.

Ulex Europaeus, the botanical name for gorse or furze.

Ultima Thule (*DR*.viii.4), extreme edge. The term was used by classical writers for the most northerly regions.

Ulunda (*TT*.xxxii), east of modern Angola.

Ulysses before Melanthus (*OMC*4.I.iv), on his return home after the Trojan war; cf. Homer's *Odyssey* xvii (Chapman's translation, ll.313–14).

un-words, coined by Hardy as negatives, e.g. **unbe**, not be, do not exist; **unblooms**, does not bloom; **unknows**, does not know.

unbelieving husband . . . (*TD*.xlvi), I Cor.vii,14.

The Unborn (*TL*). Written at least as early as 1903; 1905 may be the date of the revised version, in which the final stanza was changed (Purdy, 147). *all-immanent*, residing or active throughout the universe; cf. the 'Immanent Will' of *The Dynasts*, more expressive than the abstract 'First Cause'.

The uncertain glory of an April day (*FMC*.xviii), *TGV*.I.iii,85.

Uncle Toby (*L.*III.iv; PRF), a leading character in Laurence Sterne's extraordinary novel *Tristram Shandy*, 1760–7. After being wounded in the Netherlands, he finds his hobby in studying the science of attacking fortifications, using the bowling-green for the construction of miniature defences such as counterscarps and ravelins.

uncribbed, uncabined (*TD.*ii). See **cribbed and confined.**

Under High-Stoy Hill (*HS*). Hardy probably recalls returning from Melbury Osmond, his mother's village (*Ivelwards*, in the Yeovil direction), in company with his parents and sister Mary (d.1915). The poem may well have been written after his 1922 excursion (*Life* 417/450).

Under the Greenwood Tree (title of *UGT* and of its last chapter, which includes the 'Come hither' from Shakespeare's song), *AYL.*II.v,1 (*G.T.*).

Under the Greenwood Tree (1872) originated from the Christmas scenes which a publisher's reader praised in *The Poor Man and the Lady*, and was under way before *DR* was undertaken; it was completed in the summer of 1871, after Hardy's third visit to Cornwall. Unlike *DR*, it presents a simple, uncomplicated story, with unity of tone and no ulterior satirical motivation. Though light and humorous, it is steeped in provincial wisdom. George Eliot's praise of rural life in Dutch paintings (*Adam Bede* xvii), and her portrayal of the old village instrumental choir in 'Amos Barton' had made Hardy realize the fictional possibilities of the Stinsford choir he had heard so much of in his boyhood. Hints for the tranter's party came from the New Year's Eve dance in *Silas Marner*, which also suggested a rustic group as chorus or commentators on principal events, an emergent role in *UGT*, richly developed in *FMC* and *RN*. The story, set perhaps in the late 1840s (the 1896 preface reads 'fifty years ago' – not 'fifty or sixty' – in the 1903 edition; cf. **Queen's Scholar**, and the reference to 1839 and 1843 in I.iv), owes much to Hardy's happy prospects of marriage. The clouds which pass in this idyll (cf. *Life* 86/88) arise from playful exploitation of the jealousy he had felt from Emma's former attachment to a churchwarden farmer, and of the vanity he had noticed in her, 'a young lady in summer blue', who played the church harmonium at St Juliot. Unlike the heroine of another pastoral, *The Woodlanders*, Fancy Day makes the right choice, despite her education; there is an irony in the ending (no more threatening than a similar one at the end of

Jane Austen's *Emma*), but the swarming bees and the nightingale (linked by its 'come hither' to Shakespeare's 'no enemy But winter and rough weather') are good omens.

Under the Waterfall (*SC*), a rather Proustian recollection of an incident in the Valency valley. Hardy's sketch, showing Emma trying to retrieve the glass, is dated 19 Aug 1870 (cf. *Life* 71/74). The use of 'chalice' and 'wine' is sacramental, suggesting that love is divine (cf. the ending of *SC*.Self-Unconscious).

the Unfulfilled Intention, the idea, arising from a Darwinian view of nature, that the Creator had either forgotten to remove the defects of internecine nature or been wrong in allowing, 'beyond all apparent first intention', man to become percipient and sensitive to the cruelty of nature. Cf. *Life* 149/153; Clym Yeobright (*RN*.II.vi,III.i, opening); Hardy's comment on the First Cause (*RN*.VI.i); *W*.vii; *JO*.VI.iii, opening; and such poems as *HS*.'Freed the fret of thinking', An Inquiry, The Aërolite.

unguibus et rostro (*W*.xxx), with claws and beak, Ovid, *Ibis*,169.

Union. See **workhouse** and map B.

the Universal Sympathy of human nature . . . (*D*.pr.), from A. W. Schlegel (a German professor of literature, 1767–1845), *Lectures on Drama* v.

University boat-race (*HE*.xxii), on the Thames, an annual event between Oxford and Cambridge; witnessed by Hardy in March 1875 (*Life* 103/106).

Unkept Good Fridays (*WW*). Good Friday, though no fixed day of the year, is regarded as the anniversary of the Crucifixion (recalled in 'mockeries', 'bloody sweat', 'sepulchres', 'cross and cord'). Humanity has been served by many 'Christs of unwrit names', who have died horrible deaths for their faith or some good cause. The ending is obscure: *As little . . .* , as high as those proclaimed by true Christians. It asserts a Positivist belief, that there are others besides Jesus who, for their example and self-sacrifice in great causes, deserve to be honoured.

The Unplanted Primrose, an uncollected poem on unprized love, written some time from 1865 to 1867 when Hardy was lodging at Westbourne Park Villas, London.

un'ray (unarray), undress.

unreave, unravel, fray (a **marline-spike** is used to separate the strands of rope in splicing, *TM*.xix).

unrecked (archaic), uncared for, unappreciated, not considered.

unreformed Church (*L*.v.x), the Catholic, unchanged after the

Protestant Reformation.
unrind (colloquial), undress.
unruth, lack of pity.
unshent (archaic), unharmed, uninjured.
unvarnished tale (*TT*.xxxii), plain, unadorned, *Oth*.I.iii,90.
unweeting, unwitting (archaic), not knowing.
unwomb, give birth to.
up, stand up, rise, ascend.
An Upbraiding (*MV*), from Emma, in her grave, to Hardy.
upclomb, climbed up ('clomb', archaic).
up-country London ink-bottle chaps, far-off learned Londoners.
upland lawn (*W*.viii), from Gray's 'Elegy' (*G.T.*).
Uplandtowers, Lord (*GND*2), the fifth Earl of Shaftesbury, who married Barbara Webb in 1786.
Upon the Hill he turned (*TM*.xxi title), untraced.
uppingstock, stone or steps for mounting a horse.
upsides with, to be, to hold one's own with.
Uriah, wife of . . . queen (*TD*.liii), Bathsheba, II Sam.xi,14–27.
use, do, are accustomed to do; interest paid on a loan (the principal) as in **use-money, use and principal**.
Utilitarianism, a well-known treatise on (*HE*.xxxvi), *Utilitarianism* (1861) by John Stuart Mill, a radical reformer and philosopher whose influence in changing Hardy's philosophical and social outlook in the 1860s was deep and lasting.
Uz, sorely tried man in the land of (*CM*2.vii), Job i,1 and xxiii,1–10; quoted (*TD*.xix), Job vii,15–16.

V

Vagg Hollow (*LLE*). The dip is in the old Roman road which runs NNW from a point west of Yeovil to Ilchester, to the west of which, on the Yeo river at Load-Bridge, barges from Bristol were unloaded; see *Life* 314/337–8.
vair, squirrel-fur for lining.

Valenciennes (*WP*). For Corporal Tullidge and the battle (near the north French frontier), see *TM*.iv. If S. C., in memory of whom the poem was written, was Samuel Clark (*D*3.VII.v), Hardy's memory was unusually faulty; in a footnote to this scene, he states that Clark (buried locally, at West Stafford) died in 1857. See **Pensioner**.

Vallency, the Valency river, which flows down the valley below St Juliot to Boscastle harbour.

Valley of Humiliation (*W*.xxxvii; *TD*.xix), where Christian meets Apollyon (cf. *Life* 441–2/476): John Bunyan, *The Pilgrim's Progress*, Part I.

Valley of the Shadow of Death (*TM*.xxxv), Psalm xxiii.

vallie (dial.), value.

vamp, foot of stocking or sock; (vb.) walk, tramp.

The Vampirine Fair (*TL*). MS title 'The Fair Vampire'. See **Wingreen**.

van, wing; **vanned**, winged.

Van Alsloot (*RN*.III.iii; *TD*.xvi). See **Sallaert**.

Van Amburgh (*LLI*.8d), an American circus manager and exhibitionist (1801–65) who travelled with his 'show' in England and on the Continent.

Van Beers (*TD*.xxxix), Belgian painter, 1852–97. His London exhibition of November 1886 was compared unfavourably with the work of Wiertz by one reviewer.

Vandal (*HE*.xliv; *L*.II.i), barbarian, marauder, destroyer of beauty (from the characteristics and habits of an early German tribe).

Vandyck, Vandyke (*L*.I.iii,xv,III.ii,VI.v; *W*.v; *GND*6; *Life* 13/18), Van Dyck, Flemish painter, 1599–1641. **vandyked**, with deep indentations like those in the lace collars of portraits by Van Dyck.

vanity and vexation (*HE*.xxxi), Eccl.i.14.

Vanity Fair (PRF), the first thirty chapters (almost half of Thackeray's novel) 'well-nigh complete in artistic presentation'. **Vanity Fair** (*LLE*.A Gentleman's Epitaph . . .), see Bunyan, *The Pilgrim's Progress*, Part I.

the vanmost, those in the forefront (of the battle).

Var (*TD*.xvi,xxv), the old British name for the Frome river.

varden (dial.), farthing.

varmint, varmit (dial.), vermin, objectionable thing or person.

Vashti (*W*.xxxi). See **Esther**.

Vassal unto Love (*PBE*.xxx ep.), Tennyson, *In Memoriam* xlviii.

Vaterland (*TM*.x, Germ.), 'Fatherland', native country.
'vation, 'pon my, as I wish for salvation (after death).
Vega (*FMC*.ii), the brightest star in the northern sky.
veil . . . temple . . . rent (*W*.xxxvi; *JO*.VI.iii), Matt.xxvii,51.
Velasquez (*TD*.xxv; *D*3.II.iii), Spanish painter, 1599–1660.
vell (dial., 'vell or mark'), trace, sign; fell (vb.).
ventru (Fr.), pot-bellied.
Venus knot (of hair), coiled and knotted as in classical statues of Venus, goddess of love and beauty.
Venus, temple to (*WB*.II.iii), at Jordon Hill, near Weymouth, the site for *PPP*.The Well-Beloved in two editions.
Venus Urania (*JO*.III.vi), goddess of heavenly or spiritual love, her earthly or sensual counterpart being found in Shakespeare's V and A. See Shelley's *Adonais*, and cf. Shelleyan love, *TD*.xxxi.
vérité vraie (SF), not the truth of realism, but the higher truth discussed in PRF, the selection 'with an eye to being more truthful than truth (the just aim of Art)' (SF); cf. *Life* 228–9/239.
vermiculated, decorated in a style which suggests worm-tracks.
Veronese (*WB*.I.viii), of Verona in north Italy, scene of the *RJ* story.
vers de société, verses on topics provided by polite society.
verses turned into prose (*WP*.pr.). Cf. **She, to Him**.
Vespasian (*CM*6; *GND* conclusion). See **Embarcation**.
vesper, sing an evening song (cf. 'vespers' = evensong).
Veteris vestigia flammae (*SC*.Poems of 1912–13 ep.), traces of the old flame, Virgil, *Aeneid* iv,23.
Via (Lat.), Roman highway; see **Icen**.
Via Lactea (Lat.), the Milky Way (*TT*.xli); for Swithin's shock on seeing Viviette aged, cf. **Amabel**.
Via Sacra . . . Phryne (*JO*.v.iii): **Via Sacra**, street in ancient Rome; **Octavia**, sister of the emperor Augustus and wife of Mark Antony; **Livia**, wife of Augustus; **Aspasia**, a teacher of eloquence at Athens who became the mistress and wife of Pericles; **Praxiteles**, a Greek sculptor who made a statue of the beautiful courtesan **Phryne**, said to have been his model for Aphrodite (**Venus**) of Cnidus.
Vic., cap. eighty-five (*W*.xxxvii), the 85th statute passed during the parliamentary session in (as stated) the 20th and 21st years of Queen Victoria's reign (cap. = Lat. *caput* or chapter). The reference is to the 1857 Matrimonial Causes (or divorce) Act, which ended divorce by private bills in Parliament (*W*.xxxviii), a practice which only the rich could afford. Hardy makes Beaucock

quote the title of the act in the above detail to alert the reader, who knows that the American who had left the States on the failure of the Southern cause (in 1865, at the end of the Civil War), and has spent a number of years in south Europe, appeared on the scene much more than a year earlier (before the act was passed, according to Beaucock, who suggests it came into effect 'last year'). How much for his own ends Beaucock misrepresented ignorantly or deceptively was never ascertained, Hardy states. If the statute-title was not abracadabra to him, it was to Melbury. At the time ('then') the act was 'new' only as 'imparted by Beaucock to his listener'. The new court in London which it had set up in 1857 did not change the conditions for divorce, and it certainly did not make divorce possible for the poor, as Beaucock claimed. Had he known the law, he would have realized it offered nothing to raise Melbury's hopes, and he would have taken care not to risk consulting a London lawyer on the case. The period of the novel is probably the early 1870s, as Hardy seems to imply in a letter of 1926 (*Life* 432/466), where 'fifty' in 'fifty years ago' is a round or approximate number.

vicinage, adjacent area, neighbourhood. **vicinal way**, local road.

A Victorian Rehearsal, an uncollected poem, which hints at greater tragedy in the lives of the performers than in the tragedy being prepared for London audiences; based perhaps on insights Hardy gained from his limited stage experience (*Life* 54/55–6).

victorine, fur tippet, fastened in front below the neck, with the two ends hanging at length.

Video . . . deteriora sequor (*MC*.xxx), I see and approve better things, but follow worse, Ovid, *Metamorphoses* vii,20–21.

Vieux Manoir de François premier (*L*.VI.i), 'old manor-house of Francis I' (King of France, 1515–47), with carvings of satyrs (part-human, part-animal creatures) and griffins (creatures with the body of a lion and head and wings of an eagle).

view-halloo, the huntsman's cry when a fox breaks cover.

Vilbert, 'Physician' (*JO*). Hardy had probably heard of the quack 'Dr' Gilbert, an itinerant pill-doctor, and a centenarian when he was in the infirmary at Bridport workhouse.

vill, village, mansion (villa).

villanelle, a poem with a rural subject, usually in five tercets followed by a quatrain, with only two rhymes throughout.

villeins, serfs in Norman times (in England).

Villeneuve, French admiral. After being worsted in the fight with

Calder off Cape Finisterre, he had put back to Ferrol in the NW of Spain (*TM*.xxx; cf. *D*1.III.i). Later he withdrew to Cadiz, emerging from which, with his French and Spanish fleet, he was defeated by Nelson off Cape Trafalgar.

Vindilia Island (*WB*.I.i), the Roman name for Portland.

Viney (*UGT*.IV.iv,v.i), probably named after John Vine of Lower Bockhampton Dairy.

vinger (dial.), finger.

vinnied. See **blue-vinnied**.

viol, violin; play the violin.

violet . . . shade (PRF), Wordsworth, 'She dwelt among . . . ways' (*G.T.*).

A violet in the youth . . . (*PBE*.title-page), *Ham*.I.iii,7–10.

virginibus puerisque (*HE*.ix), for girls and boys, Horace, *Odes* III.i.

virtuous woman . . . rubies (*TD*.xxxix), Prov.xxxi,10–29.

vis-à-vis (Fr.), opposite, opposite number, partner (in a jig).

visit the sins . . . fathers . . . children (*TD*.xi), Exod.xx,5.

Visitation, ecclesiastical inspection. See **Diocesan Synod . . . .**

Visiting the bottom . . . world (*WB*.II.iii), Milton, 'Lycidas' (*G.T.*), an elegy on his friend Edward King, drowned while crossing the Irish Sea.

Vitae post-scenia celant (*HE*.title-page), men conceal the back-scenes of life, Lucretius, *De Rerum Nature* iv,1182.

Vittoria (*TM*.v), in Spain, where the French were defeated in 1813; cf. *D*3.II.i–iii.

vitty (dial.), fitting, just so, proper.

Vive l'Empereur! (*D*), Long live the Emperor!

vivâ voce (Lat.), by word of mouth, orally.

vlankers (dial.), outflying flakes of fire, sparks.

v'la! (*HE*.xxxiii), Coming! (Fr. *Voila!*).

vlee (dial.), flee.

vlock (dial.), flock.

The Voice (*SC*). Hardy travelled by rail to Launceston, Cornwall (cf. his first visit, *Life* 65/67; the 'air-blue gown' denotes his second visit, August 1870, *Life* 78/81).

The Voice of the Thorn (*TL*). Cf. 2 Oct 1887 (*Life* 202/211).

The Voice of Things (*MV*). Hardy thinks of three stages in his relations with his dead wife: August 1870, in Cornwall; a period soon after 1890, when love died between them (the visit is imaginary); and another more than twenty years later, when he revisited Cornwall after her actual death. *huzza'd*, cf. **The Wind's**

Prophecy. *Confession*, made in the hope of forgiveness for things done and left undone (cf. C. of E. Morning, or Evening, Prayer).

Voices from Things Growing in a Churchyard (*LLE*). Cf. *MV*.Transformations. *Fanny Hurd*, Fanny Hurden of Higher Bockhampton, who went to school with Hardy at Lower Bockhampton, and whom he remembered regretfully (cf. *Life* 413–14/446–7 and Millgate,41); she was delicate, and died in 1861. *Bowring*, of Kingston Maurward House (d.1837). *Thomas Voss* (*UGT*.I.iv). *Lady Gertrude*, of the Grey family who lived at Kingston Maurward. *Audeley Grey*: his mural memorial in Stinsford Church overlooks the pew where the Hardys sat.

voidless, unavoidable.

volk (dial.), folk.

Voltaire (*JO*.III.iv; *PPP*.The Respectable Burgher). See **Panglossians**.

volte-face (Fr.), complete change of attitude or view.

voot (dial.), foot.

Voorwärts! (Germ.), Forward (march)!

Voss, the only real name in *UGT* (*Life* 92/95); see **Voices** above.

vox et praeterea nihil (Lat.), a voice and nothing more.

V. R. 1819–1901 (*PPP*; V. R. = Victoria Regina), written shortly after the death of Queen Victoria, who had reigned from 1837. No doubt a tribute to the dead Queen seemed indispensable in a volume of poetry which appeared in 1901. 'A Reverie' is Hardy's way of excusing a rather conventional grand attribution to the Absolute, though he finds something nearer the truth when he states that the Queen's real achievement may lie hidden at present, 'as in the All-One's thought lay she'. (Thought does not become an Absolute or First Cause which Hardy believed to work mechanically, by rote.)

Vye, Captain (*RN*). Originally named Drew, he probably owes something to the old naval lieutenant (named Drane) who lived near the Hardys (*Life* 3/7).

Vye, Eustacia. For the origin of 'Eustacia', see *Life* 117/120 or the 1912 preface to *RN*.

wadden, wadn' (dial.), was not.

wafer, small gelatinous disk used for sealing letters.

Wait . . . Till my change come (*HS.*Waiting Both), Job xiv,14, a text remembered from a sermon by the Revd Henry Moule, vicar of Fordington, about 1860 (*Life* 390–1/423).

The Waiting Supper (*CM*2). Written in the autumn of 1887, it takes its theme from Browning's 'The Statue and the Bust' (which appeared in *Men and Women*, 1855); cf. the ending and *PPP.*Long Plighted. The chronological point of introducing a quotation from Browning's poem, and the late presentation of some of the place-names (e.g. 'Casterbridge' for the market-town), suggest that Hardy did not give his story the care it deserves.

waits, musicians and carol-singers at Christmas.

Wakely, Samuel (*MC.*xxxiii), composer of hymn-tunes, ?1805–81.

The Walk (*SC*). It began across the road from Max Gate, and continued to the top of Conygar Hill (map A).

walk wi' God (*TT.*xvi), from William Cowper's hymn 'Oh! for a closer walk with God'.

walked round love . . . (*RN.*I.vii; cf. *LLI.*1), Psalm xlviii,12–13.

Walkingame (*FMC.*viii). Cf. **He Revisits His First School**.

walm (dial.), rise, well up.

Walpolean scandal (*HE.*xxxviii), in the voluminous letters of Horace Walpole, 1717–97. Hardy's knowledge of them (cf. *HE.*Sequel and *Life* 361/389,376/406) was not limited to the six volumes to Sir Horace Mann he read in London (*Life* 59/61). See *Life* 9/13,163–4/170 on Lady Susan, and **The Doctor's Legend**.

Walton, Izaak (*GND*6), torture and love simultaneously, a recurrent thought (for example, in baiting with a live fish without 'hurting him') in *The Compleat Angler*, 1653–1676.

wamble (dial.), walk unsteadily, wobble, totter.

Wandering Jew (*WB.*II.ii). See **Ahasuerus**.

A wandering voice (*PBE.*xv ep.), Wordsworth, 'To the Cuckoo' (*G.T.*).

wanzing (dial.), wasting away, decaying.

War Poems (*PPP.*). This series, occasioned by the Boer War in

South Africa (1899–1902), proceeds chronologically, with strong anti-militarist and anti-Church bias. 'I am happy to say that not a single one is Jingo or Imperial', Hardy wrote. He cycled to Southampton to see troops embark, and watched them in rain marching late at night to the Dorchester railway-station (The Going of the Battery). Notes on some of the poems are given under their titles.

Warborne (*TT*; *GND*2), Wimborne Minster, north of Poole.

Ward (*JO*.II.iv), W. G. Ward, 1812–82, a Balliol theologian and Tractarian who became a Roman Catholic.

Wardour Castle (*JO*.III.ii), SW of the railway-station at Tisbury, which is 12 m. west of Salisbury.

Warm'ell (Warmwell) Cross (*WT*7.vii; *LLE*.At Lulworth Cove . . .), crossroads where the road from Warmwell meets the old turnpike road from Dorchester to Wareham (map D).

The War-Wife of Catknoll (*WW*): at Chetnole (map C) during or at the end of the 1914–18 war.

wash, liquid food, swill.

A Wasted Illness (*PPP*). Hardy probably wrote this in the kind of mood which prompted *PPP*.In Tenebris, with recollections of his illness at Upper Tooting (*Life* 145–6/149–50). '(Overheard)' was added to the title for the 1920 edition.

water (request for, *JO*.VI.xi), part of the Crucifixion theme (John xix,28).

watering-place, seaside resort; and **George III's summer residence** (*D*.pr.), Weymouth, Hardy's **Budmouth**.

Waterloo (near Brussels), where the French under Napoleon were finally defeated (by Wellington, 1815) at the end of the long war with England: *OMC*4.I.v; *RN*.III.i; *L*.I.viii; *CM*4; *D*3.VI.viii,VII.i–viii. Cf. *Life* 284/301–2.

Waterston(e) Ridge (*LLI*.8d; *TL*.The Revisitation), the ridge followed by the Ridge Way on either side of Slyres Lane (map A).

W.D., War Department.

'We are getting to the end' (*WW*). The image of man in the cage of Necessity (cf. *Life* 171/178) comes from Carlyle's 'Goethe's Helena', an essay Hardy first read when he was a young man.

We are made a spectacle . . . (*JO*.VI.ii,iii), I Cor.iv,9.

We are such stuff as dreams . . . (SF; *LLE*.Apology), *Tem*.IV.i, 156–8.

We Field-Women (*WW*). One of Tess's companions, after returning to the Valley of the Great Dairies (the Frome valley), recalls the winter at Flintcomb-Ash (*TD*.xliii) and Tess's misfortune in love at Talbothays.

We frolic . . . May (*PBE*.xiv ep.), Gray, 'On the Spring' (*G.T.*).

we have wronged no man (*JO*.v.vi), II Cor.vii,2.

'We sat at the window' (*MV*). In July 1875, almost a year after their marriage, the Hardys were at Bournemouth (*Life* 107/110), before settling at Swanage. The rain is ominous; see **St Swithin**.

the weariness, the fever . . . fret (*PBE*.ii). See **fever and fret**.

weasand, weazand (dial.), throat, gullet, windpipe.

Weatherbury (*UGT; FMC; MC; WP*.In a Eweleaze . . . ; *WW*.In Weatherbury Stocks), Puddletown, 5 m. NE of Dorchester; it takes its name from the hill fortress Weatherbury or Weatherby Castle, 3 m. ENE. Bathsheba's house is drawn to some extent from Waterston House (map A) but imagined near the village; Boldwood's farm is based on Druce Farm, near **Weatherbury Bottom**. The great barn owes many of its features to the tithe-barn at Cerne Abbas. The stocks stood in the square near St Mary's Church.

web, the network of cause and effect in time and space (cf. *W*.iii; *Life* 177/183 and *D*1.Fore Scene). Hardy's more scientific philosophy on this issue never changed; the question was how much freedom circumstances left the individual. Undoubtedly Shelley and Carlyle influenced him strongly; cf. *Adonais* liv, 'web of being', and **Goethe**. In 1876 he noted from J. A. Symonds' *Studies of the Greek Poets* that 'each act, as it has had immeasurable antecedents, will be fruitful of immeasurable consequents; for the web of the world is ever weaving'.

weedery, weeds (archaic), mourning dress.

ween (archaic), think, believe, imagine, surmise.

weet (archaic), know; **weetless**, ignorant, unaware (of the future).

weigh, heave up anchor, sail.

weigh . . . balances . . . found wanting (lacking: *FMC*.lv), Dan.v,27.

weird, determined by destiny, or helping to determine destiny (cf. Hardy's footnote to *RN*.VI.iii); **weirdsome**, fateful, casting a spell; **weird-wed**, wedded by fate. Cf. the weird sisters, the three witches in *Macbeth*.

Welcome, proud lady (*PBE*.xl ep.), from 'Proud Maisie is in the wood' (*G.T*), taken from Scott, *The Heart of Midlothian* xl.

welkin (archaic), the region of the air in which clouds float.

Welland (*TT*). Hardy's map is misleading: the tower in Charborough Park suggested the story, but his observatory is placed on the old fortress hill Weatherby Castle (cf. **Weatherbury**). To reach it Lady Constantine crossed the old Melchester road (the Roman road) and walked across a field. The village must be largely imaginary; the demolition of cottages to extend the park refers, however, to what happened at Charborough.

The Well-Beloved. First written for serial issue considerably before *JO* was begun, and published as *The Portrait of the Well-Beloved* from October to December 1892, it was revised in 1896 for publication in book form (Mar 1897). Although the initial story was conceived years earlier, when he was 'interested in the Platonic Idea' (*Letters* II,156), the final form combines concepts which occurred to Hardy in March 1884 and February 1889, of *Time against Two*, with *RJ* antagonisms, and of the story of 'a face which goes through three generations or more' (*Life* 164/171,217/226). The Idea (first projected in *W*) which makes the lover find the Well-Beloved in one woman after another is linked with the pursuit of artistic beauty; Pierston is a development (as the name suggests) of Fitzpiers. The serial anticipates the bitterness of *JO*: Pierston marries Marcia, but the subjective illusion of the Well-Beloved is dissipated by the marriage-tie; many years later, assuming Marcia is dead, he marries Avice of the third generation, to release her in Phillotson fashion when he discovers that she and Leverre are in love. The protest against the 'barbarism' of a legal Church ceremony which seeks to perpetuate the suffering of incompatible couples discloses Hardy's private feelings climactically in Pierston's attempt at suicide. The ending is improbable, and the whole is an unsatisfactory grouping of diverse tones, from the light and engagingly fantastic to the morbid and depressing. The novel is more considered, homogeneous, and felicitous, uniting realism and the whimsical. The former includes elegiac testimony to Hardy's regard for his cousin Tryphena Gale, née Sparks (II.iii), and observations of London society (cf. 'a leading actress of the town', II.ii, and Ellen Terry, *Life* 232/244), Hardy making use of notes which he thought it prudent to keep for novel-requirements (cf. *Life* 104/107,291/309–10,305/328). Time is the burden of the novel, taking its dominant image from the tink-tink of chisels in the local quarries, as in *WP*.In a Eweleaze (1890). The Well-Beloved Idea is treated recurrently and variously with ridicule. Artistic genius is a curse (as Shelley sees it in 'Alastor') which drives Pierston continually in search of the 'prototype of his conception'. That he is finally freed does not relate to the end of Hardy's novel-writing; he could pursue his ideals with fewer restraints in poetry. *The Well-Beloved* is an imaginative exercise in deromanticising a kind of subjectivism which Hardy had often fancifully indulged; his final debunking of Shelleyan–Platonic idealism could well have been influenced by the conclusion of Goethe's *Faust*, certainly by Benthamism, possibly by a comment in Mrs Humphry Ward's *Robert Elsmere* (1888): 'It seems to me', said Langham, musing, 'that in my youth people talked Ruskin; now they talk about drains.' For the reception of the novel, cf. *Life* 285–6/303–4 and III.vii, on the unfleshliness of the Idea (no woman had ever been wronged by Pierston); for its places, see map H.

The Well-Beloved (*PPP*). For the subject, see the above note; for the references, see separate notes. *the Pagan temple* (to Venus): Hardy knew from Hutchins that a Roman camp and temple had stood on Woodbury Hill near Bere Regis. See **Venus, temple to**.

Wellbridge (*TD*), Wool, formerly Woolbridge, 10 m. from Dorchester on the Wareham road. The railway runs on the south side of the river; on the other side, beyond the Elizabethan bridge, stands the manor-house which belonged to the Turbervilles (copies of the fading portraits of the two Turberville ladies may be seen in the Dorset County Museum). East of the village are the remains of Bindon Abbey, where the open stone coffin may be seen by the north wall of the chancel. Just across the stream on the northern side of the main Abbey site are buildings which indicate where the old flour-mill stood.

Wellesley, General (*CM*4), Arthur Wellesley, made Field-Marshal the Duke of Wellington in 1814. He was on service in India from 1797 to 1805.

weltbürgerliche (Germ.), cosmopolitan and rootless.

Weltlust (Germ.), worldly pleasure and pride.

Went up the hill . . . bride (*FMC*.lvii), from 'Patty Morgan the Milkmaid's Story' in R. H. Barham, *The Ingoldsby Legends*.

Wertherism of the uncultivated (*L*.III.iv), a phrase taken with reference to Methodism (and its emotional appeal) from Karl

Hillebrand's 'Familiar Conversations on Modern England' in *The Nineteenth Century*, June 1880. The allusion is to Goethe's early novel on the sorrows of Werther, 1774.

Wesleyan (*WT7*). The Methodist movement, begun by Charles and John Wesley as a C. of E. revival in the eighteenth century, led to the formation of the nonconformist Wesleyan Methodist Church.

Wessex, a separate kingdom, south of the Thames and stretching from east Cornwall to Sussex, when England was divided into seven kingdoms (the Heptarchy) in Anglo-Saxon times. Not until three of his novels had been published, and he was writing *FMC*, did Hardy see the advantage of adopting the name for the expanding regionalism of his novels. Place-names in the earlier novels were subsequently altered in conformity with his fictional background scheme. 'Wessex' had the additional advantage of suggesting fiction which transcends realistic presentation. Cf. *FMC*.pr; *Life* 122–3/126,351/378–9; *TD*.1892 pr.; Gen.Pr.

Wessex (the dog). See **A Popular Personage at Home**.

Wessex Heights (*SC*). The poem refers to the period of Hardy's deep depression in 1896 (the MS gives 'December'), particularly as a result of the harsh criticism he incurred following the publication of *JO*. *after death may be*, a less certain note than in earlier poems such as *PPP*.His Immortality; *Her who . . . is kind*, Charity (I Cor.xiii,4); *mind-chains*, thoughts from which he cannot free himself elsewhere. The *great grey Plain* is Salisbury Plain; the *tall-spired town* is Salisbury. In these places (with Tess at Stonehenge, Jude in 'Melchester'), Hardy cannot avoid thinking of scenes in the two novels which had brought him into disfavour. He then thinks of four people. On 6 Dec 1914 Florence Hardy wrote that they were all women; three of them were living when the poem was written in 1896; 'now only one is living'. There are undoubted recollections of Tryphena Sparks (d.1890) in *JO*, though they are not of major importance; she lived at Puddletown and may be the ghost of Yell'ham Bottom. The ghost in the Frome valley is probably that of Hardy's mother, who may have remonstrated with him on some aspects of *JO* at one of their meetings during the winter of its publication, when the meadows between Lower Bockhampton and Max Gate were white with mist; the one in the railway train is almost certainly Emma Hardy. The 'one rare fair woman' is Mrs Henniker; whatever Hardy thought at this juncture, their friendship lasted until her death in 1923. For *Ingpen* or Inkpen in Berkshire, and *Wylls-Neck* or Wills Neck in the Quantock Hills, see Hardy's map of Wessex. **Bulbarrow** and **Pilsdon Crest** (or Pen) are noted separately.

Wessex Poems (1898). Hardy's first volume of published verse is an extraordinary miscellany, from poems of his earliest apprenticeship to his most recent, from the grim to broad humour, with clear Darwinian insights and bias, and a large admixture of tales, some of which must have been intended for prose. Some are Gothic; a few occasioned by the death of his cousin Tryphena are of an inventive kind. Several ballads testify to Hardy's continued interest in the vast evolving plan of *The Dynasts*. The verse is variable, from the lyrical and idiomatic to the rough and laboured, with awkward inversions and neologistic forms. Chance and irony, Time, change, and disillusionment characterize the subjects, in which Wessex settings are repeatedly a strong component. Hardy's illustrations enhance the interest of this volume.

Wessex Tales (1888) contained only *WT*1,4,5,6,7. For the sake of homogeneity *WT*2 and 3 were added in 1912 (after being included in *LLI*.1894), being interchanged with 'An Imaginative Woman', which had been added in 1896.

west, move (or appear to move) west.

Westcombe (*OMC*4.I.vii), an imaginary town introduced merely to fictionalize Hardy's resentment of class-discrimination.

the Western Duchy (*CM*.11.iv), the Duchy of Cornwall.

Westminster Abbey, going in for (*HE*.vii), aiming at fame as a poet, and a memorial in Poets' Corner, Westminster Abbey.

The West-of-Wessex Girl (*LLE*), Emma Gifford/Hardy; see *Life* 66/67–8. *squired*, escorted; *marbled ways*, streets of hewn stone in Plymouth (cf. **The Marble-Streeted Town**); *Andrew's*, see **Places**.

A Wet August (*LLE*). By contrast the weather recalls August 1870 with Emma Gifford in Cornwall fifty years earlier. The light of love and hope contrasts with *the waste world*, as in Shelley, *Prometheus Unbound* II.i,126.

A Wet Night (*TL*). The route is one frequently followed by Hardy in his youth, from Dorchester via Fordington Moor (i.e. by the Frome) to Stinsford, then across the eweleaze to Cuckoo Lane, and on to Higher Bockhampton.

wet old garden (*DR*.xii.6), cf. Swinburne 'Ilicet' in *Poems and Ballads*, 1866, and **the garden**.

Weydon-Priors (*MC*; *GND*5; *HS*.A Last Journey), Weyhill, west of Andover, Hampshire, once famous for its centuries-old fair, which coincided with farm-sales, particularly of sheep.

Weymouth. Hardy lived there while working for the architect Crickmay from the summer of 1869 to February 1870. During this period he began *DR* and wrote a number of poems. It is mentioned in *OMC*2 and *MV*.Great Things; it is 'the town by the sea' in *MV*.Molly gone; see **Budmouth**. Poems where the Weymouth setting is not acknowledged: *SC*.At a Watering-Place, The Newcomer's Wife (cf. *WB*.I.vii); *MV*.At a Seaside Town in 1869; *HS*.On the Esplanade (cf. *DR*.iii.2).

The Whaler's Wife (*WW*). Possibly at Bridport, where there is an inn called 'The Five Bells', with a sign showing church-ringers. *Ring*, see **Inscriptions . . . Bells**. *anyway*, in any case (colloquial).

what a gift life . . . (*FMC*.xlix), Browning, 'The Statue and the Bust'.

What great ones do . . . prattle of (*HE*.vii), *TN*.I.ii,33.

What sport . . . garden . . . bias (*TT*.xxvii: *rubs*, unevennesses, obstacles; *bias*, a leaden weight on one side of the bowl which makes its course curve as it loses pace), *R2*.III.iv,1–5.

What the Shepherd Saw (*CM*7; written for Christmas 1881). The setting was transferred from an area SW of Salisbury (near Cranborne Chase) to a point west of Marlborough (where the trilithon may be seen; cf. **Shakeforest Towers**). Ogbourne is the name of two villages north of Marlborough.

Whatman's paper (*L*.I.xi), a brand of drawing-paper.

the Wheel (*D*2.VI.v). Cf. **Turner of the Wheel** and **primum mobile**.

When I look . . . tombs . . . (*JO*.II.i), from *The Spectator*, no. 26, 30 Mar 1711, by Joseph Addison, on Westminster Abbey; *motion*, emotion.

When I set out for Lyonnesse (*SC*). See *Life* 65–6/67 and **Lyonnesse**.

When I would pray . . . Isabel (OMC4.I.i ep.), *MM*.II.iv,1–4.

When Oats Were Reaped (*HS*). Hardy, when fields below Max Gate are being harvested, walks across the Frome valley towards Stinsford; cf. *MV*.The Wound, which suggests that Emma wounded his feelings along this road.

When the fair apples . . . (*W*.xxv), from the third minstrel's song in *Aella* by Thomas Chatterton, 1752–70; cf. the **marvellous boy**.

where angels fear to tread (*W*.xxxvii), Fools rush in . . . , Pope, *Essay on Criticism*, 625.

Where Duncliffe . . . Paladore (*JO*.IV.iv), quotations (the first should be 'While Duncliffe . . .') from William Barnes, 'Shaftesbury Feäir'; *cloty*, water-lilied. See **Shaston**.

Where heaves the turf . . . heap (*PBE*.iv ep.), Gray's 'Elegy' (*G.T.*).

Where love is great . . . grows there (*PBE*.xxvii), *Ham*.III.ii,166–7.

Where once . . . debate . . . (*LLE*.Apology), Tennyson, *In Memoriam* lxxxvii.

Where Stour . . . fed (*JO*.IV.iv). See **From whose foundation**.

Where the Picnic Was (*SC*). The poets Henry Newbolt and W. B. Yeats, who travelled from London to present Hardy the gold medal of the Royal Society of Literature on his 72nd birthday (2 June 1912; see *Life* 358/385), were special guests. The 'strange straight line' suggests a point high up towards Abbotsbury, where Chesil Beach can be seen as a straight line running along the shore, with water on both sides of it, towards Portland.

Where They Lived (*MV*). The bank, the summer-house, and 'March' in the 1913 MS date (the month of Hardy's return, *Life* 361/389), show that he was thinking of the rectory at St Juliot.

'Where three roads joined' (*LLE*). The MS gives 'Near Tresparret Posts, Cornwall'; see map E. Hardy, on his return to Cornwall, contrasts happiness with Emma before marriage with what succeeded. The words of the title spell doom, being borrowed from J. A. Symonds, who, in *Studies of the Greek Poets*, 2nd series, uses them to indicate the spot where Oedipus sets his tragic destiny in motion by unknowingly killing his father.

Wherefore . . . light . . . misery . . . (*RN*.V.i title), Job iii,20.

wherrit (dial.), worry.

Which fashion hails . . . scenes (*HE*.xxix), Byron, 'The Waltz'.

whicker (dial.), snigger, giggle.

while, until; pass. **the while**, during which time.

While Drawing in a Churchyard (*MV*). Cf. *WP*.Friends Beyond and *MV*.Jubilate; the yew suggests Stinsford (Mellstock) churchyard. *diurnal round*, an echo of Wordsworth's 'A slumber did my spirit seal' (*G.T.*); *no God . . . rise*, see **Trumpet**.

whilom (archaic), formerly.

whindling (dial.), dwindling, declining, unimportant.

whirligig of time (*TT*.xli. Cf. 'Time . . . revenges' later in *TT*.xli, and *WB*.III.vii), *TN*.V.i,363.

white feather, cowardice.

White Horse Hill (*TM*.viii). The name seems anachronistic, as the equestrian figure of George III, midway between Bincombe and Poxwell, was cut out later (*TM*.xxxvii–xxxviii), in 1808.

White Tuesday, Whit Tuesday (cf. **White Monday**, *FMC*.viii).

white witch, white wizard, a person who claimed magical curative powers, and to whom the superstitions turned when they were physically afflicted. See **conjurors**.

whited sepulchre (*JO*.IV.iii), hypocrite, Matt.xxiii,27.

white-pot (*TM*.xvi), a flavoured mixture, chiefly of milk and egg, baked on thinly sliced bread.

White's club-house (*RN*.III.vii). Hardy had referred to the name of Sir Thomas Rumbold, a Governor of Madras in the eighteenth century. He withdrew the name in response to protests against the story that Sir Thomas had been a waiter at a fashionable club, though it was to be found in several books (*Letters* I,64).

Whitesheet (*MV*.Molly Gone), the hill west of Maiden Newton. **Whit'sheet** (*TL*.The Homecoming), west of Toller Down. See map C.

The Whitewashed Wall (*LLE*). The first version was written for John Galsworthy's second number of *Reveille* (Nov 1918), a Government quarterly for disabled sailors and soldiers. Cf. Mrs Martin (*TT*.xxxviii).

Whiting, John (*D*1.II.v), his actual name (Hardy's notebook).

Whitman, Walt (American poet, 1819–92; cf. *Life* 59/61): quotation from 'So long!' at the end of *Songs of Parting* (*DR*.viii.3); from 'Crossing Brooklyn Ferry' (*TD*.xxv).

Whittle, Abel (*MC*). The similarity of his name to the old English word 'wittol' (a half-wit or fool) suggests that his loyalty to his master on the heath is intended to recall that of the Fool in *King Lear*.

Who dragged Whom . . . What? (*W*.iv), Achilles dragging the slain Hector round the walls of Troy.

who hath gathered the wind . . . garment (*W*.xvi), Prov.xxx,4.

Who lay great bases . . . ruining (*TT*.x), cf. Son.125.

The Whole Duty of Man (*TM*.vi; *MC*.x), a popular devotional work, first published in 1658.

whop and slap at, proceed energetically with.

'Who's in the next room?' (*MV*). Hardy stated that the scene was at Max Gate. *Polar Wheel*, the Arctic zone, revolving around the North Pole; *him*, Death.

whose gestures beamed with mind (*MC*.xlv). See **Female forms**.

Whoso prefers either Matrimony . . . Pharisee (*JO*.IV ep.), Milton, preface to *The Doctrine and Discipline of Divorce*.

'Why do I?' (*HS*). Hardy addresses himself. *dinning gear*, machinery making din; cf. 'mechanic repetitions'.

Why should we faint . . . die? (*JO*.II.i), John Keble, 'Twenty-fourth Sunday after Trinity' in *The Christian Year*, 1827.

wicked man . . . turned away . . . soul alive (*TD*.xlv), Ezek.xviii,27.

wideawake, soft, wide-brimmed felt hat. **wide-awake**, clever.

Wide-O, **Wide-oh** (*TD*.xxi; *MC*.xxvi). Although people were superstitious and ready to believe him, they pretended not to, declaring (behind his back) that his advice was 'wide o (of)' the mark.

The Widow Betrothed (*PPP*). The MS opening 'By Mellstock Lodge and Avenue' indicates that the house is Stinsford House; see Map A. Hardy told Edmund Gosse that he thought of the poem about 1867, and that it was written after studying Wordsworth's preface to *Lyrical Ballads* (on the language of poetry), 'as you can see for yourself'.

Wiertz Museum (*TD*.xxxix). This developed from the studio built in Brussels for the Belgian artist Antoine Wiertz, 1806–65. Hardy stayed in Brussels in 1876.

wight (archaic), man, person.

wile-weaving Daughter of high Zeus (*WB*.I.ii,II.vi). The phrase comes from an ode to Aphrodite by Sappho, as in the translation which appears in J. A. Symonds, *Studies of the Greek Poets*, 1893 (appendix).

William and Mary, the time of (*W*.xvi), during the reign of William III (of the Orange dynasty in Holland) and his cousin Mary, daughter of James II of England, whom he was invited to replace in 1688. William and Mary (who died in 1694) were proclaimed King and Queen of England in 1689; cf. **William's Mary** (*SC*.The Coronation).

William the Conqueror (*RN*.I.vii), of Normandy; after defeating the English king Harold at Hastings in 1066, he occupied England.

wimble, twist bands for hay-trussing; instrument for this.

Wimborne Minster (MCR). See **The Levelled Churchyard**, **Copying Architecture in an Old Minster**, **Warborne**.

win, reach, arrive at.

wind and rain, symbols of life's trials (from the clown's song at the end of *Twelfth Night*. For notable examples, cf. *RN*.III.vi,V.vii–ix (combined with darkness); *JO*.VI.viii–ix; *MV*.During Wind and Rain; LLE.An Autumn Rain-Scene.

wind, tameless . . . (*DR*.x.3), Shelley, 'Ode to the West Wind'

(*G.T.*).

winder (rustic pronunciation), window.

windling (dial.), delicate, wasting away; cf. **whindling**.

windows of [the] soul (*W.*xviii), the senses, chiefly sight; cf. William Blake, *The Everlasting Gospel*.

windrow, row into which mown grass was raked for drying.

The Wind's Prophecy (*MV*), a mixture, it seems, of fact and fancy for the sake of antithetical design. Hardy's first journey to Cornwall is recalled. As a contrast to the fair Emma Gifford, he may have had in mind Jane Nicholls or Martha Sparks (with whom he had been friendly in London) or her younger sister Tryphena, who was at Stockwell (teacher-training) College in March 1870 (cf. the last three but two paragraphs of *DR.*x.4, however). *waves . . . Huzza . . . multitude*, an image used in *HE.*xlv; cf. *MV.*The Voice of Things. *each pharos-shine*, each of the revolving beams from the lighthouse on Lundy Island, with flashes, perhaps, from Hartland Point and Trevose Head.

wind-up, as a, to conclude, or round off, things.

Wingreen (*TD.*viii; *TL.*The Vampirine Fair), a high hill SE of Shaftesbury and NE of Melbury Down; Manor Court could be Rushmore (cf. *Life* 269/286).

Winstanley (*TT.*xv), the architect who perished in his Eddystone lighthouse when it was destroyed by a gale in 1703.

winter. For its symbolical use, see **frost**.

Winter, Jack (*LLI.*8g). The events which led to his hanging are basically similar to those in *JO.*v.iv with reference to the traditional gibbeting of an ancestor of Jude and Sue. The details of the hanging were related by Hardy's father of a youth who was arrested for reasons given in *WT*4. See **The Withered Arm**.

Winter Night in Woodland (*HS*). The woodland is near Hardy's birthplace, but, as the presence of members of the Mellstock 'quire' (*UGT*) indicates, the activities described belong to a period before his boyhood; he probably heard accounts of them from his father. During his grandfather's occupation of the Hardy home, tubs of smuggled spirits in transit had been hidden there.

winter wind and neglect (*DR.*x.1), cf. *AYL.*II.vii,174–90.

Winter Words (posthumously published, 1928), another miscellany of poems, with few outstanding but no pronounced decline, on subjects from a gentleman's suit and gruesome marital reality to sensational love-stories and defiant suggestions that Jesus Christ was mad, and God (the Immanent Will) without moral sense.

Hardy protests that his thought is misunderstood by reviewers who are no better than 'licensed tasters'. Seeing another European conflict looming, instead of condemning an abstract First Cause in his old style, he sensibly, almost at the outset and emphatically at the end, denounces the 'hideous self-treason' of nations which impels history with 'demonic force'. His symbolical title indicates the poetry of old age (cf. *MV*.The Five Students) and, even more, a sense of developing disaster.

Winton, **Wintoncester** (*GND*4; *TD*.lix; *JO*.IV.iv; *SC*.The Abbey Mason), Winchester, Hampshire. The cathedral, St Thomas's Church, the gaol, the college (school), and training-college for teachers are referred to; the 'ancient hospice' for pilgrims and wayfarers is the Hospital of St Cross, to the south.

Winwood, Oswald (*OMC*2). His success in the India Civil Service examination was based on that of Hardy's friend Hooper Tolbort (*Life* 32/37).

wis (archaic), know, perceive, imagine or guess; see **I wis**.

wise in her generation (*MC*.xxxii), cf. Luke xvi,8.

wisht (archaic), sad, mournful.

wist (archaic), knew, known; **wistlessness**, unawareness, ignorance.

wit (archaic), know; **witlessly**, unknowingly; **witlessness** = **wistlessness**.

witches . . . pricked . . . ducked (*TD*.l). To counteract the malign spells of 'witches', waxen images of them were pricked (cf. *RN*.v.vii); or they were punished by being ducked in water. See **black witch** *and* **white witch**.

Witenagemote, 'assembly of wise men', i.e. of the Wessex or more local supreme council in Anglo-Saxon times.

With mirth . . . wrinkles come (*CM*2.viii), *MV*.I.i,80.

With the rose . . . go (*UGT*.I.i), from an old folk-song.

The Withered Arm (*WT*4). Written in 1887, it combines local superstition (probably from Hardy's mother; cf. *WT*.pr.) with the story his father told of a youth hanged for being 'present by chance' when a rick was fired during the period of agricultural unrest in the 1820s. Originally Farmer Lodge lived at Stickleford, and the dairy-farm was in the Swenn valley.

withering fast (*FMC*.xliv), Keats, 'La Belle Dame sans Merci' (*G.T.*).

without (archaic), outside; cf. **withoutdoors**, **withoutside**.

Without, Not Within Her (*LLE*). In their earlier years Hardy valued Emma's zest for life (not her intellect, ll.7–8); her liveliness and gaiety (cf. *LLE.*'If you had known') dispelled his fits of gloom. The corn-chaff simile implies 'purged' (Matt.iii,12).

withwind, withywind, bindweed.

withy, willow.

withy-bed, plantation of willows (in a damp, low-lying situation).

witted (archaic), knew.

woak (dial.), oak.

wold (dial.), old.

the Wold Hundredth (*LLI.*7), the old tune which was retained (after being sung to the Sternhold and Hopkins version) for the Tate and Brady metrical form of Psalm c; cf. **Tate-and-Brady** and *Life* 10/16.

Wolfe (*PPP.*The Sick Battle-God). Thomas Wolfe died in the hour of victory (on the Heights of Abraham, 1759) which was critical in wresting Canada from the French.

woll, wool (dial.), will.

A woman . . . compass a man (*DR.*ix.2), Jer.xxxi,22.

. . . woman deliberates (*RN.*I.v). Cf. Joseph Addison's *Cato* IV.i,31, 'The woman that deliberates is lost.'

The Woman I Met (*LLE*). Cf. *Life* 235/247. *the Lock*, a London hospital for those suffering from venereal disease; *our kind . . . feather*, people of all kinds; *Juans*, rakes, libertines.

woman taken (in adultery: *TD.*liii), John viii,1–11.

A Woman's Trust (*LLE*), on Emma's faith in Hardy when he began novel-writing. The poem refers to her childlike qualities and her trust in his fidelity. *scathless*, unharmed (by early criticism; cf. *Life* 84/86–7,507; *aurore*, dawn; *crueller*, cf. *LLE.*'Where three roads joined'.

A woman's way (*PBE.*xxii ep.), untraced.

Wonderful Women (*TT.*xli), an arch reference to the movement for women's rights (supported by Emma Hardy).

wonders of the deep (*HE.*xxxi), Psalm cvii,24.

wont, custom, manner. **wonted**, customary.

wonted fires . . . ashes (*FMC.*xliii), cf. Gray's 'Elegy',92 (*G.T.*).

The Wood Fire (*LLE*). Hardy's protest at the removal and burning of crosses, commemorating British soldiers killed on the Western Front (in France and Belgium), after the First World War, is represented by the burning of the three crosses on Calvary after the Crucifixion. *Galilee carpenter's son*, Jesus whose mother Mary was married to the carpenter Joseph; they lived at Nazareth in Galilee. For this ascription of human paternity and *boasted he was* *king*, Hardy was charged with blasphemy.

The Woodlanders (serialized May 1886 to Apr 1887) was finished in February 1887 (*Life* 185/192), Hardy having gone back to his original main plot (*Life* 176/182; cf. 102/105). This hinged on the misfortunes of marriage when artifical middle-class values are preferred to partner-choice by natural inclination, a subject brought to mind by Hardy's own engagement (cf. *PBE*), and felt even more keenly by the time he settled at Max Gate. The title-page epigraph which he composed (see **Not boskiest bow'r**) is inseparable from his tree-planting there (*Life* 173/509), from which originated the scene between Marty and Winterborne (viii; cf. *TL*.The Pine Planters). The theme of the novel is unfulfilment, both in nature (vii; *Life* 149/153) and with reference to all the major characters. It is reinforced by grey wintry scenes, fog, tree-dripping elegiac tones, and Norse imagery (cf. **Niflheim**), much of which was suggested by Matthew Arnold's 'Balder Dead'. Hardy's sympathies are with those who endure and show spiritual virtue (xlii); the ending emphasizes the heroine's weaknesses (cf. *Life* 220/230–1). Despite changes in place-names, the setting of the first edition remains almost wholly unaltered; it is the woodland country near Melbury Osmond (his mother's village) and Melbury House (disguised by placing it 'in a hole', like Turnworth House, near Blandford Forum), with Bubb Down ('Rubdown') as its focal point; see **the Hintocks**. For the date of the action, see **Vic**. Fitzpiers' romantic illusions, his subjective view of love and the universe – the 'Me' and 'Not Me' (vi,xvi) – came from Carlyle's essay on Novalis. Hardy's attitude towards the illusory 'rainbow iris' or 'iris-bow' had its future in *WB* and poems on love and a non-Darwinian view of nature. Browning uses the same image for the first time, and comments on its implications, in the Prologue to *Asolando*, 1889.

Woodwell, Mr (*L*), based on Mr Perkins, minister of the Baptist Chapel at the east end of Dorchester; see *Life* 29–30/33–5,424/458.

Woodyates Inn (*TM*.xi; *LLI*.8h), once a splendid coach-inn, 10 m. SW of Salisbury on the Dorchester road.

Woot hae me? (dial.), Will you have me?

words that burn (*PBE*.xviii), Gray, 'The Progress of Poesy' (*G.T.*).

Wordsworth, Captain John (*D*1.I.i), a younger brother of the poet. Early in February 1805 his ship *The Earl of Abergavenny*, which belonged to the East India Company, drifted in a calm on to the Shambles, where it foundered. (The indications in the text seem to be wrong; cf. map H.)

Wordsworth, William (1770–1850): and **the Wandering Voice** *DR*.xii.3), 'To the Cuckoo' (*G.T.*); his **astringent ode** (*PBE*.xx), 'Ode to Duty' (*G.T.*); sonnets in the style of Wordsworth's (*L*.I.i); his preface to *Lyrical Ballads* quoted twice (*LLE*.Apology).

workhouse. From the end of the eighteenth century workhouses were instituted by parishes for housing and employing paupers and unemployed. When provided by groups of parishes, they were called Unions (*FMC*.xxxix; DLa).

The world and its ways . . . (*OMC*4.I.viii ep.; *DR*.xiii.4; *CM*2.iv; *JO*.VI.iv), Browning, 'The Statue and the Bust'.

worm (*TM*.xxvii), a screw fixed to the end of a rod for removing the charge or wad from a muzzle-loading gun.

worm i' the bud (*PBE*.xxxi ep.; *MC*.xxxiv), *TN*.II.iv,109–11.

wot (archaic), know, knows; what (as pronounced).

Would God it were evening . . . (*TT*.ii). See **Deuteronomy, woman in.**

The Wound (*MV*), a memory of Emma Hardy; cf. *HS*.'When Oats Were Reaped' (Aug 1913). The setting image is repeated from *TD*.xxi.

Wouvermans (*W*.xxviii), Wouwerman, a Dutch painter (1619–68) whose scenes are characterized by hilly country with horses, one usually white.

wrack (archaic), wreck, ruin, disaster.

Wren, Christopher (*DR*.iii.2; *JO*.V.vi,VI.i) was given his great architectural opportunity during the rebuilding of London, after much of it had been destroyed by the fire which started in Pudding Lane, 1666.

wriggles (dial.), sand-eels.

wring-house, a building to house the cider-press. **wrings**, cheese-presses; tortures, pains; (vb.) causes deep pain.

wrinkles, tips, useful bits of information.

wroth (archaic), wrathful, angry.

wuld (dial., cf. **wold**), old.

Wyatt, Sir Thomas (*HE*.ii), courtier and lyric poet, 1503–42.

Wycliff (John Wycliffe), **Huss**, **Luther**, **Calvin**, prominent figures in Protestant revolts against the Catholic Church (*TD*.xxv).

Wyndway House (*HE*.iv–v). Largely imaginary, though its setting near 'a sheet of embayed water' suggests Upton House near Holes Bay, Poole.

Xantippe, shrewish, ill-tempered wife (of Socrates).
Xenophanes, the Monist of Colophon (*HS*), a Greek philosopher who believed that God and the universe are one (monism). He is imagined speaking in his 92nd year, about 480 BC, after being banished for heresy from Colophon in Asia Minor to Elea in south Italy by the Tyrrhenian Sea. His view coincides with Hardy's (cf. the Immanent Will). *codes*, most probably the complexities of Church beliefs.
X's, four large letter (*HE*.ii), indicating the strongest malt brew; for **XXX**, see **Cupid**.

Y

Yahoo (*MC*.xxix), showing the worst in human nature; cf. Swift's satire in Part *iv* of *Gulliver's Travels*.
Yalbury (*UGT*.v.i; *FMC*), an imaginary village on the northern side of 'Yalbury Wood', near Troy Town. **Yalbury Hill**, **Yalbury Wood** (*UGT*; *FMC*; *MC*.xxxvi,xl,xliv; *LLI*.8g; *HS*.At the Mill), Yellowham Hill and Wood. The road from Puddletown to Dorchester, as it runs from 'Yalbury Brow' down 'Yalbury Hill' to 'Yalbury Bottom', bisects the wood, with the keeper's cottage in the woodland on the northern side.
yap . . . away, frighten off (as if by barking sharply).
yaw (nautical), a deviation from the direct course.
yclept (archaic), called, named.
Yea, happy . . . served us (*PBE*.xxxiv ep.), Psalm cxxxvii,8.
Yea, many . . . do thus? (*JO*.I.ep.), I Esdras iv (Apocrypha).
yean, bring forth a lamb (or lambs).

The Year's Awakening (*SC*). For the theme, see the last line of *PPP.*An August Midnight. About the middle of March the sun seems to pass from the Fishes (Pisces) into the Ram (Aries); see **zodiac**. *merest rote*, mechanically, by fixed natural laws.

years . . . drawing nigh . . . no pleasure in them (*TD*.ii), Eccl.xii,1.

Yellowham. See **Yalbury**.

The Yellow-Hammer, an uncollected poem by Hardy for *The Book of Baby Birds* by Florence Dugdale, 1912.

Yeobright, Clement (*RN*). Intellectually and in preferring rural virtues to city and professional values, he has much in common with Hardy, and is associated with light (cf. II.vi). For 'Clement', see *Life* 117/120.

Yeobright, Mr. His playing of the bass-viol (violoncello) at Kingsbere (I.v) is based on traditions about the performances of Hardy's grandfather 'as locum tenens' (*Life* 12/16).

Yeobright, Mrs. Her disappointment when Clym gives up his city career is probably based on that of Hardy's mother when he gave up architecture in London for an uncertain career as a novelist, and returned to Higher Bockhampton in 1867.

Yeobright, Thomasin, suggested to some extent by Mary Hardy.

yester, last; yesterday, **yestertide**. **yestreen**, yesterday evening.

Yewsholt Lodge (*GND*2), Farrs House, $1\frac{1}{2}$ m. west of Wimborne.

Yorkist (*L*.I.xiv), of the house of York, which had as its emblem the white rose; the sun was another. Edward IV reigned after his victory in the Wars of the Roses (against the house of Lancaster, with the red rose as its emblem).

The Young Churchwarden (*MV*), based probably on the knowledge (revealed in *S.R.*) that Emma 'disappointed' a young farmer when she met Hardy. Combined with a note in his prayer-book, a deleted MS note shows that the occasion was evening service on 14 Aug 1870 at Lesnewth, the parish paired with St Juliot for Church duties.

The Young Glass-Stainer (*MV*), written when Hardy was still planning *JO*, where the Swinburnian theme of Greek joyousness against Christian abstinence, here presented by a glass-stainer working in a church of Gothic design, is put forward by Sue before her tragedy. *Hera*, the Greek queen of heaven, wife of Zeus; the Roman Juno. *Martha, Mary*, John xi–xii,9.

Your Last Drive (*SC*). As Emma returned to Dorchester, after visiting her friend Mrs Wood Homer beyond Puddletown, she passed not far from Stinsford churchyard, where, near the large yew at the entrance, she would soon be buried.

The Youth Who Carried a Light (*MV*). The poem it follows suggests that Hardy was thinking of his own youthful hopes; cf. the boy Jude (*JO*.I.iv, 'Through the intervening fortnight . . .'). *apogee*, highest point.

Yuletide in a Younger World (*WW*). *Younger*, when we were young; *still small voices . . . fire-filled prophets*, I Kings xix,12 and Jer.v,14.

Z

Zacharias, son of (*TT*.i), John the Baptist, Luke i,5–25.

Zamsummins (*HE*.xxv), giants, Deut.ii,20.

zeed (dial. vb.), saw.

zell (dial.), sell.

Zenobia (*RN*.I.x; *WT7*.i), princess of Palmyra in the Syrian desert. After the death of her husband (which she is said to have expedited) she ruled unchecked in the east of the Roman empire, while the Romans were occupied with trouble in the west.

Zermatt: To the Matterhorn (*PPP*). Hardy heard the story of this tragedy from Edward Whymper, the sole survivor of the four English climbers (*Life* 264/280; see 294/312–13 for Hardy's visit). *atomies*, minute creatures (*RJ*.I.iv,57). For the supernatural references of the sestet, which show how Hardy the rationalist yielded to the imaginative, see Josh.x,12–14; *JC*.II.ii,8–31; and Mark xv,33 (the Crucifixion). *ninth hour*, 3 p.m., the Jewish day beginning at 6 a.m.

zero (*TT*.iv), the point at which visibility will begin.

Zeus, chief of the gods of ancient Greece (the Roman Jupiter).

zhinerally (rustic pronunciation), generally.

zid (dial. variant of **seed** or **zeed**), saw.

Zion, Jerusalem (strictly, the upper part of the old city).

zodiac . . . heaven (*W*.xvii). In ancient astronomy the Zodiac is the celestial belt round which the sun appears to move annually.

It extends eight or nine degrees on each side of the **ecliptic**, and is divided into twelve signs (named after their chief constellations, e.g. the Fishes, the Ram, the Bull, the Twins, the Crab), through one of which the sun passes in a twelfth of the year.

Zola, and other novelists (SF). Émile Zola (1840–1902) was one of the leading novelists of the French 'natural' school (see **naturalism**); he was particularly interested in heredity and 'a certain cerebral infirmity'. *Germinal* is a study of the miner; *La Faute de l'Abbé Mourat*, of celibacy. **Dumas *père***, i.e. Alexandre Dumas (1802–70), the French novelist and playwright, and **Mrs Radcliffe** (1764–1823), the English novelist, are cited as examples of writers of romance, as opposed to 'scientific realists'.

zot (dial.), sat.

Zouga (*TT*.xi,xxxii), the Botletle river in Botswana.

Zounds, an ancient oath (by God's wounds, i.e. Christ on the Cross).

zull (dial.), plough.

zummat (dial.), something.

Zurbaran (*D*3.II.iii), Spanish painter, 1598–1664. Hardy, whose interest in his work began about January 1905, thought his paintings might one day be ranked above those of Velasquez (*Life* 323/347).

zwail (dial.), sway from side to side, move unsteadily.

Maps

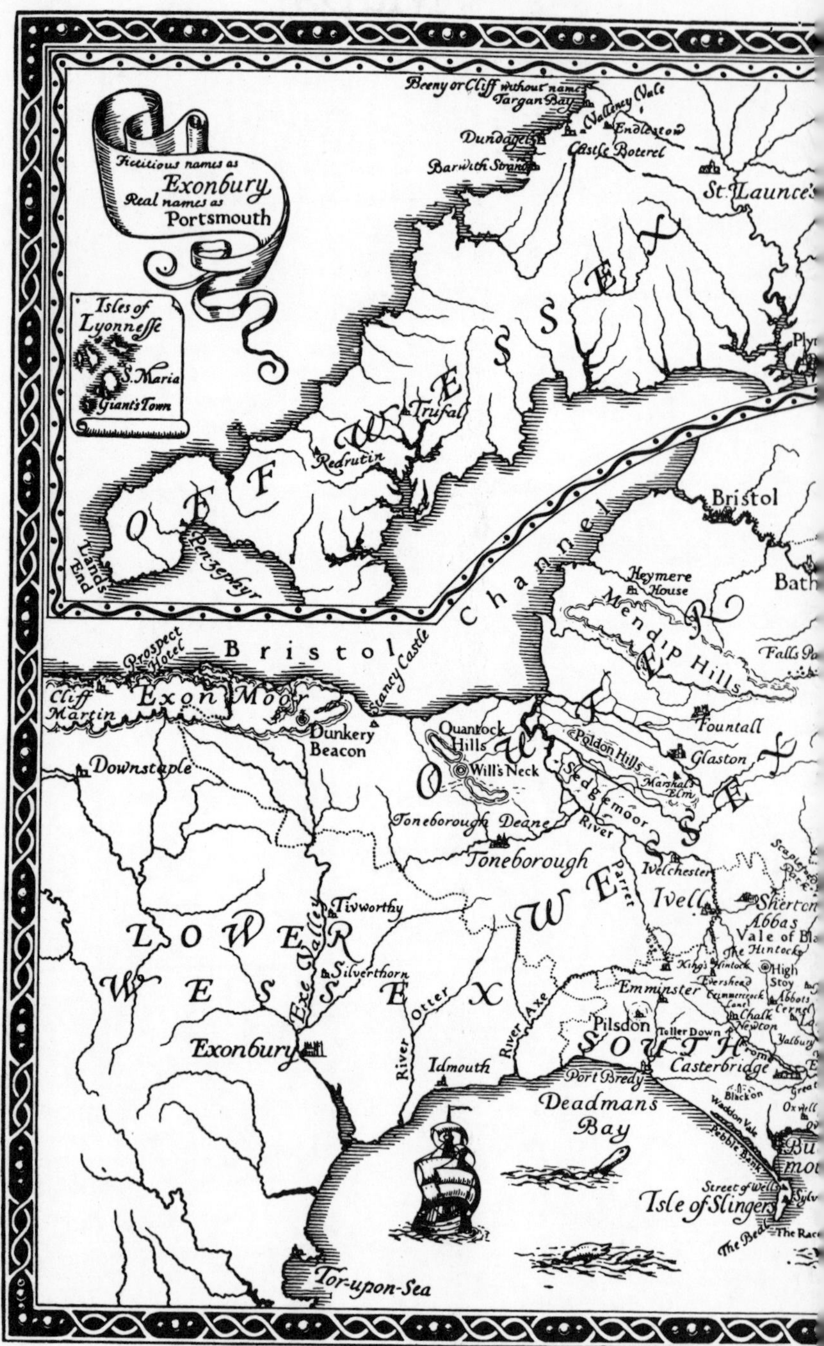

Hardy's General Map of Wessex

Map of the
WESSEX
of the
Novels and Poems
Scale of Miles
Christminster
Lumsdon
R Thames
NORTH
Alfredston
The Brown House
Cresscombe
Marygreen
River Thames
MID
WESSEX
Marlbury
Downs
Castle
Royal
Gaymead
Kennetbridge
Aldbrickham
Batton Castle
Inkpen Beacon
Stoke Barehills
Quartershot
Weydon
Priors
Icenway
House
Stonehenge
UPPER
Wintoncester
Melchester
Fernel Hall
WESSEX
Wingreen
Deansleigh
Park
The Slopes
Chaseborough
Southampton
Portsmouth
The Great
Bramshurst
Forest
Cornton
Inn
Warborne
Chene
Manor
Solentsea
Havenpool
Sandbourne
The
Island
Corvsgate
Knollsea
The Channel
Emery Walker, sc.

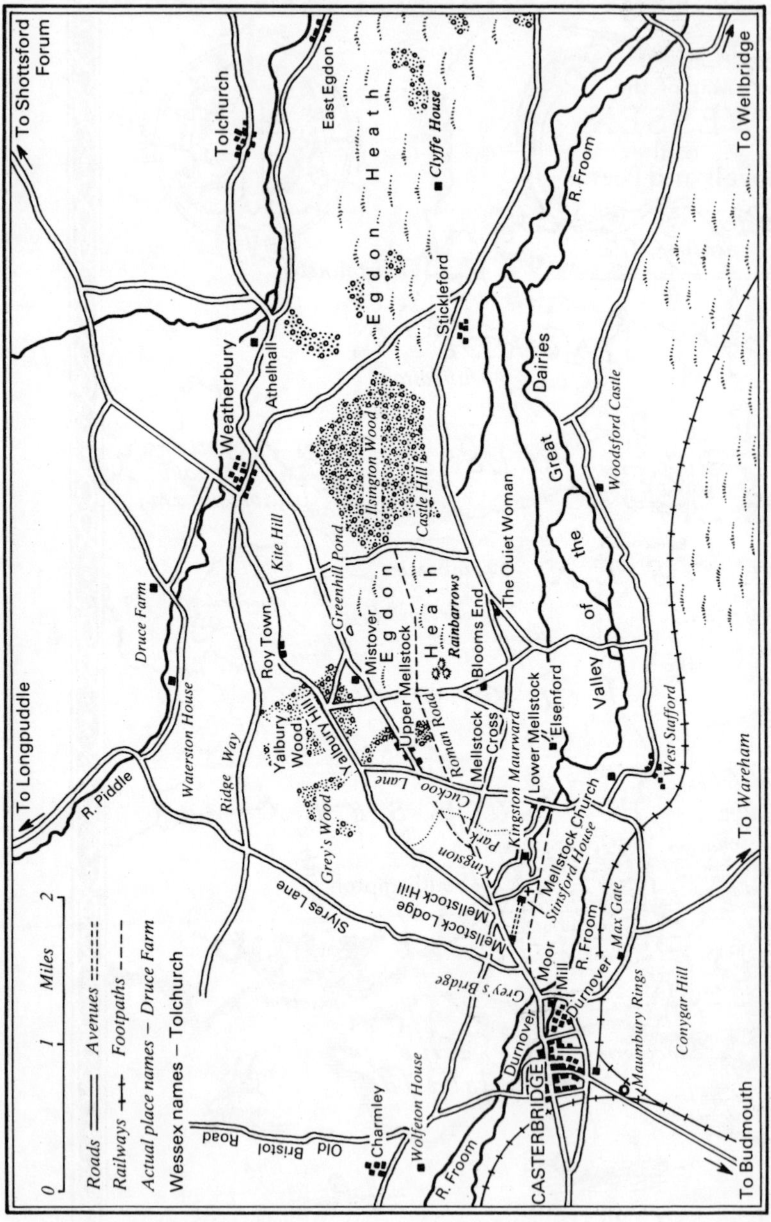

A The Heart of Wessex

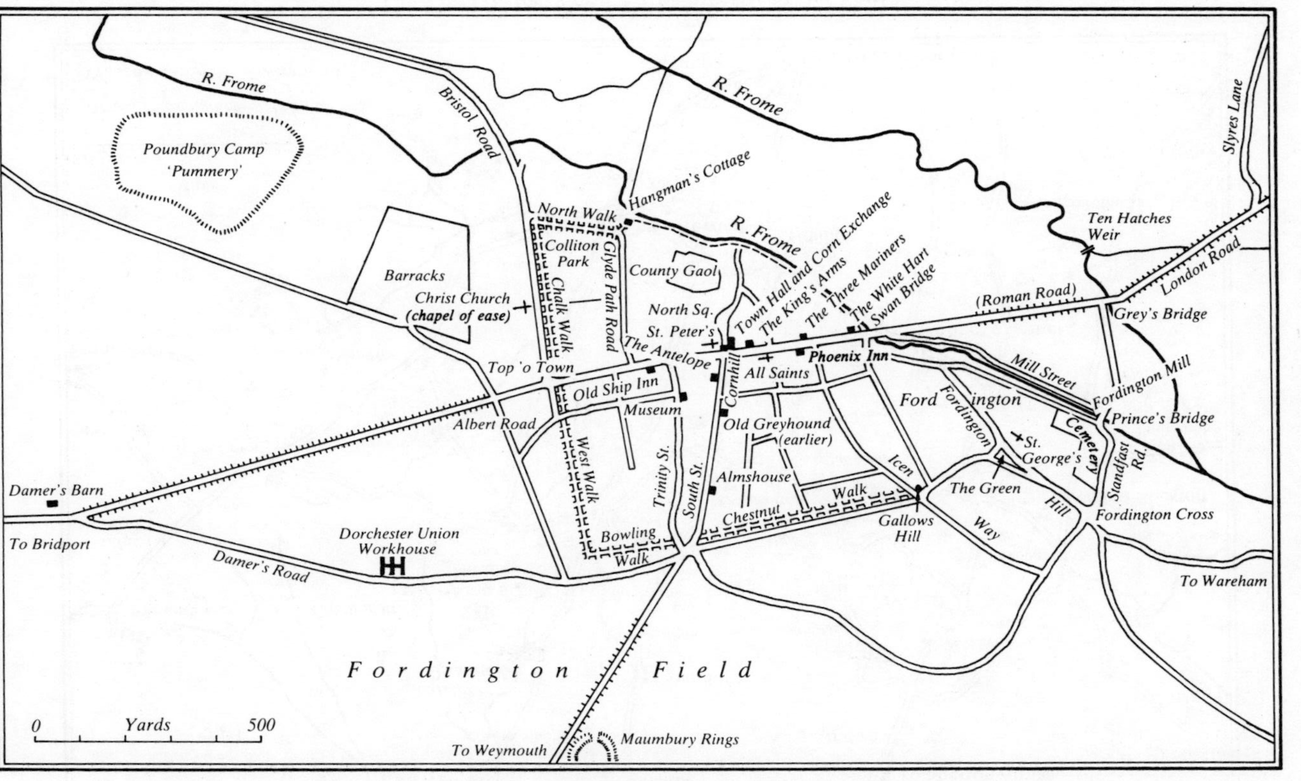

B. The Dorchester of Hardy's Boyhood

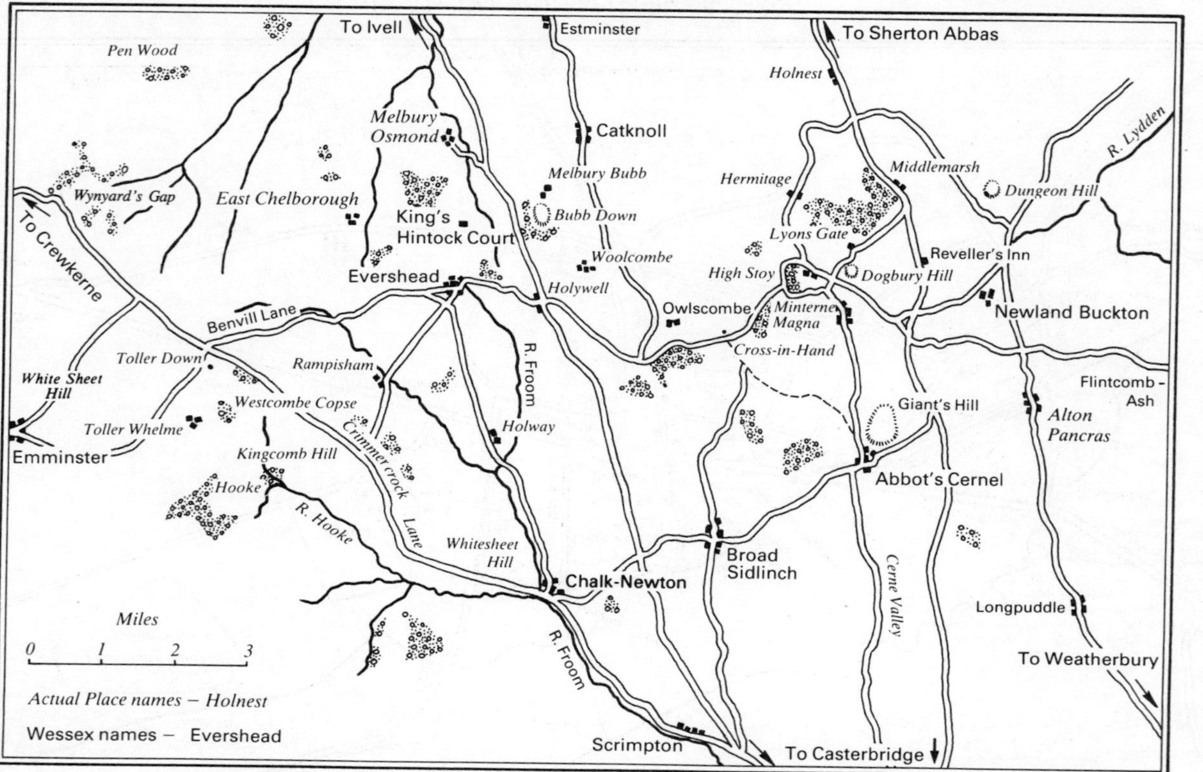

C. The Hintocks and Hill Country to the South

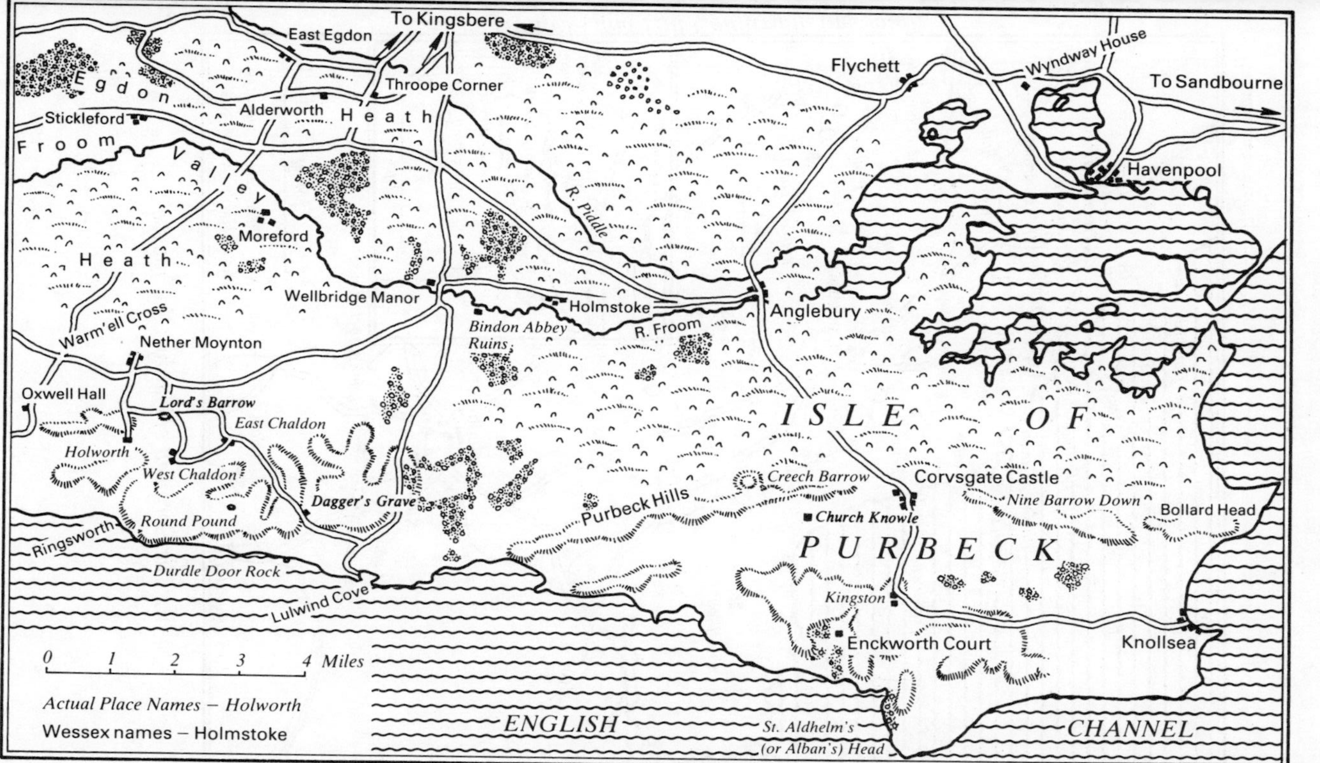

D. Egdon and Purbeck

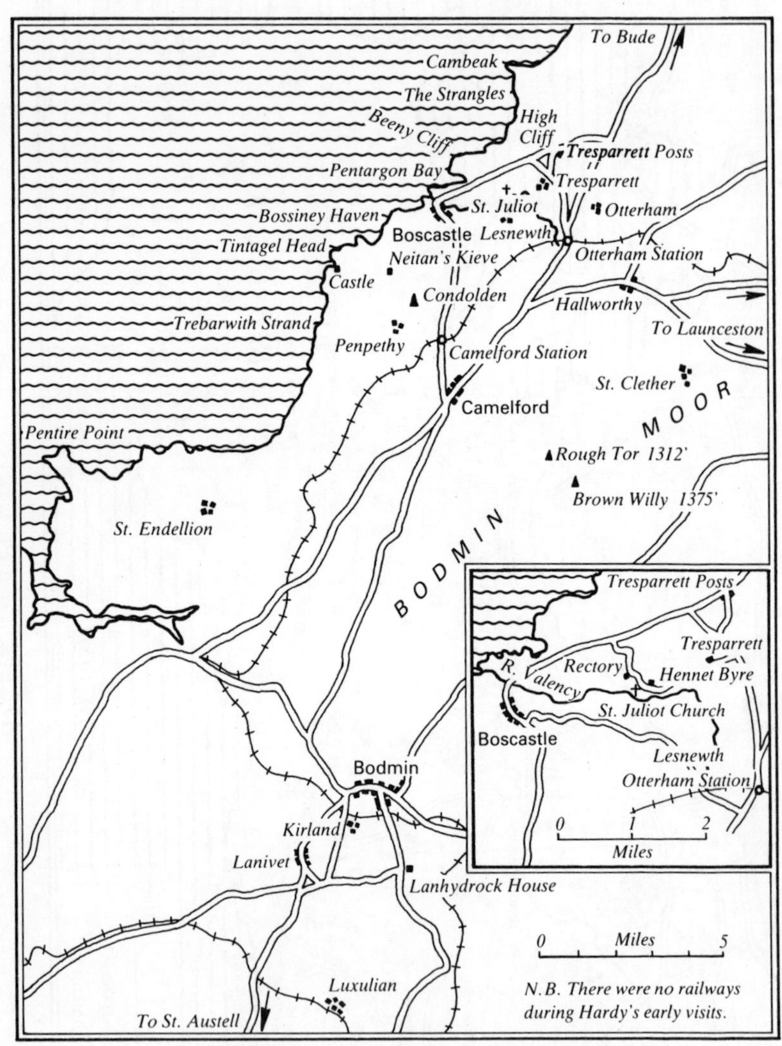
To Bude
Cambeak
The Strangles
Beeny Cliff
High Cliff
Tresparrett Posts
Pentargon Bay
Tresparrett
Bossiney Haven
St. Juliot
Otterham
Boscastle
Lesnewth
Tintagel Head
Neitan's Kieve
Otterham Station
Castle
Condolden
Hallworthy
Trebarwith Strand
To Launceston
Penpethy
Camelford Station
St. Clether
Camelford
Pentire Point
MOOR
Rough Tor 1312'
Brown Willy 1375'
St. Endellion
BODMIN
Tresparrett Posts
Tresparrett
R. Valency
Rectory
Hennet Byre
St. Juliot Church
Boscastle
Lesnewth
Otterham Station
0 1 2
Miles
Bodmin
Kirland
Lanivet
Lanhydrock House
0 Miles 5
Luxulian
N.B. There were no railways during Hardy's early visits.
To St. Austell

E. *The Cornwall of Hardy's 'Lyonnesse'*

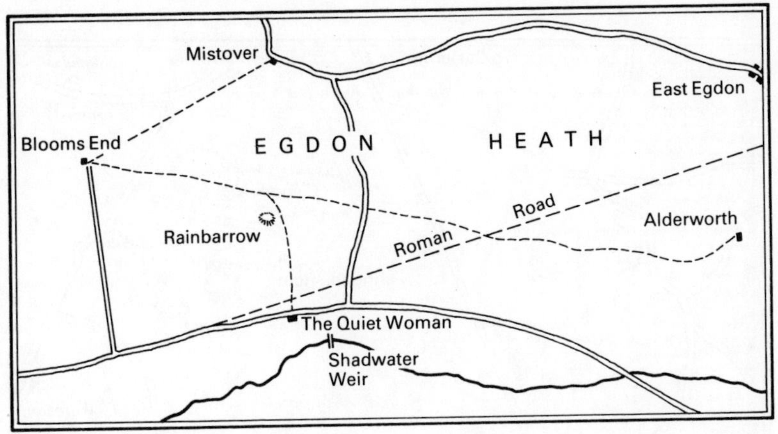

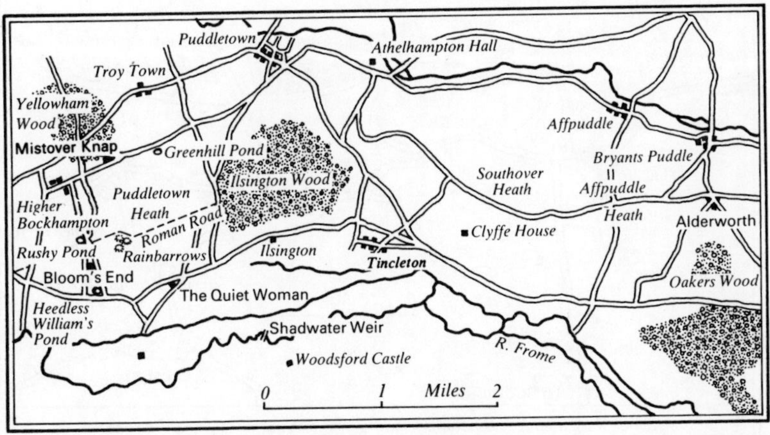

F. *'The Return of the Native'*
above: *setting, from Hardy's map*
below: *country of its origin*

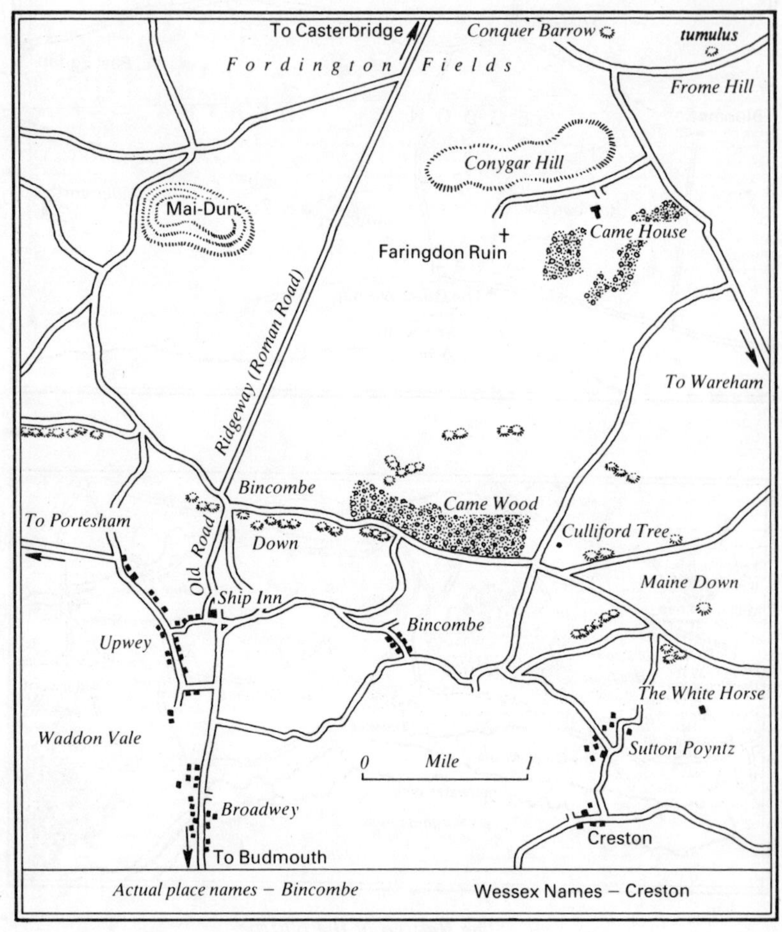
To Casterbridge
Conquer Barrow
tumulus
Fordington Fields
Frome Hill
Conygar Hill
Mai-Dun
Came House
Faringdon Ruin
Ridgeway (Roman Road)
To Wareham
Bincombe
Came Wood
To Portesham
Old Road
Down
Culliford Tree
Maine Down
Ship Inn
Bincombe
Upwey
The White Horse
Waddon Vale
0 Mile 1
Sutton Poyntz
Broadwey
Creston
To Budmouth
Actual place names – Bincombe
Wessex Names – Creston

G. *Around Ridgeway*

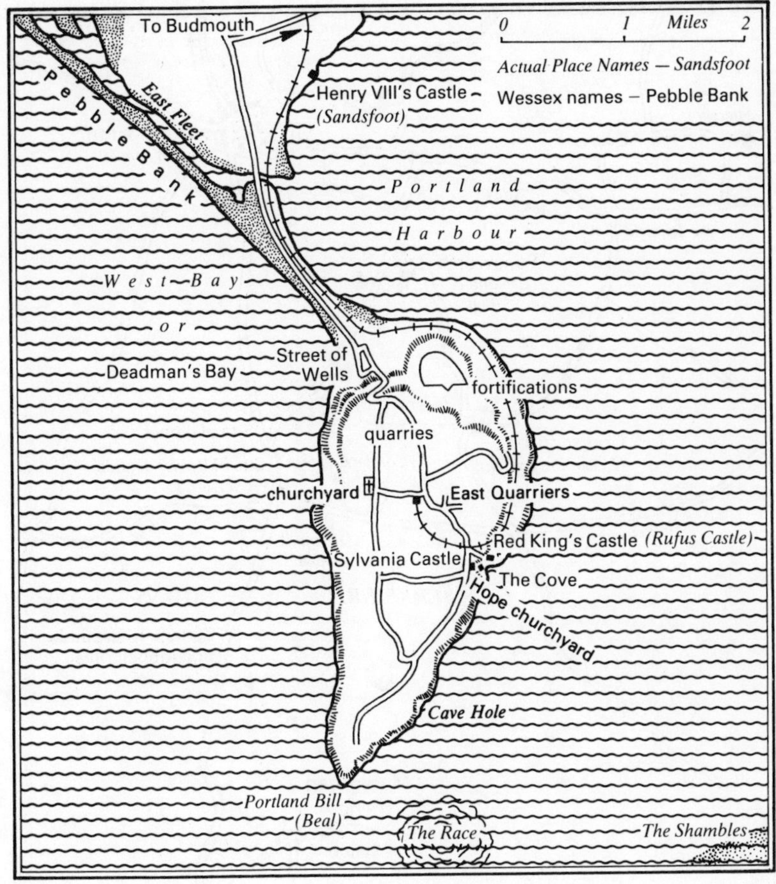
To Budmouth
0 1 Miles 2
Actual Place Names — Sandsfoot
Wessex names – Pebble Bank
Henry VIII's Castle
(Sandsfoot)
East Fleet
Pebble Bank
Portland
Harbour
West Bay
or
Deadman's Bay
Street of Wells
fortifications
quarries
churchyard
East Quarriers
Red King's Castle (Rufus Castle)
Sylvania Castle
The Cove
Hope churchyard
Cave Hole
Portland Bill
(Beal)
The Race
The Shambles

H. Portland

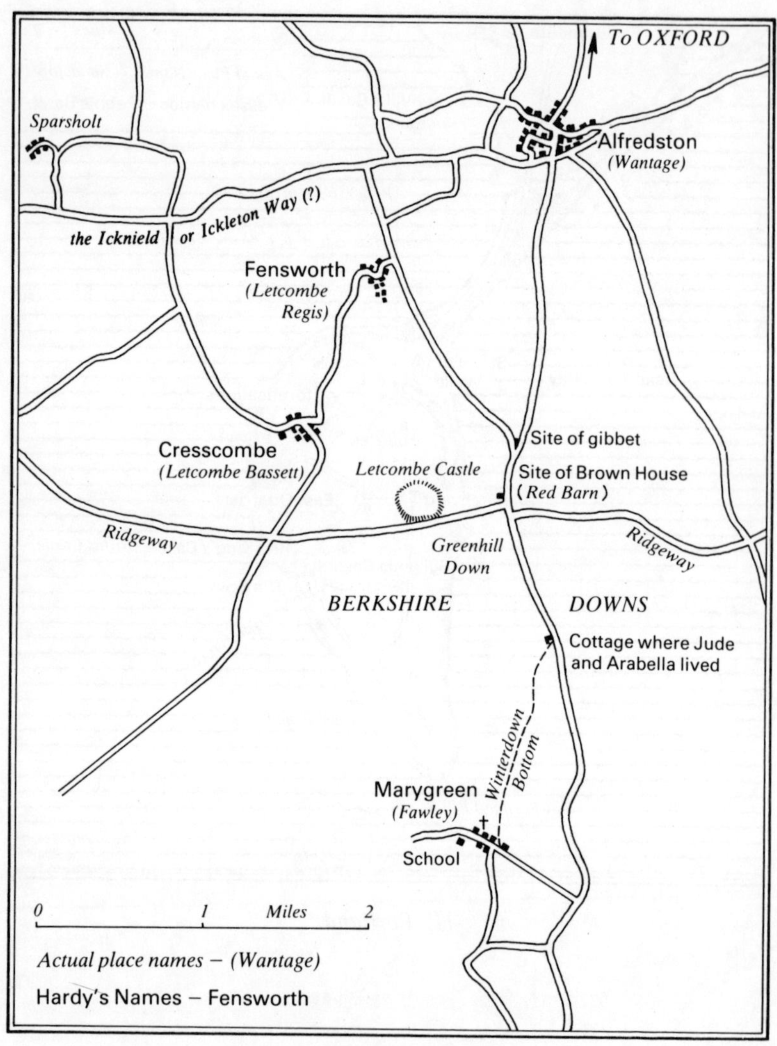

I. *Marygreen and Alfredston*